Cognitive
Development

Cognitive Development

Infancy Through Adolescence

Kathleen M. Galotti
Carleton College

Los Angeles | London | New Delhi
Singapore | Washington DC

For information:

SAGE Publications, Inc.
2455 Teller Road
Thousand Oaks, California 91320
E-mail: order@sagepub.com

SAGE Publications India Pvt. Ltd.
B 1/I 1 Mohan Cooperative
    Industrial Area
Mathura Road, New Delhi 110 044
India

SAGE Publications Ltd.
1 Oliver's Yard
55 City Road,
London EC1Y 1SP
United Kingdom

SAGE Publications Asia-Pacific Pte. Ltd.
33 Pekin Street #02-01
Far East Square
Singapore 048763

Printed in the United States of America

Library of Congress Cataloging-in-Publication Data

Galotti, Kathleen M., 1957-
Cognitive development : infancy through adolescence / Kathleen M. Galotti.
    p. cm.
Includes bibliographical references and index.
ISBN 978-1-4129-6666-5 (pbk.)
  1. Cognitive psychology. I. Title.

BF201.G35 2011
155.4'13—dc22   2010003000

This book is printed on acid-free paper.

10   11   12   13   14   10   9   8   7   6   5   4   3   2   1

Acquisitions Editor:	Vicki Knight
Associate Editor:	Lauren Habib
Editorial Assistant:	Ashley Dodd
Production Editor:	Brittany Bauhaus
Copy Editor:	Melinda Masson
Typesetter:	C&M Digitals (P) Ltd.
Proofreader:	Jenifer Kooiman
Indexer:	Author
Marketing Manager:	Stephanie Adams

BRIEF CONTENTS

DETAILED CONTENTS

PREFACE

My academic research in psychology began with my senior honors thesis at Wellesley College—looking at how preschoolers come to learn the difference between pairs of terms like *big* and *little*, *tall* and *short*. I really enjoyed planning the study, collecting the data, writing up the results, and defending my thesis before my committee—so much so that I decided to go to grad school in psychology. But, I decided, I wanted to change to a more "rigorous" focus—no more "kid stuff" for me—I was now going to do cognitive psychology and hang out with the more hard-core science-y types. Well, my heart never let me let go of kids and their language and reasoning abilities, so while my dissertation was on adult reasoning, I kept doing side projects on little kids' reasoning. And when I got my PhD, I got hired to teach developmental psychology at Carleton.

I later added in cognitive psychology to the mix of courses I teach, and started focusing much of my research on the decision making of older adolescents and adults. But, when I became a parent, my fascination with cognitive development once again came to center stage. The point I'm trying to make here is that my academic interests have long straddled both cognitive psychology and cognitive development. And, I've come to appreciate that the study of children's cognitive development can be every bit as elegant and sophisticated as the research in adult cognition.

Kids are fascinating people to hang around, to teach, to parent, and to observe. It is so very clear that their thinking is often very different from mine—and whether those differences are qualitative or quantitative, innate or learned, and domain-specific or general-purpose are rich questions that philosophers and psychologists continue big debates on even today. One of my biggest goals for this book, then, is to give you the background knowledge to be able to think about those great debates and participate intelligently in those conversations.

In many larger schools, cognitive psychology and developmental psychology are taught by different faculty and cover very different sets of topics. In the smaller schools I attended and where I currently teach, there's a lot more overlap. When I teach one course, I frequently bring up topics and research from the other. My first textbook was one in cognitive psychology—but from the first edition it had a chapter on cognitive development as well as many other developmental examples throughout. In this book, you'll see the reverse—a lot of discussion of topics from mainstream cognitive psychology. My firm belief is that to really understand cognitive development, you need a good grasp of where it is going. (Of course, I also tell my cognitive students that to really understand how cognition works, you have to understand its development!)

In any event, writing this book has been a 6-year project. I've learned a *lot* about topics that are far from my own research areas, and that has been great fun. I've also had the luxurious opportunity of immersing myself in the literature around topics closer to my own—often, whole afternoons would go by with my scarcely noticing it was time to leave, so caught up could I get in another fascinating study. I hope I've conveyed some of my own excitement and enthusiasm to you. Enjoy.

PLAN OF THE BOOK

Developmental textbooks typically come in one of two kinds: those organized topically and those organized chronologically. Chronological organization means that all the developments of infancy, say, are discussed together before moving on to consider all the developments of toddlerhood, then the preschool period, and so forth. In other words, the book is organized into chapters based on the age of the children being discussed.

Topical organization, which is a little more common in current cognitive developmental textbooks, arranges chapters by subject. So, for example, there might be a chapter on perception, covering its development from infancy through the oldest age group the book includes, and another chapter on attention (again covering the full span of ages the book encompasses).

I've chosen more of a hybrid organization. The heavier emphasis of the book is chronological, although some of the chapters highlight particular topics (such as language, academic learning, or moral development). I like a chronological arrangement because I believe it helps students see the infant, toddler, child, or adolescent more holistically. That is, I think your understanding of infant memory, say, is more complete when it's discussed just after a presentation of infant attention and perception. Some special topics, however, don't seem to be as effective when broken up across chapters, and these are the ones that are treated more topically.

Many books in cognitive development end their coverage with childhood. I've chosen to include adolescence for a number of reasons. First, I find this just a fascinating period of transition and growth, with a lot of exciting developments happening in higher-order cognitive abilities. Second, I think including it presents a more complete picture of cognitive development. Third, my own students seem to find this developmental period the most interesting and compelling, probably because they were so very recently in it!

The book is divided into five sections, with two or three chapters per section. The first section (Chapters 1 and 2) provides general overview information on what cognition is, what the major theoretical approaches to cognitive development are, and what the more common research methods and approaches in this field are. Plan to refer back to these two chapters a lot as we examine different developmental periods.

The rest of the book has more of a chronological flavor. The second set of chapters (Chapters 3, 4, and 5) encompasses infancy and toddlerhood; the third set (Chapters 6, 7, and 8) early childhood spanning roughly from age two and a half to about six years. Next comes middle childhood (Chapters 9, 10, and 11), which corresponds roughly to the ages during which children attend elementary school (in Western cultures). Finally, the last section (Chapters 12 and 13) covers adolescence (which, in the United States, would translate to middle and high school students, with some extension to college students).

Cognition does not occur in a vacuum, of course. For this reason, I've tried to bring in other areas of psychology that impact, and are impacted by, cognitive development. Among these are neurological development, social development, and cross-cultural psychology (to remind us all that the way cognitive development proceeds in the United States is only one possible way it can and does unfold). Of course, each of these topics is covered more thoroughly in other whole books or even book series, so I am only able to touch on relevant topics and themes. I've tried to provide interested students with places to go for further information.

I'm writing this paragraph as one of the last pieces of the book (even though it will be the first thing many of you read). It strikes me that this book is like a complex symphony or musical—with lots of interrelated parts that have to come together to present a unified picture. I hope when you come to the end of the book that you have an appreciation for the complexity, subtlety, and wide-ranging nature and creativity that comprise cognitive development.

ACKNOWLEDGMENTS

I've had a lot of help writing this book. Thanks first to my own kids, Timothy and Kimberlynn, for being a part of my life; giving me many, many examples to write about; being patient with my need for time to write; and mostly just being great human beings. They've been an inspiration to me, and not just for this book.

Many of my students or former students pitched in to help me with this project at various points. Laura Nathan and Lacey Dorman read early drafts of many or all chapters and provided feedback from an undergraduate point of view. Lacey also spent the better part of a summer helping me figure out what pieces of the book I needed to request permissions for, as well as organizing lists of, all the tables, figures, photos, and quotations I used. Katie Stinebargh, Blair Nyline, and Andrea Rockwood helped with the thankless task of checking my references. All of these folks also helped me secure books and articles that were needed. Stephanie Moberg did a lot of high-resolution scanning of many of the figures, and stayed calm when I would ask her to get 20 things together in a single day. Beth Lavin, a former student, didn't hesitate when I called her frantically to request she run her infant son out to a restaurant to get a particular kind of photo, when an appropriate one couldn't be located from a photo bank.

Lots of other colleagues also helped out. Lorie Tuma, administrative assistant extraordinaire, supervised all of the students and made a lot of suggestions especially over scanning. Her delightful sense of humor is a godsend when it comes to keeping setbacks in perspective. Plus, she is nice to my kids and keeps a stash of chocolate in her desk for emergencies—what a pal! Nancy Ashmore, friend and photographer, once again avoided rolling her eyes when I thought up another weird photo idea and just came over and started (photographically) shooting. Diane Kinneberg, a former principal at my children's elementary school, read the sections on academic learning from a professional educator's point of view.

The Faculty Grants Committee at Carleton College, including President Rob Oden and Dean Scott Bierman, provided me with salaried released time from teaching to work on this book, and that resource was invaluable. Other Carleton faculty colleagues, including Roy Elveton, Susan Singer, Marion Cass, Will Hollingsworth, Deanna Haunsperger, Stephen Kennedy, Steve Kozberg, and many others, make my working life a good one and my day-to-day experience well worth getting up for.

Vicki Knight, my editor, has worked with me on two different books now. Vicki's associate editor Lauren Habib and editorial assistant Ashley Dodd also provided assistance in locating some of the photographs that Nancy didn't take and in obtaining permissions. And, in one act going way above and beyond the call of duty, Ashley and Lauren posed for a re-creation of a photo we really needed and couldn't otherwise obtain!

I also have to mention the production staff, including Brittany Bauhaus and Laureen Gleason. I'm especially pleased with the work of the cover designer, Arup Giri, who listened to my ideas and feedback carefully and produced a really effective cover (my daughter likes the goat photo the best). Melinda Masson did the copyediting, and Jenifer Kooiman worked on proofreading. Finally, the following reviewers provided feedback on one or more chapters at different draft stages:

Holger B. Elischberger, *Albion College*

Alycia M. Hund, *Illinois State University*

Virginia T. Mayer, *Troy University Dothan*

Mary Michael, *University of North Carolina at Charlotte*

Gayathri Narasimham, *Vanderbilt University*

Patricia E. Ragan, *University of Wisconsin Green Bay*

Greg D. Reynolds, *University of Tennessee*

Liat Sayfan, *University of California, Davis*

David Sobel, *Brown University*

Kaveri Subrahmanyam, *California State University, Los Angeles*

Kristen Weede Alexander, *California State University, Sacramento*

ABOUT THE AUTHOR

Kathleen M. Galotti holds a BA in psychology and economics from Wellesley College, as well as an MA and a PhD in psychology and an MSE in computer and information sciences from the University of Pennsylvania. At Carleton College she holds the title Professor of Cognitive Science and serves as the director of the interdisciplinary Cognitive Science program, which she helped establish in 1989. She also is a former chair of the Psychology Department. She teaches courses in cognitive and developmental psychology and cognitive science and has also taught courses in statistics and introductory psychology.

Dr. Galotti is the author or coauthor of dozens of studies in cognitive and developmental psychology. Her research centers on the development of reasoning and decision-making skills from the preschool period through adulthood and on the styles with which adolescents and adults plan for the future, make important life commitments, and learn new information. Her research has been funded through the National Science Foundation, the Spencer Foundation, and the National Institutes of Health. She is the author of *Making Decisions That Matter: How People Face Important Life Choices* (2002), as well as a textbook, *Cognitive Psychology In and Out of the Laboratory* (4th ed., 2008). She has also authored or coauthored dozens of articles in peer-reviewed journals.

Dr. Galotti is the parent of two children, Timothy and Kimberlynn, and spends much of her time enjoying their youthful exuberance and energy. In her spare time, she raises and trains Bernese mountain dogs, shows them in competition in licensed obedience trials, and is an approved obedience and rally judge for the American Kennel Club.

To Tim and Kimmie, thanks for being exactly who you are, and for developing in such interesting ways!

CHAPTER 1

INTRODUCTION AND OVERVIEW

WHAT IS COGNITIVE DEVELOPMENT?

By way of introduction, I want you to think for a minute about children you know well. They might be your siblings, your nieces or nephews, your cousins, your neighbors, or even your own children. Or maybe they are children of friends, children you babysat for or tutored or worked with at a summer camp. Focus on a couple of these children, preferably ones of very different ages, and consider their intellectual capabilities.

The two children foremost in my mind are my son and daughter. When I began the first draft of this book, Tim(my) was 10 years old and Kimberlynn just shy of her second birthday. Tim at that time was going into fifth grade, was a skilled reader and speaker, and enjoyed and was pretty darn good at verbal endeavors: creating riddles, writing stories, taunting his sister. He could pay attention in school for sustained periods (on most days!); he could remember lots of events that happened to him 5 or 6 years ago; he could solve fairly sophisticated problems both of the school variety (in math class) and in real life (how to get a phone number of a friend when he, Tim, was out of town and without a local phone book).

Kimberlynn, by contrast, at that time was in many ways almost a different creature from her brother. She had just learned to talk, and most of her utterances were quite short ("No!" "Shoe!" "Mama!"), so conversations with her tended to consist of her naming someone or something ("Dog!") and her conversational partner carrying the bulk of the burden of conversation ("Yep—that's a dog, all right! His name is Tackle. Can you say 'Tackle'?").

Kimberlynn could recognize things and people she'd seen before, but her retention interval was shorter than her brother's—if she hadn't seen someone for a couple of months, the chances of her reacting to the person as familiar were quite low. Her attention span was short—she might have played with a toy for 15 minutes but quickly lost interest after that, especially if she was playing alone. Her most frequent problem-solving strategy was to cry and point to what she wanted, waiting for others to get it for her.

Two different children, at two different ages, show us a variety of differences in cognitive abilities. Of course, this is what developmental psychologists would call a **cross-sectional comparison**—contrasting different individuals at different ages and drawing inferences about development. The problem with cross-sectional comparisons is that some of the differences we see might be individual differences, independent of developmental status. For example, the two children happen to differ genetically—Tim is my biological child, while Kimberlynn was adopted in infancy. Or the differences I see could stem from specific cognitive abilities such as spatial memory or verbal fluency.

Happily for this example, it's taken me over 6 years to get to revising this chapter. Tim is now 16. He's become politically active and interested in social justice issues. In math class, he's learning to solve problems involving ellipses and hyperbolas. Last month he got his driver's license, and now he spends much time constructing elaborate arguments for why I should soon buy a second "family" car. He's developed a love of theater, particularly acting, writing, and directing. He'll even sing and dance in musicals, though his first love is comedy.

Kimmie, in turn, is an outgoing member of Mrs. Down's second-grade class. She is an avid reader and even better at math stuff—not just the basic arithmetic facts, but noticing and creating patterns, solving logic puzzles, and thinking spatially. Her attention span is incredible and her spatial memory particularly impressive—perhaps accounting for her ability to learn new dance routines for various recitals—she does jazz, tap, and ballet, as well as hip-hop.

When I compare each child now with each child at an earlier age, I'm making what developmental psychologists call a **longitudinal comparison**. In contrasting 10-year-old Tim with 16-year-old Tim, for example, I'm in some ways controlling for Tim's personality, intelligence, interests, and preferences. I'm seeing the early verbal abilities Tim had in reading and writing stories morph into a quite developed talent in theater. I'm seeing his "practical problem-solving" skills come in handy as he organizes study sessions, directs rehearsals, and figures out strategic ways of approaching me to get what he wants. Moreover, Tim can now give a detailed plan for his next year or two, in terms of how he will likely be spending most of his time; at age 10, his time horizon was much shorter and more driven by circumstance or by parental direction.

Likewise, Kimberlynn has shown a lot of growth in the intervening 6 years. She used to have few verbal skills; now there are evenings where I long for a few minutes of lack of speech! Her memory abilities sometimes amaze me, particularly for things like dance routines, song lyrics, and stories. She is extremely focused in school and well able to complete homework quickly and thoroughly—even the challenge problems. Indeed, I see less similarity between 2- and 8-year-old Kimmie than I do between 10-year-old and 16-year-old Tim.

In this book, we'll be taking a detailed look at the intellectual competence of infants, toddlers, children, and adolescents. We'll examine changes in various kinds of competence, and we'll consider different possible explanations for what drives these changes in **cognitive development**. We'll look first at different realms of cognition—different cognitive tasks or processes. We'll consider how these realms are manifested in infants, toddlers, children, and adolescents, and we'll examine theories of how the developmental changes come to be. In this way, we'll be attempting to accomplish two major tasks: (a) describing major developmental landmarks in each realm and (b) explaining how children at one developmental moment evolve more advanced capabilities and performances.

COGNITIVE REALMS: AN OVERVIEW

The term cognition encompasses a broad range of intellectual activities. In fact, whole textbooks exist on the topic of the cognitive area of psychology (e.g., Galotti, 2008; Matlin, 2004; Reed, 2006). Consequently, condensing a whole, diverse, and multifaceted field into a thumbnail sketch is quite a challenge. Cognitive psychology has to do with how people (almost always adults) obtain, retain, use, and communicate information. Alternatively, you can think of cognition as comprising the various parts of our mental life: what goes on inside our heads when we perceive, attend, remember, think, categorize, reason, decide, and so forth.

Here, I'll give just a brief synopsis of some of the major cognitive processes we'll be discussing throughout the rest of the book. In this chapter, I'll be mostly describing the adult forms of each cognitive realm. My goal here is to sketch for you the mature form of each cognitive area. This should provide you with two things: (a) a snapshot of the "endpoint" toward which cognitive development is driving and (b) an understanding of the different realms of cognition. It may seem backward to you to start with a description of endpoints, but my hope is to offer you an overall framework and some basic vocabulary as we start the journey. Rest assured, then, that we will spend portions of each of the remaining chapters examining the realms we talk about here in much more developmental detail.

Perception

Much if not all of the information we acquire from the world initially arrives through one of our senses. We might see, hear, smell, taste, or touch new information. Depending on the sensory modality being used, the information will have a different nature—light waves in the case of vision, sound waves in the case of audition, chemical molecules if the sensory modalities are smell or taste. These channels of input bring us a wealth of information. However, the information they provide is in relatively raw, unprocessed form. Perception refers collectively to the cognitive processes used to interpret sensory information.

For example, when an observer looks at the scene outside a window, he may be bombarded with visual information—information about objects, the size of those objects and their distance the amount of light upon those objects, and so forth. But the act of recognizing the parts of the visual scene *as objects* requires perception. The observer needs to somehow *segment* the information, figuring out which parts relate to other parts—which parts cohere into unified objects. To even recognize a single object, the observer needs to figure out what the boundaries around that object are, in a process known as *figure-ground discrimination*. We'll see in the chapters to come that even though perception seems to happen almost instantaneously much of the time, it actually requires quite a lot of complicated cognitive processing. We will see that while infants, in particular, bring a lot of probably innate competence to this task, there is still much growth and change in perceptual abilities, at least through early childhood.

Attention

When we work on a complicated cognitive task, we often need to focus or concentrate our mental energy on that task to complete it successfully. That can require ignoring or shutting out distractions. This description captures the essence of what cognitive psychologists call attention, the ability to allocate mental resources to certain tasks. By selectively attending to one conversation in a room, for example, we are able to focus on more aspects of the exchange—nuances in a speaker's voice, the exact wording being used, and the connections a speaker draws between ideas, to list some specifics. It's very likely as well that we will have a richer memory of a conversation to which we paid close attention.

Selective attention has its costs as well. When we focus on one thing, we stop attending to other stimuli. When I attend to one conversation at a party, I seem to stop hearing others—I typically don't know what they are about and won't remember much if anything about them later. One interesting exception to this idea is something called the "cocktail party" effect (Cherry, 1953), and it works as follows. If I'm paying attention to one speaker, I don't hear other conversations, *unless and until* someone in a nonattended conversation says my name (or something else of great personal importance to me). In that case, the sound of my name being pronounced seems to "pop out" of the background blend of noise, capturing my attention, at least momentarily.

No doubt you've noticed something else about attention as well: The need for it varies from task to task. Difficult, unfamiliar, and complex tasks require a lot of mental concentration; easy or well-practiced things don't. Cognitive psychologists are very familiar with the so-called practice effect, which states that the amount of practice given to a task decreases the amount of mental effort required to complete it. For example, as you practice playing a particular piano piece, it becomes easier and easier to play, requiring less and less of your attention, until you reach the point where so little attention is required to play it that the task is said to have become an **automatic process**. An automatic task can often be performed while you engage in a second, simultaneous task. That is, depending on the demands of the tasks involved, you can sometimes divide your attention among them, a phenomenon known as **multitasking**.

We will see in the chapters to come that growth in attention span and growth in the ability to regulate attention are very important bedrocks of cognitive development. We will see first that children become increasingly able to attend to a stimulus for a longer period as they get older. More than this, though, we will see that children and adolescents come to exert increasing amounts of control over their attention—that is, they develop an ability to focus their attention more clearly and develop better strategies for resisting distraction. Finally, we will devote a lot of time to considering how children come to allocate their mental energies to tasks that may not be immediately or inherently interesting—a skill that comes in very handy when children encounter formal schooling!

Memory

Information that we perceive and attend to often needs to be stored or filed away for future use; **memory** is the term we use to refer to those storage places and processes. There are long-standing and wide-ranging debates among cognitive psychologists over the nature of the storage places (e.g., are there many or only one?), as well as the kinds of memory processes and how they operate. For now, we'll focus on three different general findings about the nature of memory, ones that most cognitive psychologists, whatever their theoretical orientation, would agree with.

First, much of memory is limited, especially memory for currently active information. In a landmark study, George Miller (1956) argued that the "span" (i.e., capacity) of immediate (or short-term) memory was about seven (plus or minus two) for most adults of normal intelligence. That is, in general, the number of pieces of unrelated information you can "keep in mind" at one time is somewhere between five and nine. These capacity limits appear to increase with age. For a preschooler, the "magic number" might be three or four rather than seven.

A second general description of memory that almost every psychologist would acknowledge is that memory is often constructive, rather than being an accurate rendition of the past. This means that memory traces can and are affected by other information and that we are often not aware of this. Sometimes when we recall an event that happened to us, we infer or "fill in" missing information, making plausible guesses as to what was likely to have happened. The problem is that it is often impossible to separate out what we actually recall from what we have inferred or hypothesized. For this reason, eyewitness reports are often problematic. We will see that current work on children's eyewitness memory suggests that preschoolers might have especially suggestible memory systems.

A third point to make: The memory process of encoding (i.e., forming an initial memory trace) seems to be especially important in how and whether a memory is actually retrieved. Various studies have shown that being in the same location, the same mood, or the same state of chemical consciousness (drunk or sober) can affect one's ability to recall information. One widely accepted explanation for this is the *encoding specificity* principle, which states that when we initially form a memory trace, it stores not only that information but also the information including our personal circumstances at the time the memory trace is formed. Thus, learning information when we are in a sad mood makes it easier to recall when we are again "blue." Walking through an old neighborhood, school, or playground might bring back a lot of memories that you have forgotten you have stored—when the "learning" context is reinstated, recall seems to become much easier. Again, we'll come back to this point in several of the chapters to come.

Knowledge Representation and Categorization

One of the things that distinguishes younger children from older children is that older children know a lot more about a lot more subjects than do younger ones. Older children are better spellers, have larger vocabularies, know more math facts, know more games, have seen more movies and television programs, and have more elaborate understandings of societal conventions and customs.

Of course, the more knowledge an individual has, the more crucial it is that the information be organized for easy retrieval. The system of organization makes some kinds of retrieval almost effortless but some others harder. Take, for example, your mental lexicon—the storage of the knowledge of all the words in your vocabulary. Try to list 10 words (any words) that begin with the letter *w*. Pretty easy, right? Now try to list 10 words with *w* as the fourth letter. Much more difficult, no? This thought experiment indicates that our lexicons seem to be stored alphabetically by first letter—thus when we are asked to retrieve words by their first letter, several seem to pop to mind. However, when we need to retrieve by an internal letter (e.g., a *w* in the fourth position) the retrieval is quite arduous. This indicates that information in the lexicon is not stored by fourth letters.

In the chapters to come, we'll be looking at the ways in which infants, toddlers, children, and adolescents organize their knowledge and how this changes (or doesn't change) with cognitive development. We will also try to tease apart how knowledge representation changes with increasing levels of expertise in a particular domain (e.g., chess, dinosaurs) as opposed to increasing levels of cognitive development.

Language

One of the most striking cognitive developmental changes from infancy to childhood is that children communicate in words and sentences, while infants are limited to producing (at most) strings of sounds. It's typically not until around their first birthday that toddlers produce their first recognizable word; by the age of 6, most children's vocabularies are in the neighborhood of 5,000 word families (Bauer & Nation, 1993). By *word family,* I mean the base form of a word (e.g., *walk*) as well as its inflections and derivations (e.g., *walked, walking, walks, walker*). Language, the ability to produce and comprehend an infinite number of utterances using only a finite base of units (e.g., sounds or words) that follow a system of structure rules known as grammar, is argued to be the most distinctive aspect of human cognition (James, 1890/1983).

As with all of the other cognitive realms described previously, there is much to say about human language. A brief summary of the most important points will have to suffice for now. One important point is that language is *structured*—it has a regular system of rules that, while perhaps impossible to state explicitly by most speakers, are nonetheless followed or implicitly understood. For example, native speakers of English recognize that the sentence "I ain't gonna do my homework and I ain't gonna do my chores, neither" might violate a principle of politeness (e.g., don't say "ain't"), but it is nonetheless a legal sentence. By contrast "Dinner to be I'd if you'd come honored" is not a legally allowable sentence. We can rearrange the words to form a (very polite) utterance, but as it is presented the "sentence" doesn't constitute a legal thing to say in English. Likewise, some strings of letters don't happen to be existing English words (e.g., *plickit, dinlorp*), but they follow English spelling rules and therefore could conceivably become English words someday (perhaps they might name a new, as-yet-uninvented robotic device). Other letter strings (e.g., *tlumfpt, ndichz*) don't follow those spelling rules and are very unlikely to ever become actual words.

These examples illustrate another aspect of language—it has several different levels. There are rules pertaining to the sounds of a language (corresponding to the level of phonetics); there are rules pertaining to word meaning (studied in the field of morphology); there are rules governing the arrangement of words in a sentence (syntax). Some have even argued for the existence of rules (maxims) of cooperative conversations (Grice, 1975). Speakers and listeners of a language somehow have to develop an understanding of the rules governing all different levels of language and determine some means of coordinating them all.

A third general point to make about language is that most people's understanding of rules is implicit rather than explicit. That is, people generally either follow the rules and/or notice violations of the rules, even though they can't fully state exactly what the rules are. Indeed, branches of the field of linguistics are devoted to trying to figure out just what the rules are, and experts in the field often have strongly held disagreements!

Language acquisition shows its most dramatic effects in toddlerhood and the early preschool period, and you will see that we will be devoting an entire chapter to this aspect of cognitive development in Chapter 5. However, although language acquisition phenomena are concentrated in this developmental period, language skills are far-reaching ones, so aspects of language, including the perception of sounds, reading, and constructing arguments, will be touched on in several different places.

Thinking, Reasoning, and Decision Making

We've already discussed (very briefly) how information is perceived, attended to, stored, mentally represented, and communicated, all of which are important cognitive realms. But information must often later be used to solve problems, make plans, draw conclusions, or choose options. The processes that are involved in these kinds of information usage are thinking, reasoning, and decision making.

Of the three, *thinking* is the broadest term, meant typically to refer to any mental manipulation of information. It includes calculating sums or multiplying products, searching for a correct entry in a crossword puzzle, creating a plan for a picture, and solving a detective story, to name only a few examples. The term *reasoning* is typically reserved for types of thinking that involve some sort of logical inference, drawing a conclusion from given information (often called premises). *Decision making* typically refers to the mental activities that surround a person making a choice from among different options.

Information usage can demand a lot of cognitive resources, depending on the amount of information that needs to be kept in mind and actively processed simultaneously. We will examine the developmental course of children's and adolescents' ability to grapple with these tasks and biases in many of the chapters to come, starting with the preschool period. To preview themes, we will see that adolescence represents a time where these abilities, in particular, seem to blossom and become relevant to several aspects of a person's life.

Academic Skills

Skills and abilities that develop in formal educational settings, or **academic skills**, affect, and are affected by, cognitive development. Formal schooling in most cultures does not begin until middle childhood (when children are 5 to 7 years of age, typically). But we will see, especially in Chapter 11, that the ability to read, to write, and to do 'rithmetic, the so-called "3 Rs" of Western education, require some fairly complex cognitive abilities and, in turn, help other even more complex skills and abilities develop.

Social Cognition

When psychologists speak of cognitive abilities and skills, or **social cognition**, they typically mean to draw a distinction with social, emotional, or personality aspects of a person's functioning. Thus, courses in cognitive development often contrast with courses in social and personality development. But, of course, this division is somewhat fictional in actual children. As we will see, cognitive development touches on, and is touched on by, lots of different other kinds of development.

Unfortunately, a thorough examination of all the ways social and cognitive development intersect would be a whole other book. But we will at least catch some glimpses of the intertwining in several chapters. In Chapter 8 we'll take up the topic of how children come to be able to see other points of view and come to understand how other people may have different thoughts, beliefs, intentions, and emotions. Moreover, we'll take a detailed look at the role of play in cognition. Finally, we'll come back to the social/cognitive intersection quite a bit in Chapter 13, when we examine achievement motivation, the development of moral reasoning, and epistemological development. Other chapters will also touch on this intersection.

BROADER IMPACTS OF AND ON COGNITIVE DEVELOPMENT

Throughout the book, as appropriate, we will reflect on the role of education as it relates to cognitive development—how education might enhance development and how development might enable certain kinds of educational intervention. We'll also contemplate the influence of culture on cognitive development, trying to separate which aspects of development appear to be universal to human beings across the globe and which aspects are more typical of individuals living in certain cultural milieus.

Educational Implications

Education has a pervasive influence on many aspects of a child's development. In this book, I'll be talking about two different kinds of education. **Formal education** might be the kind that comes to mind first—students in a classroom, learning from a teacher who sets the curriculum and prepares lessons and assignments, which are then graded or assessed in some other way. Often, the learning pertains to academic topics—for example, literacy, mathematics, history, or philosophy—that do not have immediate practical application. The idea behind this kind of instruction is to inculcate general-purpose skills (e.g., reading, arithmetic computation, computer skills) that presumably will be used in a wide variety of real-life tasks.

Photo 1.1 Formal educational settings, such as this classroom, are contexts for learning general literacy and quantitative skills.

This kind of education is very familiar to students who have grown up in Western schools. In fact, it is so familiar that it might be easy to overlook the fact that not all children receive this kind of formal instruction. But the fact is that worldwide, not all children attend formal schooling, especially if they come from impoverished families and/or if formal education is not valued in, or an integral part of, their surrounding culture.

Another kind of education we will talk about, therefore, is **informal education**, the kind that occurs as children serve as apprentices to masters in learning skilled trades such as weaving, hunting, farming, or the like. Psychologist Barbara Rogoff uses the term *guided participation* to talk about informal education. By this term, she means that children receive guidance, either physical or verbal, in culturally valued activities and that children participate collaboratively in this endeavor (Rogoff, 1990).

Consider a familiar example: baking cookies. This is an activity that parents often involve their children in, and it illustrates the guided participation concept well. Imagine trying to involve a 2-year-old in the process. What parts of the activity would be delegated to him, and which parts not? Well, for starters, wise parents would keep him away from the hot oven and probably would not put him in charge of putting baking trays in or taking them out of a heated oven, for safety's sake.

Photo 1.2 Cooking with children represents a form of informal education, where a more experienced baker guides the participation of a younger novice or apprentice.

However, a parent might very effectively involve the child in measuring out the flour or sugar, adding these ingredients, or stirring or mixing ingredients together. Depending on the age and dexterity of the child, the parent might physically guide the child's participation, placing a hand over the child's hand or helping the child hold the spoon. As the child gains proficiency, the parent is likely to start to "back off" the assistance, allowing the child to independently measure, add, or stir.

Cognitive psychologists have long known that the way in which a task is performed can vary greatly with the context. For example, one study of Brazilian street children (ages 9–15) compared their ability to calculate sums correctly when the task was part of a selling transaction on the street versus their ability to perform the same problems on a school-like test (involving the same problems). Psychologists approached the child vendors, asking them questions such as "If a large coconut costs 76 cruzeiros, and a small one costs 50, how much do the two cost together?" finding their average performance to be 98% correct. In contrast, when given a formal version of the same problem ("How much is 76 + 50?"), the children answered correctly only 37% of the time (Carraher, Carraher, & Schliemann, 1985).

Thus, we will be considering the role of informal as well as formal education in developing cognitive skills in the chapters ahead. We will see that different kinds of skills might be shaped and developed by each kind of experience.

Photo 1.3 Tasks such as calculation of sums of items being sold are sometimes carried out differently than the calculation of those same sums on an abstract classroom math test.

Cognition in Cultural Context

Western psychological theory emphasizes the individual more than the environment. That is, the focus is on the individual infant, toddler, child, or adolescent and on how he or she navigates different tasks. When Western developmental psychologists perform studies, they typically treat each individual infant, child, or adolescent as the unit of study, or the "case," when they perform statistical analyses.

This view of psychology is so pervasive that it is all too easy to overlook the fact that this is only one possible approach. In fact, cultures in Eastern countries such as Japan and Korea emphasize the group rather than the individual (Nisbett, Choi, Peng, & Norenzayan, 2001). Another way to draw this distinction is to differentiate between analytic cognition, said to be characteristic of Western cultures, and **holistic cognition**, which processes the entire field surrounding an individual—his or her environment, culture, landscape, and philosophical or religious milieu.

As a culture emphasizing the individual over the group, we also pay close attention to individual achievements. Students typically turn in "their own" work and receive grades that are based largely on their individual performance and mastery, and collaboration, say, on homework or a test is often frowned upon or forbidden as "cheating." In contrast, a more collectivist culture might welcome and foster group work, emphasizing skills of interdependence and harmony. We will be returning to the theme of cultural contexts for cognition throughout the chapters to come. For now, the important point to keep in mind is that cultures play a role in selecting and encouraging some cognitive abilities but not others.

GOING FORWARD

Chapter 2 will continue your "big-picture" orientation to the field of cognitive development, presenting major theories and research methods that researchers who study cognitive development often use. The remaining chapters are organized mostly chronologically, beginning with infancy and moving forward through the other major periods of development: early childhood, middle childhood, and adolescence. Within each major period of development, we will look first at the basic cognitive abilities of perception, attention, and memory before turning our attention to the so-called higher-order cognitive processes such as categorization, problem solving, reasoning, and decision making. The distinction between basic and higher-order cognitive processes is a bit murky, but the general idea is that the higher-order processes make use of multiple basic processes in order to function.

However, the organization of the book will not be strictly chronological. Certain topics, such as language or the development of academic skills, will be discussed in a single chapter, even though they span a few developmental periods. My aim in doing this is to improve the coherence of the book—though these special topics are especially prominent during one developmental period (language development in toddlerhood; academic skills in middle childhood), these aspects of cognition do show some development in other periods, and I'll mention that development too, to round out the picture of the topic.

Cognitive development is, for me, one of the most fascinating aspects of psychology. I hope to spark your interest in it and to whet your appetite for grappling with important and fundamental questions concerning how and why the transformations occur that cause infants with limited cognitive means to eventually evolve into adolescents with dreams, goals, values, and philosophies of their own.

SUMMARY

1. Cognition includes processes by which organisms obtain, retain, use, and communicate information.

2. Major cognitive processes in humans include perception, attention, memory, knowledge representation and categorization, language, and thinking.

3. Formal, classroom-style education can be contrasted with informal, apprentice-style education. Both likely influence cognitive development, though plausibly they have different effects and/or influence different realms.

4. It is also likely that cognitive development is affected by a child's cultural context. For example, Western cultures emphasize the functioning of individuals, while Eastern cultures are more likely to emphasize the group rather than the individual. Cultural differences may end up promoting either more analytic or more holistic cognition.

REVIEW QUESTIONS

1. Choose a realm of cognition (perception, attention, memory, knowledge representation, thinking, or language) and describe some of the changes occurring in it as a child develops in infancy, the preschool period, middle childhood, and adolescence.

2. What aspects of cognitive development are more likely to be affected by formal schooling, and what aspects by informal schooling? Marshal an argument to defend your point of view.

3. Discuss the claim that Western culture is more likely to promote analytic cognition and Eastern culture holistic cognition.

KEY TERMS

Academic Skills

Analytic Cognition

Attention

Automatic Processes

Cognition

Cognitive Development

Cross-Sectional Comparisons

Decision Making

Encoding

Formal Education

Grammar

Holistic Cognition

Informal Education

Knowledge Representation

Language

Lexicon

Longitudinal Comparisons

Memory

Multitasking

Perception

Practice Effect

Reasoning

Social Cognition

Thinking

CHAPTER 2

MAJOR THEORIES, FRAMEWORKS, AND RESEARCH METHODS

THEORIES OF COGNITIVE DEVELOPMENT

We've touched briefly on a number of cognitive realms, and hinted at some of the changes that occur in each as a child develops. Of course, later chapters will fill in details of all of these topics. The question now is "What is the best way to describe the nature of the *overall* cognitive changes?" In this section, we'll consider a number of different general theories and frameworks cognitive developmental psychologists have used to understand the "big picture."

This won't be the only time you encounter any of these theories, however. Specific aspects of a theory that are particularly relevant to a specific age group will be discussed in the relevant chapters. This chapter, then, serves as a general introduction to major theories of cognitive development. To make an analogy to the visual arts: Think of coverage here as a broad sketch or outline. We'll return to this outline again and again throughout the book to add texture, shading, and detail.

Piagetian Theory

The most well-known theory of cognitive development was developed by Jean Piaget (1896–1980), whose first scientific work concerned the development of mollusks. In later years, Piaget became absorbed by the question of how intelligence and cognitive functions develop, drawing parallels between these processes and those he saw in his biological work, specifically, environmental adaptation—the way organisms evolve to better fit their biological niche (Miller, 2011). Piaget believed that children were not passive recipients of cognitive development, but rather active participants in the creation of new mental structures that provided a better fit with their cognitive environment. This construction of mental structures involves children integrating their existing mental

Photo 2.1 Jean Piaget is shown here interacting with a group of children.

structures with their experiences in the world to evolve new, more complex, and more stable mental structures.

Piaget proposed what developmental psychologists call a **stage theory** of cognitive development. Stage theories, in general, are those that view development as proceeding in qualitatively different steps, each one occurring in a set order, and typically with an associated age range. Different stages build on one another, implying that the gains in one stage make possible the development in the next. For this reason, stage approach theorists believe that it is impossible for a child to skip stages, or to go through them in any but the typical order. The commonsense maxim "You have to walk before you can run" captures this idea.

Table 2.1 lists criteria for a stage theory. *Qualitative change* means that the differences between individuals in different stages are differences in kind or type, not simply differences in amount of something. For example, older children (say, 10 years of age) are typically taller than younger children (say, 2-year-olds), but this is a quantitative difference. Qualitative differences in development might best be illustrated by the difference between a caterpillar and a butterfly—it isn't simply that the butterfly is bigger; it's that the butterfly has a completely reorganized structure.

Unified structures means that underlying the performance that children or adults show on a variety of tasks are one or more cognitive structures. For example, a child's production of sentences is guided by his or her grammar, or underlying and implicit set of syntactic rules. Differences between a toddler's demand of "more cookie" and an adolescent's version of the request "Is it okay if I have a cookie?" is explained largely in terms of the difference

Table 2–1   Criteria for a stage theory of cognitive development

Qualitative change	Each stage is held to involve differences in kind, rather than differences in amount.
Unified structures	Each stage is characterized by the existence of an integrated cognitive structure or structures that guide and constrain an individual's acquisition and processing of information.
Progression	Each stage builds on the previous ones.
Stable order	Stages must be experienced in a fixed order, with each stage a logical prerequisite for the next.
Universality	Stages are fundamental to human nature and occur in basically similar ways across cultures.

in their grammar, and perhaps as well by their underlying mental models of their parents' nutritional goals and proclivities.

Progression means that each stage yields achievements that are necessary to enable the next stage to begin. That is, a child needs to be able to master the tasks characteristic of one stage before being able to tackle the challenges of a next stage. Each succeeding stage is thought to incorporate the gains of previous stages. For this reason, an individual is constrained to go through stages in a set, or *stable order*. There can be no skipping of stages, and typically, no regression of stages, as once a higher-order set of structures emerges, those structures govern one's cognitive life.

Finally, the characteristic of *universality* implies that stages are experienced in fundamentally similar ways by individuals across the globe. Stages are thought to be an inherent part of human nature and thus not subject to very much environmental influence, although the performance of different stage-related tasks could presumably show up. We'll explore this seeming contradiction in just a bit.

I said earlier that Piaget's theory focused on the development of qualitatively different mental structures. Just what are these mental structures? Curiously enough, the first structures are not mental at all but rather behavioral—the few reflexive behaviors newborns display. These include such things as grasping and sucking, and are the precursors to later mental structures.

From day one, the structures start to evolve or adapt, through two processes Piaget termed **assimilation** and **accommodation**. Piaget (1970/1983) defined *assimilation* as the "integration of external elements into evolving or completed structures" (p. 106). So, the idea is that a child takes an existing structure and applies it to a new object. For example, the child who has a grasping reflex (the structure) applies it not only to familiar objects (a rattle, a finger), but to new objects as well—a blanket, a teddy bear.

Accommodation, the other process involved in adaption, involves the changing of the structures to fit new objects. The way one grasps a blanket is very different from the way one grasps a finger, so the structure (grasping) has to undergo alteration in response. Each time an infant grasps a new object, she changes her grasping reflex, even if only by a very small amount. That change of structure is the accommodation. According to Piaget, assimilation and accommodation are always present, at least to some degree, in every act of adaptation because it is impossible for one to exist in the absence of the other. Optimally, the two are balanced, or in equilibrium.

Piaget described four major stages of development, some of which also have substages. For right now, we will only briefly review the four stages, but we will elaborate on each in the chapters ahead.

The first stage of cognitive development begins at birth and lasts until about 18–24 months. It is called the **sensorimotor stage** because Piaget believed that infants in this period operate cognitively based almost entirely on their sensory experiences and motor responses. Put more starkly: Piaget held that infants lack a capacity for **mental representation**, meaning all of their "knowledge" during this period consists of sensation/perception or action. Thus, all experience must happen in the here and now and must be centered on things that are present.

Notice the implications of this belief. Infants, lacking a capacity for mental representation, necessarily lack the ability to have thoughts that are not acted upon; conscious memories of past events, plans, or strategies for dealing with problems; or even a complicated system of communication such as language.

One of the most well-known Piagetian demonstrations of aspects of the sensorimotor stage is that of an infant's lack of understanding of object permanence. The demonstration works as follows: Take a young (say, 5-month-old) infant, and seat him facing a desirable object or toy. Watch as he gazes at and perhaps tries to reach for it. Now, block his view and grasp of the object (and make sure he can't hear or smell or in any other way have any sensory or motor contact with it). Typically, the child will fairly immediately appear to lose all interest, as if the object or toy has somehow ceased to exist! Piaget's explanation is that objects out of sensorimotor contact are truly "out of mind," because the infant has no capacity for mental representation.

The second Piagetian stage of cognitive development is known as the **preoperational stage**, which lasts from about 18 months until the child is approximately 6 years old. Preoperational children have finally acquired the ability to mentally represent objects, events, and ideas, which broadens their cognitive abilities considerably: They can use language, can pretend, and can use what Piaget called the *semiotic function,* using one thing to represent another, as when a child uses rocks as hamburgers during a play episode, or

 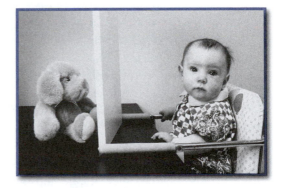

Photos 2.2a and 2.2b   According to Piaget, until object permanence develops, babies fail to understand that objects still exist when no longer in view.

when a child uses the name of a friend who isn't present to bring up the friend in conversation.

Despite these myriad impressive achievements, the preoperational child still seems somewhat deficient, cognitively speaking, when she is compared with an older child in a higher stage of cognitive development. These children are said to lack reversible mental operations (those possessed by concrete operational children that allow them to think about how an action can be undone), which means that their thinking is distorted in several predictable ways.

One striking characteristic of children of this age is their inability to keep straight the distinction between the way things look and the way things truly are, something known as the *appearance/reality distinction* (Flavell, Green, & Flavell, 1986). Thus, for example, a preschooler is likely to be shaky on the concept that a person dressed up as Mickey Mouse is really not a mouse but a human being wearing a costume.

A second characteristic of preoperational cognition is **egocentrism**, or a tendency to see the world only through one's own perspective. For example, a 4-year-old might not understand that the new babysitter doesn't know all of his friends, or what his favorite snacks are. After all, the 4-year-old knows this information, and therefore he assumes that everyone else shares that knowledge.

Preoperational children have also been described as having centered, rigid thought (Miller, 2011). That is, they pay attention to only one salient aspect of a situation or object, and ignore others. Their thought is also described as static (focusing on end states rather than the transformations that have brought about those states) and lacking *reversibility,* the ability to mentally simulate the inverse of a transformation.

A famous demonstration of preoperational thinking comes from Piagetian *conservation* tasks, of which number conservation is perhaps the best known. They work as follows: The experimenter sets two rows of checkers in front of the child, one set black and one red, each containing five checkers. Initially, checkers in each row are set out in one-to-one correspondence (i.e., each black checker is lined up with a red checker), and the child judges both rows of checkers to be equal in number. Next, the experimenter spreads out one of the rows of checkers (see Figure 2.1), and asks the child which row has more, or if the two rows still have the same number of checkers. The typical 4-year-old responds that the longer row has more checkers than the shorter row. He has failed to appreciate the fact that operations such as moving checkers around the table are number-irrelevant: They do not affect the numerosity of the rows.

Instead, it seems as if the child focuses solely on the length of the row of checkers (ignoring the density) and on what the final state of the transformed

Figure 2–1   Depiction of conservation of number task

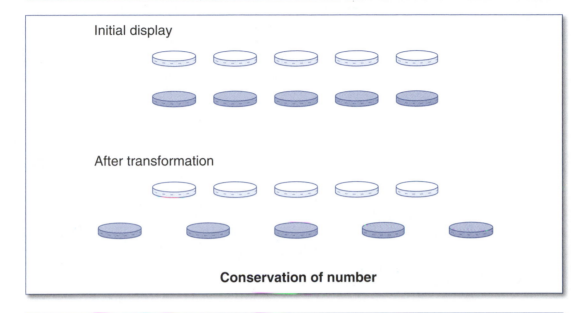

SOURCE: Galotti (2008, p. 508).

row is (longer) rather than what the transformation was (rearranging, which does not affect number), and neglects to think about the fact that the transformation is reversible (the longer row can be rearranged back into its original configuration).

From about the age of 6 years until early adolescence and puberty (say, around age 11 or 12), children enter the third stage of cognitive development, concrete operations. During this stage, children develop

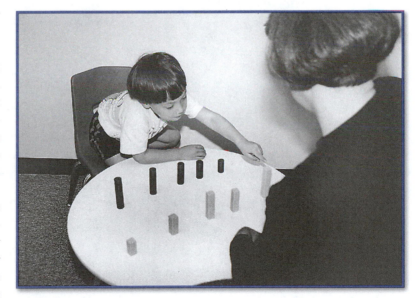

Photo 2.3   According to Piaget, this preoperational child might believe that the row closest to him contains fewer blocks than the row farther away.

more comprehensive and stable mental operations, such as the ability to conserve, or classify, or put objects in order, which allows them to process information in more sophisticated ways. Unlike younger children, concrete operational children can pay attention to more than one aspect of a situation, which in turn allows them to conserve number, quantity, area, and so forth. Concrete operational children are also quite capable of making the appearance/reality distinction, and are not so overwhelmed by their immediate perceptions.

Concrete operational children are becoming more aware of the relationships among different transformations. Take the domain of arithmetic, for example. Basic operations such as addition, subtraction, multiplication, and division are interrelated, with some operations (e.g., subtraction) the inverse of others (e.g., addition). Concrete operational children become better able to understand these interrelationships.

Concrete operational children are also more adept at seeing other interrelationships, for example, those among different sets, subsets, and supersets. Asked to classify a group of objects into categories, the 9-year-old is much better able to consistently sort (e.g., all of the round things, all of the square things; or all of the blue things, all of the red things). According to Piaget, this consistency stands in contrast to the performance

Photo 2.4 According to Piaget, concrete operational children are positioned to understand relationships between addition and subtraction facts or multiplication and division facts.

of the younger, preopera-
tional child, who starts out
sorting wooden blocks on the
basis of shape but midway
through the task switches to
sorting on the basis of color.

The final Piagetian stage
of cognitive development,
which begins around puberty,
is that of **formal operations**.
Adolescents operating in this
framework show thinking
that is much more systematic,
reflective, and scientific than
the thinking of younger children. This makes possible
greater understanding of logical reasoning, and of the
logic of scientific experiments, according to Piaget.

Photo 2.5   According to Piaget, hypothetical and deductive
reasoning typical of that required for scientific experimentation awaits
the development of formal operations.

Adolescents, unlike younger children, understand how to vary one independent variable at a time, how to list and test every possible combination
of variables, and how to think *counterfactually*.

The cognitive abilities of the adolescent are not restricted to the classroom or the science laboratory, however. For the first time, adolescents are
said to be able to see reality as only one logical possibility. Thus, they can
(and do!) question social norms, rules, and systems—including school poli-
cies, religious teachings, and political processes.

This new liberation of thought has been described as one of the
sources of adolescent idealism and political awakening, as they are now
capable of seeing a variety of possible futures for themselves and for others (Moshman, 2005).

Researchers studying the ability of people to reason logically also typically report an increase in this ability during the adolescent years
(Moshman, 2005). Adolescents are better able to see that some conclusions are demanded by premises by virtue of the abstract structure of an
argument, and not simply as a function of the truth of the premises. To
illustrate this point, I will ask you to consider the following categorical syl-
logism. The task is to determine whether the conclusion logically follows
from the premises—that is, *must* the conclusion be true if the premises
are true?

Premises:
Dogs are bigger than elephants.
Elephants are bigger than planets.
Conclusion:
Dogs are bigger than planets.

Adolescents can see, as younger children sometimes cannot, that the conclusion is logically true, even though it is empirically false. That is to say, the conclusion is false in the real world because the premises are false in the real world, *not* because of the form of the argument.

Piaget's theory of cognitive development thus describes how thought evolves from simple reflexes to an organized, flexible, logical system of internal mental structures that allows thinking about a wide variety of objects, events, and abstractions. A child at each stage of development has a remarkable set of abilities, but often (especially in stages before formal operations) faces several limitations in thinking. The mental structures that allow and organize thought develop slowly through the child's active exploration of the world.

Piaget's is not the only stage theory of cognitive development, as we will see in the chapters to come. Nonetheless, his is the broadest, both in terms of realms of cognition addressed and in terms of age range of children it applies to. However, we will visit other stage theories pertaining to specific aspects of cognitive development in the chapters ahead.

Piaget's theory has not been without its critics and its alternatives, some of which we will explore in the remaining sections. However, we will first briefly examine the contributions of a group of developmental psychologists known as the **neo-Piagetians** (Miller, 2011). These psychologists retain Piaget's commitment to the idea of qualitatively different stages, but pair this commitment with some of the ideas from information-processing theory (which we will review below). For example, Robbie Case, one of the most famous neo-Piagetian theorists, explains much of cognitive development in terms of increases in working memory capacity—the amount of mental "space" a person has with which to, say, remember bits of information for a short time, or reorganize information while solving a problem. Other neo-Piagetians, such as Michael Commons, have focused on cognitive development after adolescence.

Vygotskian Theory and Sociocultural Influences

Russian psychologist Lev Vygotsky (1896–1934) is credited with helping develop the sociocultural approach to the study of cognitive development. Vygotsky held that all humans are inextricably part of a matrix that surrounds them, and their behavior cannot be analyzed or understood without simultaneously understanding and analyzing that matrix (Miller, 2011). The cultural background, an important component of this matrix, is one that defines the sorts of abilities, skills, and habits children need to acquire. It also provides them with tools that help or hinder different cognitive tasks. It is not that the child develops internal mental structures "inside his head," the way Piaget might view it, but instead that the child and his environment (including important other people, such as parents, siblings, and teachers) together co-construct the child's mental structures. It is not that (as in most Western psychological theories) the environment *affects* development, but rather that the environment and the child together are the appropriate unit of study. The social activities that the child engages in—play, or formal schooling, or using a computer, or navigating through woods—shape the mind and the cognitive structures.

Vygotsky bestowed on developmental psychology the important concept of the **zone of proximal development**. By this he meant the range of cognitive functioning a child is capable of. At the bottom of the zone, the lowest level of performance, is the child's ability to function independently, with no help. At the upper end is the performance a child is capable of either with help from an adult or experienced older child, with the right set of props or tools, or in play (Miller, 2011). This zone represents potential development.

Photo 2.6   Lev Semenovich Vygotsky

Here's an example of the zone of proximal development. My daughter, Kimmie, is currently beginning to learn about multiplication. She loves doing multiplication facts in the car as we drive to school. One day, I threw out the problem, "7 times 3." "I can't do that one, Mom!" she wailed. "OK," I said, "can you do 3 times 7?" "Sure," she said, "that one is easy." Since then, I have to help her with the "hard problems" (the ones where the first number is greater than 5) by reminding her that she can simply swap the two numbers' order to find the right answer. In doing this, I am **scaffolding** my daughter's performance—providing aids that let her tackle and succeed at more complex problems she can do on her own.

The zone of proximal development is not simply a function of an adult or older child teaching or demonstrating a new skill for a younger one. Instead, Vygotsky intended the zone to capture "any situation in which some activity is leading children beyond their current level of functioning" (Miller, 2011, p. 380). As we will see in a few chapters, children's play can also create a zone of proximal development for different cognitive abilities.

Vygotsky also placed great emphasis on the role of culture in cognitive development. Cultures bestow on individuals a variety of tools, and this in turn shapes the cognitive skills that are enabled. In our Western culture, for example, we place great value on literacies of all kinds—reading, numerical, technological—to give some examples. We also value formal education that goes beyond teaching practical job-related skills. These values drive the setup of our educational programs and institutions—elementary and secondary education is publicly funded and available for free; lessons in the elementary grades focus heavily on teaching children to read, write, and do arithmetic (these "3R" subjects being seen as fundamental to schooling). Increasingly, technology such as calculators and computers is included in the curriculum whenever possible, with many kindergarten classrooms equipped with one or more computers, and all of them with books and writing materials.

Vygotskian theory is undergoing a renaissance of sorts among both developmental psychologists and educators. We will discuss this theory in more detail in the chapters ahead.

Information-Processing Theory

A third theoretical perspective on cognitive development comes from information-processing theory, a description of human cognition that borrows heavily from computer architecture. This approach was developed in the 1960s, as the computer revolution was in full swing. Although many psychologists contributed to developing the main ideas, the two who are most often credited with the initial formulation of the information-processing approach are Richard Atkinson and Richard Shiffrin (1968).

Figure 2.2 depicts a general model of information processing. It contains boxes, which represent memory stores—structures that hold onto information for some period of time—and arrows, which depict processes that operate on the information. Those of you with computer programming experience might be reminded of a flowchart, an apt analogy for this kind of model. The general notion of an information-processing model of cognition is that information flows through a system, being stored and transformed in various places as different processes take place. A goal of the information-processing framework, then, is to specify precisely what these storage places and processes are—how many; when, where, and how they operate; and most important for our purposes, how they change with development.

Information-processing theory does not argue for the existence of qualitative differences among children at different developmental points. Instead, information-processing theorists locate cognitive developmental differences as stemming from quantitative differences in some aspect of cognitive functions.

Figure 2–2   A typical information-processing model

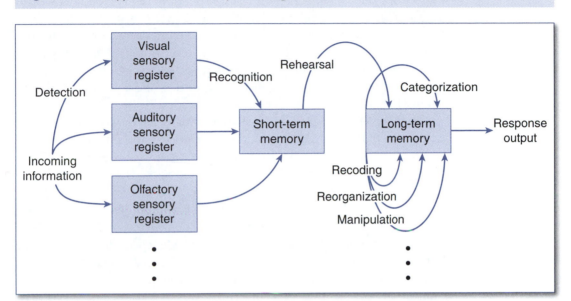

SOURCE: Galotti (2008, p. 25).

What might such aspects be? One might be in perceptual processing, as children become more sensitive to subtle distinctions between stimuli. Consider, for example, the lowercase letters *b, d, p,* and *q.* Each of these consists of a half-circle abutting a vertical line. In other words, the differences among these four letters are quite small. Little wonder, then, that beginning readers in kindergarten and first grade often confuse them, reading "bab" instead of "dad."

Processing speed is another possible factor explaining some aspects of cognitive change in children. We know that as children mature, more of the **neurons** in their brains become myelinated (Couperus & Nelson, 2006). **Myelin** is a fatty substance that wraps around the long axons of neurons, the basic cells that transmit information throughout the body and the brain. The function of myelin is to speed the nerve impulses. Essentially, this means that as a child matures, he can process more information in the same amount of time or the same amount of information in less time. Thus, older children are able to respond to stimuli and to process information about the stimuli more quickly than younger children.

Attentional control surely also contributes to cognitive development. We will see in the chapters to come that **attention spans** increase as children age. An individual's attention span governs the amount of time she can focus on a task; having a longer attention span would in turn make possible an ability to work on a wider variety of tasks, especially complex ones. A second aspect of attention that shows developmental change is in children's ability to direct (and redirect) their attention—to shut out distractions and to concentrate on a particular task, and to respond more quickly to the things they are focusing on (Plude, Enns, & Brodeur, 1994). Developmental psychologists use the term executive functioning to describe a person's ability to control her attention and direct processing resources.

Younger children have been shown to have lower working memory spans than older children. That is, the number of unrelated pieces of information they can hold in mind is much lower than the number for adults. Having a larger memory capacity again would allow children to work on harder tasks and to process more information.

Younger children are also less likely to plan ahead or to use strategies, or deliberate plans of problem solving, on cognitive tasks. For example, if given a set of stimuli and asked to study them, older children are much more likely to adopt useful study behaviors, such as rehearsal (repeating the information, either aloud or silently), than are preschoolers (Flavell, Beach, & Chinsky, 1966).

The knowledge base is another aspect of cognitive development that various psychologists examine as an explanation of cognitive development. In a landmark case study, psychologists Michelene Chi and Randi Koeske (1983) studied a then four-and-a-half-year-old, a known dinosaur fancier. The child had spent the previous 18 months acquiring information about dinosaurs from books read to him by his parents, and from playing with the various plastic models he owned. Some dinosaurs were very familiar to him and were ones he had detailed knowledge of; other dinosaurs were less well known. On a variety of standard psychological memory tests, it turned out that the child performed much better when the stimuli were familiar dinosaur names than when the stimuli were less familiar dinosaur names. This result suggested that simply having more expertise in a domain enhances performance generally on tasks involving that domain. When we consider that older children typically have more expertise in almost every realm than younger children do, it suggests that a larger knowledge base might provide much of the explanation of cognitive differences.

Certainly the ability to process and produce language has been touted as a crucially important cognitive ability that in turn might affect cognitive processing generally. Being able to use language to direct one's attention and performance on a task—that is, being able to "talk oneself through" a task—has been regarded as a major achievement.

Name means pierced lizard.

Photo 2.7   Information-processing theory notes that during middle childhood, children acquire a great deal of knowledge about a variety of topics, facilitating their cognitive processing of information within those domains.

Learning Theory

Psychologists who study learning (both animal and human) focus on how an organism's experience causes changes in the way that organism responds to future events. In order for this past experience to have an influence, of course, there must be some means of the organism representing past experience—perhaps through a change in the basic neural wiring or some other connections that the organism may or may not have explicit awareness of. Learning theorists initially believed that the laws of learning were ones that applied to all kinds of learning and all kinds of organisms—a dog learning to bark on command, a child learning when a favorite television program comes on, a scientist learning a new principle of thermodynamics.

Although this belief in one set of learning laws for all kinds of learning has been largely rejected by most psychologists (Gleitman, Fridlund, & Reisberg, 2004), many of the basic principles of learning discovered do have wide applicability to many kinds of learning. Here, we will concentrate on two major forms of learning, classical and instrumental learning (or conditioning).

Classical conditioning builds on the hardwired reflexes an organism is born with. As you may recall, reflexes have two parts—(a) a stimulus, which elicits (b) a response. In order for something to be considered a hardwired reflex, the stimulus must always automatically elicit the response, regardless of the animal's prior experience or current beliefs. Consider, as an example, the reflexive kick your leg gives when your knee is tapped in just the right spot. The tap to the knee is the stimulus, and the kick of the leg is the response.

Ivan Pavlov (1849–1936), a Russian physiologist, was the first to discover that an organism could acquire, or learn, new reflexes, which, although more fragile than hardwired ones, could come to work just as automatically. Acquired, or conditional (later mistranslated as "conditioned"), reflexes were built upon the hardwired reflexes by pairing a previously neutral stimulus, called a *conditioned stimulus,* with the eliciting stimulus from the hardwired reflex, called the *unconditioned stimulus.* After a number of such pairings, a new, conditioned reflex is built, such that the conditioned stimulus presented alone comes to elicit the conditioned response (which in most cases is similar to the unconditioned response).

So, for example, suppose that we arranged for you to have 50 exposures of a knee tap but, each time, arranged to sound a bell just before the hammer tapped your knee. According to the principles of classical conditioning, the 51st presentation of the bell (without the hammer this time) should be sufficient to cause your knee to kick.

Classical conditioning has been shown in infants. One of the most famous, and controversial, demonstrations of this came in the case of Little Albert. Psychologist John B. Watson and his graduate student Rosalie Rayner (1920) tested 11-month-old Albert B., pairing the sight of a white rat (CS, or conditioned stimulus) with the unexpected and loud sound of a steel bar being struck behind him (UCS, or unconditioned stimulus) in order to produce a conditioned fear response. They later found that this fear response generalized (that is, started to appear in response) to other, similar stimuli, including a white rabbit and a Santa Claus mask. Although Watson and Rayner were not the first to demonstrate classical conditioning in children (Windholz & Lamal, 1986), their case study is undoubtedly the most well known. Later studies have established (with fewer ethical issues) that given the right stimuli, even hours-old newborns can be classically conditioned (Rovee-Collier & Barr, 2001).

Although classically conditioned responses are fairly easy to establish, they don't explain a wide range of learned behaviors, simply because all classically conditioned responses must be built upon existing hardwired reflexes, the repertoire of which is fairly limited. Fortunately, there exists another route to establishing new behavioral responses, known as **instrumental** (sometimes operant) **conditioning**. Instrumental conditioning relies on a principle known as the law of effect (Thorndike, 1898): Responses followed by rewards tend to be strengthened, while those followed by no reward or punishment are weakened. So, for example, if a toddler throws a hissy fit in the grocery store (response) and that response is followed by something "rewarding" (e.g., the parent buys her a candy bar at the checkout lane, just to quiet her), the tantrum response is likely to become more frequently emitted in the future. On the other hand, a toddler whose fits go unheeded is, according to this account, likely to show this response less frequently in the future. We'll see examples of instrumental conditioning used to investigate especially the cognitive capabilities of infants, in Chapters 3 and 4.

Learning theory, as just reviewed, represents an **empiricist** tradition in psychology. Empiricism is a philosophical tradition that places much less emphasis on inborn, hardwired cognitive architecture, and much more emphasis on acquired behavior, learned from the environment. If you think about the traditional "nature–nurture" question, empiricism is on the end of the "nurture" dimension. Philosopher John Locke (1632–1704), for example, bequeathed us the metaphor of the mind as a blank slate (*tabula rasa*) at birth—with one's individual experiences doing the writing.

A Nativist Perspective

The corresponding philosophical position, **nativism**, places much more emphasis on knowledge structures that an infant is, in some sense, born with. As such, nativism falls on the "nature" end of the nature–nurture continuum. Philosophers such as John Stuart Mill (1806–1873) and Immanuel Kant (1724–1804) discussed the existence of preexisting categories of knowledge. Sometimes, this knowledge takes awhile to mature or unfold, but the idea is that the knowledge is genetically programmed to appear at some point, given a normal environmental experience.

As we will shortly see, some investigators researching infant perceptual abilities rely heavily on the nativist perspective to explain young infants' remarkable perceptual abilities. We will also see a strong nativist influence on many researchers who study language development. Noam Chomsky, arguably the most famous modern linguist, for example, has argued that human beings come equipped with a **language acquisition device (LAD)** that programs them to acquire a human language by the end of early childhood (Chomsky, 1968). His argument was that while the child's environment dictated *which* human language would be acquired, the LAD constrained the learning to a human language, as opposed to an artificial one (such as, let's say, HTML or C++).

Nativists like Chomsky therefore don't necessarily argue that specific knowledge is innate. Rather, the argument goes something like this: Part of what it means to be human is to have certain structures programmed into us that constrain and direct our learning. Thus, we come "prepared" to learn some things, like language or perception rather easily, when compared with other domains. This explains, for example, why a 3-year-old has learned a lot of sophisticated information about her native language but has learned very little about calculus or formal logic.

We'll be discussing some very modern programs of research in infant cognitive development in Chapters 3 and 4 that come under the nativist umbrella. That is, they emphasize the amount and range of innate, or inborn, knowledge infants arrive in the world with on the day they are born.

A Cognitive Neuroscience Perspective

Many of the general age-related changes in cognitive development are believed to stem from underlying changes in neurological development (Johnson, 1998). Certain brain structures such as the cerebellum, hippocampus, and cerebral cortex don't assume their final mature state until well into childhood or adolescence. As brain structures mature, certain cognitive achievements in such realms as vision, face recognition, and visual tracking are observed. So-called higher mental processes, such as planning and goal setting, have been linked to the final maturation of the frontal cortex during the adolescent years. And as we will see, neurological development of the prefrontal cortex has been tied to development of executive functioning (Casey, Giedd, & Thomas, 2000).

Of course, the topic of brain development and its relationship to cognition is itself a vast and complex one, and only brief highlights are given here. The interested student is referred to other in-depth treatments of the topic (e.g., Johnson, Munakata, & Gilmore, 2002). First, some growth statistics: The weight of the brain grows from 0 to 350 grams (350 grams is a little less than 13 ounces) during the prenatal period, but doesn't stop then. The maximum brain weight of 1,400 grams (a little more than 49 ounces) is achieved when the individual is about 11 years old (Nolte, 2009). Most of the postbirth growth takes place before the child's fourth birthday, although some changes continue through adulthood, with a slow decline setting in at about age 50.

There are obviously a lot of different structures to talk about when we talk about the brain. Figure 2.3 shows various structures of the brain,

Figure 2–3   Development of major structures of the brain

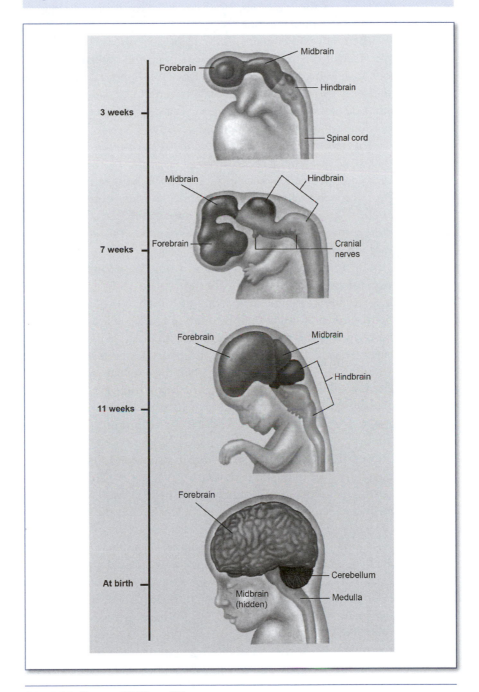

SOURCE: Garrett (2009, p. 53).

including the hindbrain, midbrain, and forebrain, and how they develop prenatally. In our brief discussion, we will focus specifically on the cerebral cortex, a part of the forebrain. However, it is worth briefly talking about the hindbrain and midbrain first.

The hindbrain contains three major structures. The *medulla* transmits information from the spinal cord to the brain and regulates life support functions such as breathing. The *pons* also acts as a neural relay center, facilitating the "crossover" of information between the left side of the body and the right side of the brain and vice versa. The *cerebellum* contains neurons that coordinate muscular activity and coordination.

The midbrain is "a small region of enormous importance" (Nolte, 2009, p. 675). Many of the structures (e.g., the *inferior* and *superior colliculi*) are involved in relaying information between other brain regions (e.g., the cerebellum and forebrain). Another midbrain structure, the *reticular formation,* helps keep us awake and alert and is involved in the sudden arousal we might need to respond to a threatening or attention-grabbing stimulus.

The forebrain also consists of a number of structures. The *thalamus,* for example, is yet another structure to relay information, especially to the cerebral cortex, about which more is given below. The *hypothalamus* controls the pituitary gland by releasing hormones, specialized chemicals that help regulate other glands in the body. The hypothalamus also controls so-called homeostatic behaviors, such as eating, drinking, temperature control, sleeping, sexual behaviors, and emotional reactions (Wilson, 2003). Other structures, such as the *hippocampus, amygdala,* and *septum*, have to do with memory and emotional experience and regulation, and the *basal ganglia* are involved in the production of motor behavior.

We will focus here on the *cerebrum* (from the Latin word for brain), the largest structure in the brain. It consists of a layer called the cerebral cortex, consisting of about a half-dozen layers of neurons with white matter beneath, which carries information between the cortex and the thalamus or between different parts of the cortex.

Figure 2.4 presents a more detailed diagram of the cerebral cortex, which neurologists divide into four lobes: frontal (underneath the forehead); parietal (underneath the top rear part of the skull); occipital (at the back of the head); and temporal (on the side of the head). Actually, since our heads have two sides, right and left, we have two lobes of each kind—the right frontal, left frontal, right parietal, left parietal, and so forth. The left and right hemispheres are connected by either the corpus callosum (in the case of the frontal, parietal, and occipital lobes) or the anterior commisure (in the case of the temporal lobes; Nolte, 2009).

Figure 2–4 Cerebral lobes and functional areas on the surface of the cerebral hemispheres

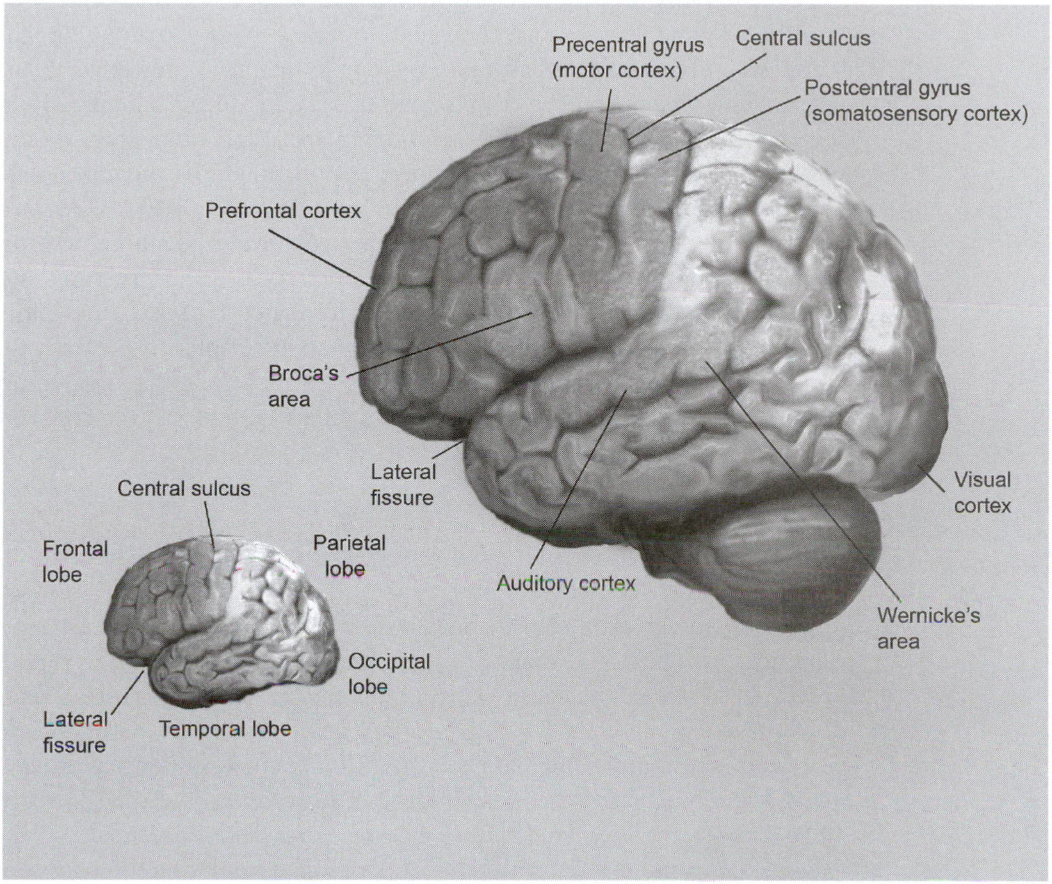

Precentral gyrus (motor cortex)
Central sulcus
Postcentral gyrus (somatosensory cortex)
Prefrontal cortex
Broca's area
Lateral fissure
Central sulcus
Visual cortex
Frontal lobe
Parietal lobe
Auditory cortex
Occipital lobe
Lateral fissure
Temporal lobe
Wernicke's area

SOURCE: Garrett (2009, p. 56).

The parietal lobes contain the somatosensory cortex, involved in the processing of sensory information from the body—for example, sensations of pain or pressure, touch or temperature (Garrett, 2009). The occipital lobes process visual information, and the temporal lobes process auditory information, as well as information from the senses of taste and smell (Nolte, 2009). The temporal lobes are also right above structures such as the amygdala and hippocampus, both involved in memory, so damage to the temporal lobes can result in memory disruption as well.

The frontal lobes have three separate regions. The motor cortex directs fine motor movement, while the premotor cortex seems to be involved with planning such movements. The prefrontal cortex or lobe is involved with what neuropsychologists call executive functioning—planning, making decisions, implementing strategies, inhibiting inappropriate behaviors, and using working memory to process information (Nolte, 2009).

The prefrontal cortex also shows the longest period of maturation, and it appears to be one of the last brain regions to mature (Casey et al., 2000). Interestingly, this region may also be one of the "first to go" in aging effects seen toward the end of life. It has been hypothesized that brain regions that show the most plasticity over the longest periods might be the most sensitive to environmental toxins or stressors.

The cognitive neuroscience approach to studying cognitive development is to chart the growth of these various brain regions and structures, and to try to relate their growth directly to performance on specific cognitive tasks. For example, a developmental cognitive neuroscientist might study the brain changes that accompany, or predict, the development of memory strategies in school-age children. We'll see specific examples of the cognitive neuroscience approach in the chapters to come.

Dimensions of Cognitive Developmental Theories

The theories we have covered share similarities and differences. Here, I want to highlight three major dimensions along which theories can be ordered. The first is the nature–nurture dimension, which essentially has to do with how much emphasis the theory places on innate, or inborn, structures versus how much emphasis the theory places on experience and learning. Obviously, learning theories are on the "nurture" end of the spectrum, while nativist theories are on the "nature" end; other theories, such as Piaget's, fall in the middle, with other theories also somewhere in between.

A second important dimension is the continuity–discontinuity dimension. This has to do with how much a theory postulates continuous, incremental, gradual change versus how much it regards development as having abruptly appearing qualitative change. Here, stage theories are likely to fall closer to the "discontinuity" end of the spectrum, and learning theories closer to the "continuity" end.

Finally, a third dimension of difference is the universal/culture-specific dimension. This has to do with whether a theory is assumed to hold across all cultures and time periods or whether it is to be offered as a description of development specific to one or more particular contexts. Theories that posit general laws or axioms fall more toward the first end; theories that don't fall toward the second.

RESEARCH METHODS FOR
STUDYING COGNITIVE DEVELOPMENT

Throughout the book, I will be presenting a number of studies in developmental psychology, some of them in great detail. When reading about a study's conclusions, it is essential to keep in mind how those conclusions have come about. Doing this requires an understanding of research methods. Whole courses in research methods exist in almost every psychology department, and therefore my treatment of the topic in one section of one chapter will necessarily be brief. If you'd like to follow up on any issues I touch on here, I'd refer you to a textbook on research methods in developmental psychology, such as S. Miller (2007).

Longitudinal Versus Cross-Sectional Designs

I presented the terms *longitudinal* and *cross-sectional* back in Chapter 1 but will provide a brief reminder here. In a longitudinal design, a researcher gathers a group of participants and follows them over time, noting changes in whatever is being studied as the group of participants ages. Longitudinal designs are expensive to run and subject to problems in interpretation if too many participants drop out of the study. Moreover, they are often problematic in confounding history with development. For example, children first recruited in 2005 in New Orleans are likely to be forever changed by their experiences living through Hurricane Katrina—a historical event that other similarly aged children from, say, California or Massachusetts didn't experience. Similarly, individuals who grew up during an economic depression or a world war are likely to be affected by those historical events in ways that are not readily detangled from other, routine developmental influences.

On the plus side, longitudinal designs do help a researcher control for a variety of individual differences. Stable aspects of a participant—certain personality characteristics or certain intellectual characteristics—presumably remain fairly constant over time and are thus not likely to explain changes in cognitive functioning over time.

In a cross-sectional design, different groups of participants of different ages are tested and compared—for example, one group of children aged 4 in the year 2010 is compared with another group of children aged 10 in 2010. Cross-sectional designs are subject to so-called cohort effects. Imagine a study comparing current (in 2010) 5-year-olds with current (in 2010) 20-year-olds on their memory for traumatic events. The older group lived through the events of 9/11, for example, and arguably experienced a national tragedy that "left its mark" on them in a way that the younger group did not. Thus, what might look like a developmental effect—that older individuals have different memories for trauma—might instead reflect a cohort effect: People who've lived through a tragedy remember other tragedies differently than people who haven't. Cross-sectional designs typically are cheaper and faster to run than longitudinal ones, however, so we will see several examples of these kinds of studies in the book.

Observational Studies and Clinical Interviews

As the name itself suggests, **observational studies** are those in which the researcher observes children and records some aspect of their behavior. For example, the researcher might "hang out" in a preschool and record the number of times one child tries to mislead or deceive another one (we'll talk about some actual studies like this in Chapter 8). Ideally, the observer remains as unobtrusive as possible, so as to disrupt or alter the behaviors being observed as little as possible. In this example, for instance, the investigator might spend several days in the classroom with the children, so that they can get used to her presence, and stop "performing" for her audience.

Observational studies have the advantage that the things studied really do occur in the real world and not just in an experimental laboratory. Psychologists call this property **ecological validity**. Furthermore, the observer has a chance to see just how cognitive processes work in natural settings: how flexible they are, how they are affected by environmental changes, how rich and complex actual behavior is. Observational studies are relatively easy to conduct and don't typically introduce ethical issues. We'll see many examples of observational studies throughout the book.

Clinical interviews are one extension of observational studies, where the investigator exercises a little more direction and influence than in observational studies but tries very hard to allow the participant to respond freely and normally. The investigator begins by asking each child one or more open-ended questions. For example, the interviewer might ask a child how he or she typically tries to pay attention to the teacher in school. The child gives an open-ended response, but the interviewer may follow up with another set of questions. Depending on the child's responses, the interviewer may pursue one or another of many possible lines of questioning, trying to follow each participant's own thinking and experience while focusing on specific issues or questions. We'll see shortly that the clinical interview was a method favored by Piaget in his work with his own infant children—although in this case, the "questions" he asked were actually nonverbal stimuli he presented. He then watched and recorded how his children responded to these stimuli.

Correlational Studies

Correlational studies are related to observational studies, in that measures of behavior are observed. Correlational studies typically involve an investigator measuring two or more things and assessing the degree of linear relationship between them. For example, a cognitive developmental psychologist might measure both the attention span and the working memory capacity of a group of children and compute the correlation, or degree of linear relationship, between these two dependent variables.

Correlational studies are observational, in that the investigator simply observes and records the dependent variables. This kind of study is good for establishing the existence of relationships between different measures. However, correlational studies are limited in that they cannot establish causal relationships. If a researcher finds that Measures A and B have a strong correlation (correlations range from an absolute value of 0 to an absolute value of 1), he cannot tell if A causes B, if B causes A, or if some other variable causes both A and B.

Experimental Studies

Experimental studies are ones in which an investigator exercises some degree of *experimental control*. Having experimental control means the experimenter can assign participants to different experimental conditions so as to minimize preexisting differences between them. Ideally, the experimenter can control all variables that might affect the performance of research participants *other than* the variables on which the study is focusing. A true experiment is one in which the experimenter manipulates one or more independent variables (the experimental conditions) and observes how the recorded measures (dependent variables) change as a result.

For example, an experiment in cognitive developmental psychology might proceed as follows: An experimenter recruits a number of same-aged children for a study of voluntary attention span; randomly assigns them to one of two groups; and presents each group with exactly the same stimuli, using exactly the same procedures and settings and varying only the instructions (the independent variable) for the two groups of children. The experimenter then observes the overall performance of the participants on a later test of attention span (the dependent variable).

This example illustrates a **between-subjects design**, wherein different experimental participants are assigned to different experimental conditions and the researcher looks for differences in performance between the two groups. In contrast, a **within-subjects design** exposes experimental participants to more than one condition. For example, participants might perform several attention span tasks but receive a different set of instructions for each task. The investigator then compares the performance of the participants in the first condition to the performance of the *same* participants in another condition.

Quasi-Experimental Studies

Some types of studies, especially those in developmental psychology, preclude random assignment (that is, having the experimenter assign a research participant to a particular condition in an experiment). For example, experimenters cannot assign participants to different ages or developmental statuses. They have to take people as they come with respect to age. Studies that appear in other ways to be experiments but that have one or more of these factors as independent variables (or fail to become true experiments in other ways) are called **quasi-experimental designs** (Campbell & Stanley, 1963).

Scientists value experiments and quasi-experiments, because they enable researchers to isolate causal factors and make better-supported claims about causality than is possible using observational or correlational methods alone. However, many experiments fail to fully capture real-world phenomena in the experimental task or research design. The laboratory setting or the artificiality or formality of the task may prevent research participants from behaving normally, for example. Further, the kinds of tasks amenable to experimental study may not be those most important or most common in everyday life. As a result, experimenters risk studying phenomena that relate only weakly to people's real-world experience.

Studies of Brain Functioning

Up until fairly recently, researchers interested in how a brain functioned usually had to wait until a patient died to perform an autopsy to correlate, say, his or her cognitive problems with a particular area of brain damage. Early in the 20th century, more information was gleaned from the reports of neuro-surgery, performed on patients who had severe epilepsy or a suspected tumor in a particular location. Notice, though, that the brains of healthy people were not explored (fortunately for them, unfortunately for science!).

In the last few decades, however, researchers have developed a number of relatively noninvasive techniques for studying the brains of healthy individuals, including infants. Collectively, these are known as brain imaging techniques. There are various kinds of techniques that differ in their use of radioactive materials, the relative degree of clarity of the output, and the amount of time it requires to obtain a scan. Among the older techniques are such things as PET scans (PET is an acronym for positron emission tomography) and CT or CAT scans (CAT stands for computerized axial tomography). PET scans require injection of a radioactively labeled compound, and CAT scans require exposure to X-rays, so neither one is appropriate for casual repeated use. We will focus here on two more commonly used and more recently developed techniques, MRI and fMRI.

MRI is an acronym for *magnetic resonance imaging*. Like CAT scans, MRI provides information about neuroanatomy. Unlike CAT scans, however, MRI requires no exposure to radiation and often permits clearer pictures as you can see in Figure 2.5, which shows an MRI scan of a brain.

Someone undergoing an MRI typically lies inside a tunnel-like structure that surrounds the person with a strong magnetic field. Radio waves are directed at whatever body structure is being scanned, causing the centers of hydrogen atoms in those structures to align themselves in predictable ways. Computers collate information about how the atoms are aligning and produce a composite three-dimensional image from which any desired cross section can be examined further.

MRI scans are often the technique of choice, as they now produce incredibly clear (relative to PET and CAT scan) images of the brain. However, MRI scans can't be used on some people (those with metal embedded in, or attached to, their bodies, such as a pacemaker or surgical clips). Because MRIs require people to lie very still in a tunnel-like machine that often leaves little room for arm movements, people with claustrophobia are also not good candidates for this technique.

MRI scans yield still pictures of the anatomy of a particular region of the brain. As such, they give good information about neuroanatomical structures of an individual's brain. Physicians and researchers can use these pictures to pinpoint areas of damage or other abnormality. However, these scans provide relatively static pictures of the parts of a brain and do not give much information about how a brain functions—that is, what areas of the brain show activity when people perform different tasks.

Figure 2–5 Patient readied for MRI brain scan

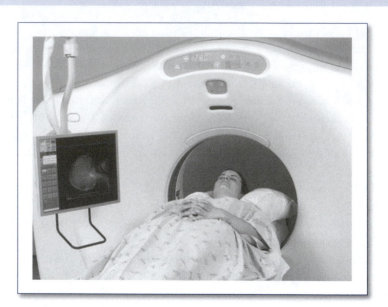

To address this need, other techniques are used, among them **fMRI**, which stands for functional magnetic resonance imaging (Nolte, 2009). fMRI uses the fact that blood has magnetic properties. Areas of the brain that are active while an individual completes a cognitive task (such as perceiving a stimulus) have an increase in blood flow, and thus a higher concentration of oxygen, relative to inactive areas of the brain. fMRI picks up on the ratio of hemoglobin to deoxyhemoglobin and generates a picture (usually in color) depicting which areas are especially active. An example is presented in Figure 2.6. fMRI scans use existing MRI equipment but provide clinicians and investigators with a noninvasive, nonradioactive means of assessing blood flow to various brain regions. fMRI techniques require a certain amount of cooperation from the experimental participant, and thus they are not used typically in children younger than about age 4 (Nelson, Moulson, & Richmond, 2006). So we won't be talking about fMRI studies for a few chapters.

The second technique we will talk about involves taking recordings of electrical activity in the brain from sensors attached to the scalp. This

Figure 2–6   An fMRI scan

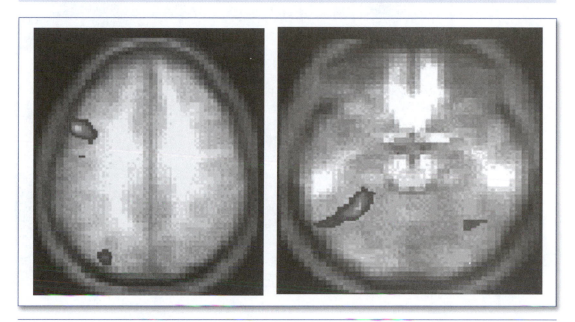

SOURCE: Garrett (2009, p. 105).

recording of so-called **event-related potentials**, or **ERPs**, measures an area of the brain's response to a specific event. Participants are presented with a stimulus, usually either visual or auditory. The recording measures brain activity from the time before the stimulus is presented until some time afterward. The brain waves recorded also have predictable parts, or components. That is, the shape of the waveform can vary depending on whether or not the participant expected the stimulus to occur or was attending to the location in which the stimulus appeared and whether the stimulus is physically different from other recent stimuli. ERPs do not provide the excellent spatial resolution that fMRIs do, but they are entirely noninvasive and very easy to use with infants (Nelson et al., 2006).

ERP recordings show an averaging of the electrical activity occurring in the brain, relative to the time of presentation of a stimulus. Thus, the researcher averages, over a number of trials, the electrical activity in the brain say, 100 milliseconds after a stimulus presentation. Random electrical activity gets "filtered out" in the averaging, leaving a smooth curve

Photo 2.8   This photo shows a baby wearing a so-called ERP cap that allows electrical recordings to be taken from the scalp.

such as the one shown in Figure 2.7. You'll notice that in this figure there are various deflections or curves above the line (known as N responses) and also ones below the line (known as P responses; Luck, 2005). P and N are traditionally used to indicate what researchers call positive-going and negative-going peaks. The number after the P or N indicates if it is the first, second, or third observed peak. As Luck (2005) summarizes: "The sequence of ERP peaks reflects the flow of information through the brain" (p. 11).

The initial peak (P1) happens on just about every trial with every participant—it is often called an "obligatory" response to the stimulus. Changes in the stimulus, such as brightness or loudness, affect the size (amplitude) of the P1 peak but not whether or not it occurs. In contrast, other deflections such as the P3 or N1 often depend upon what kind of processing the participant is doing on the stimulus—they don't always occur. We'll talk more about specific peaks when we get to discussions of particular research studies.

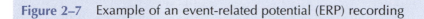

Figure 2–7   Example of an event-related potential (ERP) recording

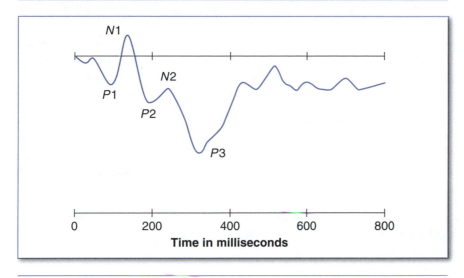

SOURCE: Luck (2005, p. 8).

❖ ❖ ❖

Given this brief look at several different research methods used by cognitive developmental researchers, I want to make an important general point. The general point here is that no research method is perfect for all questions. It helps a researcher to have a variety of methods in her toolbox if she wants to be able to investigate a wide variety of questions. Ultimately, the goal is for different research methods to be used in a variety of settings, yielding results that converge on similar answers or explanations. We will see examples of all of the research methods described here throughout the book.

SUMMARY

1. Stage theories view cognitive development as proceeding through qualitatively distinct stages that occur in a stable order, show progression, and posit unified cognitive structures.

2. Piagetian theory holds that cognitive development proceeds through four distinct stages: sensorimotor, preoperational, concrete operations, and formal operations.

   Infants in the sensorimotor stage of cognitive development (0–18 or 24 months, approximately) lack the capacity for mental representation. Young children in the preoperational period (ages 18 months to 6 years, approximately) achieve the capacity for mental representation but are easily overwhelmed by their perceptual experience and have difficulty understanding the appearance–reality distinction or taking another person's perspective. Concrete operational children (aged 6 to 11 or 12 years, approximately) are better able to classify and order information. They conserve many properties, such as quantity and number, and are able to think about the relationships among different transformations. Adolescents who have achieved formal operations (after age 12 or so) are able to think hypothetically, systematically, logically, and abstractly.

3. Vygotsky takes a different view of cognitive development. He views the development of mental structures as a by-product of social and environmental interactions. Vygotsky invokes the concept of the *zone of proximal development* to describe a mechanism by which infants and children practice with and refine their emerging cognitive structures, using scaffolding from adults or older children or in play.

4. The information-processing approach to cognitive development focuses on quantitative differences among children of various ages (e.g., differences in memory span, attention span, processing speed, knowledge base, strategies).

5. Classical and instrumental conditioning represent two major forms of learning theory, which holds that a simple set of laws applies to the learning of animals and humans of all ages.

6. Nativism is the idea that at least some knowledge is inborn, or that hardwired structures constrain and direct the acquisition of certain kinds of knowledge.

7. Understanding the development and functioning of the brain is becoming an increasingly important task for cognitive developmental psychologists. The cerebral cortex can be divided into several lobes, and some cognitive processes have been associated with neural activity in certain areas of these lobes. For example, the prefrontal cortex, thought to play an important role in executive functioning (including planning ahead, making decisions, and inhibiting inappropriate behaviors), is one of the last to mature.

8. Theories differ on at least three different dimensions: the nature–nurture dimension, the continuity–discontinuity dimension, and the universal/culture-specific dimension.

9. Finally, we reviewed several different research methods used by cognitive developmental researchers. Observational studies involve recording responses as they naturally occur. Clinical interviews allow children to provide open-ended responses, which are followed up by specific questions. Correlational studies establish the existence of linear relationships among different dependent measures. Experiments require the investigator to control all influences except the variable of interest. Quasi-experiments are structured like experiments, except that one or more variables (such as age or developmental level) cannot be randomly assigned. Two major techniques to study brain functioning include brain imaging and event-related potential (ERP) recordings.

REVIEW QUESTIONS

1. Briefly define and discuss the criteria for a stage theory of cognitive development.

2. What is the Piagetian conservation task, and what does it reveal (according to Piaget) about preschool children's cognition?

3. What aspects of the stage of concrete operations make school-aged children particularly ready for formal schooling?

4. Compare and contrast Piaget's account of cognitive development of early childhood with that of Vygotsky.

5. Describe one possible explanation a psychologist in the information-processing tradition might give to explain one major phenomenon of cognitive development.

6. Contrast learning theory with nativist explanations of cognitive development.

7. Describe the major cognitive functions localized in the four cerebral lobes (frontal, parietal, occipital, temporal).

8. Consider the three dimensions of theories of cognitive development. Choose one of the theories we have reviewed, and locate that theory on each of the three dimensions, offering support for your view.

9. Explain the major differences between fMRI and ERP recordings to study the developing brain.

10. (Challenging) In this chapter, we have reviewed six major theoretical frameworks and five major research methods used in cognitive developmental psychology. Which pairing of a theoretical framework and research method fits best, and why?

11. Explain why, all other things being equal, researchers prefer experiments to other kinds of studies.

KEY TERMS

Accommodation	CAT Scan
Assimilation	Cerebral Cortex
Attention Span	Classical Conditioning
Between-Subjects Design	Clinical Interviews
Brain Imaging	Cohort Effects

Concrete Operations

Correlation

Correlational Studies

Ecological Validity

Egocentrism

Empiricism

Event-Related Potentials (ERPs)

Executive Functioning

Experiment

Experimental Studies

fMRI

Forebrain

Formal Operations

Frontal Lobe

Hindbrain

Information-Processing Theory

Instrumental Conditioning

Language Acquisition Device (LAD)

Mental Representation

Midbrain

MRI

Myelin

Nativism

Neo-Piagetians

Neurons

Observational Studies

Occipital Lobe

Parietal Lobe

PET Scan

Prefrontal Cortex

Preoperational Stage

Quasi-Experimental Design

Rehearsal

Research Methods

Scaffolding

Sensorimotor Stage

Stage Theory

Strategies

Temporal Lobe

Within-Subjects Design

Working Memory

Zone of Proximal Development

CHAPTER 3

INFANCY

Perception and Attention

In this chapter and the next, we'll take a closer look at **infancy**, which we will define as lasting from a child's birth to her second birthday. As we will see, these (and any) age boundaries are both approximate and debatable. Some researchers would argue that the end of infancy occurs at around 12 or 18 months; others might extend the period to 30 months. Moreover, some of the development we will look at under the infancy heading, especially in the realm of neurological development, takes place well before the milestone of birth, during the prenatal period of gestation.

Breaking infant cognition into subtopics always has some degree of arbitrariness to it. So, although I've chosen to focus on infant perception and attention here and to defer discussion of infant memory and categorization to Chapter 4, we will soon see that the topics have fuzzy boundaries. What I might call "infant perception" another psychologist might classify as "infant attention" or "infant classification." Our discussion of infants' understanding of what objects are and what properties they have relates strongly to some of the issues of infant perception discussed here. However, I'm deferring that presentation until Chapter 4 because the topic also draws on issues of infant memory and categorization. And, I'm putting off discussion of language acquisition (which begins in infancy and incorporates infant auditory perception) until Chapter 5. There's no perfect way around this problem, but I hope by the end of Chapter 5, after I've presented all the strands, you will have a fairly thorough picture of infant cognitive abilities.

THEORETICAL PERSPECTIVES

In Chapter 2, we looked at a number of broad theoretical perspectives. In the following section, I'll continue to draw on some of these, focusing more specifically on how they apply to infancy. You'll note that not all perspectives will be covered here—some will be more relevant to topics in Chapter 4, and others won't have very specific things to say about infancy at all.

A Piagetian View

According to Piaget, the first stage of cognitive development, the sensorimotor stage, occurs from birth to about 2 years. Piaget's description of this stage stems largely from his careful observations and clinical "interviews" of his own three children, Lucienne, Laurent, and Jacqueline. Although normally psychologists avoid studying their own children, due to fears of bias in interpretation or report, and although normally psychologists want to see conclusions drawn on large rather than small samples of children, Piaget's observations have been widely replicated by psychologists in different laboratories (although Piaget's *interpretations* of his observations have been hotly debated).

We have already seen the basic description of the sensorimotor stage—marked by the absence of the capacity for mental representation. That is, the newborn infant is thought to "know" and "understand" the world only through his sensory reception of information (i.e., the things he sees, hears, smells, tastes, feels) or his motoric actions in the world, which at the beginning of infancy (birth) consist of a number of reflexes.

Reflexes are automatic, hardwired muscular responses to external stimuli. Some examples are the *grasping reflex,* in which an infant grips tightly whatever object touches his palm; the *rooting reflex,* in which an infant turns his head toward a stimulus that touches his cheek, in an attempt to place the stimulus in his mouth; the *sucking reflex,* in which an infant sucks on an object placed in his mouth (be it a nipple, a pacifier, a finger, or some other object entirely).

How is it, then, that an infant with only a small set of reflexes in his repertoire evolves into a cognitively more sophisticated information processor? Drawing on his early training in biology and ethology, Piaget invoked the mechanism of adaptation. In particular, Piaget believed that there were two processes of adaptation, called assimilation and accommodation, which we

Photos 3.1 and 3.2 Basic reflexes such as sucking and grasping are the basic building blocks of cognition, according to Piaget.

already defined in Chapter 2. These processes typically occur together and cause cognitive structures (at first, reflexes; later, mental operations) to evolve.

Of course, even very young infants have a variety of reflexes in their behavioral repertoire. Through assimilation and accommodation, these reflexes evolve into more flexible schemes. They also become coordinated with other schemes, making further adaptation possible. For example, an infant's grasping scheme eventually becomes coordinated with his looking scheme, enabling him to use visual and haptic (pertaining to touch) information to guide his reaching out for objects and bringing them toward himself for further visual and oral exploration. Ideally, cognitive structures evolve into a state of equilibration or stability. They are able to handle the stimuli the infant explores without requiring radical modification. At the same time, they are useful enough to help the infant master a wide series of cognitive goals.

Piaget identified six substages during the sensorimotor period. These are summarized in Table 3.1. The first substage lasts from birth until the infant is approximately 1 month old. During this period, the infant is cognitively limited to reflexive behaviors, of the sort described earlier. The reflexes are uncoordinated and initially "wired-in" to the infant's intelligence (Flavell, 1963). Over the course of the month the reflexes become triggered by a wider variety of stimuli, although little change is shown in the behaviors themselves.

Substage 2 begins at about 1 month and ends at about 4 months of age. One indication that a new stage has been entered is the emergence of reflexes that become altered with experience. Another is the emergence of what Piaget called *primary* circular reactions—behaviors that randomly lead to an "interesting" result for the infant, which are then prolonged or repeated.

Table 3–1   Piagetian sensorimotor substages

Substage	Age range	Brief description of cognitive mechanisms
1	birth–1 month	newborn reflexes
2	1–4 months	primary circular reactions
3	4–8 months	secondary circular reactions
4	8–12 months	coordination of secondary circular reactions
5	12–18 months	tertiary circular reactions
6	18–24 months	beginnings of mental representation

For example, consider an infant who is moving her hands and arms around her head in a random way. Accidentally, her thumb may brush her lips and end up in her mouth, eliciting a sucking reaction. According to Piaget, the infant may find this result an "interesting" one and will prolong or repeat it, continuing to suck the thumb. As a result of the repetition or practice, the "thumb sucking scheme" becomes more refined: It lasts for longer amounts of time, occurs more frequently, and becomes smoother and easier to execute.

The third substage, which lasts from about 4 months until about 8 months, is marked by the appearance of what Piaget called *secondary* circular reactions. Like primary circular reactions, these are repeated behaviors that seem to be "set off" without the infant's intending them. The difference between primary and secondary circular reactions, then, is that the former tend to revolve around actions of the infant's own body—sucking, grasping, looking, or listening—while the latter seem to be aimed at making interesting environmental events continue or recur. Thus, for example, Piaget's son Laurent gradually learned to rub a paper knife against the wicker side of his bassinet to make an interesting sound occur; later he rubbed other objects, such as dolls and rattles, against the bassinet.

Infants in this stage seem to be transitional between nonintentional creatures, who give no evidence of having their own goals or plans, and intentional creatures, who seem to act in pursuit of specific objectives (e.g., grab that toy and put it in the mouth). Piaget described 4- to 8-month-old infants as "semi-intentional"—like older infants, they direct behavior to the external environment and act seemingly to make interesting events occur or recur. On the other hand, there is no clear evidence that infants at this stage begin a behavioral sequence with a specific goal in mind from the start—only that as interesting sights and sounds occur in the environment, they act to prolong or reinstate them.

Another important development during this substage is a noticeable improvement in visual tracking. Infants can not only follow a moving object but start to anticipate where the object will end up when it momentarily goes out of view. For example, an infant watching a toy train enter and exit a tunnel will, over time, come to move her eyes toward the exit of the tunnel, anticipating the reemergence of the train. Infants at this stage also begin to recognize objects that are partially occluded—a dropped toy partially visible under a sweater, for example.

The fourth substage covers the period from about 8 months until the infant's first birthday. John Flavell, a major expositor of Piagetian theory, describes the major achievements of the stage as showing the first "unmistakably intentional, means-end behavior" with actions that are "unquestionably purposeful and goal-directed," ones that "look more 'intelligent,' more 'cognitive' than those of previous stages" (Flavell, Miller, & Miller, 1993, p. 52). For example, an infant in this stage may use one object to get to another—pushing one object out of the way to reach a favorite toy behind it. He can also anticipate future events in the environment. Or, a 1-year-old may quickly figure out that when Mommy puts on her coat and grabs her briefcase, it means she is leaving for work and therefore it is time (in the infant's mind at least) to begin to cry or tantrum.

What makes this substage so exciting, from a cognitive standpoint, is that it marks the first appearance of unequivocal *intentional* behavior, according to Piaget. Up until now, it is hard to be sure when an infant acts that his behavior is guided by a specific goal. However, in this period, the ability to anticipate future events and to put schemes together to avoid obstacles makes it clear that the infant is deploying behavior in the service of a goal. In part, this becomes possible because the secondary schemes that have developed previously now become more general in function and less tied to specific contexts.

Other milestones are achieved in this substage with respect to the infant's developing concept of **object permanence**. In Substage 3, as we've seen, infants can recognize partially occluded objects—one's teddy bear partially covered by a blanket, for example. However, one of Piaget's most dramatic demonstrations was that infants in the fourth substage would stop searching for an object that was fully hidden.

For example, my daughter Kimberlynn loved her pacifiers as an infant and would try to keep them nearby whenever possible (we bought a lot of pacifier clips to avoid traumatic losses). One day while playing with her I had her watch while I covered a pacifier with a washcloth. Following Piagetian predictions, Kimberlynn looked at the pacifier with great interest (and even, some would say, desperate attention), but the instant it was covered she looked away. Maxims such as "out of sight, out of mind" truly do seem to capture Piaget's ideas about what infants know about the continual existence of unseen objects.

At about the time of her first birthday, the infant enters the fifth substage of the sensorimotor period. The defining aspect of this substage is the emergence of what Piaget called a *tertiary* circular reaction. As with primary and secondary circular reactions, tertiary (third-level) circular reactions are repeated behavioral patterns. Tertiary circular reactions, however, involve the deliberate, intentional incorporation of novelty into the routine. The child is in many ways acting as a junior scientist, exploring the world and injecting variation to see what will happen.

My favorite setting to observe tertiary circular reactions is in family restaurants. The subjects to watch are families with a year-old infant.

Typically, the family enters and is seated in a booth with the infant in a wooden high chair at the end of the booth. Dad or Mom begins unpacking the requisite diaper bag, unloading a number of colorful plastic toys to set in front of Junior. Junior grabs one, shakes it around a bit, and drops it on the floor. The parent or sibling seated closest to Junior then picks up the dropped toy, handing it back. Junior drops it again. The parent or sibling again retrieves it. Many repetitions of the "game" ensue, often with Junior trying out different variations: dropping the toy on different sides of the high chair, perhaps, or from different heights. Another favorite is to drop different toys and then to try different objects—say, a salt shaker, an eating utensil, a glass of water (it's amazing the reaction Junior provokes when he tries that last one!).

These various dropped object/foodstuff experiments have a cognitive point to them (beyond providing sheer amusement for the infant). In Piaget's view, they allow the child to invent the means of solving problems. So, for example, an infant in this substage can learn to pull on a blanket in order to bring a toy on top of it into reach; he can learn to tilt objects at a certain angle in order to get them through the bars of the crib.

Photo 3.3   Tertiary circular reactions can be observed in restaurants, where older infants repeatedly drop toys to see what happens.

The capacity for mental representation makes its initial appearance during the sixth substage, which lasts from roughly 18 to roughly 24 months. It is during this period that Piaget described the toddler as first having the ability to "think," meaning to have a cognitive realm distinct from the sensory or behavioral realm. It is the basis of all subsequent sophisticated cognitive activities, including planning, remembering, forming strategies, and imagining alternatives.

Almost every modern cognitive developmental psychologist acknowledges a huge debt to Jean Piaget's contributions, whether or not he or she agrees with Piaget's characterization of cognitive development. One psychologist asserted that assessing the extent of Piaget's contribution to the field is like assessing the contributions of Aristotle to philosophy or

Shakespeare to literature—completely impossible (Haith & Benson, 1998). It was Piaget who first paid attention to the cognitive lives of infants, who first developed methods of studying infant cognition, who carefully and painstakingly charted the day-to-day changes in his own children's functioning, and who put the pieces of data together into a theory.

Nonetheless, as we will soon see, more recent work in infant cognition changes the picture that Piaget first painted. Instead of the "grand theory," which purported to explain many different types of infant cognition with a few general principles, today there are many so-called "minitheories" of infant cognition, each focused on a specific aspect of infant cognition—say, visual perception or auditory memory. The trade-off is that the different subfields comprise research enterprises that are often isolated from one another and lack the unifying descriptions Piaget once provided (Haith & Benson, 1998). Many of them have uncovered much more cognitive competence in infants at various ages than Piaget described, as we shall soon see.

A View From Learning Theory

Learning theory, as we discussed in Chapter 2, makes predictions about an individual's current performance based on that individual's past experiences. The general idea is that most of the reason an organism does what it does, or experiences what it experiences, has to do with what its prior encounters have been.

Learning theory was developed largely in animal laboratories. This makes good sense, as experiments in learning laboratories typically measure behavioral responses—either heart rates or eye blinks or lever presses— rather than long verbal reports on feelings or thoughts. It's no surprise, then, that learning theory provides developmental psychology with a variety of useful methodologies for studying the preverbal infant.

Take, for example, the question "What capabilities do newborn infants have to see, hear, taste, smell, and feel, and how do those capabilities change in the months after birth?" Although the question seems straightforward, it's a lot harder to answer than it might first seem. The challenge, of course, is that infants don't communicate in language, making standard approaches to sensory testing unusable. We can't have them read an eye chart or raise their hand when they hear a tone. Therefore, researchers studying infant perception have to devise clever means of detecting what kinds of stimuli the infants detect.

Animal researchers in the learning theory tradition got around this dilemma by using a well-known finding from the laboratory: Organisms show **habituation** to familiar stimuli. That is, when they repeatedly encounter the same stimulus, they appear to "tune it out" and pay less attention to it.

This finding can be exploited in research to ask if an animal can discriminate between two stimuli as follows: First present Stimulus A and note the animal's reaction (e.g., by recording heart rate, measuring how long the animal looks at it, or rating the apparent attention to it). Then continue to present Stimulus A until the animal "shows less interest" (e.g., heart rate decelerates to a baseline level, the animal looks away, or the raters judge the animal to not be paying attention). Now either present Stimulus A again (if this is a "control" trial) or present Stimulus B. If the animal does detect a difference between the two stimuli, the reaction to Stimulus B ought to be different from the reaction to the repeat presentation of Stimulus A. If the animal looks longer at B, shows an increase in heart rate when presented with B (relative to when presented with A), or seems more interested in B than A, researchers conclude that the animal perceives a difference between A and B. We say that the animal has "dishabituated" to Stimulus B. Now, substitute the word *infant* for *animal* in the above description, and you have a recipe for how experimenters can "ask" nonverbal infants about whether they perceive two stimuli as the same or different.

BASIC SENSORY ABILITIES IN INFANCY

A variation of the habituation technique, known as the **visual preference paradigm**, works as follows: Infants who show a preference to look at one stimulus over another are showing an ability to make a reliable discrimination between the two. By measuring the total time spent looking at each stimulus, an investigator can assess whether the infant is showing a reliable preference (Cohen & Cashon, 2003).

Robert Fantz (1958, 1963; Fantz & Ordy, 1959) developed and used such a method to examine young infants' visual acuity as well as their ability to detect the differences between two- and three-dimensional stimuli. Infants were placed in a hammock inside a small square chamber, facing up. Stimuli were presented about a foot from the infant's face, on either side and a foot apart. A quarter-inch hole in the ceiling of the chamber allowed an observer to peek through to see which direction the infant was looking in. Observers checked to be sure a reflection of the stimulus was visible in the infant's pupil and then recorded the amount of time the infant gazed at each stimulus. Figure 3.1 presents one example of stimuli Fantz used with infants from about 1 to 6 months of age.

Results showed that infants looked longer at the three-dimensional spheres than at the two-dimensional circles, with infants over 3 months of age showing a pronounced looking preference for the spheres. Fantz interpreted these results as showing that infants use both texture and brightness cues to detect the dimensionality of the stimuli.

Figure 3–1 Stimuli used by Fantz (1961) to study the depth perception of young infants. Three-dimensional spheres (on left) are presented next to two-dimensional circles with the same texture.

Other investigations by Fantz (1963) showed that even very young infants (less than 48 hours old) show more interest in more complex stimuli, showing preferences to look at faces and concentric circles rather than at a circle of newsprint or unpatterned white, yellow, or red circles. Other work by Fantz and Ordy (1959) showed that over the first 4 months of life, infants gradually show more of a preference for finer gradations of patterns, suggesting greater visual acuity over this period.

More recent research confirms many of Fantz's original findings. The picture that emerges is that first, newborns are quite limited in their visual acuity, which is so low that they would be classified as legally blind (Kellman & Arterberry, 2006). By 4 months infants' visual acuity is much improved, and by 7 or 8 months it is very close to adult levels. Table 3.2 presents a description of various visual indicators over the first 2 years of life. Figure 3.2 presents an example of how the same visual scene would appear over the course of early infancy and in adulthood.

Table 3–2   Visual indicators in the first 2 years

Monitoring Visual Development

In the early months of life, the visual system is still maturing; it is not fully developed at birth (and is even less developed in the premature infant). From birth to maturity, the eye increases to three times its size at birth, and most of this growth is complete by age 3; one third of the eye's growth in diameter is in the first year of life. Some knowledge of normal visual development is necessary if abnormalities are to be noted. The following information gives indicators of normal visual development in young children from birth to three years.

In **a premature infant** (depending on the extent of prematurity): The eyelids may not have fully separated; the iris may not constrict or dilate; the aqueous drainage system may not be fully functional; the choroid may lack pigment; retinal blood vessel's [*sic*] may be immature; optic nerve fibers may not be myelinized; there may still be a pupillary membrane and/or a hyaloid system. Functional implications: lack of ability to control light entering the eye; visual system is not ready to function.

At birth: The irises of Caucasian infants may have a gray or bluish appearance; natural color develops as pigment forms. The eyes' pupils are not able to dilate fully yet. The curvature of the lens is nearly spherical. The retina (especially the macula) is not fully developed. The infant is moderately farsighted and has some degree of astigmatism. Functional implications: The newborn has poor fixation ability, a very limited ability to discriminate color, limited visual fields, and an estimated visual acuity of somewhere between 20/200 and 20/400.

By 1 month: The infant can follow a slowly moving black and white target intermittently to midline; he/she will blink at a light flash, may also intermittently follow faces (usually with the eyes and head both moving together). Acuity is still poor (in the 20/200 to 20/400 range), and ocular movements may often be uncoordinated. There is a preference for black and white designs, especially checkerboards and designs with angles.

By 2 months: Brief fixation occurs sporadically, although ocular movements may still be uncoordinated; there may be attention to objects up to 6' away. The infant may *follow* vertical movements better than horizontal, and is beginning to be aware of colors (primarily red and yellow). There is probably still a preference for black and white designs.

By 3 months: Ocular movements are coordinated most of the time; attraction is to both black and white and colored (yellow and red) targets. The infant is capable of glancing at smaller targets (as small as 1"), and is interested in faces; visual attention and visual searching begins. The infant begins to associate visual stimuli and an event (e.g., the bottle and feeding).

(Continued)

Table 3–2 (Continued)

By 4 months: "Hand regard" occurs at about 15 weeks; there is marked interest in the infant's own hands. He/she is beginning to shift gaze, and reacts (usually smiles) to familiar faces. He/she is able to follow a visual target the size of a finger puppet past midline, and can track horizontally, vertically, and in a circle. Visual acuity may be in the 20/200 to 20/300 range.

By 5 months: The infant is able to look at (visually examine) an object in his/her own hands; ocular movement although still uncoordinated at times, is smoother. The infant is visually aware of the environment ("explores" visually), and can shift gaze from near to far easily; he/she can "study" objects visually at nearpoint, and can converge the eyes to do so; can fixate at 3'. Eye-hand coordination (reach) is usually achieved by now.

By 6 months: Acuity is 20/200 or better, but eye movements are coordinated and smooth; vision can be used efficiently at both nearpoint and distance. The child recognizes and differentiates faces at 6', and can reach for and grasp a visual target. Hand movements are monitored visually; has visually directed reach. May be interested in watching falling objects, and usually fixates on where the object disappears.

Between 6 and 9 months: Acuity improves rapidly (to near normal); "explores" visually (examines objects in hands visually, and watches what is going on around him/her). Can transfer objects from hand to hand, and may be interested in geometric patterns.

Between 9 months and a year: The child can visually spot a small (2–3mm) object nearby; watches faces and tries to imitate expressions; searches for hidden objects after observing the "hiding"; visually alert to new people, objects, surroundings; can differentiate between known and unfamiliar people; vision motivates and monitors movement towards a desired object.

By 1 year: Both near and distant acuities are good (in the 20/50 range); there may be some mild farsightedness, but there is ability to focus, accommodate (shift between far and near vision tasks), and the child has depth perception; he/she can discriminate between simple geometric forms (circle, triangle, square), scribbles with a crayon, and is visually interested in pictures. Vision lures the child into the environment. Can track across a 180 degree arc.

By 2 years: Myelinization of the optic nerve is completed. There is vertical (upright) orientation; all optical skills are smooth and well coordinated. Acuity is 20/20 to 20/30 (normal). The child can imitate movements, can match same objects by single properties (color, shape), and can point to specific pictures in a book.

By 3 years: Retinal tissue is mature. The child can complete a simple formboard correctly (based on visual memory), can do simple puzzles, can draw a crude circle, and can put 1" pegs into holes.

SOURCE: Texas School for the Blind and Visually Impaired (2007).

Figure 3–2 Infants' visual capacity increases dramatically over the first few months of life, as seen in this artist's conception of the appearance of a visual scene for infants of different ages.

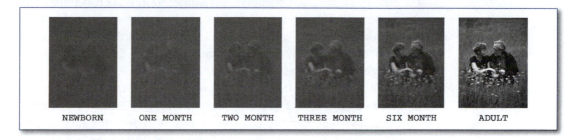

NEWBORN   ONE MONTH   TWO MONTH   THREE MONTH   SIX MONTH   ADULT

SOURCE: Cole, Cole, & Lightfoot (2005, p. 123).

What about color vision? Kellman and Arterberry (2006), reviewing the literature on infant visual perception, conclude that there are no rigorous demonstrations that infants younger than about a month are able to make discriminations solely on the basis of color (as opposed to brightness), although by 4 months of age, they do. By about 4 months of age, infants also seem to group various hues together the way adults do. By this I mean that various shades of, say, blue that we would all agree are a kind of blue, even though they differ in exact wavelength, would also be grouped together into one category by infants. Work by Marc Bornstein and colleagues (Bornstein, Kessen, & Weiskopf, 1976) habituated infants to a certain hue (e.g., greenish blue). They then presented infants with one of two different stimuli, both an equal "distance" away (in terms of wavelength) from the original. One stimulus was in the same "color" category as the original stimulus (e.g., a different shade of blue) while the other would be regarded by adults as a different color (e.g., a shade of green). Four-month-old infants dishabituated only to the second stimulus. This suggested that they saw the second stimulus as a different kind of color from the habituation stimulus, whereas they treated the first stimulus as a familiar one.

Although most psychologists agree that vision is the dominant sensory system, it is by no means the only important one. Psychologists studying the development of hearing and audition remind us that this sensory system plays a "powerful role in initiating infants into a social world" (Fernald, 2001, p. 37). Hearing can be said to begin prenatally, as the organs of the inner ear start to function during the sixth month of fetal life, and the fetus shows heart rate changes in response to loud sounds (Fernald, 2001).

Again, the experimental methods used to investigate hearing in infants are of necessity indirect, as infants cannot cooperate with a standard hearing test. Moreover, unlike in the case of vision, there is no specific behavior (e.g., looking at a stimulus) that directly reflects an underlying sensory process (e.g., vision) in the case of audition. Thus, many researchers have taken to measuring involuntary physiological responses in young infants, such as changes in heart rate or changes in event-related potentials (ERPs), to study infant hearing (Saffran, Werker, & Werner, 2006).

The thresholds at which infants detect simple sounds such as pure tones have been shown to look very similar to the thresholds adults show for those same sounds, as shown in Figure 3.3. That is, adults and infants show greater sensitivity to sounds at the middle range of auditory frequency than to extremely high or low sounds. However, infants' thresholds are higher than those of adults, suggesting that their hearing may be less acute. This seems to improve over the first 2 years of life, although by 6 months, infants' absolute thresholds are close to those of adults. Moreover, the infants' ability to localize sound—that is, to determine from where a sound is coming—improves substantially during their first 11 months (Fernald, 2001).

Figure 3–3 Mean thresholds for detecting pure-tone stimuli at different frequencies for 3-, 6-, and 12-month-old infants and for adults (adapted from Olsho et al., 1988)

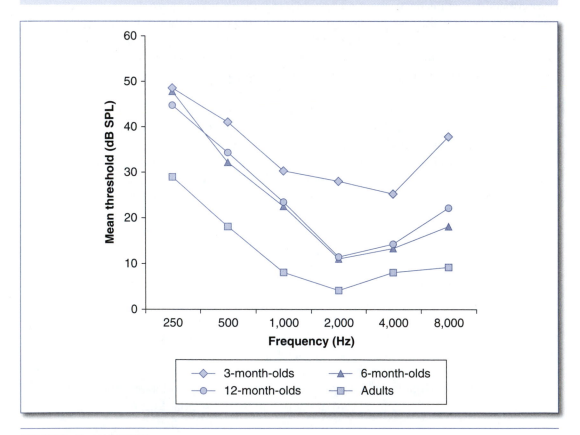

SOURCE: Fernald (2001).

With regard to taste and smell, even newborns show mature abilities to detect differences and express preferences. Rosenstein and Oster (1988) recorded facial expressions newborns made in response to different tastes (e.g., sweet, salty, bitter) that are very similar to the facial expressions made by adults to those same tastes. Figure 3.4 provides some examples. Newborns

Figure 3–4 Newborn facial responses to (a) sweet, (b) sour, and (c) bitter tastes

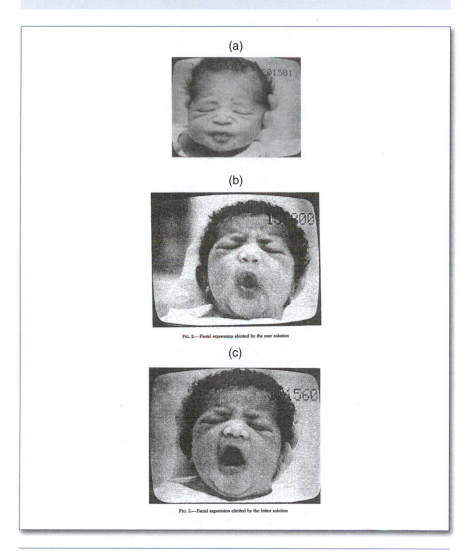

(a)

(b)

Fig. 2.—Facial expression elicited by the sour solution

(c)

Fig. 3.—Facial expression elicited by the bitter solution

SOURCE: Rosenstein & Oster (1988, pp. 1561–1563).

also show sensitivity to very slight touch (e.g., from a slight puff of air barely detectable by adults) and to changes in temperature as well as abrupt changes in their physical position.

Overall, even very young infants have a surprising amount of sensory competence, when their ability to detect and differentiate among stimuli is compared with that of older children or even adults. Nonetheless, this competence undergoes a lot of development, even in the first months. Moreover, sensory detection is just the first in a series of tasks infants (or, for that matter, adults) need to carry out in order to understand information in the world around them. Taking this raw sensory input, and making some meaningful interpretation of it, is the topic of perception, a topic to which we now turn.

We will concentrate in the rest of the chapter on visual perception, the ability to make sense of visual sensory information. One reason is that this sensory system is arguably the dominant system for humans. A second, and related, reason is that this perceptual system is the most well studied by cognitive developmental psychologists. However, the topic of infant auditory perception will be taken up in Chapter 5, as it is so heavily intertwined with speech perception and the beginnings of language acquisition.

VISUAL PERCEPTION

The visual cortex has been shown to develop early, relative to other parts of the cortex. The generation of **synapses** (connections between neurons) begins around birth and reaches a lifetime peak by about the infant's first birthday. This is in contrast to, say, parts of the frontal cortex, which don't reach a peak of synaptic density until about the end of the second year (Johnson, 2001). During this first year of life, as these brain changes are occurring, a lot of perceptual development is enabled.

Pattern and Face Perception

As mentioned before, the pioneering work of Robert Fantz described many of the early visual perceptual abilities of infants. In a classic study, Fantz (1958) showed that by 8 weeks of age, infants showed a clear preference to look at a patterned checkerboard rather than to either a small or a large square (see Figure 3.5). In contrast, infants showed no such preference for either of two identical triangles or for a plain circle and cross presented together. Moreover, for reasons Fantz could not account for, infants showed a preference for a bull's-eye pattern over a pattern of horizontal stripes,

Figure 3–5   Stimulus patterns from Fantz (1958)

SOURCE: Fantz (1958, p. 44).

NOTE: The stimulus patterns are drawn to scale; the large squares measured 5 inches on a side. Shaded areas were bright red; blank areas were gray to match the background. Adjacent patterns were presented together; the checkerboard was paired with either a large or a small plain square on a given exposure.

although the preference only became strong after 8 weeks. Fantz concluded that visual patterns could be discriminated from an early age (a little less than 2 months of age) and that the early emergence of such preferences argued against an extreme empiricist view that all perceptual abilities were learned.

Another of Fantz's classic findings was that from the age of just a few days, infants seemed to show a preference for faces over a control stimulus that was equated for the same amount of light and dark regions. Interestingly, infants also showed the same preference for "scrambled" faces over the control stimulus (scrambled faces contained features like eyes, nose, mouth, and hair, but with these features randomly mixed, as shown in Figure 3.6). Later research has shown that infants prefer to look at moderately complex visual stimuli, with lots of boundaries and edges (Kellman & Arterberry, 2006).

Figure 3–6 Fantz's (1961) test of young infants' pattern preferences

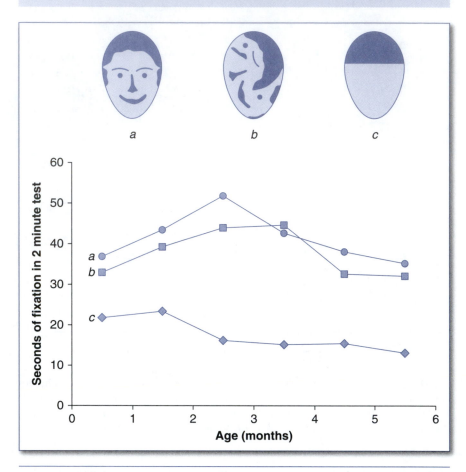

SOURCE: Adapted with permission from D. R. Shaffer's *Developmental Psychology,* 6th edition (2002), and R. L. Fantz in *Scientific American,* 204 (1961).

NOTE: Adaptive significance of form perception was indicated by the preference that infants showed for a "real" face *(a)* or a scrambled face *(b)*, and for both over a control *(c)*. Infants preferred to look at complex stimuli rather than at a simple oval.

Other classic work by Philip Salapatek and colleagues (Maurer and Salapatek, 1976; Salapatek & Kessen, 1966) focused on the way young infants scan visual stimuli. These researchers used an apparatus to record the eye movement of young infants as they looked at a stimulus. As you can see in Figure 3.7, which is based on results reported by Salapatek (1975), 1-month-old infants are likely to scan only a small portion of a visual stimulus—say, one corner or one feature of a face—while even slightly older infants—say, 2 months of age—are already scanning more thoroughly, focusing especially on the eyes (Maurer & Salapatek, 1976).

Figure 3–7 By recording eye movements, investigators can see where infants are fixating their gaze. Very young infants scan only portions of a visual display; 2-month-olds scan more thoroughly and examine internal features more so than do 1-month-old infants.

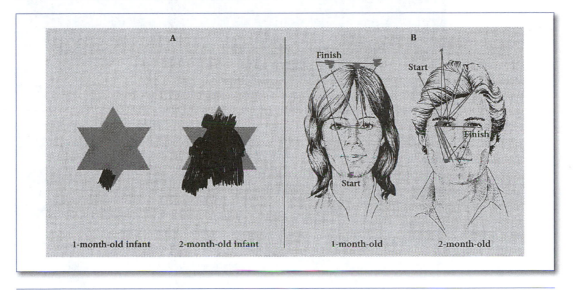

SOURCE: Shaffer (2002, p. 190); Adapted from Salapatek (1975).

More recent work by Leslie Cohen and Cara Cashon (2001a) has examined more closely whether and when infants process faces "configurally"—that is, as elements set up with certain relationships kept constant (two eyes at the top, a nose in the middle, a mouth above the chin) or instead as simply a set of individual features (eyes, nose, mouth, eyebrows, etc.) arranged in no particular way. These researchers used 7-month-old infants and presented them with female faces. First, they habituated them to two female faces, until the infants' looking time decreased to about half of the time they initially looked at the faces. Then, the experimenters presented three test faces: (a) one of the two faces previously shown (familiar face condition), (b), a novel face not shown during habituation, and (c) a "switched" face, created using computer software that combined the hair and outline of one habituated face with the internal features—eyes, nose, and mouth—of the other habituated face.

Results showed that the infants looked longer at the switched and novel faces than they did at the familiar faces, so long as the faces were presented in an upright position. This suggests that infants, like adults, were processing these faces "configurally," paying attention not only to the individual features but to the relationships of the various features to one another. However, when faces were presented in an inverted, upside-down position, infants (like adults) processed only the features and looked no longer at the switched faces than they did at the familiar faces.

Photo 3.4   Research suggests that even very young infants enjoy looking at faces.

Disagreements exist among infant perception researchers over how younger infants process faces and when faces become of special interest to infants (Cohen & Cashon, 2003; Kellman & Arterberry, 2006). Some researchers propose that even a few weeks after birth (and perhaps as early as the first day of life), infants can not only discriminate between a schematic face and a scrambled face but can also recognize their own mother's face when it is presented together with the face of a stranger (Bushnell, 2001). Cognitive neuroscience investigations of face processing in infants (see Nelson, Moulson, & Richmond, 2006, for a review) show that as early as 3 months, infants show distinctive ERP responses to faces relative to other stimuli (e.g., inverted faces, houses, animals). However, not until 12 months do infants respond to inverted faces as distinctive stimuli (as do adults and older children). This evidence suggests that face perception is not fully functional at birth. Despite the controversies, it appears to be clear that by the second half of the first year, infants are looking fairly adult-like when it comes to the perception of faces, at least.

Perceptual Constancies

Adults perceive the world using a variety of constancies. For example, the shape of an object projected to the retina changes as one's angle of view to the object changes. As shown in Figure 3.8a, for example, as you stand in front of a door that is in the process of being opened, the shape of that door actually changes from a rectangle to a trapezoid. Despite this objective change, your perception of the door is that it retains its rectangular shape. This is called shape constancy.

Similarly, as objects come nearer to us, the actual size of the object projecting to the retina becomes bigger, as shown in Figure 3.8b. Nonetheless, we don't perceive the object to be changing in size—a phenomenon known as size constancy. Constancies aid our perception of the world immeasurably— imagine the chaos that would ensue if we thought that objects changed size,

Figure 3–8a   Shape constancy: We perceive all three doors as rectangles.

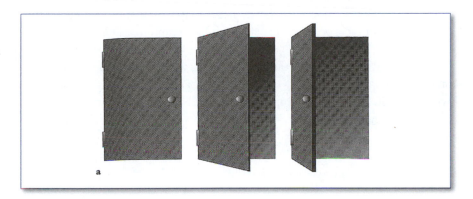

SOURCE: Kalat (2003, p. 147).

Figure 3–8b   Size constancy: We perceive all three hands as equal in size.

SOURCE: Kalat (2003, p. 147).

shape, or both every time we moved or they did! The question is "When do infants seem to show evidence of having these perceptual constancies?"

Some landmark studies by psychologist T. G. R. Bower (1966a, 1966b) attempted to address just this question. Bower framed the issue as follows: In order for a person to perceive either shape or size as a constant, he has to know that the information that comes to his retina is impoverished—the retinal image, after all, is two-dimensional, while the world that is being perceived is three-dimensional. So then the question becomes "Do babies learn, from their experience in the world, to use the two-dimensional cues from the retinal image to judge distance, size, and shape?" Such a proposition would fare well with psychologists with an empiricist orientation, and it might also be quite consistent with a Piagetian, constructivist account. On the other hand, if it can be shown that *very* young infants demonstrate shape or size constancy, that might indicate that at least some of their perceptual abilities are innate and that little learning from the environment is necessary in order to perceive certain aspects of objects.

Bower (1966b) used operant conditioning to investigate perceptual constancies in infants as young as 6 weeks of age. First, the infant was presented with a stimulus and trained to make a certain behavioral response—in this case a turn of the head—when the stimulus was presented. Figure 3.9 presents an

Figure 3–9 Bower's (1966b) experiment on infants' ability to differentiate between different shapes and orientations

SOURCE: Bower (1966b, p.81).

example. The correct response was reinforced by an experimenter popping up in front of the infant and cooing "peekaboo," as shown in Figure 3.10.

> **Figure 3–10** Bower (1966b) used a "peekaboo" from an experimenter as a reinforcement for responding correctly.

SOURCE: Bower (1966b, p. 81).

Once the infant was responding reliably to this conditioned stimulus, the experimenter presented other stimuli and recorded the rate of responses to them (see Figure 3.11). Some of these other stimuli were the same size as the original conditioned stimulus but presented at a different distance. Some of these stimuli were other sizes from the original stimulus, presented at a distance such that the retinal image of the stimulus would be the same in size as the original stimulus, as shown in Figure 3.12. The question was "Which stimuli would the infants discriminate among?"

Findings showed that the infants tested made 98 responses to the original conditioned stimulus, with 58, 54, and 22 responses to Test Stimuli 1, 2, and 3, respectively (see Figure 3.12). Notice that Test Stimulus 1 has the same true size as the original conditioned stimulus, and Test Stimulus 2, while having a different size, is presented at the same true distance. Infants responded more to these test stimuli than they did to Test Stimulus 3, which had a

Figure 3–11   Bower's (1966b) experimental procedure used operant conditioning to train an infant to respond to a rectangle at a certain orientation by using "peekaboo" reinforcement (top). After training, the experimenter changed the orientation of the rectangle (center), and then looked to see how the infant responded to the new stimulus (bottom).

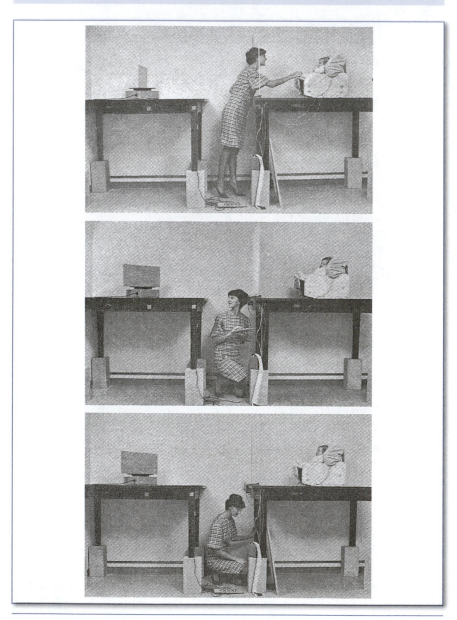

SOURCE: Bower (1966b, p. 84).

Figure 3–12   Size constancy was investigated with cubes of different sizes placed at different distances from the infant. The conditioned stimulus was 30 centimeters on a side and 1 meter away; test stimuli were 30 or 90 centimeters on a side and 1 or 3 meters away. The chart shows how test stimuli were related to the conditioned stimulus in various respects.

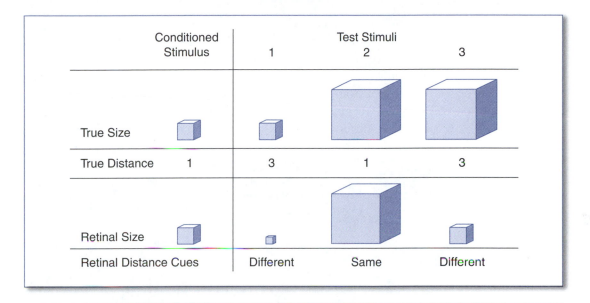

SOURCE: Bower (1966b, p. 82).

different size and was presented at a different distance but led to the same size retinal image as the original stimulus did.

Bower concluded from these results that 6- to 8-week-old infants were showing at least some ability to perceive size constancy. In fact, later work by Slater and colleagues (Slater, Mattock, & Brown, 1990) showed good evidence for size constancy in infants as young as 2 days old! Bower (1966a) also performed very similar studies showing that 50- to 60-day-old infants show some evidence for shape constancy as well.

Thus, taken as a whole, the evidence suggests that even very young infants show some evidence of size constancy. They do not rely strictly on the images projected to their retinas to judge true size and true distance—instead, they seem to be able to judge these two things correctly, at least under some conditions. Bower (1966b) believed that such findings refuted a radical empiricist or constructivist view of infant cognitive development (such as Piaget's) that held that the initial perceptions of infants were disorganized retinal "snapshots" of the world that only became organized and coherent with lots of visual practice in the world. Just as a heads-up, these findings from the constancy studies will be important when we consider the infant's ability to understand and mentally represent objects, a topic we will consider in Chapter 4.

Depth Perception

A classic study in infant perception was carried out at Cornell University by psychologists Eleanor ("Jackie") Gibson and Richard Walk (1960). They first constructed an apparatus they called the "**visual cliff**," which is depicted in Figure 3.13. Essentially, this consisted of a heavy sheet of glass with a board on top in the center. A patterned cloth laid underneath the glass created the appearance of a "cliff," although the presence of the heavy glass protected any experimental participant from taking a tumble. Another patterned sheet lay on the "deep" side of the cliff, on the floor, so that the visual cues to depth were fully present.

Figure 3–13   Experimental apparatus used in the classic "visual cliff" experiments

SOURCE: Biophoto Associates / Photo Researchers, Inc.

Thirty-six infants, aged 6 to 14 months, were tested. Each was initially placed on a slightly raised center board. The infant's mother called the infant to her first from the cliff side (i.e., the side that looked as though the infant was crawling off into space) and then from the shallow side. The results were compelling:

> All of the 27 infants who moved off the [center] board crawled out on the shallow side at least once; only three of them crept off the brink onto the glass suspended above the pattern on the floor. Many of the infants crawled away from the mother when she called to them from the cliff side; others cried when she stood there, because they could not come to her without crossing an apparent chasm. The experiment thus demonstrated that most human infants can discriminate depth as soon as they can crawl. (Gibson & Walk, 1960, p. 64)

Infants behaved in interesting ways while in this experiment. Some would look down the steep side of the "cliff" and then back away. Others would pat the glass with their hands, thus getting tactile information that there was firm support, yet still they would refuse to cross the cliff.

Gibson and Walk (1960) point out that although their results are consistent with a nativist perspective, the data are not definitive. An empiricist could make the argument that during the first 6 or so months of life, infants learn what depth is and what the visual cues to it are. Human infants do not have the ability to locomote (e.g., crawl) until several months have elapsed. However, Gibson and Walk tested a variety of nonhuman species, each of which has much earlier locomotion—chickens, goats, sheep, turtles, pigs, cats, dogs, and rats. Kids (baby goats, in this case), lambs, and chicks all are able to stand within about a day—and none of them ever crossed the visual cliff (though they would readily move about on the shallow side). Not coincidentally, the authors pointed out, these animals all rely on vision as their dominant sensory system. In contrast, rats, which are nocturnal, rely more on tactile cues from their whiskers when roaming around in the dark—and rats did not avoid the visual cliff, as long as their whiskers made contact with the glass.

ATTENTIONAL DEVELOPMENT

Although we have divided this chapter into separate topics—perception versus attention, for example—it's very important to remember that in practice, these different cognitive processes are not so separable. We've already seen, for example, that infant perceptual abilities are typically investigated by measuring the infant's attention to different stimuli and making inferences from the pattern of their relative attentiveness or lack of attentiveness about what stimuli they perceive or prefer (Colombo, 2002). We will see in Chapter 4 that infant attention is also used to study what infants remember, how they form categories, and what they know about objects.

Cognitive psychologists who study the topic of attention in adults and older children define "attention" in terms of the deployment of mental resources to one or more tasks. To pay attention to something is, in this view, to concentrate on it, to devote mental energy to it, and to stop attending to other, distracting stimuli in order to focus on the attended stimulus. We call this last process (where we stop attending to other stimuli) *disengagement* of attention.

As with other areas of research with infants, it is hard to be certain of what they attend to. We can (with some training) record what they look at, but this may not be synonymous with what they are mentally processing (e.g., have you ever stared at a professor who is lecturing at the front of the room but had your mind wandering elsewhere?). However, since infants don't communicate in language, sometimes the best we can do is see whether or not they differentially look at different stimuli. Bear in mind, however, that a lot of interpretation then has to be made about whether looking means actively attending to something (Haith & Benson, 1998).

Cognitive neuroscientists are developing alternative measures of attention. Recording changes in ERP patterns and recording changes in heart rate are two alternatives (Colombo, 2002). For example, Figure 3.14 shows a typical pattern of heart rate as a measure of visual attention. You can see three different phases of heart rate in this figure. The first, labeled OR in the figure, corresponds to infants' initial look at the stimulus—in other words, their orienting response toward the stimulus. As they continue to look, they show sustained attention (labeled SA), during which their heart rate decelerates and then recovers. Colombo, Richman, Shaddy, Greenhoot, and Maikranz (2001) argue that this deceleration corresponds to the infant encoding the stimulus. The final phase, labeled AT, corresponds to the infant disengaging his attention from the stimulus and redirecting it elsewhere.

Colombo and colleagues have found three distinct phases of visual attention over the first year of infancy. From birth until about 10 weeks, there is an increase in the amount of time infants typically look at visual stimuli, perhaps reflecting more general increases in infant alertness. From 10 weeks until about 5 or 6 months, the amount of time infants spend visually attending to a stimulus gradually declines, perhaps as infants get better at disengaging their attention from one stimulus and refocusing on another. Finally, from about 7 months onward, infants' average duration of looking plateaus or even gradually increases. Colombo (2002) interprets this phase as the beginning of sustained, voluntary attention—that is, of the infant "deciding" to focus on stimuli, rather than having his attention passively captured by stimuli.

Figure 3–14 Results from Colombo et al. (2001)

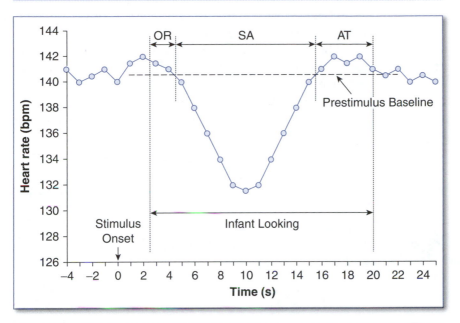

SOURCE: Colombo, Richman, Shaddy, Greenhoot, & Maikranz (2001, p. 1609).

NOTE: Schematic representation of how orienting (OR), sustained attention (SA), and attention termination (AT) were coded within a single look. Stimulus onset occurred at the point designated on the x-axis as 0: The infant began looking at approximately 2.75 s and ended looking at approximately 20 s. The heavy black line shows infant heart rate (HR), and the dotted horizontal line represents the baseline HR level derived from a prestimulus period. SA was coded if the infant showed at least five consecutive beats below baseline level during a look. The period between the start of the look and the onset of SA was coded as OR, and the period after HR returned to baseline, but while the infant was still looking, was coded as AT.

Cohen (1991) makes the point that infants attend most to stimuli they can see clearly or follow easily (if the stimulus is moving) rather than to units they have difficulty seeing or following. Further, as they develop, infants become able to process the relations among lower-order units into more complex units. So, instead of processing parts or features of a stimulus (e.g., head, tail, paws) individually, they perceive a whole object or stimulus (e.g., a dog). The change in processing from features to whole objects seems to occur sometime between 4 and 7 months; however, the changeover from features to whole patterns occurs earlier (between 1.5 and 3 months) when the stimulus is more simple (e.g., a geometric angle).

MEDIA EXPOSURE DURING INFANCY

A recent study by Zimmerman, Christakis, and Meltzoff (2007) surveyed 1,009 parents of children aged 2 to 24 months by telephone to measure how much television or how many DVDs those children viewed. Their findings are somewhat startling, at least to me. By 3 months of age, about 40% of infants regularly watched either television, DVDs, or videos. By 24 months of age, this figure rose to 90%. By about 9 months of age, about half of the infants had regular exposure to media. Infants younger than 12 months who had exposure to media had it for about an hour per day; the corresponding figure is 90 minutes for older toddlers aged 24 months.

Table 3.3 presents the reasons parents gave for why their infants were watching television, DVDs, or videos. As you can see, parents most frequently

Table 3–3 Reasons parents gave as being the most important for their children watching television or DVDs/videos

Reason	Most important reason, %	Of total cited reasons, %
The television and video programs that I have my child watch teach him/her something or are good for his/her brain	28.9	22.4
It is something he/she really enjoys doing	22.7	23.3
I need some time to get things done on my own	20.5	19.7
It is time he/she spends together with a sibling	9.1	12.8
The child needs or wants to relax	4.4	10.9
It teaches the child to get along well with others	1.4	8.0
It is family time, bonding time, or quality time	0	1.0
It grabs and holds my child's attention	0	0.7
Other reasons	13.0	1.4

SOURCE: Zimmerman, Christakis, & Meltzoff (2007, p. 476).

cited that the programs their infants and toddlers were watching had some educational value or would be "good for the brain." Indeed, a number of DVDs and videos market the message that viewing will promote vocabulary growth and cognitive skills and even spur better brain development (Courage & Setliff, 2009).

The claim for brain development is an extrapolation from work with juvenile rats (and other species). Individuals raised in so-called enriched environments had more dendrites, synapses, and other features of their neurons and performed better on some learning tasks (see Greenough, Black, & Wallace, 1987, for a more complete review). However, the complexity in this case consisted of having more objects in a cage or daily exposure to a maze or to other animals. In other words, no specific results of exposure to educational DVDs, videos, or television have been reported (for either human or rat babies!).

Others have claimed that too early exposure to television can lead to problems in the development of attention spans. Again, however, this claim is an extrapolation from studies showing a positive correlation between TV viewing in children younger than 3 and subsequent attention problems (Christakis, Zimmerman, DiGiuseppe, & McCarthy, 2004). However, as we discussed in Chapter 2, the demonstration of a correlation does not support the inference of causation. It could be, for example, that parents of children who will later be diagnosed with attentional disorders are more likely to "park" their children in front of a TV screen just to get a little rest for themselves (Courage & Setliff, 2009).

Research on how well infants and toddlers can learn from a television screen also presents a mixed picture. Work by psychologist Rachel Barr and her associates (e.g., Barr, Muentener, & Garcia, 2007) have demonstrated the existence of something they call a *video deficit effect*. What this means is that 1- and 2-year-olds learn less from watching a televised model carry out some action than they do from watching the same action modeled by a live actor. This deficit is especially evident when the test occurs 24 hours after exposure to the model.

Taken together, the results do not yet support any firm conclusions. In a review of this literature, Courage and Setliff (2009) conclude that "it is premature either to condemn television and video material as a source of harm to the developing infant brain or to promote it as a viable source of early learning" (p. 76). The need for further research is significant and timely, as the issues at stake are certainly important ones.

❖ ❖ ❖

In this chapter, we've examined infants' ability to perceive and attend to information. Many would regard these cognitive processes as the most basic ones for acquiring and using information. But we will see in the next chapter that perception and attention are very hard to separate from other fundamental cognitive processes such as memory and (in the case of infants, perhaps) thinking. We will also look more in depth at the Piagetian notion of the object concept—infants' knowledge about the properties of objects in the world—as a vehicle for examining the integration of different cognitive processes.

SUMMARY

1. We began our look at cognitive development in infancy by considering the Piagetian description of the sensorimotor stage of development. This view holds that infants lack a capacity for mental representation and are thus limited to sensory impressions and motor behaviors.

2. Piaget divided the sensorimotor period into six substages. The first substage is indicated by the restriction of the infant's cognition to reflexive behavior. With development, behavior becomes less reflexive, more complex, and more intentional and eventually gives rise to mental representation in Substage 6.

3. Researchers examining infant cognition often use tools developed by learning theorists. Specifically, habituation paradigms, created initially in animal learning laboratories, are often employed to investigate infants' perceptual and attentional capabilities.

4. While newborns are severely limited in their visual acuity, by the end of their first year the clarity of vision approaches that of an adult. Likewise, newborn infants do not appear to discriminate colors very well, but 4-month-olds seem to make color discriminations the way adults do.

5. Infants' hearing shows less absolute sensitivity than adults' but similar kinds of sensitivities to tones of various pitches. Likewise, even very young infants have been shown to have fairly sophisticated abilities to detect basic tastes (sweet, sour, bitter, salty) and odors and even very slight touches.

6. Infants show reliable preferences for complex visual patterns from a few months of age. Their ability to visually scan a stimulus shows tremendous improvement over the first 4 months. By the latter half of the first year, infants appear to be scanning human faces in an adult-like manner.

7. Even very young infants have been shown to observe perceptual constancies of size and shape and to perceive depth. This has been taken to suggest that some of infants' perceptual abilities are innate, rather than learned.

8. Infants' attentional abilities have been described as becoming more controlled and voluntary over time. In particular, somewhere around the middle of the first year, infants appear to develop the ability to disengage their attention from one stimulus and redirect it to another.

9. Infants and toddlers get a surprising amount of exposure to television, DVDs, and videos. Many parents buy specially designed DVDs and videos hoping they will provide a "jump start" to their child's education or cognitive development. However, scientific evidence that early exposure to media either helps or hinders cognitive development is currently lacking.

REVIEW QUESTIONS

1. Describe different kinds of *circular reactions* (e.g., primary, secondary, tertiary) and discuss their role in infant cognitive development, according to Piaget.

2. Explain what the visual preference paradigm is and how infancy researchers use it to investigate infant sensation and perception.

3. What basic sensory capabilities does a newborn infant show?

4. Why is it important, in your view, to study how infants scan visual stimuli? Why is it important to know how they scan faces in particular?

5. Discuss findings from studies of infants' perceptual constancies and what these might tell us about infant cognition.

6. Describe and critique the classic Gibson and Walk (1960) experiment testing depth perception in infants.

7. Describe some methodological challenges in studying what infants perceive and what they attend to. What sorts of measurement techniques seem to be best suited to this kind of research? Justify your answer.

8. Describe the most useful study you can design to answer the question as to whether DVDs or videos designed to enhance infants' cognitive development really work.

KEY TERMS

Adaptation	Object Permanence
Circular Reaction	Shape Constancy
Constancies (perceptual)	Size Constancy
Equilibration	Synapses
Habituation	Visual Cliff
Infancy	Visual Preference Paradigm

CHAPTER 4

INFANCY

Memorial and Conceptual Development

I n Chapter 3, our focus was on the perceptual world of infants—the information they acquire from the world, and the stimuli they attend to. In this chapter, we will continue to examine the cognitive abilities and changes occurring during the first 2 years of life, but our focus will be slightly different. Here we will center our attention on how infants come to remember information they have previously had exposure to—how they form and retain memory traces, either explicitly or implicitly. Secondly, we will examine how infants categorize information—mentally grouping some things together and treating them as similar. Finally, putting together the topics of perception, attention, memory, and categorization, we will conclude by examining what infants seem to know about objects—their properties, their existence, and their behavior.

THEORETICAL PERSPECTIVES

As I did in Chapter 3, I'll be picking up on the discussion of different theoretical frameworks from Chapter 2. Because I talked at length about the Piagetian perspective on infancy in Chapter 3, the discussion here will be quite short. Ditto for the discussion of the nativist perspective. However, I'll spend a fair amount of time talking here about the view from the information-processing perspective on infancy, as its concepts and ideas have important things to say to help us put research on infant memory in particular into perspective.

A Piagetian View

You will recall from our discussion in Chapter 2 that, according to Piaget, most infants lack the capacity to form mental representations, which, in turn, should suggest that they are unable to form memory traces that persist for a period of time longer than a minute or two. It might be helpful for you to review the section on Piagetian theory in Chapter 3, particularly focusing on the last three substages of the sensorimotor period. You might recall from that section that Piagetian theory posits that before the age of about 8 months, infants appear to have no coherent understanding of what objects are, what properties they have, and how they behave. We will see in this chapter in particular much recent research disputing all of these claims.

Piaget has more to say about older infants' knowledge about objects as well. You'll recall that Substage 4 infants don't easily fall for the "object under the washcloth" trick, and they quickly (and often with great glee) investigate a suspicious lump under a cloth, retrieving the hidden object. This might lead you to believe that a 10-month-old infant has a mature understanding that objects have continued existence even when unseen. However, another Piagetian demonstration, known as the "A not B" task, casts some doubt on this interpretation.

The task is performed as follows. The infant is seated between two cloths or other types of covers—Cover A on the left and Cover B on the right, let's say. You entice the infant to try to grab for an interesting toy, and then have her watch as you hide it under Cover A. She should by this point be able to uncover the toy quickly, and may very well enjoy doing so. You repeat this sequence a few more times, always making sure that she watches you hide the toy under Cover A. Then, you introduce a change in the game. With the infant watching you carefully, you this time hide the toy under Cover B.

Often, the infant's response will surprise you. Having carefully visually tracked your hand holding the object go under Cover B and emerge empty, the infant will immediately turn back to Cover A to look for the object! Moreover, when she doesn't find it there, she will often call off the search! According to Piaget, this is because the infant's grasp of object permanence still has some maturing to do.

It is in this fifth substage when infants gradually come to perform "correctly" (according to adult standards) on the A not B task, being able to overcome the behavioral "habit" of looking for the object in A regardless of where they saw the object hidden. However, infants even at this age show limits in understanding of object permanence, being still unable to solve the riddle of invisible displacements.

For example, imagine I was to take my 1-year-old daughter's pacifier and hide it in my hand, then put my closed hand into my pocket, and then withdraw the hand, opening it to show that it was empty. This "trick" would not fool you (I assume), but it would mystify a young toddler. Piaget's explanation goes back to the name of the stage—the infant is bound by his sensory and motor interactions with the world, and lacks the capacity to mentally represent or imagine a location of the object that he hasn't directly seen.

We will see in this chapter, however, many demonstrations that challenge Piaget's view. Work by Rovee-Collier and Bauer in particular has posed strong challenges to traditional Piagetian views of younger infants' abilities, and we will explore that work very shortly. Moreover, we'll review work by other researchers that suggests that infants know quite a bit more about objects than Piagetian theory credits them with.

A Nativist View

Piaget's views seem to suggest that infants need a certain amount of experiences (say, 8 months' worth) to learn about objects in their world. Developmental psychologists in the nativist tradition reject this view in particular. As we'll see in the descriptions of work by Elizabeth Spelke and Renée Baillargeon, much younger infants seem to know a lot more about objects than Piaget's view (or a learning theory view) would predict. In fact, Spelke and Baillargeon currently focus on describing the knowledge infants have about objects in terms of a small set of hardwired principles or constraints.

Psychologist Elizabeth Spelke (1994, 2000) suggests that infants arrive equipped with two principles: those of continuity and cohesion. The *principle of continuity* states that objects exist and move continuously in time and space (i.e., they can't pop in and out of existence). The *principle of cohesion* describes the idea that objects cannot spontaneously disintegrate or meld with other objects—they have firm boundaries that contain them. These principles, Baillargeon (2008) proposes, are but two corollaries of a more general principle of persistence: "Objects persist, as they are, in time and space" (p. 3). We'll explore each of these proposals toward the end of the chapter.

For now, I want to explore the meaning it has to say that an infant possesses a hardwired principle or constraint. Obviously, it cannot mean that an infant can articulate that principle in words. What it does mean, in contrast, is that infants come into the world prepared to make certain assumptions, entertain certain hypotheses, or hold certain expectations of the way objects will or won't behave. Spelke and Baillargeon believe that infants have these expectations or hypotheses that guide what they pay attention to and what kinds of information surprises them, from the time they are born. By the way, you might be curious about how researchers assess "surprisingness" in infants. We'll see in the last section of the chapter how these nativist theorists determine just what surprises an infant and what does not.

A View From Information-Processing Theory

Recall from Chapter 2 that information-processing theorists make analogies between human cognition and computer architecture. Figure 2.2 (see page 29), which presents a general overview, depicts with boxes various memory stores. Information-processing theorists view memory as storage and are concerned with both the number of different stores (memory systems) an individual has and how these stores operate.

Notice that this view opens the door to a number of different possibilities for developmental change. Infants could develop more and more varied kinds of storage, for example. Or, they could become more efficient in the way they use their memory stores. Or, the capacity of the memory storage could grow with development. Or, the duration with which information can be stored could grow with development. Or, some combination of some or all of these possibilities could provide the best explanation of memory development.

Before turning to the work on infant memorial development, let's first take a look at proposals for different kinds of memory stores. Cognitive psychologists have long debated whether different *kinds* of memories exist. In other words, the question is whether or not there are different memory systems that operate according to different principles, use different processes, and/or store different kinds of information. Many such distinctions have been proposed.

One of the first distinctions proposed was between long- and short-term memory (Atkinson & Shiffrin, 1968). The proposal was that there was one kind of system for one's immediate memory (e.g., your "memory" for the beginning of the sentence you are currently reading) and a different one for the kinds of memories one has "shelved away." Short-term memory was thought to be strictly limited to about seven plus or minus two pieces of unrelated information (Miller, 1956), and to encode information by its acoustical sound (Baddeley, 1966). Long-term memory, in contrast, was thought to have a very large and perhaps infinite amount of storage, and to encode information based on its meaning (Atkinson & Shiffrin, 1968). More recently psychologist Alan Baddeley (1986) has proposed a newer concept of working memory to replace the traditional description of short-term memory. Working memory emphasizes the idea that people have to have a mental workspace in which to encode, transform, and manipulate information, and that they use this mental workspace not only to store information briefly but to solve problems, create sentences, and reason from premises to conclusions, to name just a few important cognitive tasks. We'll explore working memory in much more detail in Chapter 8.

Another distinction commonly proposed is that between recognition and recall. Both are retrieval processes—that is, processes by which information that has been stored in memory are brought back to conscious awareness (Galotti, 2008). The difference is in whether or not the individual must fully re-create the stored information, in the case of recall, or whether the individual must simply show awareness that the presented information has been previously encountered. A familiar example might be a test—the essay questions would be instantiations of recall questions, while most multiple-choice questions allow the test taker to recognize the correct answer. Most of the time, recognition processes are thought to be less cognitively taxing than recall processes, although exceptions have been noted (Klatzky, 1980). We'll look at research suggesting that, even in infancy, both kinds of memory exist.

Finally, many psychologists distinguish between **implicit memory**—that is, memory that one isn't explicitly aware of having but that affects one's current behavior—and **explicit memory**, in which the person shows clear evidence of conscious or deliberate recollection or recall of previously experienced events (Roediger, 1990). We'll see that there is reason to believe that this distinction is also a useful one to draw in the study of infant memory. To preview: Many developmental psychologists believe that as infancy progresses, infants move from showing only implicit memory to showing both implicit and explicit memory.

MEMORY DEVELOPMENT IN INFANCY

How and when do infants remember previous experiences? How can we tell whether or not an infant remembers a past experience? As with the study of infant perception and attention, the study of infant memory cannot rely on verbal questioning. Instead, developmental psychologists who study infants must devise nonverbal approaches to asking such questions of infants. Often, these approaches make use of instrumental conditioning, which we reviewed in Chapter 3.

Instrumental conditioning can be used to bring about a number of new behaviors, and the techniques are widely used by animal trainers working with a variety of species. They can be used quite successfully with humans of all ages, although in general it takes younger infants longer to learn the same task than it does older infants (Rovee-Collier & Barr, 2002). For the cognitive developmental researcher, instrumental conditioning provides a way of sidestepping the problem that infants do not produce or understand language. Instead of asking infants if they remember something, then, researchers can provide experience in the form of classical or operant conditioning, and then see how long discernable effects of the training last.

A Demonstration of Infant Memory

Rovee and Fagen (1976) used an instrumental conditioning paradigm to see whether or not young infants could form and store memory traces. They placed infants aged 2 to 6 months in a crib, over which was hung a mobile, decorated with certain symbols. At first, one of the infant's ankles had a ribbon tied to it, with the other end of the ribbon tied to a hook. The baseline level of kicking was recorded—that is, how frequently the infant just happened to kick. Next, the ribbon was attached to the mobile, such that kicks caused the mobile to move. The harder the kick, the greater the movement of the mobile, and infants demonstrated interest in and enjoyment of this relationship, suggesting that the moving mobile functioned as a positive reinforcer of the response of kicking.

Later, the ribbon was switched back to the original hook so that kicks did not produce reinforcement. This served as a measure of learning and memory with no delay in testing called the *immediate retention test*. Moreover, sometime later (days or weeks), the same crib, mobile, and ribbon (not tied to the mobile) were again presented, and the level of kicking was measured. If infants kicked only at baseline level, investigators inferred that they did not remember their training. If infants kicked at a rate substantially above baseline (and close to the immediate retention test), investigators interpreted this as evidence of long-term memory.

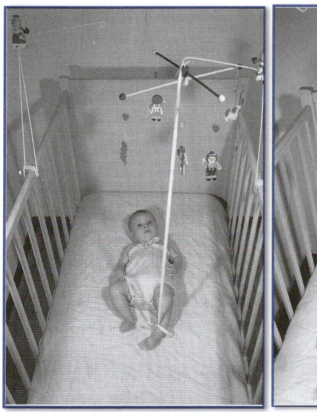 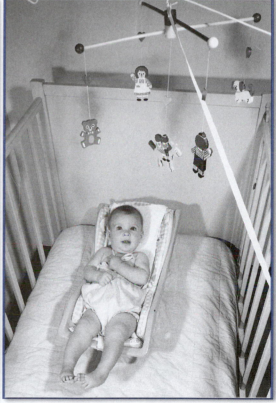

Photos 4.1a and 4.1b The experimental arrangement used with 2- to 6-month-olds in the mobile conjugate reinforcement task, shown here with a 3-month-old. (a) *Acquisition phase*: The ribbon and the mobile are attached to the same overhead hook so that kicks move the mobile. (b) *The delayed recognition test*: The ribbon and mobile are attached to different hooks so the kicks cannot move the mobile.

SOURCE: Rovee-Collier & Barr (2001).

Rovee and Fagen (1976) found that 3-month-old infants, trained for 9 minutes a day for 3 days, showed clear recognition of a previously presented mobile after 24 hours—however, they did not show elevated rates of kicking to a new mobile. Thus, not only did they remember the original mobile for 24 hours; they showed evidence that they could discriminate between a previously seen stimulus (the original mobile) and a new one.

Older infants show less interest in the mobile-kicking task, and so Rovee-Collier and her colleagues devised a more interesting task for older infants (aged 6 to 18 months), known as the train task. Infants were seated in front of a toy train on a circular track. A large lever was at the front of the display. As in the mobile kicking task, there was first a baseline phase, during which the lever was deactivated and did not produce any effect. Next, during the learning phase, every lever press by the infant resulted in the train moving briefly down the track. The learning phase was followed by

Photo 4.2 The experimental arrangement used with 6- to 18-month-olds in the train task, shown here with a 6-month-old. During baseline and the delayed retention test, the lever is deactivated so that presses cannot move the train. Note the complex array of toys in the train box.

SOURCE: Rovee-Collier & Barr (2001).

one or more retention phases, which, like the baseline phase, had the lever deactivated.

Six-month-old infants perform identically on the mobile-kicking and train task, which provides evidence of some comparability across tasks (Hartshorn & Rovee-Collier, 1997). Using data from these two tasks, Rovee-Collier and colleagues have shown that the maximum duration of retention rises with age, as is shown in Figure 4.1. Infants of 2 months seem capable of retention of information for a few days at most; in contrast, 18-month-olds remember how to work the train for 13 weeks—roughly the length of time of a college semester!

Figure 4–1 The maximum duration of retention (in weeks) of independent groups of infants over the first 18 months of life in studies using one of two operant tasks. Six-month-olds were trained and tested in both the mobile and the train tasks.

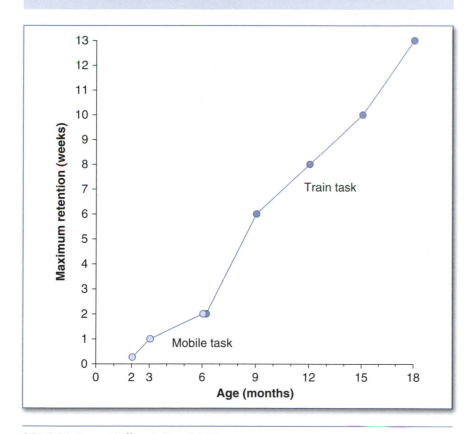

SOURCE: Rovee-Collier & Barr (2001).

Recognition Memory

In a sense, one could argue that the results just discussed along with the results of studies of classical and instrumental conditioning discussed earlier represent tests of recognition memory, or at least of implicit recognition memory. After all, the evidence that conditioning has occurred is that the infant emits trained behaviors in response to a cue. In order to respond to the cue, the infant has to have some sort of memory trace formed. A critic might take issue, however, with whether or not conditioned responses always indicate memory. That critic might argue, instead, that conditioned responses simply show that an infant has acquired a motor habit, a physical response that does not indicate an explicit memory trace.

Therefore, it would be helpful to see whether infant memories could be indicated with methods other than conditioning. Another test of recognition memory that does not involve conditioned responses is known as the **visual paired comparison task**, or VPC (Pascalis & De Haan, 2003). This task was

Figure 4–2 Visual paired comparison task (VPC): An infant is presented with the sample for a familiarization period. Thereafter, the participant is confronted with the familiar stimulus and a new stimulus. The time spent fixating on each stimulus is recorded.

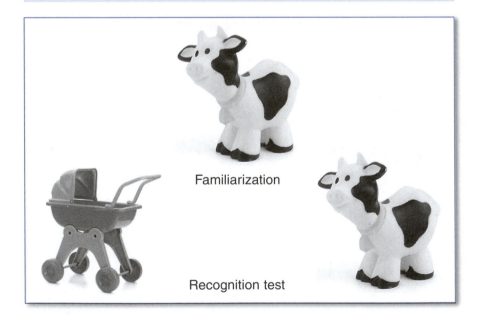

Familiarization

Recognition test

SOURCE: Pascalis & Dettaan (2003, p. 86).

also developed by psychologist Robert Fantz (1964) and, like the habituation procedures he used in his studies of infant perception, relies on people's tendency to pay more attention to novel, rather than familiar, objects. Figure 4.2 depicts stimulus presentation in the VPC. First, the infant is presented with a single stimulus, say, a toy cow, during what is called the *familiarization phase,* which lasts for some predetermined amount of time. Next comes a *recognition phase,* which presents the familiarization phase stimulus along with a novel stimulus. Observers, blind to which stimulus is on which side, observe the infant's eyes from behind a screen and record the amount of time the infant spends fixating on each stimulus, as shown in Figures 4.3 and 4.4. Longer duration of fixation to one stimulus (typically the novel stimulus) than the other is thought to indicate recognition memory.

You might be wondering how it is researchers can be sure that longer looks at novel stimuli measure recognition memory. If so, your skeptical response is appropriate—preferential looking in infants could mean a number of different things. The answer is that researchers employ a number of

Figure 4–3   Example of the experimental setting. The infant is watching pictures, and a camera located above the screen records her eye movements.

SOURCE: Pascalis & Dettaan (2003, p. 82).

Figure 4–4 Video frames (3/100 s) of an infant's eye movements during the retention tests of the VPC task. From top to bottom, the corneal reflections of the two stimuli (two white bars inside the infant's pupils) indicate that the child looked at the stimulus on its left, then at the center, and finally at the stimulus on the right.

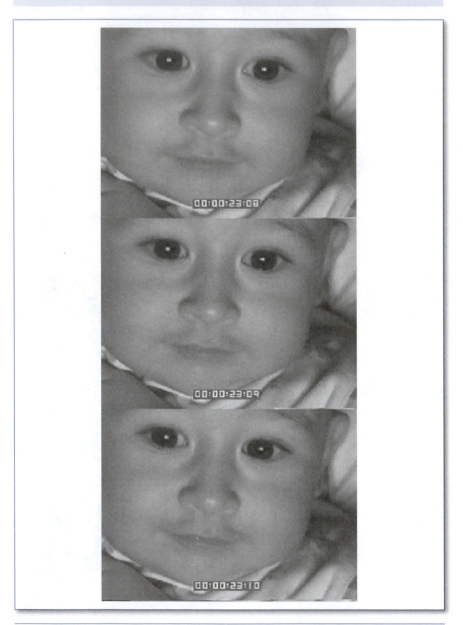

SOURCE: Pascalis & Dettaan (2003, p. 83).

controls to ensure that preferential looking at the novel object isn't due to some extraneous factor:

> To help ensure that novelty scores reflect processing and recognition memory, and not methodological factors, several controls are generally incorporated into VPC tasks. First, preliminary testing is done to ensure that, at the outset, members of each pair are approximately equal in attractiveness. Thus, the paired test stimuli are presented without any prior familiarization. If they are equivalent in attractiveness, infants' attention to each member of the pair will be roughly equivalent. Second, the familiarization stimuli are counterbalanced, so that each member of the pair serves equally often as familiar and novel across infants in a group. Third, on test, the left-right placement of the novel and familiar stimuli are reversed midway through to control for position preferences. (Rose, Feldman, & Jankowski, 2004, p. 75)

Using this methodology, researchers have shown that even very young infants show clear evidence of recognition memory. For example, 3-day-old infants were shown to recognize stimuli presented 2 minutes earlier (Pascalis & De Schoen, 1994), and by the age of 3 to 6 months, infants can show recognition memory after retention intervals of days or weeks (Fagan, 1973; Pascalis & De Haan, 2003; Rose et al., 2004). The amount of information infants seem to be able to hold in visual recognition memory also grows over the first year, as demonstrated in a number of studies (Rose et al., 2004). Older infants show a preference for more complex stimuli than do younger infants, such as those with more lines, or parts, or patterning. Most intriguingly, infant visual memory as measured in the latter half of the first year of life shows moderate correlations with various cognitive measures, including IQ scores, much later in development (e.g., during the preschool or even the elementary school years; Rose et al., 2004).

Recall Memory

The studies described above speak to the idea that infants show an ability to recognize previously presented information. As I mentioned earlier, however, recognition is often thought to be easier than recall, in that the person recognizing information doesn't have to construct a full rendition of the stored information but instead can simply respond to a second presentation of it. The question then becomes "Do infants show evidence of recall memory?" Work from the laboratory of psychologist Patricia Bauer suggests the answer is yes.

To demonstrate recall memory in infants, Bauer faced a familiar problem: Most psychologists who study recall rely on verbal reports of their participants, but infant researchers do not have this option. So, together with one of her mentors, Jean Mandler, Bauer developed an **elicited imitation task** to do this (Bauer, 2002a, 2002b). In essence, the infant is presented with objects and shown a unique sequence of actions using those objects. For example, infants might be shown a plastic car, a miniature plastic Big Bird character, a base for the car to be inserted into, and a plunger that, when pushed, causes the car to ride down the base and turn on a light (Carver & Bauer, 2001). Figure 4.5 provides an illustration. The general point here is that the actions performed on objects were not ones that would be likely for infants to spontaneously do—hence, when infants performed them, the investigators could be fairly sure it was due to their prior exposure to a model, and not because the objects somehow "invited" the infant to produce them.

Figure 4–5   Example two-step sequence: Turn on the light. To reproduce the sequence, infants had to first put a toy car down a vertical compartment of an L-shaped apparatus and then push a rod into the horizontal compartment, thereby causing the car to roll to the end and turn on a light. Note that infants could push the rod before putting the car into the vertical compartment. However, doing so would not cause the light to illuminate.

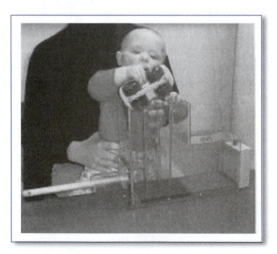

SOURCE: Bauer, Wiebe, Carver, Waters, & Nelson (2003).

Recall that in Piagetian theory described in Chapter 3, infants would not be capable of this kind of **deferred imitation** until they reached Substage 6 of the sensorimotor period—at about age 18–24 months. However, findings from Bauer's research laboratory suggest that under certain conditions, even infants aged 9 months can show evidence of recall memory in the elicited memory task when tested after a 1-month delay (Bauer, 2002a, 2002b). During the second year of life (i.e., with toddlers aged 13 to 24 months), long-term recall becomes even more stable and lasts for longer periods of time. For infants shown a three-step sequence of actions when they were 20 months old, for example, over 60% showed evidence of recalling those actions 12 months later (Bauer, 2002a; Bauer, Wenner, Dropik, & Werweka, 2000). Remember that the objects Bauer used and the actions performed on them were fairly unique and idiosyncratic, so the infant's ability to reproduce those actions on those objects months or years later is fairly impressive!

Based on her own results and those from neurological studies of infants, Bauer (2002b, 2006, 2007) argues that long-term recall ability emerges around 9 months, when brain structures in the medial temporal lobe including the **hippocampus** (see Figure 4.6) become functional. Development of related structures in the prefrontal cortex continues in the second year, and full maturation does not occur until adolescence. Thus, Bauer would assert that the development of recall memory continues to improve throughout childhood. We will see in the chapters to come that this assertion has a great deal of supporting evidence that has accrued from various laboratory findings.

Much of the work in infant memory research requires a great deal of creativity in setting up studies that allow nonverbal infants to demonstrate whether or not they possess a memory trace of a previously experienced event. There are controversies among different researchers over which techniques work best, how data should be collected and analyzed, and what interpretations can be drawn from research findings.

A current controversy has erupted over the question of whether there are different kinds of memory systems (e.g., recall vs. recognition, or implicit vs. explicit) or not. Rovee-Collier and Cuevas (2009) take issue with the postulation of multiple memory systems, and with the idea that explicit memory (typically indexed by recall memory tasks, such as those used by Bauer) develops later and out of an earlier-appearing implicit memory system (typically measured by recognition memory tasks, such as the VPC task described earlier). Instead, Rovee-Collier and Cuevas argue that even very young infants can learn and remember many associations or links that can become part of an elaborate memory network. As the network grows, and as elements of the network become increasingly interconnected, infants show increasingly flexible memory performance.

Figure 4–6   Location of the hippocampus

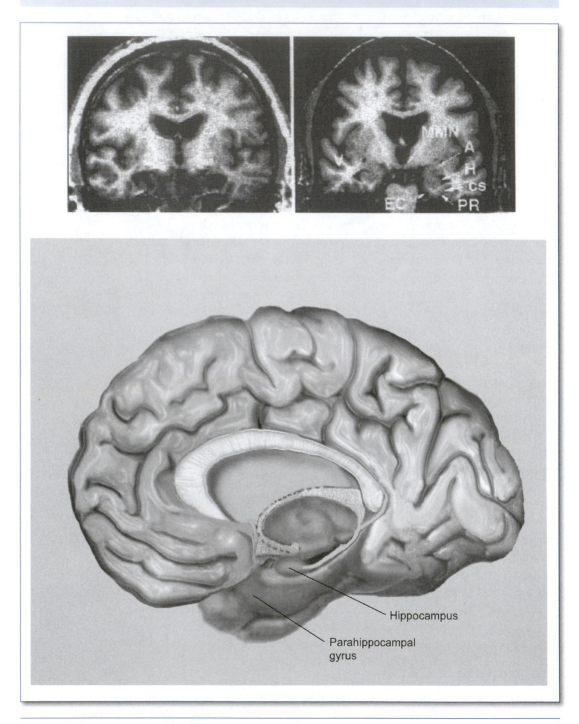

SOURCE: Garrett (2009, p. 365).

But despite the theoretical disagreements over how many memory systems infants have, some general principles about memory in infancy can be drawn from the findings of different researchers in different laboratories using different experimental techniques. These principles, summarized by Hayne (2004), include the following:

1. Older infants encode information faster than younger infants.

2. Older infants remember information longer than do younger infants.

3. Older infants use a wider range of cues for retrieval than do younger infants.

Our look at infant memory has so far focused on what some cognitive psychologists would call episodic memory. Psychologist Endel Tulving (1972) proposed the existence of two separate memory stores—one that contains information about general knowledge and one that contains memory traces of information from one's personal experience. Episodic memory is thought to contain your memories that trace to a specific event—your recollection of your first day of kindergarten, or the time you dressed up your kitten to look like a rock star—in other words, memories for events that you remember occurring at a particular time and place (even if you don't remember exactly what that time and place were).

Semantic memory, in contrast, contains your general knowledge—for example, that Boston is the capital of Massachusetts, that 6 times 7 is 42, and that school usually starts in August or September and goes until May or June. You may remember all of this but have not a clue as to when you first encountered or experienced the presentation of this information. Some cognitive psychologists would refer to semantic memory as the knowledge base.

We will segue, now, into looking at infant versions of semantic memory. That is, we will look at the infant knowledge base. We'll begin by looking at how infants categorize stimuli—mentally classifying different stimuli into categories of "same" or "different." Next, we'll examine more broadly the issue of infants' developing knowledge of objects.

CATEGORIZATION IN INFANCY

The importance of categorization to infant cognition was stated especially vividly by Haith and Benson (1998):

Imagine an infant who must learn anew its parent's face for each perspective rotation, each expression, and each change of hair style. Or, consider the task of an infant who must acquire a new knowledge base for each separate cat that it encounters—that each meows, drinks, eats, and so on. And, one can appreciate the utility of categorization. By incorporating individual percepts of the mom's face into a mom-face category and individual cats into a cat category, infants gain enormous leverage in accumulating knowledge. Each piece of information one acquires with an individual exemplar can generalize to the whole set, permitting appropriate expectations and behavior in encounters with completely new instances. (p. 229)

Categorization is defined in slightly different ways by different investigators, but a typical definition is the idea that infants group certain objects together in the time it takes to view these objects, based on their perceptions of similarities and differences (Oakes, Horst, Kovack-Lesh, & Perone, 2009). So how do infants group things together, or at least recognize different instances as belonging to the same category? Once again, researchers need to come up with ways of asking such a question of preverbal infants. And once again, some very clever researchers have created some very intriguing paradigms.

Eimas and Quinn (1994), for example, showed photographs of cats and horses to infants 3 or 4 months of age. Infants were tested in a visual preference procedure, where they sat in a parent's lap and saw two pictures or photographs at a time. One group of infants first viewed various pictures of cats (in various poses and of various colors); the other group first viewed pictures of horses (again, of various stances and colors). Two different animals of the same kind were shown on each trial (which lasted 15 seconds), and there were six trials (with a total of 12 different animals, either horses or cats) presented.

Next came the preference test trials. Infants who had first seen cats were now presented with six trials in which a novel cat was paired with a novel horse, a different novel cat was paired with a novel tiger, and a still different novel cat was paired with a female lion. The infants who initially saw horses saw, on their test trials, a novel horse with a novel cat, a different novel horse with a novel zebra, or a still different novel horse with a novel giraffe.

Looking times to each picture on the trials were recorded. Infants initially familiarized with horses were significantly more likely to look at the photographs of cats, zebras, or giraffes than they were to look at photographs of never-before-seen horses. In contrast, infants initially familiarized with cats were significantly more likely to look at the photographs of horses and tigers (but not female lions) than they were to look at photographs of never-before-seen cats. The authors took the significant looking preferences to indicate that the infants somehow recognized that the novel animals from the familiarization category were "more of the same" category of animals previously seen. Therefore, the infants paid more attention to the "new" animals—those they perceived to be from a different category.

Eimas and Quinn (1994) were not claiming that infants had a lot of knowledge about what horses or cats were. However, what they showed was that infants could mentally group together instances (different photographs) of horses and distinguish them from various instances of cats. In later work, Quinn and Eimas (1996) tried to key in on what cues infants were using to categorize. They presented 3- and 4-month-old infants with pictures of cats and dogs. In one condition, infants saw photos of entire animals; in another, just the heads of the animals (with the bodies occluded, or covered up); and in still others, just the bodies (with the heads occluded). Infants in the first two conditions were successfully able to categorize dogs versus cats, but infants in the third condition, who saw only bodies, did not make this categorization. This work and another follow-up (Quinn, Doran, Reiss, & Hoffman, 2009) using eye-tracking equipment suggested strongly that infants focus on heads, and particularly faces, in making classifications, at least of animal stimuli.

Other investigators found infants less able or willing to categorize when presented with actual objects (e.g., miniature horse and dog figurines), or when presented with pictures of items one at a time instead of in pairs (see Kovack-Lesh & Oakes, 2007, for a description). This in turn suggests that the way especially young infants carry out categorization depends heavily on the way the infant encounters the stimuli, and on what the stimuli are. Said another way, the kind of stimuli used and how they are presented makes a big difference in the results of infant categorization experiments.

What do infants do with non-animal stimuli? A study by Baldwin, Markman, and Melartin (1993) suggested that infants categorize objects primarily on the basis of physical appearance and expect exemplars within a category to share properties. Their research participants were infants aged 9 to 16 months. They were shown "a number of unusual objects possessing a range of relatively idiosyncratic nonobvious properties" (p. 714), including a cylinder whose ends slid apart while making a sound and a can that, when turned, produced a "wailing" sound. The point here is that the objects had properties that weren't visually obvious (to an adult observer).

Infants, seated in their parent's lap at a table facing the experimenter, were offered a toy while the experimenter made several general exclamations to attract their interest. They were given 30 seconds to explore the toy in whatever way they wished. Then a second toy was held up and given to the infants while the experimenter took back the first toy, placing it nearby. The two toys were similar in appearance (e.g., had different colors or patterns but very similar shapes).

In a baseline condition, neither of the two toys exhibited the nonobvious property, as the experimenters disabled those features on the toys. In the fulfilled expectations condition, both toys had the nonobvious property. The violated expectations condition was the one most of interest to the experimenters—in it, the first toy had the nonobvious property, but the second toy did not. The question was whether in this condition infants would persist in trying to make the second toy exhibit the property the first toy had.

In fact, they did: Infants in the violated expectations condition showed more attempts to make the second toy produce the interesting sound or movement than did infants in either of the first two control conditions (baseline or fulfilled expectations conditions). In a second study, the authors showed that if the two toys presented were radically different in appearance (e.g., the wailing can described earlier, followed by a cube), then the infants did not try to make the second toy (e.g., the cube) exhibit the interesting property (e.g., the wailing sound) the first one had displayed. These results, taken together, imply that infants who discover a nonobvious property in one object expect a perceptually similar object to share that surprising property. That is, the infants were able to categorize objects together quickly, based on their physical similarity.

Psychologist Amy Booth (2008) showed in a recent study that somewhat older infants (aged 14–18 months) could categorize using a much more abstract basis—that of causal relationships between objects. Her study has a very complex design, which will only be partially reviewed here.

Infants were shown 32 novel three-dimensional objects, all made out of clay and brightly colored. These are depicted in Figure 4.7 (although the figure is reproduced in black and white). These objects were grouped into sets. In Figure 4.7, each set is in a row. The first four objects in each row (the familiarization objects) as well as one of the test items (in Figure 4.7, the seventh object in each row) had similar shapes and colors.

Infants were randomly assigned to the causal, noncausal, or no-outcome condition. Infants in all conditions received the familiarization training, in which they were shown the first four objects in each set, two at a time. These were presented in the presence of an "outcome box"—a box constructed of smoky glass that hid a toy inside. When the box was illuminated, a noisy toy (a neighing horse, a spinning pinwheel, a quacking duck, or a flashing ball of lights) appeared. This box was controlled by the experimenter and always placed out of reach of the curious infant.

In the *causal* condition, the experimenter placed a pair of familiarization objects on the table. She picked up one of them, holding it 2 inches from the box; touched the object to the box while simultaneously illuminating it; and then removed the object from the box while deactivating the illumination.

Figure 4–7   Familiarization, contrast, and test stimuli for each set. The target object is pictured in fourth position for each set. Set 1 objects were shades of blue and green, Set 2 objects were shades of pink and purple, Set 3 objects were shades of brown and gray, and Set 4 objects were shades of yellow and orange.

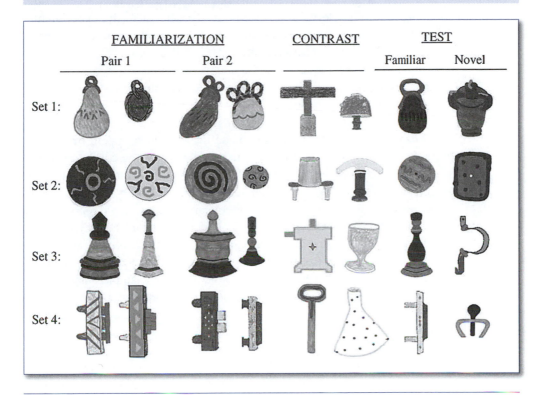

SOURCE: Booth (2008, p. 987).

The idea here was to imply to the infant that the familiarization object some-how "caused" the box to light up. The experimenter next repeated this sequence with the other familiarization item in the pair. Later, the same pro-cedure was repeated with the other pair of familiarization objects.

The other two conditions, *noncausal* and *no outcome*, were both con-trol conditions. In the no-outcome condition, the outcome box was never illuminated. In the noncausal condition, the box was illuminated, but not when the familiarization object was touching it. All infants then saw a con-trast item. Even when the contrast item was touched against the box, the box did not illuminate. The idea here was to show infants in the causal condition that not all objects activated the box. Booth (2008) was showing that it is not simply the presentation of an object together with the box that causes infants to categorize them together—infants need to detect a causal relationship to use as the basis of forming the category.

Last came the test phase. Infants were presented with two novel objects—one that looked similar to the familiarization objects and one that was different. The infants played with both test items for a few seconds, after which they were retrieved and placed out of reach. Next, the experimenter brought out a previously seen familiarization item and reminded the infant what it could do (in the causal condition). She then asked the infant, "Can you find me another one of these?" while placing both test items within the infant's reach. The session was videotaped, and research assistants coded to see which item the infant selected (either by placing it in the experimenter's hand or touching it).

Infants in the causal condition chose the familiar test item 62% of the time. In contrast, infants in the noncausal and no-outcome conditions chose the familiar item only 43% or 46% of the time, as shown in Figure 4.8. The effect was slightly more pronounced for older infants. Booth (2008) interprets these results as showing that at least older infants can use causal relationships, a fairly abstract connection, as a basis for forming categories of objects.

Taking all the studies on categorization together, there is some suggestion that infants first categorize by using perceptual information about objects—what they look like, their overall shape or texture. For example, infants might categorize different individual cats into the category "cat" on the basis of what the animals look like—size, fur, paws, tail, facial features. As they develop, infants become less dependent on perceptual similarity and are able to categorize on more abstract bases (such as causality).

But not all psychologists subscribe to this theory of how categorization works. Jean Mandler (2000), for example, believes that there are two separate and independent processes of categorization that infants use by the time they reach the ripe old age of 9 months. The first is the *perceptual categorization* already described—grouping together items on the basis of general physical appearance. The second, called *conceptual categorization,* is one infants use to sort items together based on some aspect of the "meaning" of the category.

Mandler and her associates (Mandler & Bauer, 1988; Mandler, Bauer, & McDonough, 1991) have used a simplified sorting task with their young research participants, called a **sequential touching task**. Essentially, items from two contrasting categories (e.g., miniature animal figurines and miniature car figurines) are presented, and the infants are encouraged to interact with the items. The experimenter avoids naming or labeling any of the objects and merely records the order in which the infant touches different objects.

Figure 4–8 Means and standard errors for the proportion of trials in which infants selected the familiar test object in each condition. The * indicates responding that exceeded both chance (0.50) and performance in the noncausal and no-outcome conditions. The ~ indicates responding that exceeded performance in the noncausal and no-outcome conditions but only marginally exceeded chance.

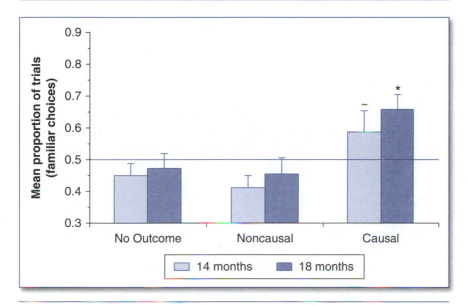

SOURCE: Booth (2008, p. 991).

Amazingly, infants show a tendency to touch objects within the same category (e.g., different animal models) in sequence at well above chance levels of performance. This behavior has been taken to show a primitive kind of sorting items into categories. Similarly, infants can be handed models of objects one at a time, and the amount of time they actively explore each item is recorded. If infants categorize one object into the same category as the previous several items they've explored, then they should show less time exploring it relative to an object handed to them that they regard as belonging to a different category.

Using this methodology, Mandler and McDonough (1993) studied infants 7 to 11 months old. These infants were shown to differentiate between animals and vehicles. More surprisingly, 9-month-old infants were shown to differentiate airplanes from birds, even though the overall shapes and perceptual similarity were high (one airplane even had a face painted on it).

Mandler (2000) concluded from this work that infants must "know" something about what airplanes and birds are to be able to differentiate between them. Although granting that infants' knowledge of these categories is likely to be crude and incomplete, she argues that they do go beyond what things look like in their mental grouping of objects in the world. This proposal is a very controversial one and has attracted a great deal of spirited commentary (e.g., Carey 2000a; Gibson, 2000; Nelson, 2000; Quinn & Eimas, 2000; Reznick, 2000), and the issue of whether infants begin with one or two systems of categorization is very much alive in the field today.

KNOWLEDGE OF OBJECTS

We saw in Chapter 3 that Piaget placed a lot of importance on infants' knowledge about objects in their cognitive development. Much of infants' growing maturity was indexed by their ability to track objects, indicate awareness that hidden objects continued to exist, and find objects that were hidden in new locations. Piagetian theory held that as infants attain new levels of cognitive development, they develop more sophisticated assumptions about the nature of objects, what properties they have and what physical laws they obey.

In this section, we will examine recent work showing that at least some investigators believe that younger infants have a great deal more sophisticated understanding of objects and their properties than Piaget credited them with. These issues speak directly to issues of whether infants learn about objects and their properties or whether they have some innate knowledge about objects that guides their perceptions of what information to pay attention to.

Object Permanence

Piaget claimed that before they were about 8 months old, infants lacked a concept of object permanence, a sense that physical objects with which one is not currently in sensory or motor contact continue to physically exist. Presumably, this lack was tied to infants' overall lack of ability to mentally represent things. After all, if an infant cannot mentally represent an object, there should be no way to imagine it when it is out of sight or hearing.

Work by psychologist Renée Baillargeon and her collaborators during the past two decades has challenged this Piagetian orthodoxy. We begin with a classic study reported by Baillargeon performed with infants aged 6.5 to 8 months (Baillargeon, 1986) and later extended to even younger 4-month-old infants (Baillargeon & DeVos, 1991). In these studies, infants sat in front of a screen set up to the right of an inclined ramp, as shown in Figure 4.9. During the habituation phase, infants saw the screen raised and lowered. Behind the screen was a track. After the screen was lowered, infants saw a small toy car go down the inclined ramp and to the right, behind the screen.

Next, infants were given the **impossible/possible events task**, in which they were tested with one of two events—the first, a "possible" event, is shown in the second row of Figure 4.9. In this event, when the screen was raised, it revealed a box sitting behind the track. As in the habituation event, after the screen was lowered, the car rolled down the ramp and across the track behind the screen. The second, "impossible" event was very similar to the possible event, *except that* the box was actually placed *on* the track instead of behind it. This event is depicted in the bottom row of Figure 4.9.

Figure 4–9   Schematic drawing of the habituation and test events used by Baillargeon (1986).

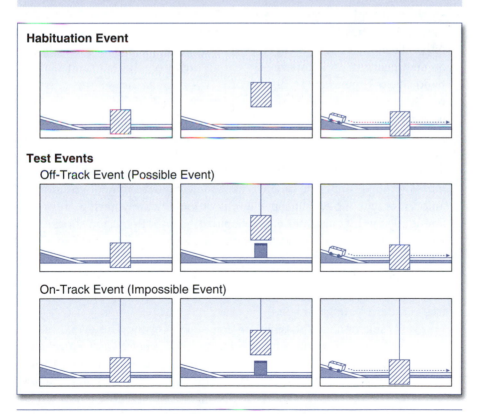

SOURCE: Baillargeon (1999, p. 129).

Now, according to Piaget, 6-month-old infants ought not to react any differently to the "possible" than to the "impossible" event. Lacking a sense of object permanence, they should be just as unsurprised to see a car roll in front of a box as "through" a box—after all, if infants have no expectations of objects continuing to exist when hidden behind a screen, then they would have forgotten all about the existence of the occluded box anyway. But Baillargeon's results showed something clearly at odds with Piagetian predictions. Her 6.5- and 8-month-old participants, as well as her 4-month-old female participants, looked longer at the "on-track" "impossible" event. Baillargeon interpreted this result to mean that the infants "(a) believe that the box continued to exist, in its same location, after the screen was lowered; (b) believed that the car continued to exist, and pursued its trajectory, when behind the screen; (c) realized that the car could not roll through the space occupied by the box; and hence (d) were surprised to see the car roll past the screen when the box lay in its path" (Baillargeon, 1999, p. 128).

In another study, Baillargeon and DeVos (1991) studied infants three and a half months old. They presented them with the stimulus display shown schematically in Figure 4.10. Each infant saw one of two habituation events first. These events presented either a short carrot or a tall carrot moving behind a large yellow screen, followed, a few seconds later, by the an emergence of an identically appearing carrot emerging from the right-hand side of the screen. In other words, it looked as though the same carrot simply traveled behind the occluding screen (although actually there were two different carrots used). After a 1-second pause, the experimenter slid the carrot back (to the left) behind the yellow occluding screen, paused for 2 seconds, and then slid the leftmost carrot out from behind the left edge of the occluder. This cycle of carrots disappearing and reappearing continued until the infant reached a predetermined criterion of amount of time looking at the stimulus or looking away having previously attended to it. Infants experienced habituation to both tall and short carrot stimuli before the next phase of the experiment began. (Incidentally, Baillargeon and DeVos used carrots as stimuli because pilot testing convinced them that a stimulus shaped like a rabbit they had used in previous work with older infants [Baillargeon & Graber, 1987] actually appeared to frighten these younger infants.)

Next came either a "possible" or "impossible" event. This event was the same as the corresponding habituation event, *except that* the occluding screen had a new shape, as shown in the bottom panels of Figure 4.10, and a new color, blue, meant to draw infants' attention to the fact that the screen was new. The idea was that short carrots ought to fit behind the new screen, and thus the possible event ought not to have been perceived as all that

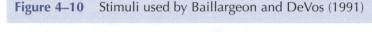

Figure 4–10 Stimuli used by Baillargeon and DeVos (1991)

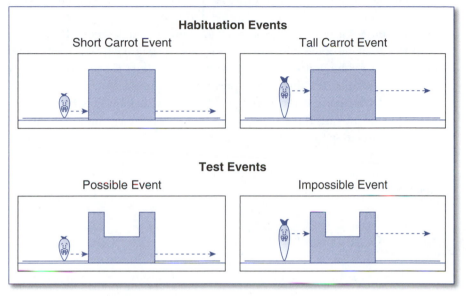

SOURCE: Baillargeon & DeVos (1991, p. 1230).

NOTE: Schematic representation of the habituation and test events shown to the infants in the experimental condition in Experiment 1.

surprising. However, a tall carrot would *not* have fit behind the new screen—its top ought to have been visible if it were moving from one end of the screen to the other. Thus, the tall carrot moving behind the new screen ought to have been an impossible event.

Results showed that although infants looked for an equal amount of time at the two habituation events (i.e., tall vs. short carrots moving behind the rectangular yellow screen), they looked longer at the impossible than the possible test event. Baillargeon and DeVos (1991) took this result as evidence that their three-and-a-half-month-old infants "(a) realized that each carrot continued to exist after it slid behind the screen, (b) assumed that each carrot retained its height behind the screen, (c) believed that each carrot pursued its trajectory behind the screen, and therefore, (d) expected the tall carrot to be visible in the screen window [the opening in the blue test screen] and were surprised that it was not" (p. 1233). These conclusions strongly suggest that even fairly young infants possess a fair amount of knowledge about what objects are and how they behave.

Not all investigators agree with Baillargeon's conclusions about infants' competence, however. Some have argued that Baillargeon did not use stringent enough habituation criteria for the infants in her studies, so they were not fully habituated before the possible and impossible events were tested (see Cohen & Cashon, 2003, for a review, and see Baillargeon, 1999, for a response to many of the criticisms). Critics also question why it is that infants don't reach for hidden objects before 8 or 9 months if they truly have a sophisticated understanding of the permanence of objects.

The debate comes down to a matter of how evidence is interpreted. Does longer looking time at one stimulus display really indicate that an infant's expectations about an object's existence have been violated? Is there a simpler, more perceptual explanation? What are the appropriate experimental controls? As we have seen, infancy researchers have to face and debate such issues regularly.

Object Coherence

Imagine a woman standing behind a table. You would see the top half of the person and part of her legs and feet, but the middle of her body would not be visible, being occluded by the table. Nonetheless, in such circumstances we typically see not different "person-parts" that we somehow figure out go together but rather one object whose view is partially blocked by another object.

In a now-classic experiment, psychologists Phillip Kellman and Elizabeth Spelke (1983) set out to discover whether and when infants came to this perceptual conclusion about the coherence, or unity, of objects that are partially hidden from view (i.e., object coherence). In their study, 4-month-old infants were first habituated to a stimulus display, shown in Figure 4.11, which showed a rod partially occluded by a box in front of it. If the rod was presented moving back and forth behind the box, infants later showed habituation to a presentation of a complete rod moving back and forth, but no habituation to two rod pieces moving back and forth together. This suggested to the authors that infants were surprised to see two separate rod parts and had likely "expected" to see a single rod. In other words, Kellman and Spelke were arguing that even when the rod was partially blocked by another object, these 4-month-old infants realized that it was a single coherent object. Apparently, infants are particularly sensitive to information coming from moving objects (the results were different if infants were first presented with a static, nonmoving rod behind a box). With stimulus displays in motion, infants show the same kinds of perceptual performance that older children and adults do.

However, as Cohen and Cashon (2003) point out, the ability to perceive a coherent object is consistent with the Piagetian description of Substage 3

Figure 4–11   Stimuli from Kellman and Spelke (1983)

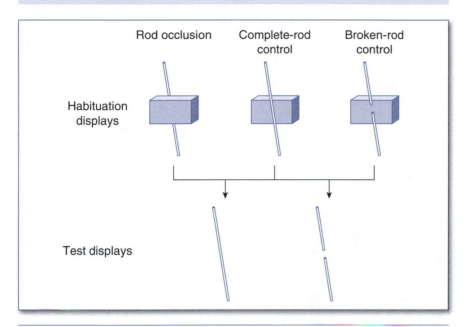

SOURCE: Kellman & Spelke (1983, p. 495).

behavior common to infants aged 4 to 8 months. It would thus be of greater interest to see how even younger infants approached this "occluded rod" task. Just such a series of studies was conducted by Alan Slater and his associates (Slater et al., 1990) with newborn infants. Contrary to Kellman and Spelke's 4-month-old infant participants (or to a new group of 4-month-olds Slater et al. tested), the newborn infants showed a decided looking preference for the coherent rod, rather than the "broken" rod, refuting the idea that infants are born with an innate idea of object unity or coherence. However, results from both laboratories show that by 4 months of age, infants do expect parts of objects that move together to be part of a single coherent object.

Object Identity

When you place an object (say, a can of Coke) on your kitchen counter in the morning and come back in the evening to encounter it, you seem to know immediately that it is the "same" object you left several hours earlier. How and when do infants come to "equate" two or more sensory encounters with a stimulus as being with the "same" stimulus? Relatedly, when infants see objects adults would recognize as distinct, when and how do they come to segregate, or individuate, those objects?

Researchers Fei Xu and Susan Carey (1996) investigated this question of **object identity** using a paradigm similar in some ways to the one used by Renée Baillargeon in her occluded objects studies. It is depicted in Figure 4.12 and works as follows: First, the infant sees one object (say, a duck) move behind an occluding screen. Next, a different object emerges from the other

Figure 4–12 Schematic representation of experimental paradigm from Xu and Carey (1996)

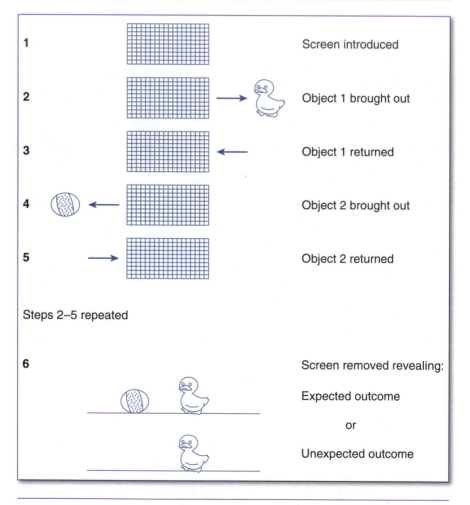

SOURCE: Carey & Xu (2001, p. 187).

side of the occluding screen. Next, the occluding screen is removed, revealing either (a) an expected event, the two different objects, or (b) an unexpected event, only one of the objects. Again, the question was "Would infants look for differing amounts of time at unexpected, relative to expected, events?"

Xu and Carey (1996) assert that in this procedure, they are never initially showing infants two objects together in time and space (e.g., in spatiotemporal proximity, to use a fancy phrase). Interestingly, although 12-month-old infants looked longer at the unexpected event, 10-month-olds did not!

What was most surprising about these results was that earlier studies that seemed very similar procedurally had yielded very different results with younger infants. Spelke, Kestenbaum, Simons, and Wein (1995) presented four-and-a-half-month-old infants with stimuli as depicted in Figure 4.13. In this case, two identical objects were used, but there were two screens not connected. No stimulus ever appeared in the gap between the two screens. After habituating the infants to the events depicted in Steps 2–5 of Figure 4.13, the screens were removed, revealing either one or two objects. Infant participants showed clear evidence that they "expected" two objects, in that they looked reliably longer at the unexpected outcome of a single object.

A replication of this finding by Wynn (1992) using slightly different procedures and different stimuli led again to the idea that even young (4- or 5-month-old) infants distinguish one object from two objects and use spatial and temporal information to draw inferences about whether there will be one or two objects behind occluding screens.

All of this work suggests that infants' knowledge of objects is more fragile than that of older children. In other words, although in some circumstances infants show what appears to be good evidence of holding certain expectations about the existence and properties of objects, in other circumstances they do not. Cohen and Cashon (2001b) suggest that with cognitive development, infants become more and more able to process information at more holistic levels—for example, to deal with whole objects rather than parts of objects. However, when the demands of a cognitive task increase, infants fall back to simpler modes of processing and attend to features or parts of objects rather than to whole objects.

Spelke and Hofsten (2001) offer an interpretation that is somewhat different. They believe that over the course of infancy, the ability to mentally represent objects becomes increasingly precise. As representations become more precise, they become less subject to disruption by other representations or by the presence of other information. Easier tasks (e.g., looking at events) require less precise representations to complete than do harder tasks (e.g., reaching for objects behind a barrier).

Figure 4–13   Schematic representation of experimental paradigm in Spelke, Kestenbaum, Simons, and Wein (1995)

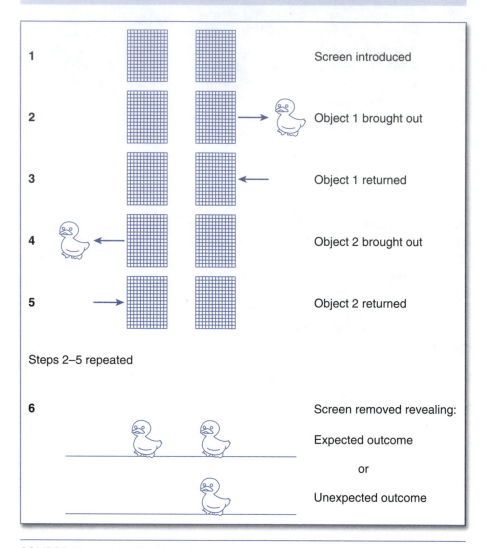

SOURCE: Carey & Xu (2001, p. 184).

Indeed, Elizabeth Spelke (1994) argues that at least some knowledge about objects emerges so early in life that it must be innately endowed. She believes that this knowledge is in the form of constraints about hypotheses infants hold about objects. For example, Spelke believes that infants know, in some sense, that objects exist continuously—they do not break apart spontaneously or blink in and out of existence. They move continuously through space.

Spelke (1994) holds that infants have to start with some knowledge to acquire more of it. They cannot learn about how objects fall to the ground, for example, unless they are first able to perceptually focus on an object. To do this focusing, they must at some level have some knowledge of what an object is. Baillargeon (2008) offers a slightly more general account, arguing that infants begin with an innate principle of persistence, "which states that objects persist, as they are, in time and space" (p. 11). From this initial knowledge, infants gather perceptual information and use it to construct more complex and detailed representations of objects and, in so doing, learn more about how objects behave and what their properties are.

Not all infant researchers accept this nativist view. Others argue that neurological development, particularly of the prefrontal cortex, helps infants better represent hidden objects, among other things. Still others describe infant cognitive development in terms of increasing organization of component systems, an idea taken from an information-processing framework. Bremner (2001) reviews these and other accounts in more detail. What is important for our purposes is the following: Piaget's original account will at least need some modification to accommodate these recent findings. Indeed, according to nativist theorists, Piagetian ideas about object permanence will simply have to be discarded. Whether the modifications are minor or merit a wholesale revision depends upon one's interpretation of what the data mean and what the tasks measure. As we have seen throughout the chapter, it takes a fair bit of ingenuity to ask infants to reveal their cognitive capabilities.

❖ ❖ ❖

I hope that this chapter and the last have convinced you that the field of cognition in infancy is an active, rapidly changing one. New findings from different laboratories are reported almost weekly and change our view of what infants are capable of and when. At the same time, infants' abilities do seem to vary widely as a function of the task they are asked to perform. One aspect of their cognitive development, then, seems to be the lack of generality of their performance in different circumstances. Because their abilities change so drastically with different circumstances, some developmental psychologists describe their emerging abilities as fragile. We will encounter this idea of fragility of abilities as we examine cognitive development in other age groups in the chapters ahead.

SUMMARY

1. The issue of what information or knowledge about objects an infant can remember and use to classify is one that theorists from different camps see very differently. In particular, nativists credit newborns with some innate knowledge about what objects are and how they behave; theorists in the Piagetian, information-processing, and learning traditions do not.

2. Using data from instrumental conditioning tasks, Rovee-Collier and her colleagues have shown that infants aged 2 months show recognition memory for about a few days, whereas 18-month-old infants remember information for up to 13 weeks.

3. Studies of recognition memory using the visual paired comparison test show evidence of recognition memory in infants a few days old.

4. Studies of recall memory in infants using an elicited imitation task suggest that infants can create and store explicit memories from 9 months of age. As infants get older, they become capable of retaining recall memories for longer periods of time.

5. Infants have been shown to categorize, or form groupings of, similar items from about 3 months of age. To what degree their groupings reflect underlying knowledge of what the categories mean is debated, with some investigators asserting that infants categorize only based on perceptual features and others arguing that in some circumstances they are capable of deeper and more meaningful differentiation.

6. Baillargeon's work has challenged Piagetian theory that infants lack object permanence before about 8–9 months of age. Her work, making use of staged "possible" and "impossible" events, suggests that infants show surprise when viewing the latter, which in turn seems to indicate that infants have specific expectations of how objects behave and that they continue to exist when out of sight. However, her conclusions have provoked controversy within the community of investigators, and much hinges on how her data are interpreted.

7. Some theorists believe that young infants possess a more fragile knowledge of objects than do older infants. This means that younger infants display their object knowledge only under very limited circumstances. Other theorists believe that what explains the different performance of younger and older infants is that as they develop, infants become more precise in forming mental representations of objects.

REVIEW QUESTIONS

1. Show how principles of classical and instrumental conditioning have been used to study the memory of very young infants.

2. Explain the distinction between implicit and explicit memory, and discuss how this distinction applies to the study of infant memory.

3. How convincing do you find evidence from the VPC task regarding infants' recognition memory capabilities? Explain your position.

4. Discuss the merits and shortcomings of the elicited imitation task used by Bauer and her associates to demonstrate recall memory in infants.

5. Compare the merits of the VPC and the elicited imitation task as measures of infant memory. What are the strengths and weaknesses of each?

6. Summarize the evidence for the proposition that even young infants can categorize (some) objects.

7. Compare and contrast findings in the infant memory and infant categorization literatures.

8. Discuss the merits and shortcomings of the sequential touching task used by Mandler and her associates to demonstrate categorization in infants.

9. Explain the distinctions among the concepts of object coherence, object identity, and object permanence.

10. Choose one of the experiments described in this chapter, and explain how the findings would be explained by (a) a Piagetian theorist, (b) an information-processing theorist, and (c) a nativist theorist.

KEY TERMS

Categorization

Deferred Imitation

Elicited Imitation Task

Episodic Memory

Explicit Memory

Hippocampus

Implicit Memory

Impossible/Possible Events Task

Knowledge Base

Object Coherence

Object Identity

Recall Memory

Recognition Memory

Retrieval

Semantic Memory

Sequential Touching Task

Visual Paired Comparison (VPC) Task

CHAPTER 5

LATE INFANCY/ EARLY CHILDHOOD

Acquiring Language

Hang around a baby or toddler for any length of time, and you'll likely come to the conclusion very quickly that they don't make wonderful conversational partners. Oh, they may be able to point to a "doggie" or "kitty" or say "bye-bye"—but conversations made up exclusively of such interchanges rapidly lose their interest for most adult speakers (even devoted parents!). Better yet, compare these conversations with those you can hold with an average 3-year-old, and you should notice an incredible difference. The 3-year-old can talk about events and people who aren't necessarily in the room—she can describe her fear of monsters or her desire to go see Santa Claus. She can instigate a game of "let's pretend" or suggest a menu for the evening meal (my 3-year-old often suggested "pink cookies" as the entrée). There's no doubt about it—language development takes a big leap between late infancy and the preschool period. In this chapter, we will review some of the major landmarks of language acquisition in the infancy and toddlerhood period.

THEORETICAL PERSPECTIVES

It will be helpful as we begin this chapter to consider first off what a language is. You might be tempted to equate language with communication (as in "My dog can tell me in his language when he wants to play" or "His body language was certainly communicating his lack of respect for me"). But as we will see, language is actually much less and much more than these two examples might imply.

The Nature of Language

Let's first take up the issue of why my dogs (I have two Bernese mountain dogs, named Tackle and Lizzy) do not have language, even though they are very communicative. My dogs can tell me when there is a squirrel in the backyard (by barking furiously by the patio door); they can tell me when they think it's dinnertime (by going to the spot at which they are fed and wagging tails furiously); they can tell me when their water dish is empty (Lizzy upends it with her paw repeatedly, clattering it across the floor). Aren't they using their language to talk to me?

Not really, at least according to psychologists and linguists who study language. Although it is true that my dogs are *communicating,* the range of messages they can express is very limited. They can't reminisce with me over what happened last Tuesday; they can't comment on whether or not they want to play with or eat the squirrel in the backyard; they can't make requests for specific meals (thankfully!).

In order for a communication system to be considered a true language, it must have two characteristics: It must be productive, meaning that an infinite number of combinations of parts can be legally created to express different ideas (with potentially very nuanced differences), and it must be regular—that is, governed by a system of rules. These two characteristics are known as productivity and regularity, respectively (Galotti, 2008), and we will consider each in turn.

First, productivity. This criterion means that from a finite number of parts, an infinite number of combinations are possible. Consider the number of possible sentences of English. You might think that there is some very large set that would encompass all of the known legal sentences of English. You would be wrong. To see why, consider the following example sentences:

Flit (one of my now-departed dogs) ate one Brillo pad.

Flit ate two Brillo pads.

Flit ate three Brillo pads.

You might see that this list could go on for a while. In fact, there will be a different sentence for each number. Because there are an infinite number of numbers, there will be an infinite number of these sentences, which are but a small subset of all sentences of English. (And for the record, Flit actually ate 15 Brillo pads. It still escapes me why. And she lived to scavenge again!)

Second, consider the following group of sentences, inspired by a children's rhyme:

This is the house that Jack built.

This is the cat that lives in the house that Jack built.

This is the dog that chased the cat that lived in the house that Jack built.

This is the flea that bit the dog that chased the cat that lived in the house that Jack built.

These sentences are built up recursively, and it should be fairly easy to see that one could extend the pattern indefinitely (Jackendoff, 1994). Based on these two examples (and there are many others) it becomes clear that the number of sentences of English (or any natural language) is infinite, despite the fact that the number of parts of a sentence (e.g., the number of words) is finite.

Now let's consider regularity, the second criterion of a natural language. Regularity means that sentences follow some system of rules, typically called a grammar. Now, to say that a speaker's language is regular is to say that it is systematic with respect to the rules—it is *not* to say that the speaker can articulate what the rules are. So, for example, a native speaker of English would immediately recognize that all of the following are "legal" sentences:

I'm going to the store to buy apples.

What I'm going to the store to buy are apples.

It's apples that I'm going to the store to buy.

This demonstrates that the same underlying idea can be expressed in different ways. However, the following sentence is *not* a legal utterance of English—even though one could probably decode the meaning if one tried long enough:

Buy to store the I'm apples to going.

Not only is it an "illegal" sentence, it is a sentence unlikely to ever be produced by a native speaker (except if she were trying to generate an example of an illegal sentence for a textbook!).

Productivity and regularity are two defining characteristics of a human language—the claim is that all human languages show these, and that anything that shows these properties is a natural language. But human languages also have some other characteristics that, while not defining, are descriptive.

We've already said that language is used to communicate. Natural languages are also often arbitrary: There's no necessary connection, for example, between the word *dog* and the canine house pet. Language is also hierarchical, with sentences breaking down into words, words into morphemes (the smallest units of language that are meaningful), and morphemes into phonemes (the units of sound that make changes to words; Gleitman, Fridlund, & Resiberg, 2004).

A Nativist Perspective

The study of language development has fascinated not only developmental psychologists but cognitive psychologists, linguists, sociologists, anthropologists, and others. Language appears to be one of the few cognitive abilities that is, many would argue, uniquely human. Moreover, famous case studies in the literature of the Wild Boy of Aveyron (Lane, 1976) and "Genie," the severely neglected adolescent discovered in the 1970s (Curtiss, 1977), suggested that language abilities develop on a fixed timetable. These two children, who apparently had minimal to no exposure to human language before they reached puberty, were unable to later make up for that deficit. Although each was able to acquire a number of words, they never mastered the syntactic fluency that a typical 4-year-old child has. Developmental psychologists and linguists (e.g., Lenneberg, 1967) thus began to speak of a **critical period** for language acquisition—a time in which language had to be mastered (before puberty) if it were ever going to reach mature levels of fluency. A related issue nativist theorists proposed was that of **encapsulation**—that is, the degree to which the mechanisms that deal with language are specialized only for language and thus separate from other cognitive processes, such as perception and attention, or instead how interactive language processes are with these other cognitive processes.

Linguist Noam Chomsky (1977, 1988) is the originator of the term language acquisition device, or LAD. The LAD is thought to be a domain-specific encapsulated device. Moreover, the LAD is thought to be unique to human beings, or species-specific.

Chomsky (1993) explained his nativist view most succinctly as follows:

> Language learning is not really something that the child does; it is something that happens to the child placed in an appropriate environment, much as the child's body grows and matures in a predetermined way when provided with appropriate nutrition and environmental stimulation. (p. 519)

Chomsky, then, is claiming that, given a relatively normal environment and absent some gross birth defect, infants' language will mature and unfold. One analogy here might be to walking: We know that, absent birth defects and given an unremarkable environment, most infants start walking around their first birthday or a little after. Although some cultural practices can accelerate or delay walking by up to a few weeks or in one reported case almost up to a year (see Lightfoot, Cole, & Cole, 2009, for discussion), walking seems to be something that infants the world over will do, regardless of the specifics of their environment, at around the same age, give or take a month or two. Walking and other motoric behaviors seem to unfold naturally as the infant gains muscle control; it does not seem to be a matter of observational or reinforced learning.

The basis for Chomsky's claim is something that cognitive scientists call the **poverty of the stimulus argument** (Behme & Deacon, 2008). Essentially, this argument goes as follows: The infant's general learning abilities and the information available in the world regarding language together can't explain the fact that language acquisition happens so fast (over the first 4 years of life) and ends up with such complex knowledge. The fact that children acquire language rapidly, easily, and without direct instruction seems to point to maturation, as opposed to learning, as the mechanism governing language acquisition.

A Learning Theory Perspective

This nativist view of language is not without its critics (see Behme & Deacon, 2008). Moreover, not all aspects of language acquisition are thought to be innate. My daughter Kimberlynn, for example, was born in Vietnam but adopted at 3 months and brought to the United States. Her first language, unsurprisingly, is English, suggesting that which language becomes a person's native language is a matter of which language she is exposed to. As we are about to see, language has many different parts to it, and there is an ongoing debate over which (if any) are innately endowed (Pinker & Jackendoff, 2004).

Michael Tomasello (2006) is one researcher who does not accept the idea of language being an innately endowed system. He believes that young children acquire syntactic aspects of language in much the same way they acquire vocabulary and knowledge of how to speak politely: through learning. By analyzing the speech that adults direct to children (so-called *child-directed speech,* or *CDS*), Tomasello reports the following: Children aged 2 to 3 years hear an average of 5,000 to 7,000 utterances per day from adults. When these utterances are analyzed, a great deal of repetition of patterns is found. For example, more than half of all maternal utterances in the sample he studied fell into one of 52 patterns, including such utterances as *Are you . . . , I'll . . . , It's . . . , Can you . . . ,* and *Here's . . . .* This level of repetition, Tomasello holds, helps toddlers and very young children learn how specific patterns in their native language work. Indeed, toddlers may hear the same patterns repeated dozens or hundreds of times in a single day. In essence, the level of repetition found undermines the poverty of the stimulus argument made by nativist theorists, at least according to Tomasello.

The nativist-empiricist controversy is thus very much in evidence when it comes to the topic of language acquisition, and we will not be able to resolve the questions definitively in this chapter. Instead, what we can do is examine all of the different parts of aspects of language and look at the development of each. We will look first at the development of sound recognition and production, then at word recognition and production, and then at sentence recognition and production. We will end by looking at the development of young children's ability to carry on conversations and to use language for communicative purposes. But it will behoove us to keep in mind that all these parts of language do work and develop in interrelated ways. Figure 5.1 provides a convenient overview of the different parts of language as they develop over the first 4 years. This will be a good summary to review as we arrive at each "piece" of language development.

PHONOLOGICAL DEVELOPMENT

In this section we will examine how infants begin to perceive and produce the sounds of speech in their native language. This issue isn't simply a question of hearing and vocalizing, as it might at first seem. Consider a foreign language that you don't speak. The sounds of the language are different, perhaps only subtly, from the sounds of your native language. For example, in English, the difference between the sound made in speaking an /r/ differ from that made in speaking an /1/ (as in *right* vs. *light*). Changing the sound from an /r/ to an /1/ changes the word. However, the /r/–/1/ distinction is one that is not made in Japanese—to a native Japanese speaker, the /r/–/1/ distinction is one that is difficult to hear.

To give just a little background, it is necessary to take a very brief detour into the domain of phonology, the study of speech sounds and sound systems of different languages. We first need to say that a speech sound is an acoustic signal that conveys some meaning. Although linguists have tallied over 200 different speech sounds in all the world's languages, no single language makes use of all 200—English, for example, uses approximately 40. Table 5.1 provides a list of these. You'll notice that English has more sounds than letters, indicating that the mapping between oral and written language is not one-to-one. In fact, there are some letters (e.g., *c*) that are associated with different sounds (e.g., *cat* vs. *cinch*), and some multiple letter patterns associated with single sounds (e.g., *th, fl, chr*). Linguists and psycholinguists call the different sounds of speech by the term phones.

Now, not all phones constitute meaningful differences in a language. For example, the /p/ sound is different in *spring* and *ping* (technically, there is more aspiration, or a larger burst of air, when you pronounce the latter word). So the term *phoneme* is reserved for sounds of the language that make a meaningful difference.

Figure 5–1 Major milestones of language development

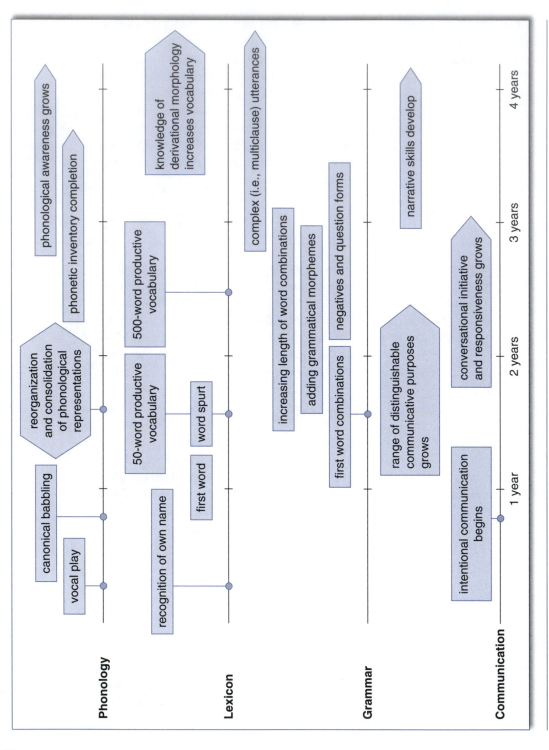

SOURCE: Hoff (2005, p. 4).

Table 5–1   Phonemic symbols for the sounds of American English

Consonants			Vowels	
/p/ pill	/t/ toe	/g/ gill	/i/ beet	/ɪ/ bit
/b/ bill	/d/ doe	/n/ ring	/e/ bait	/ɛ/ bet
/m/ mill	/n/ no	/h/ hot	/u/ boot	/U/ foot
/f/ fine	/s/ sink	/ʔ/ uh-oh	/o/ boat	/ɔ/ caught
/v/ vine	/z/ zinc	/l/ low	/æ/ bat	/a/ pot
/θ/ thigh	/č/ choke	/r/ row	/ʌ/ but	/ə/ sofa
/ð/ thy	/ǰ/ joke	/y/ you	/aɪ/ bite	/au/ out
/š/ shoe	/k/ kill	/w/ win	/ɔɪ/ boy	
/ž/ treasure				

SOURCE: Hoff (2005, p. 94).

So it's clear that different languages use different phones and have different phonemes. In addition, languages also differ in what kinds of sound combinations they allow. For example, in English we can combine /b/ and /r/ to produce *bring*, but we never combine /t/ and /l/ at the beginning of a legal English word. We also change the pronunciation of some sounds depending on their context. For example, consider two nonsense syllables, *tif* and *wug*, and pretend they each name an alien creature. Suppose there were two of each. You would form the plural of these new words by saying *tifs* (with an /s/ sound) and *wugs* (with a /z/ sound), because you'd be following, implicitly, the phonological rules of English. Jean Berko (1958) demonstrated, by the way, that even 4-year-olds are able to, rather easily, follow these rules as well.

Our next question should be "How and when do infants and children come to perceive speech sounds, somehow mentally marking as different only those ones that signify a meaningful difference in the language?" A related question is "How do infants and children produce the speech sounds of their native language?" Because, as a rule, language comprehension outstrips language production, we will consider these two issues in that order.

We might begin by looking at how infants perceive any sort of sound—that is, by examining their **auditory perception**. We talked in Chapter 3 about infants' ability to detect sounds. This ability begins prenatally. It has been shown that by about the sixth month of gestation, most fetuses can hear sounds from the mother's environment, even if what they hear is somewhat muffled. For example, fetuses appear to be able to hear speech intonation—the rising and falling of speech, as in the way we ask questions (rising intonation) or make statements (falling intonation)—much better than they can resolve the sounds that would identify which specific words are being spoken (Fernald, 2001).

After birth, infants' ability to detect sounds parallels that of adults, but their thresholds are higher. That is, the specific range of sound frequencies that infants are most sensitive to are also the ones adults are most sensitive to, although adults' hearing is more sensitive than infants' (Fernald, 2001). Newborn infants have also been shown to be able to grossly localize sound—that is, to determine, broadly, what direction a sound is coming from (Morrongiello, Fenwick, Hillier, & Chance, 1994). In general, Fernald (2001) in a review of the literature concludes that in normally hearing infants, their auditory sensory experiences are very close to adult-like by the time they are 6 months of age.

But sensory experiences are only the raw material for perceptual interpretation. We've seen in Chapter 3 in the case of visual perception that young infants can, in some instances, show a remarkable ability to go beyond the sensory input and make a rather sophisticated interpretation of the real-world source of that input. This is also true for auditory perception, especially in the perception of speech sounds.

Perceiving Spoken Language

When someone says a sentence to us (such as *This is a pen*) it might seem as though each word or syllable occurs in a definite time with pauses around it. That is, we tend to "hear" pauses in the speech stream that correspond to word or syllable boundaries—for example, we "hear" a pause between the word *This* and the word *is*. But if we examine this more closely, using sophisticated equipment known as a sound spectrogram, we find that there aren't always reliable breaks in the sound stream that occur between words or syllables, as shown in Figure 5.2. Just to help you interpret what you are seeing, let me explain that a spectrogram is a graphic representation of speech, showing the frequencies of sound, in hertz (cycles per second), along the y-axis, plotted against time on the x-axis. Darker regions in the figure indicate the intensity of each sound at each frequency. Note that the boundaries (white spaces) do not correspond to word or syllable boundaries. There is *nothing* in the physical stimulus itself to indicate where these boundaries are.

Figure 5–2   Spectrogram of a person pronouncing the indicated sentence, "This is a pen."

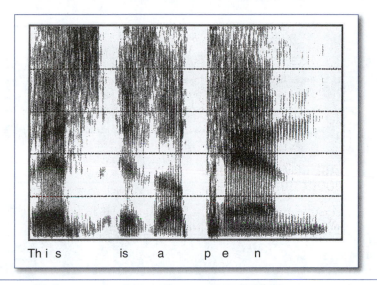

SOURCE: Galotti (2008, p. 352).

In other words, the "pauses" you hear around words when you're in a conversation really aren't there. As native speakers of the language, well practiced at hearing and interpreting speech, we somehow "insert" such boundaries as we parse, or decode, the sentence.

So one thing that infants have to learn to do is figure out where the boundaries are between segments of speech. As if this weren't daunting enough, they also have another major challenge: to figure out which sound differences signal different meanings, and which sound differences don't matter. For example, the /b/ versus /p/ distinction is an important one for English speakers—it signals different words (e.g., *bill* vs. *pill; bop* vs. *pop; buck* vs. *puck*). Yet the sounds are very similar—linguists tell us that, in fact, the two sounds share many important features, such as where and how the vocal tract is closed when the sounds are made, and differ only in a feature called *voicing*—the time the vocal cords start vibrating relative to the release of air. With the consonant /p/, the vocal cords do not start to vibrate until after the lips have released air, whereas in producing the voiced sound /b/, the vocal cords start vibrating before the lips release air (Hoff, 2005).

So far, so good, perhaps. One could assume that infants are very sensitive to the voicing aspect of these sounds and use it to make the discrimination between /b/ and /p/. However, there's a complication. Not all /b/ sounds lead to the same acoustic signal. For example, Figure 5.3 is a spectrogram of me saying three words that begin with /b/: *baby, boondoggle,*

Figure 5–3   Spectrogram of the words *baby, boondoggle,* and *bunny*

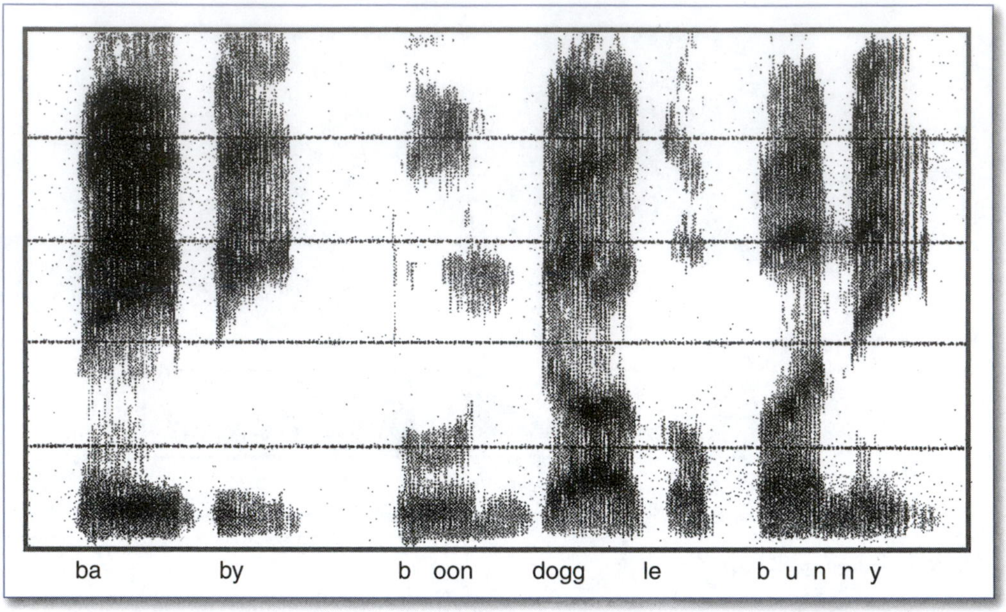

ba   by   b oon   dogg   le   b u n n y

SOURCE: Galotti (2008, p. 353).

and *bunny*. While to the casual listener these all have the same beginning sound, the spectrogram shows that the actual acoustic signal varies, depending on the context in which the sound occurs. Moreover, the acoustic signal will vary according to the pitch of the speaker's voice (women's voices typically have higher pitches). However is a baby to figure out which aspects of an acoustic signal make a meaningful difference (such as the /b/–/p/ distinction) and which don't?

It turns out that babies (and adults) get a head start on this task by perceiving sounds categorically. This means that the listener, automatically and rather effortlessly, classifies sounds like /b/ and /p/ into two categories: /b/ and /p/. Within the /b/ category, all the sounds are heard as being equally /b/-like; no further differences are heard. Likewise, once a sound is categorized as a /p/, no further distinction is made among all the /p/ sounds.

Lisker and Abramson (1970) were able to demonstrate this categorical perception of /b/ and /p/ sounds by creating some artificial (computer-generated) /b/ and /p/ sounds. These two sounds actually differ in only one feature, called *voice onset time* or VOT, which has to do with how quickly the vocal folds vibrate after a consonant sound is released. Lisker and Abramson found that any sound with a VOT of less than or equal to .03 was heard as a /b/;

anything with a VOT of greater than .03 was heard as a /p/ by their adult participants. This sort of categorical perception has been demonstrated with other consonant pairs, and it seems safe to conclude that we pay very close attention to some distinctions in speech—those that can make a meaningful difference—but ignore others.

Eimas, Siqueland, Jusczyk, and Vigorito (1971) showed with a study of infants aged 1 to 4 months that they easily discriminated between the /b/ and /p/ sounds, treating all variants of /b/ (such as *baby, boondoggle,* and *bunny)* as the same, but treating a /ba/ sound as distinct from a /pa/ sound. Further work replicated this classic finding, and researchers now believe that even infants who have not had much listening experience come prepared to make these distinctions quickly and automatically.

From a developmental standpoint, what is very interesting is that infants who are "prelinguistic"—that is, who are not using language to communicate—are also perceiving speech categorically (Aslin, Jusczyk, & Pisoni, 1998). Even more interesting, infants aged 1–4 months have been shown to be sensitive to meaningful phonetic differences that occur in languages other than their own. In this respect, infants can be better discriminators of distinctions in a "foreign" language than their parents, at least for about 6 months (Aslin et al., 1998; Werker & Tees, 1999)! This seems to imply a certain amount of flexibility in the infant language system—it does not quickly specialize to one language but retains an ability to acquire a variety of languages at least for a while.

Gradually, over the first year, infants seem to lose this ability and become "specialists" in listening only for distinctions that occur in languages they hear on a regular basis (Fernald, 2001). For example, Werker and Tees (1984) tested the ability of English-learning infants aged 6 to 12 months to hear the differences in phones in two foreign languages: Hindi (the discrimination was between the /Ta/ and /~ta/ sounds), and Nthlakampx (a Native American language; stimuli used were the /k'i/ vs. /q'i/ discrimination). Figure 5.4 shows that English-hearing infants' ability to make the discrimination declined over time, with the 10- to 12-month-old infants performing much less well than the 6- to 8-month-olds. In contrast, 11-month-old Hindi or Nthlakampx infants were perfectly able to make the relevant distinctions in their native language.

But the perception of isolated sounds is only part of the story of phonological development. Infants need to learn to discriminate sounds like /ba/ and /pa/ when they are embedded in the speech stream in actual words, and research shows that this task is much harder for infants (Hoff, 2005). It helps a little if the important syllables are stressed and are pronounced slowly—this is true not only for infants but for adults trying to comprehend a foreign language with which they have limited fluency.

Figure 5–4 The proportion of infants at each age reaching discrimination criterion on the Hindi and Nthlakampx contrasts. Far right: The performance of infants 11 months old raised in either a Hindi or a Nthlakampx environment

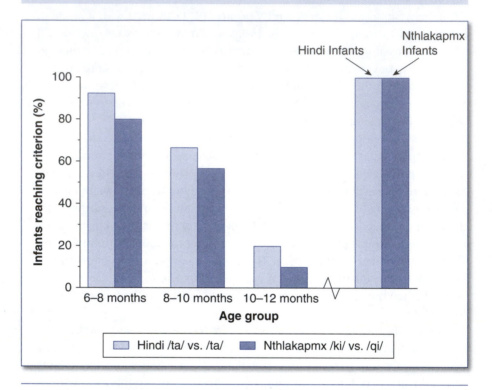

SOURCE: Werker & Tees (1999, p. 519); Adapted from Werker & Tees (1984).

Fortunately, scientists have observed a phenomenon originally dubbed "motherese" in many different cultures. Mothers typically talk to their infants using lots of repetition, with higher average pitch, with a more extreme range of pitch, and with more stress on content words, shorter utterances, and longer pauses (Hoff, 2005; Newport, Gleitman, & Gletiman, 1977). Subsequent work has shown that most all adults, not just mothers, use this kind of speech to infants, so it is now referred to as **infant-directed speech** or **IDS** (Aslin et al., 1998). So, to give yourself an example of motherese, imagine finding yourself face-to-face with an attentive, smiling, 5-month-old baby and what you would say to him and how you would say it. Chances are you would produce IDS. Infants have shown a definite preference to listen to IDS (over adult-directed speech, or ADS, which typically has lower pitch, less exaggeration, etc.). Interestingly, infants in an English-language environment have been shown to prefer IDS even in the foreign language of Cantonese (Werker, Pegg, & McLeod, 1994).

IDS seems to help infants focus their attention on the most important words or grammatical units and on the emotion of the speaker (Aslin et al., 1998). A study by Golinkoff and Alioto (1995) showed that adults learning words in a foreign language learned them better when the words were presented in IDS rather than ADS, which implies that IDS serves a function in helping infants master words in their native language.

Over time, infants also learn the general sounds and rhythms of their language—the so-called *prosody.* Imagine overhearing a conversation taking place in the next room. You might not be able to make out the specific words, but you might still hear the way the pitch of the voices rises and falls and the general overall rhythm. Nazzi, Bertocini, and Mehler (1998) created stimuli in which specific sounds were hard to determine but overall prosodic cues were left intact, and showed that newborns could discriminate between languages that were prosodically different (e.g., English and Japanese or English and Spanish) but not between languages that were prosodically similar (e.g., Spanish and Italian).

All of the studies referenced above show that infants know a lot about the sounds and structure of their language well before they show clear comprehension of what words mean and well before they produce any recognizable words. Some phonological knowledge appears either to be innate or to develop very early—other knowledge shows a lot of effects of environmental exposure. But however the knowledge is acquired, by the end of the first year, the average infant has learned a lot about his native language.

Producing Spoken Language

Those first 12 months aren't all about passively perceiving, however. Infants produce approximations to formal language well before their first birthday. Although not all infants produce spoken language (congenitally deaf children being an obvious example), most do, and these infants will be our focus in this section.

Newborn infants make a variety of sounds, although most involve some form of crying. Others, such as sneezing or burping or sucking, are called *vegetative sounds,* and although they aren't terribly language-like, they do serve a communicative function and also cause the vocal cords to vibrate and send air flowing through them, so they do "count" as prelinguistic production of speech sounds.

At about 2 months, infants exhibit a marked social change—not only do they begin to show complex and more animated facial expressions, they begin to smile (Fogel, 2001). At the same time, they begin to produce vocalizations known as cooing, sounds produced by what appear to observers to be happy babies. Cooing consists of vowel sounds produced without consonants—an "oooooo" or " aaaaah" sound—but as they develop infants produce a chain of different vowel sounds separated by in-breaths (Hoff, 2005). At about 4 months infants produce recognizable laughter and begin to produce sounds described as "squeals, growls, and friction noises" (Hoff, 2005, p. 98). Consonant sounds, especially ones such as /g/ or /k/ (produced in the back of the mouth), begin to emerge between 2 and 3 months, while front-of-the-mouth consonants such as /m/, /n/, /p/, /b/, and /d/ start being produced by 6-month-old infants.

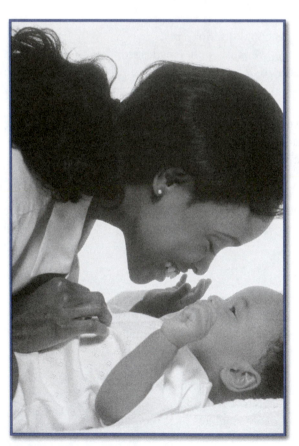

Photo 5.1 Young infants begin producing "cooing" sounds at about 2 months.

Between 6 and 9 months, infants start to babble—that is, to produce syllables with consonants and vowels. The earliest form of babbling, called reduplicated or canonical babbling, takes the form of repeated syllables—for example, *rara* or *googoo*. Infants do not seem to be producing these sounds with the obvious intention of communication—indeed, infants of this age often seem quite content to sit alone in their cribs, babbling up a storm. Nor do the vocalizations appear to have any regular meaning. However, this step is one seen in all hearing infants and marks the first divergence between the vocalizations of hearing and deaf infants (Hoff, 2005).

Between 9 and 12 months, infants begin to show increasing intersubjectivity—that is, sharing mental control, acting together, and sharing experience in harmony with other people, particularly their caregivers (Trevarthen & Aitken, 2001). The idea here is that infants begin to be able to interact simultaneously with people and objects and to use their gaze at people to direct the people to focus on an object or even to retrieve it for the infant (Lock, 2001). Although, strictly speaking, this is not the production of language, intersubjectivity is often used as an auxiliary to language—getting one's "conversational partner" to focus on the communicative exchange. Using gesture, infants at this age begin to make "requests" and issue "demands"—for example, raising their arms up to indicate a desire for an adult to pick them up, or pointing to request an object out of reach, as shown in Figure 5.5. Such gestures are thought to express an infant's goal or communicative intent and provide a bridge to more symbolic communication in the years to come (Camaioni, 2001).

Figure 5–5 Unable to reach the apple (1), the child turns to attract the adult's attention by vocalizing (2). Having established eye contact with the adult (3), the child uses a pointing gesture to direct the adult's attention to the apple (4), thereby identifying the object implied as being wanted by the tonality of the vocalization (from Lock, 1980, p. 98).

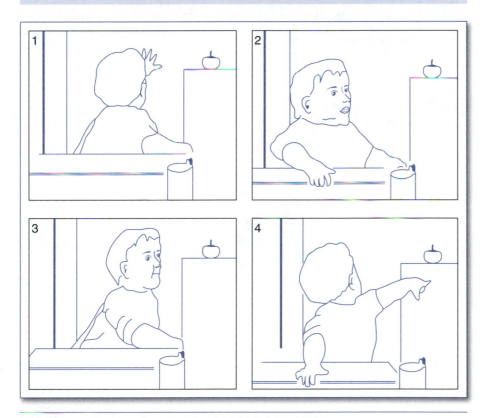

SOURCE: Lock (2001, p. 392); Adapted from Lock (1980, p. 98).

LEXICAL DEVELOPMENT

Right around the time of their first birthday, infants begin to utter their first recognizable word. It's often not pronounced exactly the way an adult would (e.g., my son's first word was *ba* for *ball*), but it bears at least a rough approximation to the adult version of the word and is used to refer to an object or event consistently. Some infants actually produce so-called protowords earlier—in between babbling and the production of their first "real word"—but the protoword is often an invented one (Hoff, 2005). **Lexical development** is the term used to describe the growth of vocabulary during language acquisition.

First words are often tied more tightly to specific contexts relative to words adults or older children use. For example, a child might use the word *duck* only to refer to a particular yellow rubber bathtub toy, not to refer to real ducks or even the same toys when played with out in the yard—suggesting that children's understanding of what a particular word means might differ substantially from that of an older child or adult. Interestingly, the "decontextualization" of words—for example, using *duck* in a wider set of circumstances—might take only a matter of a few weeks or months.

Photo 5.2 Toddlers need to learn that words such as *duck* apply to a wider set of referents than just a bathtub toy.

What Words Are Learned First

When my son and my daughter were each first learning to speak, I had hoped that the first meaningful word from them would have been a gushing *Mama*. Alas, as I mentioned, my son's first word was *ball* (followed by *balloon*, *bye-bye*, and *daiden* [for *dog*]); *Mama* was fourth or fifth. Similarly, my daughter's first words were *shshshs* (for *shoe*) and *baabaaa* (a preemptory order for me to begin yet another rendition of my infamous "Baa Baa black sheep"). For her also, *Mama* came in a bit later, although as I recall it still made the "first five." In researching the topic of children's first words, I was reassured to find that my children's focus on ordinary objects (instead of *me!*) was pretty typical. For example, Harris, Barrett, Jones, and Brookes (1988) reported on the first 10 words produced by four different children. Their findings are reproduced in Table 5.2.

Table 5–2 First 10 words produced by four children, grouped according to type of initial use

	Child			
Word type	James	Jacqui	Jenny	Madeleine
Context-bound	mummy go quack there buzz moo boo	wee hello mummy here no down more go	choo-choo bye-bye there	there hello here bye-bye
Nominal	teddy ball	Jacqui bee	teddy doggy moo shoe car	teddy shoes brum woof baby
Non-nominal	more		mummy no	yes

SOURCE: Harris, Barrett, Jones, & Brookes (1988, p. 83).

Katherine Nelson (1973) conducted a landmark study of 18 children as they acquired their first 50 words. Nelson made monthly visits to the children's homes, starting when the toddlers were between 10 and 15 months old and continuing until they reached 25 months of age. Nelson had the mothers keep track of each new word their child spontaneously produced. She then analyzed these data, classifying the words into categories as shown in Table 5.3. As can be seen, most of the children's early words were "general nominals"—names of objects, substances, animals, and people—entries such as *ball, water, doggie,* and *man.* Specific nominals were the next most frequently used

Table 5–3   Mean percentage of 50-word vocabularies by category ($N = 18$)

Category	%
I. Nominals:	
Specific:	
People	12
Animals	1
Objects	1
Total specific nominals	14
General:	
Objects	31
Substances	7
Animals and people	10
Letters and numbers	1
Abstractions	1
Pronouns	3
Total general nominals	51
II. Action words:	
Demand-descriptive	11
Notice	2
Total action words	13
III. Modifiers:	
Attributes	1
States	6
Locatives	2
Possessives	1
Total modifiers	9

Category	%
IV. Personal-social:	
Assertions	4
Social-expressive	4
Total personal-social	8
V. Function words:	
Question	2
Miscellaneous	2
Total function words	4

SOURCE: Nelson (1973, p. 18).

NOTE: Percentages do not add up to 100 due to rounding.

words—these name specific people, animals, or objects (e.g., *Mommy, Rover*). Action words came next, including such entries as *down, up,* and *see.* Modifiers (e.g., *pretty, red, mine*), personal-social words (e.g., *ouch, please*), and function words (e.g., *what, for*) were less frequently uttered.

Nelson (1973) also broke down the words into sets of 10—for example, the first 10 words acquired, the second 10 words acquired, and so on, and analyzed the categories of words according to these sets. Figure 5.6 shows the results. In general, as word acquisition proceeds, the use of general nominals becomes more frequent and the use of specific nominals less frequent.

Nelson (1973) also noted striking differences among individual children in the way their earliest vocabularies grew. Roughly half of the children she studied seemed to focus more heavily on names for objects, while the other half of the children were more likely to focus on the personal-social words. This latter group was also more likely to learn stereotyped phrases useful in social interaction, including *go away, don't do it, thank you,* and *I want it.*

As I mentioned earlier, first words often don't have the same extensions that the adult usage of the same words does. For example, I use the word *dog* to refer to all domesticated canine house pets—be they Chihuahuas or Great Danes. However, 1-year-olds are known to often overextend the word *dog* to other nondog things such as horses or cows. At issue is whether the

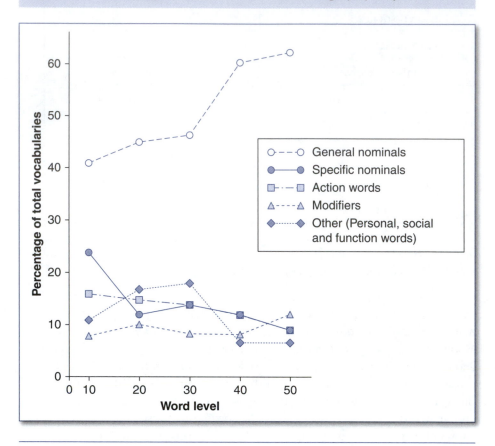

Figure 5–6   Percentage of vocabularies in each category by acquisition level

SOURCE: Nelson (1973).

overextension really indicates that the child does not distinguish between a dog and a cow or whether he uses the word *dog* to refer to cows just because he has no other word to do so early on (Rescorla, 1980). Children also produce **underextensions** of words, as in the *duck* example discussed earlier, where they use the word in much more restricted contexts than would an older child or adult.

At around 18 months, many toddlers show a phenomenon known as the "naming insight," where they appear to suddenly realize that things have names (Camaioni, 2001). This naming insight begins a vocabulary spurt. Suddenly, new words are acquired at a very accelerated rate. In the cases of my own two children, I remember not being able to write down their vocabularies after they reached this age (which, for both, was at about their 50-word vocabulary mark). Anglin (1993) estimated that by the time they reach first grade (at age 6), most children have vocabularies of about 10,000 words. Working backward from a vocabulary size of, on average, 50 words at 18 months means that they must learn the meanings of about 5.5 words a day during that interval! Other investigators have given even higher estimates—some as high as 13 new words per day up until age 18 (Bloom, 1998).

How on earth can children manage this incredible feat? I remember studying vocabulary words for the SAT, and even learning two new words a day was hard! Susan Carey (1978) describes the phenomenon using the term **fast mapping**. She and colleague Elsa Bartlett demonstrated this process in a pilot study with older preschool children aged 3 to 4 years.

They chose the color olive, which they knew that none of the children knew the name of. They chose to give this color an unknown and unfamiliar name, *chromium* (which actually is a color name). The children studied all attended a university nursery school, and Carey and Bartlett arranged to have the teacher at the school introduce the new word in as natural and casual a way as possible. They painted a tray and a cup in the school olive and placed them next to an identically shaped cup (colored red) and an identically shaped tray (colored blue). While getting ready for snack, the teacher would say to a child, "Bring me the chromium tray, not the blue one, the chromium one," or "Bring me the chromium cup, not the red one, the chromium one" (Carey, 1978, p. 271). The idea here was that both the structure of the sentence and the contrast to the known color words provided lexical cues as to what "chromium" was supposed to mean.

Now, Carey and Bartlett knew through pretesting of the children that they originally called the olive color *green* or, in a few cases, *brown*. However, only one of the children failed to understand the teacher's request. Four children spontaneously produced an approximation to *chromium* and several asked for clarification—by holding up the olive-colored cup or tray and asking, "This one?" And 6 weeks later, 8 of 14 children changed their responses (compared with their baseline responses) when asked the name of the color olive. Two no longer used *brown* or *green*, and although none of the children said *chromium*, the rest used *gray*, *blue*, or *brown* and another color.

Carey (1978) interprets these results as follows: A very informal and brief introduction is sufficient to induce at least some children to begin to restructure their lexical domains. It is as if the child comes prepared to effortlessly notice when a new word needs to be created in the mental lexicon. Thus, an entry for the new word is created, along with some of the syntactic and semantic features (e.g., adjective, a sort of shade of green).

However, along with the fast mapping comes a slower and more **extended mapping**, where the child learns the "full" meaning of the new word. The children in Carey and Bartlett's study did not remember to produce the name *chromium* when confronted with something colored olive weeks later—they just knew not to call it *green* or *brown*. Indeed, one child later seemed to equate *chromium* with *fuchsia,* acting as if the word *chromium* meant "any sort of odd color." Extended mapping, a process in which the child learns all the dimensions of meaning of a word, takes several encounters and probably several weeks, months, or even years.

Of course, the Carey and Bartlett study was performed with 3- and 4-year-olds, and you might be wondering if children of this age learn words differently than younger toddlers. After all, in order to learn a new color name, one has to have at least some color names already in one's mental lexicon. Fortunately, some work has been done with younger children to try to explain the processes by which they learn new words.

Constraints in Word Learning

The toddler learning a new word confronts a very big mapping problem. To illustrate, imagine a toddler in a stroller being pushed by her mom at the zoo. They stop in front of the giraffe exhibit, and the mom points to the giraffe and says, "Look, honey—that is a *giraffe.*" Problem of mapping solved, right? The child sees the giraffe, hears the word *giraffe,* and maps the two together.

Well, not quite. The problem is that when the mom points to the giraffe, how does the child know that she intends to refer to the entire animal—not just the long neck, or the hooves, or the animal and the house behind it? Ellen Markman (1989; Woodward & Markman, 1998) has hypothesized that children make what she called the **whole object assumption**. That is, when they hear a new word (and start fast mapping a new lexical entry), children assume that the new word names a single whole object. It isn't that they can't learn other words, such as verbs or adjectives; it is merely that, as a default, children will assume that a new word labels a whole object.

In one study, 2-year-olds were shown a novel object made of a distinctive substance (e.g., a metal *T*) and told, "This is my *blicket*" (Soja, Carey, & Spelke, 1991). Later, the children were shown two new things: a new object, made in the same shape as the first but out of a different material (e.g., a plastic *T*), and

Photo 5.3   A trip to the zoo affords young children the chance to learn many new animals' names.

pieces of the original material (e.g., metal fragments in arbitrary shapes). They were asked to indicate which of the two choices was a *blicket,* and over 90% chose the object instead of the fragments. That is, children transferred the label, *blicket,* to the new object made out of different material rather than to the old material that now did not form an object.

Another constraint toddlers are assumed to use in word learning is called the **mutual exclusivity principle** (Markman, 1989; Woodward & Markman, 1998). The idea here is that normally, toddlers assume that objects have a single label. Thus, returning to the toddler-and-mom-at-the-zoo example, imagine that the toddler knows the word for *bear* but not for *monkey,* and assume the mother and child are standing in front of two displays—one with a bear and another with a monkey. If the mother says, "Look, that's a monkey," the mutual exclusivity constraint predicts that the toddler will map this new word, *monkey,* onto the monkey rather than the bear, because he already has a verbal label, *bear,* for the bear, and assumes that each object has a single label. Littschwager and Markman (1994) showed that even 16-month-olds use the mutual exclusivity principle when learning a new word. Second labels for words can be learned, but children are more resistant to doing so.

A final principle toddlers seem to have is called the **taxonomic principle** (Markman, 1989). The idea here is that when children have a word for an object, they generalize that word to other objects that are of the same kind as the one they know about. Thus, if children have a word *dog* for an animal that lives next door—say, a poodle—they are likely to use this word also to refer to another kind of dog they encounter—say, a basset hound owned by Grandma. They are very unlikely to extend the word to things associated with the poodle they know, such as the poodle's leash or water bowl, even though they have seen those objects together with the poodle several times.

Markman and Hutchinson (1984) demonstrated this experimentally with preschoolers who were introduced to a puppet and taught to speak "puppet language." On some trials, children were shown a picture of a blue jay and told that in puppet language it was called a *sud*. Next, they were shown two other pictures—one of a duck (something in the same "category" as a blue jay, at least for adults) and the other of a nest (something that young children are shown to associate with birds)—and were asked which one was the same as the *sud*. Although when no label (*sud*) was given and children were just shown pictures they grouped things like a bird and a nest together, when given the label *sud* they were much more likely to extend it to other birds—that is, taxonomically.

So far, we have focused exclusively on how toddlers and young children learn nouns. But children don't just learn nouns—and not all the nouns they learn refer to physically present objects. How else do children learn new words, especially words that don't refer to physically present objects? How might they, for example, learn new verbs or new adjectives?

Roger Brown (1957) in a landmark study showed that 3- to 5-year-old children can use the syntax of sentences to figure out what kind of thing a word refers to. For example, he showed a picture of a pair of hands kneading some sort of red confetti-like material in a blue and white striped container. Some children were told that the picture showed *sibbing*; others that it showed *a sib*; and still others that it depicted *some sib*. The three groups of children then made very different assumptions about what the word *sib* meant, interpreting it as a verb, as a noun (the container), or as a mass noun (the material), respectively. Only the grammatical markers on the word changed, suggesting that children are sensitive to syntactic nuances. Gelman and Markman (1985) reported similar findings, depicted in Figure 5.7, that 4-year-olds use syntactic cues to distinguish between adjectives and nouns when given very ambiguous instructions to either "find the fep one" or "find the fep" with no definition given of the word *fep*.

We will explore the young child's acquisition of knowledge of syntax very soon. For the moment, it is worth pointing out that children's word learning and syntactic acquisition are related. We will also see in a later section that word learning is connected to children's understanding of pragmatics.

Figure 5–7   Syntax as a clue to word meaning. Four-year-olds pick (b) when told, "Find the fep one," and they pick (c) when told, "Now find the fep." These responses suggest that 4-year-olds can use the syntax of a sentence to distinguish between words that imply a contrast between members of the same category (adjectives) and words that do not imply such a contrast (common nouns).

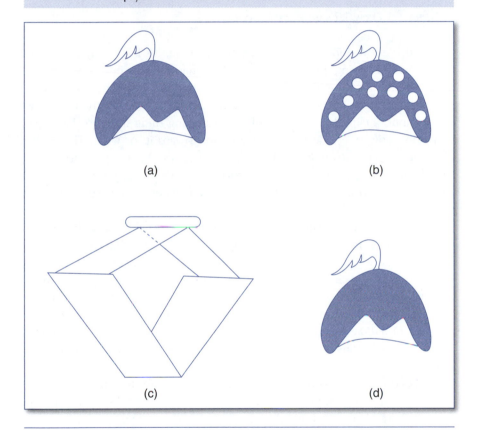

(a)   (b)

(c)   (d)

SOURCE: Gelman & Markman (1985, p. 135).

SYNTACTIC DEVELOPMENT

First words convey information, but in a very limited way. The child can point to objects in the world, and the parent or sibling or caretaker can expand on these utterances. For example, the following exchange is very typical of the kinds of conversations I had with each of my children when they were around 18 months old:

Child: Doggie.

Me: Yep, that sure is a dog, all right.

Child: Doggie.

Me: Yep, that's a doggie. Do you want to go pet him?

Child: Doggie.

Me: Okay, let's go pet the doggie.

Notice a few things about this exchange. One, it's fair to say that I was pretty much carrying the conversation. The child introduced the topic, and I "ran with it." Two, I was doing a lot of interpretation of the child's communicative intentions in this conversation. It's not clear whether the child was simply announcing the presence of an interesting thing in his or her environment, indicating a desire to move closer toward it, or what. Three, the exchange rapidly loses interest—both for you as the reader and (quite frankly) for me as the conversational partner. I have to admit that it is much more fun to converse with both children today when they have richer and more structured things to say.

Our focus in this section is on multiword utterances—that is, things that appear to be "sentence-like" for the child. Although (as with most aspects of language development) there are wide individual differences, most toddlers start producing so-called two-word utterances around the age of 18 months (Tomasello, 2006). It is only at this point when we can begin thinking about the **syntax**, or structure of the words within an utterance. It is not possible to speak of *syntax* in a toddler's language until he produces multiword utterances, simply because it is not possible to structure a one-word utterance in different ways.

If children's two-word utterances had absolutely no structure, then what we should observe are random pairings of words in a child's vocabulary. In fact, what we observe is quite the opposite: Children's two-word utterances display a considerable amount of regularity. In Table 5.4, I reproduce a sample of two-word utterances produced by my niece Brandi Lee when she was about 18 months old. This corpus of language illustrates some fairly typical phenomena of language development.

You'll notice that certain words or phrases, such as *Rockabye* and *Oh deah*, always occur initially in the utterance; that other words or phrases, such as *down* and *didit*, always occur at the end of the utterance; and that certain other words, such as *Dassie*, *Mummy*, and *Santa*, occur either initially or at the end of the utterance.

Table 5–4	Sample two-word utterances

Dassie (her word for "Kathie") down. (meaning "Kathie, sit on the floor.")
Oyd (her word for "Lloyd") down. (meaning, "Lloyd, sit on the floor.")
Mummy down.
Rockabye baby.
Rockabye turkey.
Rockabye Santa.
Oh deah (dear) Santa.
Oh deah Dassie.
Oh deah Mummy.
Oh deah turtle.
Mummy didit. ("didit" meant, roughly, to have performed an action.)
Dassie didit.
Brannie (her word for "Brandi") didit.

SOURCE: Galotti (1999a, p. 489).

Braine (1963) hypothesized a pivot grammar to account for these regularities. Braine argued that children begin to form two-word utterances by first somehow selecting a small set of frequently occurring words in the language they hear. These words are called "pivots." Children's knowledge about pivots includes not only the pronunciation and something about the word's meaning but where in an utterance the pivot should appear. Other words that the child uses are called "open" words. Braine argued from data much like that in Table 5.4 that toddlers form "syntactic" rules of the following sort: "Pivot1 + Open" or "Open + Pivot2," where Pivot1 includes all sentence-initial pivots (e.g., *Oh deah*, *Rockabye*), and Pivot2 includes all sentence-final pivots (e.g., *didit*, *down*).

Braine's (1963) pivot grammar accounts for some of the regularities apparent in the speech of some children. However, work by other investigators (Bowerman, 1973; Brown, 1973) soon showed that it fails to account for the utterances of all children. Although current consensus is that the grammar is at best incomplete and in many cases incorrect, some investigators have argued that it might provide some useful ideas about how children begin to construct a grammar from the language they hear around them (Ingram, 1989).

Tomasello and his collaborators (Tomasello, Akhtar, Dodson, & Rekau, 1997) have shown that when toddlers aged 22 months learn a novel name for an object (e.g., *wug* to indicate a stuffed animal), they can use the term correctly with other pivot-type words (to produce, for example, utterances such as *Wug allgone* or *More wug*). However, these toddlers couldn't generalize across different pivot schemes. So, for example, if a 22-month-old toddler was taught a new verb (an experimenter calls a child's attention to an action and says something like, "Look! That's called *meeking*"), that child would *not* be likely to take the new term and utter something like "Brannie meeking" when she saw Brandi carrying out the action formerly referred to as "meeking."

Brown (1973) took a different tack in accounting for regularities in children's two-word utterances. Brown asserted that children at the two-word stage are constructing their utterances *not* by following rules of syntax but by using a small set of semantic relations. Table 5.5 presents the semantic relations that he proposed are used. Brown argued that this particular set of relations is an outgrowth of the knowledge about the world that toddlers of this age should have. He believed that children at this point in development focus on actions, agents, and objects and are concerned with issues such as where objects are located and when and how they can disappear and reappear. As such, Brown's proposals fit nicely with the Piagetian view of sensorimotor development (Ingram, 1989).

One problem with Brown's approach is that it requires an adult to interpret what the child intended to communicate at the time of the utterance. It forces adults to interpret children's language in terms of adult assumptions and beliefs, and it assumes that adults and children use language to refer to events and objects in the world in similar ways. Ingram (1989) pointed out that this assumption can be erroneous.

More recent work in language acquisition has focused more specifically on how the complexity of multiword utterances (e.g., those beyond two words) arises. Researchers have paid particular attention to the emergence of *grammatical morphemes*, "little" words or prefixes and suffixes that don't typically carry as much meaning as do the early words uttered by a child but still help make a child's language more understandable.

Some examples of grammatical morphemes are determiners such as *the, a,* and *an;* verb tense markers such as *–ing* and *–ed;* and plural markers such as *–s* and *–es.* When children begin to form three-word utterances, they also begin to put in some grammatical morphemes. Roger Brown, who published a landmark study of the early language acquisition of three children (with pseudonyms Adam, Eve, and Sarah) in 1973, tracked the development of 14 different grammatical morphemes. He found that becoming a proficient user of these morphemes took quite awhile—often until the children were over 4 years old

Table 5–5   Proposed semantic relations for early grammars

Relation	Definition and examples
1. Nomination	The naming of a referent, without pointing, usually in response to the question "What's that?" Often indicated with words such as "this," "that," "here," "there." (Also see "Demonstrative and Entity" below.)
2. Recurrence	The reappearance of a referent already seen, a new instance of a referent class already seen, or an additional quantity of some mass already seen, e.g., "more" or "another" X.
3. Nonexistence	The disappearance of something that was in the visual field, e.g., "no hat," "allgone egg."
	Semantic Functions
4. Agent + Action	The agent is "someone or something, usually but not necessarily animate, which is perceived to have its own motivating force and to cause an action of process" (p. 193), e.g., "Adam go," "car go," "Susan off."
5. Action + Object	The object is "someone or something (usually something, or inanimate) either suffering a change of state or simply receiving the force of an action" (p. 193).
6. Agent + Object	A relation that uses the two definitions above. It can be considered a direction relation without an intervening action.
7. Action + Location	"The place or locus of an action" (p. 194), as in "Tom sat in the chair." Often marked by forms like "here" and "there."
8. Entity + Locative	The specification of the location of an entity, i.e., any being or thing with a separate existence. These take a copula in adult English, e.g., "lady home" meaning "the lady is home."
9. Possessor + Possession	The specification of objects belonging to one person or another, e.g., "mommy chair."
10. Entity + Attribute	The specification of "some attribute of an entity that could not be known from the class characteristics of the entity alone" (p. 197), e.g., "yellow block," "little dog."
11. Demonstrative and Entity	The same as Nomination except that the child points and uses a demonstrative.

SOURCE: Ingram (1989, p. 287).

(Brown, 1973). There also appeared to be a regular order of acquisition, with the morpheme *–ing* typically appearing first (as in *I'm eating*), followed by the use of *in* and *on,* followed by the plural marker, followed by several others.

Children's use of different sentence forms also shows regularity. Children begin by uttering simple declarative sentences, such as *I go store* or *I want some eggs*. Not until the child begins to add grammatical morphemes and construct three-word or longer utterances do other sentence forms appear, including negative sentences (e.g., *I can't see you* and *No want cereal*), questions (e.g., *I go potty?* and *Why the moon is up?*), and passive voice (e.g., *My dolly was eaten by the dog*). Such sentence forms are more complex than simple declarative sentences, in part because they often require the use of auxiliary verbs (e.g., *can, be, will*) and in part because they often require inversion of word order.

Almost always, children's language comprehension outstrips their production. What this means is that children typically show evidence of understanding more complex syntactic forms than they themselves produce (Tomasello, 2006). This finding suggests that children become sensitive to issues of grammatical structure at a very early age, arguably well before their fourth birthday.

CONVERSATIONAL/PRAGMATIC DEVELOPMENT

To become full-fledged fluent users of language, toddlers have to do more than master the phonology, acquire an appropriate lexicon, and structure their utterances appropriately. They must also master the practices of the language community in which they wish to communicate. This mastery has several components to it, including pragmatic knowledge—understanding the communicative functions of language; discourse knowledge—understanding the mechanics of conversation; and sociolinguistic knowledge—knowing how language use differs as a function of the social class or status of a conversational partner, the formality of the setting, and so forth (Hoff, 2005). We won't be able to cover each of these topics in any depth in this section, and the interested student is encouraged to consult Erika Hoff's (2005) discussion. For now, a few examples will have to suffice.

When I reread the journals I kept during my son's infancy, I rediscovered several "unusual" words he used—including *daiden* for *dog* and *fuf* for *brush*. I had forgotten about these "words" largely because, at age 16, he hasn't produced them in quite a while. However, I recall him wanting to "fuf" my hair, his hair, and his dad's hair, and I recall filling a Christmas stocking with a variety of *fufs* to his great delight—a nail *fuf,* a shower *fuf,* and several hair *fufs* in various colors and styles.

My spouse worried about this idiosyncratic usage and was unhappy to hear me repeat the word, worrying that if I reinforced usage of *fuf,* my son would never properly pronounce the word. And, had that happened (it didn't!), it would have had extremely unfortunate consequences—just imagine your reaction if your college roommate said *fuf* instead of *brush.* You would be wondering why on earth he or she used this funny word, when a perfectly available word in English existed. Your roommate would be violating the pragmatic principle of *conventionality*—the idea that other users in your language community expect you to use the standard word unless you have a good reason for doing otherwise (Clark, 1993).

Now, one good reason you might have is that you wish to draw a distinction between most ordinary brushes and some brushes with some special property—perhaps, made out of a certain material or of a certain size. In such a case, you might want to invent a new word and use it only for that special class of objects. In doing so, you would be following the pragmatic principle of *contrast,* the idea that when a speaker uses a different word, it is assumed she intended a difference in meaning.

Eve Clark (1993) gives evidence that young children honor these two pragmatic principles from at least their early productions. They attempt to model their utterances on adult speech, trying to pronounce words as adults do and rejecting adults' mimicry of their own approximations. As we saw in the lexical development section, when learning new words, toddlers assume that the new entries are not synonyms for words they already know—a pragmatic assumption.

Toddlers also need to learn to become conversational partners—to follow the "rules" of a conversation. One such rule is to take turns in speaking and listening—conversations tend to lose effectiveness when both parties speak at once (or both try to listen at once). Caretakers begin to "signal" this rule in their first conversations with their baby—pausing in their utterances to give the baby a chance to "talk"—even though the infant's contribution is at first restricted to wiggling, grunts, groans, and various digestive noises. Over time, the infant may begin to take his turn by contributing a gesture, a facial expression, and eventually a word.

Toddlers also need to learn to stay "on topic" when in a conversation. That is, if I am talking about my dogs, it doesn't work very well if, out of the blue, my conversational partner starts making observations about the weather or recounting an anecdote from her childhood. But, as we will see in the chapters ahead, this "egocentric" form of communication is quite typical of young preschoolers in their "conversations."

❖ ❖ ❖

Language acquisition is certainly not complete by the time the young child exits toddlerhood. We will return to various aspects of language acquisition in the chapters to come. The point for now is to see that language acquisition is truly a remarkable cognitive development, that it occurs on several different levels, and that much of the early development is achieved well before the child enters formal schooling.

SUMMARY

1. Language development proceeds quite rapidly over the first 4 years of a child's life.

2. Language is distinguished from other communication systems by the presence of two characteristics: productivity (an infinite number of utterances can be constructed from a finite number of parts) and regularity (legal utterances are governed by a system of implicit rules).

3. Many theorists subscribe to a nativist view of language, especially for certain aspects of it such as syntax. They believe that human beings are born equipped with a uniquely human, special-purpose language acquisition device that helps them rapidly acquire one of the possible human languages.

4. Not everyone accepts the idea of an innate LAD, however. Other theorists analyze the language utterances children are typically exposed to, and argue that this set of stimuli is repetitive enough to explain rapid language learning.

5. Phonology is the study of the speech sounds of different languages. Phonemes are the sounds of language that make a meaningful difference.

6. From about the age of 1 month, infants have been shown to perceive speech sounds categorically—that is, to treat all variants of the same sound as equivalent. At first, infants are able to categorically perceive a wide range of speech sounds, but over the first year they seem to lose this ability for speech distinctions not made in their native language.

7. In the first half of the first year, infants progress from producing vegetative sounds to cooing to babbling.

8. In the latter half of the first year, infants begin to show intersubjectivity, sharing mental and perceptual experiences with people and objects.

9. The first recognizable words are produced around the time of an infant's first birthday. Many of the first words produced refer to names of objects, substances, animals, and people. However, many first words are either over- or underextended to objects in the world, when compared with adult usage of those same words.

10. The growth of vocabulary during the toddler and preschool years is remarkable, going from an average vocabulary size of 50 words at 18 months to approximately 10,000 words by age 6 years.

11. Children's two-word utterances begin appearing around 18 months. Two-word utterances typically show regularities in word order.

12. As children begin to form multiword utterances, they begin to add in grammatical morphemes such as tense or plural markers.

13. In addition to learning phonological, lexical, and syntactic principles, young children need to acquire pragmatic, discourse, and sociolinguistic knowledge to become effective users of language in their communities.

REVIEW QUESTIONS

1. Explain the difference between a communication system and language.

2. Review the arguments for and against the proposition that language is innate.

3. What is categorical perception, and how might it make learning to understand language easier?

4. Describe the features of infant-directed speech (IDS) and how it might aid infants learning to understand language.

5. Trace the early stages in infants' production of speech during the first year.

6. What are over- and underextensions, and what might they tell us about children's understanding of words?

7. Describe the "fast mapping" study of Bartlett and Carey, and discuss its significance for the study of language acquisition.

8. Describe each of Ellen Markman's proposed constraints on word learning.

9. Contrast the pivot–open grammar approach of Martin Braine with the semantic approach of Roger Brown in explaining the regularities of children's two-word utterances.

10. What kinds of pragmatic knowledge do children need to acquire to become effective conversational partners?

KEY TERMS

Auditory Perception	Discourse Knowledge
Babbling	Encapsulation
Categorical Perception	Extended Mapping
Cooing	Fast Mapping
Critical Period	Infant-Directed Speech (IDS)

Intersubjectivity

Lexical Development

Morpheme

Mutual Exclusivity Principle

Overextension

Phone

Phoneme

Poverty of the Stimulus Argument

Pragmatic Knowledge

Productivity

Regularity

Sociolinguistic Knowledge

Syntax

Taxonomic Principle

Underextension

Whole Object Assumption

CHAPTER 6

EARLY CHILDHOOD

Perception and Attention

T he next few chapters examine early childhood—that period between toddlerhood and the beginning of formal schooling in many cultures. Chronologically, we are looking at the ages of roughly two and a half to six years old—in our culture, what would be called the "preschool" years. We begin with a look at the major developmental theorists, Piaget and Vygotsky. We then examine the perceptual and attentional developments during early childhood. We conclude this chapter with a detailed examination of the effects of different kinds of television viewing on preschoolers' cognitive development.

THEORETICAL PERSPECTIVES

Theories, as we have already seen, provide a "big picture" or overview of developmental phenomena. Here, we will look first at Piagetian views of this period of development, examining specifically Piagetian descriptions of the preoperational period. We will then contrast that view with that of Vygotsky, whose theoretical work seems particularly relevant for children in early childhood.

A Piagetian View of Early Childhood

Recall from Chapter 2 that Piaget describes this stage of development as the preoperational period. It is characterized both by gains (relative to the sensorimotor period, which precedes it) and by deficits (relative to the period of concrete operations, which occurs during middle childhood).

Compared with an infant or a toddler, the preoperational child has come a long way. Now in possession of the ability for mental representation, the young child can have a sense of the past and of the future, in addition to the present. She can think, without having those thoughts acted out behaviorally. She can form rudimentary intentions for the future, imagine a richly specified world of pretend, and plan complex sentences to communicate. She can use symbols, both in language and in play, using one object (say, a block) to "stand in for" or represent another (say, a car).

On the other hand, the preschooler typically fails a lot of tasks that the school-aged child passes easily. A 4-year-old boy is unlikely to pass the Piagetian conservation tasks described in Chapter 2. If given a bunch of blocks that differ in color, size, and shape and asked to "put together the blocks that go together," he is unlikely to consistently classify, for example, on the basis of color or shape or size. Instead, he might start with a small yellow round block and add a small green round block, a small red round block, a large red triangular block, and then a large blue triangular block—in other words evidently forgetting the overall classification basis he began with.

Children in the preoperational period are characterized as well by their egocentrism. That is to say not that they are selfish (although they often are) but rather that they are unable to distinguish between their own perspective and the perspective of others. So, for example, an egocentric child facing one way in a room is said by Piaget not to realize that a person facing him sees different things than he does. Nor does he understand that his mom may not know the other moms and dads who come to pick up his day care friends at the end of each weekday. If he knows these moms and dads, he figures, everyone else does, too.

Piaget explains these cognitive gaps as stemming from the child's lack of mental operations (Gelman & Baillargeon, 1983). Such operations allow young children to structure their knowledge of the world and to make an all-important distinction between appearance and reality. Lacking operations, the child is bound by his perceptions—and can do nothing but conclude that the way things appear is the way they really are.

The appearance–reality confusion can help explain children's failure on the number conservation task. To review, the task begins with the experimenter laying out two rows of five checkers, arranged in one-to-one correspondence, as in Figure 2.1 (see page 23). The experimenter asks the child whether the two rows have the same number of checkers in them or whether one of the rows has more, and, given this arrangement and a reasonably small number of checkers, the 4-year-old will typically readily agree that the two rows have "the same." Now, with the child watching, the experimenter spreads out one row of checkers, making it longer, and asks again whether the two rows of checkers have the same or whether one row has more. The typical response of the child will be that the longer row has more.

One explanation for the child's incorrect answer is that she is "keying in" on the length of the row and failing to notice that even though length has increased, density of checkers within the row has decreased in a compensatory way (Gelman, 1969). Another way to say this is that the child looks only at the length and does not think about the fact that spreading objects apart cannot affect their numerosity.

We will come back to discussion of the appearance–reality distinction when we discuss children's play as well as children's reasoning, in Chapter 8.

However, the topic is also very relevant to a discussion of young children's perception, as we shall soon see.

A Vygotskian View of Early Childhood

Russian psychologist Lev Vygotsky's views of cognitive development differ in several key respects from those of Piaget. Recall that Vygotsky held fast to the notion that the child is integrally a part of his environment and cannot be meaningfully studied in isolation from that environment. It is not that the child develops internal mental structures "inside his head," the way Piaget might view it, but instead that the child and his environment (including important other people, such as parents, siblings, and teachers) together co-construct the child's mental structures. It is not that (as in most Western psychological theories) the environment *affects* development but rather that the environment and the child together are the appropriate unit of study. The social activities that the child engages in—play, or formal schooling, or using a computer, or navigating through woods—shape the mind and the cognitive structures.

Vygotsky also bestowed on developmental psychology the important concept of the *zone of proximal development.* By this he meant the range of cognitive functioning a child is capable of. At the bottom of the zone, the lowest level of performance, is the child's ability to function independently, with no help. At the upper end is the performance a child is capable of, with help from an adult or experienced older child, with the right set of props or tools, or in play (Miller, 2011). This zone represents potential development. As the child develops more ability, the zone changes as well. The important point is that at any given point in time, the child's "true" ability is not one level but actually a range, depending on the circumstances in which the child is performing.

Examples of this zone abound. When I helped my then 6-year-old daughter write lowercase letters, I sometimes put my hand over her hand holding the pencil and helped her move it in the correct series of strokes. This physical guidance is what Vygotskian psychologists call scaffolding—that is, providing temporary extra structure to aid a child's fragile attempts. In providing scaffolding, I helped my daughter write more letters and do so more legibly than she was able to do on her own. Presumably this guided practice facilitated her learning to write letters so that now, a year and a half later, she can write all her letters clearly and legibly by herself. Scaffolding need not be physical or explicit; Rogoff (1990) describes several cultures in which young children learn

Photo 6.1   Helping a beginning child write by providing physical guidance is one form of *scaffolding* a developing behavior.

skills such as weaving simply by carefully observing skilled adults perform the task.

The zone of proximal development is not simply a function of an adult or older child teaching or demonstrating a new skill for a younger child. Instead, Vygotsky intended the zone to capture "any situation in which some activity is leading children beyond their current level of functioning" (Miller, 2011, p. 380). As we will see in Chapter 8, children's play can also create a zone of proximal development.

With the Piagetian and Vygotskian theories as background, we turn to the topics of perception and attention in preschool children. These cognitive activities interact heavily with memory and knowledge representation, two topics we reserve for Chapter 7. Although space constraints require the topics to be discussed separately, it is important for you to keep in mind that the various cognitive systems are heavily intertwined.

PERCEPTUAL DEVELOPMENT

In an influential theoretical paper, psychologist Heinz Werner articulated the *orthogenetic* principle of development: "Wherever development occurs it proceeds from a state of relative globality and lack of differentiation to a state of increasing differentiation, articulation, and hierarchic integration" (Werner, 1957/1982, p. 22). Certainly we can see aspects of this idea in Piagetian theory—the young infant lacks the ability to distinguish between himself and the world around him—everything exists as a giant, undifferentiated whole. We will probe this idea more carefully as we consider the topic of perceptual development.

Analytic Versus Holistic Processing

Psychologist Deborah Kemler (now Kemler Nelson) took this idea a step further in applying it to the general way that preschoolers approach a variety of cognitive tasks, including perception. Her claim was that young preschoolers initially process information in a global, holistic mode but that with cognitive development, they become more analytic and more able to focus on specific aspects of stimuli (Kemler, 1983).

Consider, as an example, the stimuli presented in Figure 6.1. If we asked you to choose the two objects that best "go together," we might find the following results. The first two objects match exactly on the dimension of size (they have exactly the same shape and area); however, they differ greatly in patterning. The second two objects do not match exactly in size or in patterning, but they overall are more similar to one another. Kemler's work would predict that most preschool children would sort these two together (sorting holistically, using overall similarity as the basis of sorting), whereas adults and older children would be more likely to sort analytically, choosing to group together those objects that have an exact match on one dimension (in this case, grouping the first two stimuli together). That is, older children and adults analyze each stimulus into separate, independent properties, such as shape and pattern, while younger preschool children are more likely to react to each stimulus as one undifferentiated whole.

Kemler (1983) argues not that preschool children are *incapable* of analytical perception but simply that their preference is to perceive stimuli as whole objects rather than to analyze the features, aspects, properties, or dimensions of stimuli. Over time, this preference shifts to a more analytic

Figure 6–1 The first two stimuli match exactly on the dimension of size but are very different in overall pattern. The second two stimuli don't match exactly in either size or pattern but have a very similar pattern.

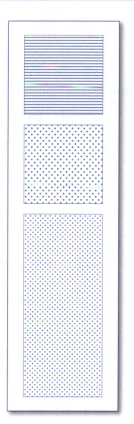

one. However, both kinds of processing are possible at either age, and which approach is taken may well depend upon the specifics of the task.

Notice that this account of holistic processing of perceptual information provides at least a partial account of why preschool children often fail the Piagetian conservation tasks. If they are inclined not to analyze stimuli into different dimensions but instead to treat them as wholes, then they are much less likely to notice that one dimension of a stimulus array varies inversely with another. For example, in Figure 2.1, the longer row of checkers is also the less dense row of checkers—the dimension of length trades off against the density. To fail to notice this trade-off might be to encourage an inappropriate focus (Piaget called this "centration") upon a single aspect or dimension of the stimuli—in this case, length of the row of checkers.

Face Recognition

When it comes to perceiving certain kinds of stimuli—namely, human faces—however, preschoolers have been claimed to focus on individual features (e.g., mouth or hair) rather than the overall, holistic facial configuration (Carey & Diamond, 1977, 1994). In a classic study, Susan Carey and Rhea Diamond (1977) presented children aged 6, 8, and 10 years with photographs of faces and of houses. Some of the photographs were presented in the normal, upright orientation, while others were presented upside down, in an inverted orientation. They later presented a series of pairs of photographs, one that had previously been presented and one that had not, always in the same orientation (upright or inverted) as the stimuli had originally been presented. Accuracy in recognizing upright faces rose with age: 6-year-olds recognized about 69% of the upright faces, compared with 81% for 8-year-olds and 89% for 10-year-olds. However, accuracy for inverted faces stayed pretty constant: 64%, 67%, and 68% for 6-, 8-, and 10-year-olds, respectively. Performance with photographs of houses showed a different pattern. There was no developmental difference in recognition of upright houses (71%, 74%, and 73% correct recognition for 6-, 8-, and 10-year-olds, respectively) but a clear improvement for older children in recognizing inverted photographs of houses (58%, 64%, and 77% for 6-, 8-, and 10-year-olds, respectively).

In a second study, children of the same ages saw photographs similar to those in the top row of Figure 6.2. Next, they were shown pairs of photographs similar to those shown in the bottom row of Figure 6.2. Note that in each pair, one depicts the model shown in the original photograph, either wearing a different article of clothing or a different expression, and the other depicts a different model displaying the same facial expression as the one displayed in the original photograph. Children were told to look carefully at the face of the first model, because her clothes, her eyeglasses, or even her hair might change.

Carey and Diamond (1977) hypothesized that younger children would have more difficulty abstracting the "facial configuration" from a single photograph than would older children. Therefore, younger children were expected to be more easily misled by similar articles of clothing or eyeglasses on different models. In fact, these were just the results they obtained. Ten-year-olds were much less likely to be fooled by clothing or eyeglasses than were 6- or 8-year-olds. The authors concluded that 10-year-olds pay much more attention to relationships among facial features—things like the distance between two eyes, or the distance from the mouth to the nose—than do younger children. Put this way, at least when it comes to faces, younger children seem to be more likely to process information analytically than holistically.

Research following up on this landmark study has produced a more complicated and nuanced picture. For example, in some studies, less pronounced age differences are found with different kinds of manipulation of faces (Carey & Diamond, 1994; Pellicano & Rhodes, 2003; Pellicano, Rhodes, & Peters, 2006). Pellicano and Rhodes presented 4- and 5-year-olds with faces such as that shown in Figure 6.3a. Immediately thereafter

Figure 6–2 Facial expression stimuli similar to those used by Carey and Diamond (1977)

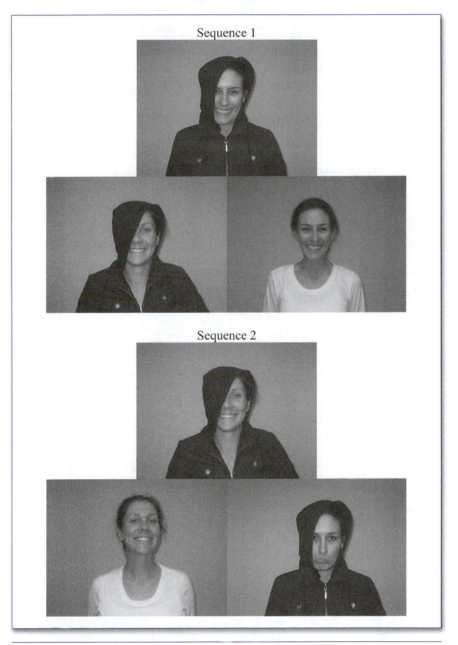

(Continued)

Figure 6–2 (Continued)

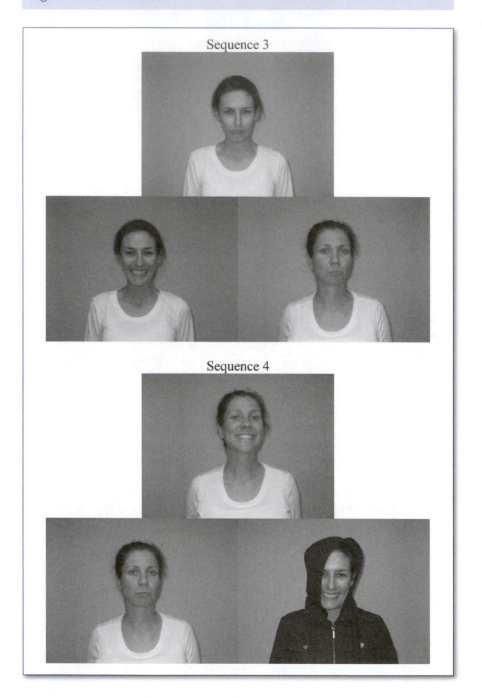

Sequence 3

Sequence 4

they were asked to recognize this face when presented with a pair of similar faces (Figure 6.3b) or (on other trials) to recognize just a part of the face (Figure 6.3c). If young children do encode faces by individual features, then they should be better than adults at the "parts of a face" task then they are at the "whole face" task. But, as Figure 6.4 shows, this pattern of results was not found. Instead, although adults were overall better at both kinds of recognition tasks, they showed the same pattern of results as younger children. Inverting the faces made recognition of parts easier than recognition of whole faces, but again, this pattern of results held for both children and adults.

Object Recognition

What about preschoolers' perception of other, nonface objects? Daniel Bernstein and colleagues (Bernstein, Atance, Loftus, & Meltzoff, 2004) have investigated how preschoolers and adults are able to identify stimuli that are degraded in various ways, such as those shown in Figure 6.5. Research participants included 3-year-olds, 4-year-olds, 5-year-olds, and adults (college students) who saw images that were initially very blurry or dark or cropped, such as those in the top panel of Figure 6.5. Gradually, and over 15 distinct steps, the pictures clarified, as partially shown in each column of Figure 6.5. On half the trials, observers were told what the object was (e.g., "a fish"), but on the other half they were not. On the first kind of trial, the observers were asked to estimate when a same-aged peer would be able to first identify the object. In general, all observers overestimated when a peer would be able to identify a degraded object. Moreover, at least some of the time, preschoolers were much more likely than adults to overestimate when a peer would be able to recognize an object (based on the average state of degradation of pictures it took the observers to recognize objects when they were not told ahead of time what the object was, a finding confirmed in a follow-up study; Bernstein, Loftus, & Meltzoff, 2005).

In general, then, we see that preschoolers perform at least some perceptual tasks in similar ways to those adopted by adults. However, the preschoolers often take longer, make more errors, and overestimate their own perceptual abilities when compared with adults on those tasks. It may be that a certain amount of experience is necessary to establish a balance or an optimal approach to holistic and analytic perceptual processing for any given task. While able to perceive in both

Figure 6–3 Example of stimuli presented in the upright task: (a) target, (b) test stimuli presented in the whole condition, and (c) test stimuli presented in the part condition

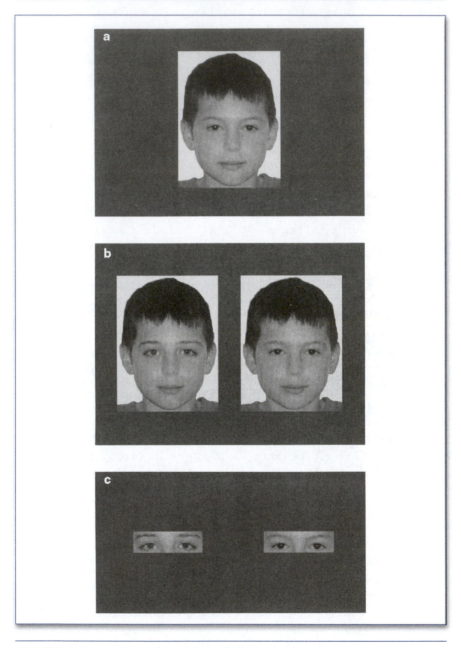

SOURCE: Pellicano & Rhodes (2003, p. 620).

Figure 6–4   Children's and adults' performance in the part and whole conditions of the upright task. Standard error bars are shown.

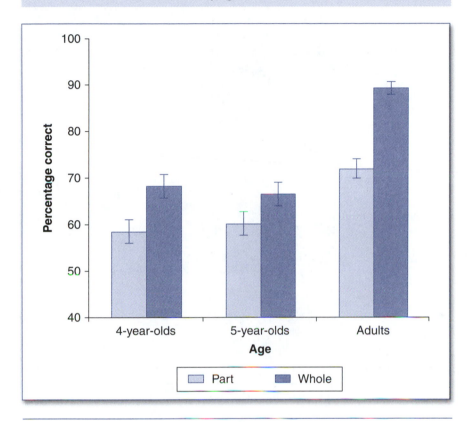

SOURCE: Pellicano & Rhodes (2003, p. 620).

modes, it may take preschoolers more time and require more practice before they can adopt the right perceptual approach.

Understanding Symbolic Representations

One of the tasks that often begins in the preschool period is the perception and use of various symbols. The most common example in our culture is the recognition of letters and numbers, a topic we'll look at in much more detail in Chapter 11. However, even the perception of pictures, photographs, or scale models is something that develops, sometimes dramatically, during this period. This topic, by the way, involves both perception (the meaningful interpretation of sensory information)

Figure 6–5 Examples of stimulus gradation

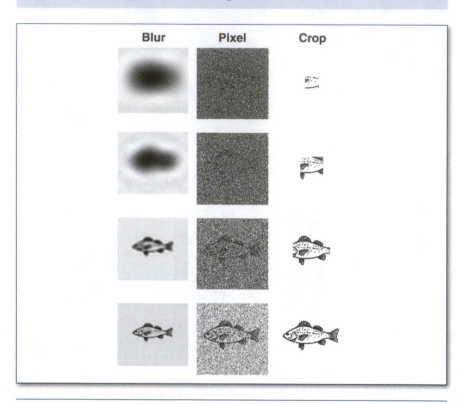

SOURCE: Bernstein, Atance, Loftus, & Meltzoff (2004, p. 265).

and higher-order reasoning of the sort we'll be looking at in Chapter 8. So I could have just as easily discussed this topic there, but I thought it interesting to contrast some of the studies with some of the other perceptual ones.

Judy DeLoache (1987) performed a landmark study looking at preschoolers' ability to perceive and interpret scale models. Children aged two and a half to three years were shown a scale model of an adjacent larger room, as depicted in Figure 6.6. The model contains the same furniture as does the larger room, and the furniture is arranged spatially the same way in both the model and the actual room. Children were shown the scale model, and watched as a miniature toy was hidden behind or under a miniature piece of furniture, and were instructed that a larger toy was hidden behind the corresponding piece of furniture—as in "Watch!

I'm hiding Little Snoopy here. I'm going to hide Big Snoopy in the same place in his big room" (DeLoache, 1995, p. 109). Then the children were asked to go into the big room and find "Big Snoopy." Results (which were later replicated in several other studies; see DeLoache, 1995, for a review) show that 3-year-olds often (about 75% of the time) immediately found Big Snoopy, whereas children 6 months younger (aged two and a half) usually performed very poorly (correct less than 20% of the time). According to DeLoache (1995):

> Failure in the task is not due to memory or motivational factors: Virtually all children can retrieve the toy they actually observe being hidden in the model. Nevertheless, the younger children fail to relate their knowledge of the model to the room. These children understand that there is a toy hidden in the room, and they readily search for it. What they do not realize is that they have any way of knowing—other than by guessing—where it is. (p. 110)

Figure 6–6   A scale model of a room placed outside the actual room

DeLoache (1995; Marzolf, DeLoache, & Kolstad, 1999) believes that several factors influence children's ability to use information from the model to find the hidden object in the room. For example, the relationship between the model and the actual room needs to be made explicit; otherwise even typical 3-year-olds will fail the task. The resemblance between the model and the room is also very important. When the "model" furniture is very similar to the actual room furniture, performance is enhanced, and when it is dissimilar, performance decreases. Moreover, if the model and room are made very similar in overall size, even two-and-a-half-year-olds can do the task (DeLoache & Smith, 1999).

At the heart of this task, DeLoache (1995) believes, is the salience of the physical properties of the symbol—in this case, the model. To be able to use a symbol (be it a model, a word, a diagram, or something else), a person must *dually represent* the symbol. That means she must realize that the symbol has, simultaneously, a concrete meaning and an abstract one—that which it refers to. Put another way, the model of a room is itself both a *concrete* object—a miniature room—and an *abstract* one—a marker or representation of something else (the big room).

DeLoache (1995) believes that **dual representation** is made more difficult when the concrete aspects of the symbol are made salient to the child. When parts of the model are made very concrete and interesting, they tend to attract the child's attention to the model itself and distract the child from thinking of the model as a model.

According to this hypothesis, children's performance should be enhanced when the model is made less salient as a concrete object. One way to do this is to use a photograph rather than a scale model. When DeLoache used photographs, young children's performance interpreting models increased. Moreover, placing a model behind a window (ensuring that children could not touch or play with it) also decreased its salience and enhanced the performance of even two-and-a-half-year-old children. Contrarily, allowing children to play with the scale model for a few minutes before beginning the main task (which presumably enhanced its salience as a concrete object) hurt the performance of 3-year-olds (DeLoache, 1995).

A dramatic follow-up study illustrated this point very nicely (DeLoache, Miller, & Rosengren, 1997). One group of two-and-a-half-year-olds performed the standard task. A second group was deceived about an "incredible shrinking machine" that could not only shrink troll dolls (as shown in Figure 6.7) but could actually shrink entire rooms. ("Shrinking" took place out of the child's sight, while the experimenter and child left the room.) By using a portable laboratory room, surrounded by curtains on three sides instead of walls, the experimenters were able to convince children that the room had actually shrunk. Next, a small toy was hidden in the small room, and the "machine" was allowed to restore the room and hidden toy to its regular size (again, with the child and experimenter out of the room, listening to computer-generated beeps). Figure 6.8 presents a schematic view of what the children experienced.

The reasoning behind the experimental design was as follows: If children believed that the room had actually shrunk and been resized, then the model would no longer be a symbol; it *would be*—in the child's mind—the actual room. In this case, finding the hidden object is simply a memory test and does not involve the use (and decoding) of symbols. Therefore, it

Figure 6–7 The incredible shrinking troll. The panel on the left shows the troll positioned in front of the shrinking machine; the panel on the right shows the troll after the shrinking event.

SOURCE: DeLoache (1995, p. 112).

Figure 6–8   The credible shrinking room. Physical arrangements for the symbolic and nonsymbolic tasks. For the symbolic task (a), the portable room was located in a large lab, surrounded on three sides by opaque curtains represented by heavy lines; the model was located in an adjoining area. The nonsymbolic task began with the arrangement shown in (b); before the first shrinking event, the portable room was located in the lab, partially surrounded by curtains, just as it was in the symbolic task. The only difference was the presence of the shrinking machine, represented by the dark rectangle, sitting on a table. In the aftermath of the shrinking event, depicted in (c), the model sat in the middle of the area previously occupied by the portable room. The sketches in (d) and (e) show Terry the Troll before and after the demonstration shrinking event.

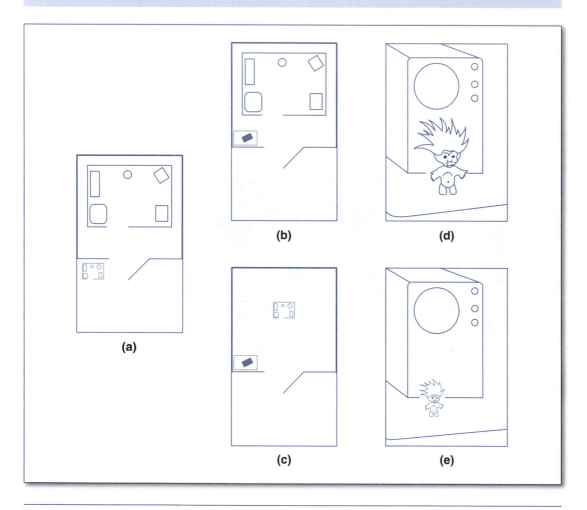

SOURCE: DeLoache, Miller, & Rosengren (1997, p. 310).

should be easier for younger children to find the hidden object in this condition. The results showed exactly this pattern. The mean number of times a child went straight to the correct hiding place was .8 (out of four trials using different hiding spots) in the standard condition, and 3.1 in the "shrinking room" condition.

DeLoache and Smith (1999) note that these results have implications for working with children in applied settings. For example, forensic interviews with children who are alleged victims of sexual abuse often use dolls as props, in the hopes of eliciting more and better information from children as to what actually happened during the original event. The assumption is that young children will be able to easily map the doll to themselves, and to point to parts of the doll that correspond to parts of their own body. DeLoache and Smith and others have found, to the contrary, that children of around 3 years of age give no more information in interviews using dolls than in those that do not. Four- and 5-year-old children, by contrast, are able to use dolls to enhance their recall. The point is, however, that the use of dolls requires a fairly sophisticated ability to deal with symbolic representation, a skill that is fragile below the age of about 4 years.

More recently, DeLoache and colleagues (DeLoache, Uttal, & Rosengren, 2004; Ware, Uttal, Wetter, & DeLoache, 2006) reported on fascinating and often comical scale errors made by very young preschoolers and toddlers (aged 18–30 months). These children first entered a laboratory playroom, which contained a large indoor slide the child could climb and slide down on, a large plastic car the child could enter and ride in (using his feet), a child-sized chair, and several other play items. The children first enjoyed a free play period, with an experimenter making sure that they interacted at least twice with each of the three objects mentioned above. Next, the experimenter and child left the room, and during their absence, the three target items were replaced with miniature replicas—a tiny slide, car, and chair. Twenty-five of the 54 children tested made what DeLoache et al. called a "scale error"—making a serious (not a pretend or humorous) attempt to slide down, ride in, or sit on the miniature slide, car, or chair, respectively. Children aged 20 to 24 months were especially likely to make these errors. Figure 6.9 presents some photographs of scale errors.

A separate group of same-aged children, shown the large and small versions of the slide, car, and chair, were easily able to discriminate between them and knew which one they could actually slide down and so forth. So, perceptually, the children can see the difference between a large and a miniature version of the objects. How, then, are the scale errors to be accounted for?

Figure 6–9 Three examples of scale errors. (a) This 21-month-old child has committed a scale error by attempting to slide down a miniature slide. She has fallen off in an effort to carry out this impossible act. (b) This 24-month-old child has opened the door to the miniature car and is repeatedly trying to force his foot inside the car. (c) This 28-month-old child is looking between his legs to precisely locate the miniature chair that he is in the process of sitting on.

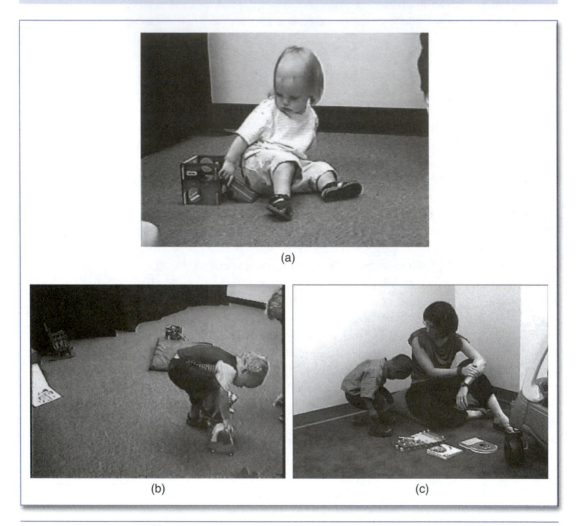

(a)

(b)   (c)

SOURCE: DeLoache, Uttal, & Rosengren (2004, p. 1027).

Interestingly, children worked hard to coordinate their actions with the size of the object. When interacting with a miniature car, for example, they would bend over or kneel down next to it and try a very precise grip to open the door, aiming their feet at the tiny opening.

DeLoache and her coauthors believe that the phenomenon of scale errors shows a dissociation between the perceptual system and the system controlling their actions. For the toddler or young preschooler, seeing a miniature object triggers the child's representation of the category of larger objects that the miniature object represents. So, for example, seeing a miniature chair activates the toddlers' representation of chairs. Included in this representation is the "motor program" for interacting with the object—that is, the typical behaviors one exhibits in relation to the object. For chairs, those behaviors typically include turning around and lowering one's bottom toward the seat of the chair.

Older preschoolers and adults at this point register the miniature size of the tiny objects and inhibit the motor program. However, younger children lack the ability to inhibit the program. Thus, they try to squeeze themselves into or onto objects where they just don't fit. Or, they try to stuff large dolls onto tiny chairs or into tiny cribs (Ware et al., 2006). DeLoache and colleagues speculate that scale errors may result from the immature functioning of the prefrontal cortex in the brain, which typically exerts inhibitory control over behavior. In addition, scale errors may signal that a brain area responsible for identifying objects, typically located in the primary visual cortex and projecting to the inferotemporal cortex, is dissociated from a second brain area, located in the posterior parietal cortex, which controls planning for movements of parts of the body.

ATTENTION AND EXECUTIVE FUNCTIONING

So far in this chapter we've looked at how preschool children interpret sensory information to come to an understanding of what a stimulus is and, perhaps, what it means. In the examples we've encountered, we have been assuming that the preschool child is in fact paying attention to whatever the stimulus is. It is time now to "unpack" this idea and explore what it means for a child (or an adult, for that matter) to "pay attention."

In Chapter 1 I said that cognitive psychologists define attention as the ability to allocate mental resources to certain tasks. Typically, this aspect of attention is known as **selective attention**—the ability to concentrate on, say, one stimulus in the environment, while simultaneously shutting out other, conflicting stimuli or resisting distracting temptations (Hanauer & Brooks, 2005; Ruff & Capozzoli, 2003). When I talk to my daughter while the radio is playing, for example, I am attending to our conversation while shutting out the music or lyrics.

Some tasks are harder for me to do than others. The harder the task, typically, the more attention I need to devote to it to get it done. So, for example, when I am driving in an unfamiliar neighborhood in the dark in bad weather, I don't have the cognitive resources left over to carry on a conversation. On the other hand, a relatively easy and well-practiced task, such as folding the laundry, is easy for me to do while I talk on the phone or watch TV. My ability to multitask, or to divide my attention across two tasks, is an aspect of attention known as divided attention.

As I become proficient at a task, it typically requires less attention to perform. This so-called practice effect is well known to cognitive psychologists. Take, for example, learning to write (print) your name. Chances are very good that at first this took a lot of your concentration and intense focus. Now, given that you've written your name so many times, you can probably do it easily while devoting attention elsewhere—for example, having a conversation, watching television, or humming a tune. Cognitive psychologists explain that with lots of practice, the performance of the task becomes more and more automatic—requiring fewer cognitive resources to carry out.

Photo 6.2 Some tasks can hold the attention of preschoolers for a surprisingly long period of time.

Development of Attention Spans

With this brief introduction to attentional concepts, we will now turn our focus to the question of how attention and attention spans develop in preschoolers. If you've ever hung around a preschooler, you know that their attention spans are typically short, and their ability to maintain focus is quite variable. A task that interests them can absorb their energy for quite a long time (my daughter at age 3 years once spent hours trying to feed a bunny at day care by holding up leaves to the side of the cage. Conversely, her interest in helping me rake leaves in the yard would typically last under 10 minutes).

In the laboratory, cognitive developmental psychologists study the development of attention with so-called *vigilance* tasks. In such a task the child watches a continuous stream of stimuli, each one presented very briefly, and is told to respond only to a certain infrequently occurring stimulus (Cooley & Morris, 1990). Figure 6.10 presents an example of a version of this vigilance task. Children view a series of pictures in this task, called the "Selector/Distractor" task. The target, a colored picture of a duck, is presented on 25% of the trials. The distractor, in this case a colored picture of a turtle, is presented on the remainder (75%) of the trials. Each picture is displayed for 500 milliseconds (a half-second), followed by a wait of another 500 milliseconds. After some practice trials (given to accustom the child to the apparatus and the procedure), each child sees four blocks of 24 stimuli each (96 stimuli total) in a task that lasts about 5 minutes (Akshoomoff, 2002).

In some studies, children under the age of about four and a half years have been found to do very poorly on the task—either not completing it at all or omitting lots of responses to the target stimuli (Akshoomoff, 2002). Of the children able to complete the task, older children (aged five to five and a half years) were significantly faster to respond than younger children (aged three and a half to almost four and a half years).

Of course, you might want to argue that children's performance on an arbitrary laboratory task is not indicative of their attentional abilities in other

Figure 6–10 Simple sequence of the stimuli used in the selective attention tasks. Arrows indicate target stimuli. Each stimulus measured approximately 3 × 3 cm.

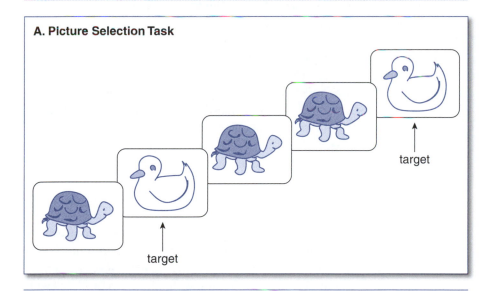

A. Picture Selection Task

target

target

SOURCE: Akshoomoff (2002, p. 631).

realms. If so, your argument would echo the findings of a study by Ruff, Capozzoli, and Weissberg (1998).

They studied the attention of preschoolers aged 30 to 54 months on three different tasks—watching a videotape, playing with toys, and performing a laboratory reaction time task. Their focus was children's sustained attention, which they defined as "the ability to mobilize and maintain selectivity and concentration" (p. 454). They were also interested in the question of individual differences—that is, whether some children were able to selectively attend to tasks more than other children across tasks.

Children first watched a videotaped "puppet show" consisting of 21 very short (15-second) skits involving puppets and dolls. The time interval between skits was variable and unpredictable—presenting each child with blank-screen gaps. Next, they performed the reaction time task, watching the videotape monitor for a rabbit and pushing a button as soon as it appeared. Last, the children were allowed to engage in a 10-minute free play period with toys provided by the experimenters.

For each task, the researchers measured the time a child spent looking at the monitor (or toys) or devoting focused attention to the monitor (or toys), meant to be a more intense kind of attention than simple looking. To measure focused attention, coders (watching videotaped sessions) relied on things the child said, the child's posture, interested facial expressions, reduced motor behaviors, and active scanning of the screen. They also measured *quiet inattention* (the duration of time a child looked away from the screen or toys) and *active inattention* (the time a child physically left the table he was supposed to sit at while performing the three tasks).

Focused attention rose with age in both the puppet show and free play tasks. Active inattention decreased dramatically over the three ages studied (30 months, 42 months, and 54 months), although quiet inattention was not significantly different for younger and older children, except in the reaction time task. The authors also noted that while attention does increase over the age range studied, increases in attention happen later on very structured tasks relative to unstructured ones. That is, attention during free play and television viewing tasks (which are relatively unstructured) showed bigger age-related changes between 30 and 42 months. In contrast, attention during the reaction time task (a structured task) showed most increases between 42 and 54 months. The authors concluded that "children in the preschool years generally become more interested in structured tasks and more willing to accept and follow instructions from adults; the results suggest that these changes translate into more prolonged attention and better performance" (Ruff et al., 1998, p. 462).

Moreover, attention in the puppet show was significantly correlated with attention in the free play task and reaction time tasks. This shows some attentional consistency in children across situations. However, the magnitude of significant correlations was only modest, suggesting that children's attention does differ significantly as a function of the task they are engaged with. Moreover, attention in the reaction time task was not significantly correlated with attention in the free play task. This in turn suggests that children's attention does vary with the task and, perhaps, with children's motivation to perform a task. That is, children in the preschool period may be showing increased willingness to perform tasks adults ask them to (such as the reaction task), rather than a better ability to pay attention in the context of such a task (Renninger & Wozniak, 1985).

Inhibitory Control

Maintaining a focus on a task at hand (especially a task that is not inherently interesting or absorbing for you) requires inhibitory control. That is, to maintain attention, you need to inhibit the temptation to let your mind wander, to look in another direction, to get up and leave, to start singing or telling stories or engaging in other off-task behavior. Inhibitory control is governed by the prefrontal cortex, along with other aspects of so-called executive functioning—self-regulation, planning, monitoring and modifying behavior, and maintaining attentional focus (Zelazo, Müller, Frye, & Marcovitch, 2003). The prefrontal cortex is not fully mature until young adulthood, and certain regions of it show dramatic changes between a child's second and seventh year (Huttenlocher, 1990).

You can see everyday examples of the difficulty preschoolers have with inhibitory control if you observe childhood games of "Red Light, Green Light" or "Simon Says." In these games, the children have to inhibit what is called a **prepotent response**. In "Red Light, Green Light," the prepotent response is running—the allowable behavior when the leader of the game declares a "green light." However, the signal "red light" is meant to evoke near instantaneous stopping, and preschoolers' frequent failure to stop quickly enough causes them to have difficulty with the game. In "Simon Says" the leader issues various commands—for example, "Touch your head." This command invites immediate action—but the preschooler has to inhibit it if the leader does not precede the command with "Simon says." Again, many preschoolers have trouble remembering this consistently enough to win the game.

Patricia Brooks and colleagues (Brooks, Hanauer, Padowska, & Rosman, 2003) studied a laboratory analog of children's inhibitory control games. They used a task called the "same–silly" card sorting task, based on the Dimensional Change Card Sort (DCCS) task (Frye, Zelazo, & Palfai, 1995).

Photo 6.3 In the childhood game "Red Light, Green Light," children have to inhibit the prepotent response of running when the leader calls "red light."

Children were instructed to sort cards into the piles indicated by target cards. So, for example, children saw two cards, one displaying a line drawing of a dog and the other displaying a line drawing of an airplane. In the "same" version of the task, children sorted all the cards with pictures of dogs on them into the pile with the target card displaying a dog and all the airplane cards into the pile containing the target airplane card. In the "silly" version of the task, children did just the opposite: putting the dog cards with the target airplane card and the airplane cards with the target dog card. Each child received five trials of either the "same" or the "silly" task in Phase 1 of the experiment, followed by Phase 2, five trials of the opposite kind of game (i.e., those who played the "silly" game in Phase 1 played the "same" game in Phase 2 and vice versa).

Even 3-year-olds (the youngest group tested) could sort the cards in either the "same" or the "silly" game, averaging about 77% correct sorting trials (children slightly older, closer to age 4, averaged about 97% correct). However, the performance of 3-year-olds was much less impressive in a subsequent experiment (with different children of the same ages) with more complex and colorful stimuli. In this experiment, the stimuli consisted of two kinds of cards, depicting socks and cups, that were colored either green or yellow. There were five cards depicting each of the following: yellow socks, green socks, yellow cups, and green cups. The colors of the cards were never mentioned to the child, and otherwise the same and silly games were explained the same way as in the previous experiment. So, for example, the child was told in the "same" version of this task to sort all the pictures of cups next to a picture of a cup and all the pictures of socks next to a picture of a sock. The "silly" version of this game worked just the opposite—cup pictures were sorted near the sock picture and vice versa. Notice here that once again the children are being asked to sort by shape, this time with the additional (implicit) requirement of ignoring the color of the object depicted on each card.

With this version of the game, only the older 4-year-olds could master the "silly" game. Even though the color was not relevant, and even though none of the children sorted the cards by color, the presence of color seemed enough to distract the younger 3-year-olds from the task at hand. Most children kept playing the "same" game even in the "silly" game condition. This suggested that the "same" responses were prepotent.

One explanation for this finding is that younger preschoolers suffer from **attentional inertia** (Kirkham, Cruess, & Diamond, 2003). That is to say younger preschoolers focus on one aspect of a stimulus display at a time (e.g., shape or color). Thus, when asked to sort cards in a way that requires them to inhibit a prepotent response (e.g., when asked to play the "silly" game), they have trouble doing so, especially if they simultaneously have to work to ignore distractions.

Notice here a connection to Piagetian theory, discussed earlier in the chapter. Piaget believed that preschoolers often became too "centered" in their perceptions—focusing only on one dimension of a stimulus and ignoring others. Attentional inertia might be another description for this inability to disengage attentional focus and redirect it elsewhere. With development of the prefrontal cortex, older preschoolers become more able to control the direction of their attention, which in turn enables them to perform more challenging tasks and to better resist or ignore distractions. This ability, in turn, allows the children a great deal more control over their cognitive activities and enables them to deal with more complexity.

TELEVISION VIEWING IN THE PRESCHOOL YEARS

So far we have treated perception and attention as completely independent cognitive activities. Of course, this is false. In the real world, these cognitive processes intertwine with each other and with other cognitive processes we have yet to examine, such as memory and language. One everyday activity in which preschoolers engage—television viewing—is a place where arguably perception and attention are two primary cognitive processes used, and we will pause in this section to consider television viewing in the preschool years.

Although children in our culture have exposure to many other different kinds of media, including computer games, the Internet, iPods, and radio, we will focus here on television because it is both more studied and more available to the preschooler in the average American home. Huston and Wright (1998) report a wide variation in the number of hours preschoolers watch television, with a range among the 320 preschoolers studied from 0 to 80 hours per week. On average, 3- to 5-year-olds watch about 2 hours a day (Wright et al., 2001). Viewing of educational programs, in particular, peaks at age 4 years.

In this section, we will focus attention on the effects of educational television such as *Sesame Street, Blue's Clues, Barney & Friends,* and other such shows that are targeted at preschoolers with the explicit goal of promoting either school readiness, prosocial interaction, or some combination of both.

Criticisms of television's effects on children, particularly preschool-aged children, have emerged since its introduction (as is the case, incidentally, with almost all new media—computers, video games, record players, iPods, etc.). These criticisms can be divided broadly into two categories: those that see the effects of any television viewing, regardless of content, and those that are aimed at certain kinds of television viewing (e.g., those that are content-specific; Anderson, Huston, Schmitt, Linebarger, & Wright, 2001).

General criticisms of television viewing generally fall into four overlapping categories: (a) the "displaced time" view, which argues that television viewing harms cognitive development because it takes away time from other, more beneficial leisure activities such as reading or pretense play; (b) the "cultivates passivity" view, which holds that because it takes so little effort to watch television, that activity instills a habit of passive, easy waiting for entertainment; (c) the "shallow information processing" view, which posits that the rapid pacing and short segments typical of many television shows result over time in shorter attention spans and difficulty sustaining focus; and (d) the "visual/iconic representation" view, which argues that television viewing selectively enhances visual information processing at the possible expense of verbal processing, which can lead to a lowered ability to imagine or infer information that is not explicitly presented (Huston & Wright, 1998).

Testing the effects of television viewing is tricky. A researcher could measure the amount of television children watch and correlate it with their attention span, the time they spend reading, or the imaginativeness of their play, for example. However, even if the correlation were strong, it would not determine the direction of causality. To establish causality, researchers sometimes study the effects of television viewing before and after television is introduced in remote parts of the world. In general, these studies (reviewed by Huston & Wright, 1998; see also Huston, Wright, Marquis, & Green, 1999) suggest very small negative effects for television viewing. For example, the amount of time spent on leisure reading has remained steady since 1945 (averaging about 15 minutes a day). The average correlation between television viewing and academic achievement is about −.05. There are few relationships reported between home television viewing and school readiness in the early years of schooling.

Of course, this lack of results might stem from the fact that there are different kinds of television to view, and there may be different effects of different kinds of viewing. Wright et al. (2001) divided television viewing into nine categories as shown in Table 6.1. This table also presents the mean number of weekly minutes preschoolers aged 3 to 5 years spent viewing each kind of program. By a large margin, preschoolers spend much more time watching cartoons and educational programs than any other type of program. It seems plausible that *what* preschoolers watch might be an important predictor of what the outcomes are (Kirkorian, Wartella, & Anderson, 2008).

Educational programs for young children, particularly preschoolers, have become more frequent since the 1970s. In the early 1990s, public policy changes mandated that television stations provide programming that serves the educational and informational needs of children. Interpretation of this mandate varies, but we will look in detail here at some clear cases of educational programs.

Sesame Street began broadcasting in November 1969. From the start the creators intended the show to help preschool children, particularly children from

Table 6–1   Number of minutes viewed per week by program type for 3- to 5-year-olds (N = 524)

	M	SD
Educational programs	240.44	281.42
Non-educational cartoons	320.05	339.54
Action programs	23.46	89.46
Comedy programs	67.42	141.87
Reality-based programs	4.45	26.66
Relationship drama programs	25.92	88.10
Fantasy programs	43.25	130.52
Sports programs	23.11	94.45
Other programs	14.05	62.55

SOURCE: Adapted from Wright et al. (2001, p. 38).

low-income and minority families, become ready for school—both academically and socially or emotionally (Fisch, 2004; Fisch, Truglio, & Cole, 1999). Academically, *Sesame Street* was intended to promote the following types of skills: letter and number recognition, names of shapes and body parts, sorting and classification skills, and knowledge of relational terms (e.g., *in, out, under, beside*). Early studies (reviewed by Fisch et al.) indicated significant gains in a sample of a thousand 3- to 5-year-olds who were either encouraged or not encouraged to watch the first season of the show. Before and after the show's first season, the children were given an extensive series of tests assessing the learning readiness skills described above.

Results showed significant gains for children who had watched *Sesame Street,* with the greatest gains exhibited by children who watched the show the most. Moreover, the concepts the show emphasized the most heavily that season (e.g., letter recognition) showed the area of greatest overall gains. A later study showed that teachers of children who had watched *Sesame Street* rated them higher than their non–*Sesame Street*–viewing classmates on such dimensions as verbal readiness, quantitative readiness, attitude toward school, and relationship with peers. The teachers did not know which children had been viewers and which had not. A 2-year longitudinal study following 3- to 5-year-olds found that watching *Sesame Street* was associated with vocabulary development when controlling for other factors such as parental education and number of siblings (Huston, Bickham, Lee, & Wright, 2007). A follow-up study of 570 adolescents who had participated as preschoolers in a study of television viewing showed that watching educational programs as preschoolers was associated with "higher grades, reading more books, placing more value on achievement, greater creativity, and less aggression" (Anderson et al., 2001, p. vii), with the results more consistent for boys than for girls.

Sesame Street is no longer the only television show aimed at nurturing preschool cognitive development, of course. In 1996, a show titled *Blue's Clues* emerged with the broad goal of teaching thinking skills:

Photo 6.4 *Sesame Street,* an educational television show for preschoolers, is aimed at promoting school readiness.

Blue's Clues is a think along, play along series specifically targeted to preschoolers. Steve, the one live character, lives in an animated world with his animated puppy, Blue. In every episode, Steve invites the home viewer in and then he and Blue set up the theme for the day. Blue wants to play Blue's Clues to figure out the problem that is set up. Throughout the episode, Blue leaves her paw print on three objects (clues) from which the child viewer is invited to make an inference about the solution. Along the way, obstacles in the form of educational games are encountered. Each game utilizes a multilayered approach to learning that provides increasingly challenging content that is developmentally appropriate for the 2- to 5-year-old audience. (Anderson et al., 2000, p. 181)

Anderson et al. (2000) report a longitudinal study of children who either did or did not watch *Blue's Clues*. Viewers performed better than nonviewers on a variety of tests of specific concepts covered in the program, including relational concepts, sequencing, patterning, and transformations; on solving "riddles" characteristic of those used on the program; and on some other measures of problem solving that were not specifically tied to the program. In another study, preschool viewers who watched the same episode of *Blue's Clues* over a 5-day period showed little decline in attention but rather more interaction with the episode (e.g., answering questions, pointing at the screen) with repetition (Crawley, Anderson, Wilder, Williams, & Santomero, 1999).

Educational television aimed at preschoolers does not focus exclusively on academic skills, such as letter or number recognition, however. Singer and Singer (1998) report on their studies of the program *Barney & Friends,* which premiered in 1993. The *Barney* show also reviews academic concepts but places a heavier emphasis on other types of skills and desiderata, including emotional awareness, social and constructive attitudes (including promotion of the values of sharing, turn-taking,

Photo 6.5   *Blue's Clues* is an educational television show aimed at teaching early thinking skills to preschoolers.

Photo 6.6 The educational television show *Barney & Friends* emphasizes emotional awareness and development.

cooperation, and self-control), and multi-cultural exposure.

Singer and Singer (1998) trained graduate and undergraduate students to rate episodes of *Barney & Friends* by a variety of variables: cognitive, social or emotional, cultural, and physical. Based on the ratings they were able to assign scores to different episodes based on how educationally "rich" they were. They later interviewed preschoolers who had just viewed one of these episodes and asked them to recall it. The findings showed that children comprehended best those episodes that had been previously rated by the graduate and undergraduate students as having the most educational elements.

Preschool viewers showed gains after watching *Barney & Friends* on such measures as counting, matching numbers, identifying colors, and vocabulary growth. Additionally, they also showed gains on awareness of manners and knowledge of the neighborhood. Singer and Singer (1998) note that the preschooler viewers showed enthusiastic responses to the videos, often jumping up to join in the dances, singing along, or shouting out the name of characters as they appeared. They write:

> The general positive feeling that characterized the children's responses to the show seems to these investigators to reflect a national phenomenon, a type of yearning of preschoolers for the good feeling and security offered by Barney and his child friends. To see as many as 10 or 12 child viewers holding hands, singing the *I Love You* song and embracing each other at the end of a viewing without adult coaxing (as has occurred in the dozens of observations) is a powerful message to us all. (Singer & Singer, 1998, p. 339)

None of these results are to be taken as endorsement of constant television viewing by preschoolers of all ages. Indeed, concerns over heavy television usage, the effects of watching non-educational cartoons, and television viewing by children under the age of 2 years have all been reported (Anderson & Pempek, 2005; Peters & Blumberg, 2002; Vandewater et al., 2005). However, the general point here is that certain educational television programs, designed for preschoolers, can have beneficial effects for both their cognitive and their social development.

Thus far we have focused on attention and perception in preschool children. To round out the cognitive picture, we will need to consider other cognitive processes such as memory, knowledge representation, thinking, and problem solving. As we will see in Chapters 7 and 8, these cognitive capacities also undergo dramatic transformations during early childhood.

SUMMARY

1. Early childhood is traditionally defined as the period covering the ages of two and a half to about six years.

2. Piaget called this the "preoperational" stage of development. According to his theory, preschoolers gain the capacity for mental representation, thus being able to store memories, comprehend and produce language, think without acting on their thoughts, and use symbols, unlike younger toddlers and infants. At the same time, preoperational children lack mental operations and thus, according to Piaget, are bound by their perceptions—they have no way to order and structure their knowledge except by relying on what their senses tell them is true.

3. Vygotsky takes a different view of cognitive development in early childhood. He views the development of mental structures as a by-product of social and environmental interactions. Vygotsky also invokes the concept of the zone of proximal development to describe a mechanism by which children practice with and refine their emerging cognitive structures, using scaffolding from adults or older children, or in play.

4. Kemler Nelson describes preschoolers as holistic processors of perceptual information—using overall similarity, rather than values on any specific dimension, to categorize. Older children and adults, she argues, are more likely to perceive analytically.

5. Some work by Carey and Diamond suggests, in contrast, that preschoolers perceive faces using features, focusing on individual parts (e.g., an eye, a nose), rather than configurally, as do adults and older children, focusing on the relationships among features. Later work has called into question the conclusion that preschoolers and older people perceive faces differently.

6. Preschoolers learn to use a variety of symbols during early childhood—including words, letters, and numbers. DeLoache's work suggests that during this period children show a great deal of development in their ability to use scale models to represent larger spaces. According to DeLoache, older preschoolers learn to use dual representation—to mentally represent the model both as its own object and as an abstract symbol.

7. Children under the age of four to four and a half years tend to show shorter attention spans on vigilance tasks. On tasks they find inherently interesting, such as playing with toys or watching a videotape, their attention spans are longer. However, even with interesting and engaging tasks, younger preschoolers show less attention and are more distracted than are older preschoolers.

8. Preschoolers develop more inhibitory control as they develop. They become better able to stop themselves from emitting prepotent responses. This control in turn better equips them to sustain attention, to resist distraction, and even to play more competitively in games such as "Simon Says" and "Red Light, Green Light." Inhibitory control is thought to stem from developments in the prefrontal cortex.

9. Television viewing is a popular activity for many American preschoolers. Some research suggests that specially designed educational programs targeted at preschoolers, such as *Sesame Street, Blue's Clues,* and *Barney & Friends,* can promote learning of academic and social or emotional concepts, thus enhancing some aspects of school readiness.

REVIEW QUESTIONS

1. Compare and contrast Piaget's account of cognitive development in early childhood with that of Vygotsky.

2. What does it mean to perceive information analytically versus holistically? How accurate is it to describe the typical preschooler's perception as either holistic or analytic? Explain.

3. Review DeLoache's work on preschoolers' ability to use scale models. What might this tell us about preschool cognitive development?

4. Define the term *executive functioning* as it applies to attentional development in preschoolers.

5. Childhood games such as "Simon Says" and "Red Light, Green Light" are fun and challenging for preschoolers. Explain, from a cognitive developmental standpoint, why this might be so.

6. What is attentional inertia, and how might it explain the performance of preschoolers on certain cognitive tasks?

7. What conclusions can be drawn (and what conclusions should be resisted) from your reading of the research of preschoolers viewing educational television programs?

KEY TERMS

Attentional Inertia

Conservation

Divided Attention

Dual Representation

Prepotent Response

Selective Attention

CHAPTER 7

EARLY CHILDHOOD

Memory and Conceptual Development

When psychologists think about cognitive processes, memory is certainly one of the first to come to mind. How people encode, store, and retrieve information about the past is central to so many different aspects of their lives. As we saw in Chapter 4, infants and toddlers have a surprising amount of competence even with recall memory from about 9 months onward. However, early memories are fragile and hard to access.

In this chapter, we will continue our discussion of memorial development that we began in Chapter 4. We'll begin by talking about capacity and processes and then turn our attention to preschoolers' strategic approaches to memory tasks. We'll also examine autobiographical memories—the sort of thing your earliest memory exemplifies.

We will also see, however, that personal narrative memories are not the only things stored. Indeed, to become a cognitively competent being, a child has to store information about the world—facts, word meanings, "common-sense" knowledge, and a host of other like entities. Collectively, these form the knowledge base, an important part of memory. Ideas in this knowledge base are often referred to as concepts, so it will be a natural segue to examine preschoolers' conceptual development here.

THEORETICAL PERSPECTIVES

Memory development seems to take a great leap forward during the preschool period. If you think about your earliest reliable memory, you are likely to find that it dates back to the time you were a preschooler (Howe, 2000). This in turn implies that it is not until children reach the preschool years that they will be able to form durable memory traces that will persist for the rest of their lives.

A View From Information-Processing Theory

We reviewed information-processing theory in a general way in Chapter 2, and in Chapter 4, we saw how parts of it apply to the study of infant memory development. You'll recall that in both places, we discussed the view held by early information-processing theorists that the basic cognitive architecture children have shares many similarities with the architecture of a computer. Most significantly, the idea was that people have a variety of memory stores that hold information for some period of time. These memory stores can have information transferred in or out of them, and information can also be transformed while being held in a particular store.

Debates within this field center over questions of how many stores there are and what defines the differences, if any. Some theorists have argued for different memory stores based on the length of time information is stored—distinguishing long-term from short-term memory, for example (Atkinson & Shiffrin, 1968; Baddeley, 1986). We saw in Chapter 4 some other proposals, in particular ones that distinguish implicit from explicit memory—that is, memory storage for things people aren't consciously aware they are storing versus storage for those things they are (Roediger, 1990). Other information-processing theorists have argued that the evidence supports only one central memory store, with different kinds of processing done on the information at the time of encoding (Craik & Lockhart, 1972).

Here, we will consider another proposal for distinct memory stores. Recall the proposal of Endel Tulving (1972). In his view, there are two separate memory stores in long-term memory—one that contains information about general knowledge and one that contains memory traces of information from one's personal experience. Episodic memory is thought to contain your memories that trace to a specific event—your recollection of your third birthday party or the time you visited Disneyland—in other words, memories for events that you remember occurring at a particular time and place (even if you don't remember exactly what that time and place was). Semantic memory, in contrast, contains your general knowledge—for example, that Harry Potter is a fictional wizard, that George Washington was the first president of the United States, or that kids usually carry backpacks to elementary school. We will make use of the episodic–semantic distinction throughout this chapter.

MEMORY DEVELOPMENT

Cognitive psychologists often consider different aspects of memory separately, in order to break a vast topic into manageable parts. One can consider memory capacity—that is, how much information can be stored. One can also consider memory *processes*—the cognitive activities that contribute to a memory trace being formed, being stored, being transformed, or being retrieved. Strategies refer to a person's deliberate plans to form or retrieve memory traces. Metacognition includes strategies but also one's other knowledge of how memory works and how it fails. To simplify our presentation, we'll take up each of these topics in turn.

Memory Capacity

I hope that you'll recall from Chapter 4 that many cognitive psychologists make a distinction between working memory, which holds information currently being processed, and long-term memory, which acts as a sort of archive for all the stored information you can access but are not currently using. One reason for making this distinction has to do with the differential capacities of the two memory stores. Long-term memory is thought to be virtually limitless, at least for adults. After all, we add information into long-term memory throughout our lives, and it never seems to get filled up.

Working memory, in contrast, is thought to have very stringent limits. Adults were shown in a classic paper (Miller, 1956) to be able to retain about seven unrelated pieces of information, without rehearsal, for up to about a minute. This "magical number seven" (plus or minus two) is often referred to as the "span" of immediate memory (Dempster, 1981). In a typical "memory span" experiment, participants are presented with a list of items (usually random digits or letters) at the rate of one every second. The first list presented is usually short (for adults, three items), and each successive list has one additional item. The participants are asked to report the list of items in order. Their span is defined as the longest list they can reliably (e.g., more than 50% of the time) report (Dempster, 1981). In adults, digit spans are moderately to highly correlated with other subtests on intelligence assessments and with other scholastic achievement tests such as the SAT.

Spans for children are smaller than spans for adolescents and adults, as the data presented in Figure 7.1 make clear. For digit span, the span most frequently studied, the average 2-year-old has a span of a little more than two, whereas 5-year-olds' "magical number" is about four and a half. Findings from word span studies show similar patterns (letter span studies aren't typically conducted with preschool-aged children, who may not recognize letters yet).

Why be concerned about children's memory spans? Recent studies suggest a connection between working memory span and executive functioning, a topic explored in Chapter 6. Espy and Bull (2005) reported that preschool children with higher and lower digit spans also differed in their performance on attentional control tasks. Those children with higher spans—that is, more working memory capacity—were better able to shift their attention from one set of responses to another as a task demanded. Put another way, bigger memory spans are correlated with a child's ability to disengage attention from one task and redeploy it to another. Children with lower memory spans have a harder time "forgetting" the old rules of the game and using new ones when the rules change.

Alloway and Gathercole (2005) have also showed that preschoolers with higher digit and word span scores were better able to remember sentences than children with lower spans, who were more likely to omit or insert words

Figure 7–1   Developmental differences in digit span, word span, and letter span

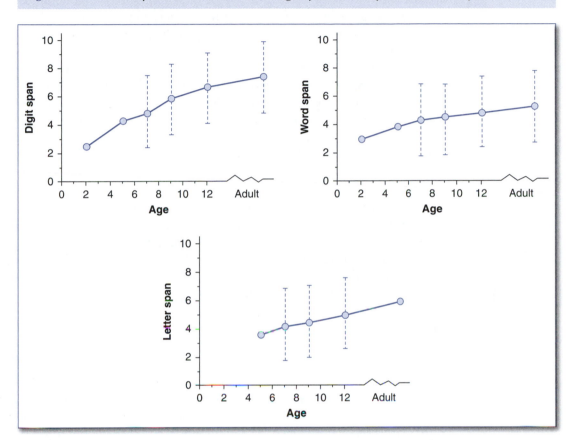

SOURCE: Dempster (1981, pp. 66–68).

or to reorder words in the sentences they tried to recall. More broadly, Alloway, Gathercole, Willis, and Adams (2004) review several studies in which measures of preschoolers' working memory capacities predict their scholastic abilities as measured by standardized tests 3 years later. It has also been seen as playing a very important role in children's vocabulary acquisition (Baddeley, Gathercole, & Papagano, 1998).

Memory Strategies and Metacognition

One of the most striking memorial developments in preschoolers is that their memory becomes more intentional, more explicit, and more strategic. If you were to have asked my then 3-year-old children to remember a list of items to buy, say, at a grocery store, they would likely have cheerfully listened to your list (however long) and then gone off and promptly forgotten most items. My daughter in particular might have entered the grocery store and sworn up and down that the list contained only the following items: M&M's, PEZ candy, animal crackers, vitamin water, lemonade, and candy kisses. I base this supposition both on my own interactions with my kids and on the results of a very similar study reported by Z. M. Istomina, a Russian psychologist (1982). Preschoolers simply don't have much of a clue about how well their memories will work or what their capacity limitations are. To use a more formal term, preschoolers have less *metacognition*, or knowledge about how their cognitive processes—in this case, memory—work. As a result, when they are in a situation in which they have to use their memories, they don't take actions that might help them remember.

This phenomenon was demonstrated in some classic studies undertaken by John Flavell and his associates. Flavell, Beach, and Chinsky (1966) conducted the first study, with children in kindergarten and the second and fifth grades. Each child was shown two sets of seven pictures and was asked to point to the pictures in the same order that the experimenter did. In one condition, the wait was 15 seconds between the time the experimenter finished pointing and the time the child was asked to re-create the order. The children wore special "space helmets" that prevented them from looking at the pictures or seeing the experimenter but allowed one of the experimenters (who was a trained lip reader) to observe whether they were verbalizing the items they had to remember. Very few of the kindergarten participants showed evidence of rehearsing the items to be remembered; a little more than half of the second graders and almost all of the fifth graders showed evidence of using rehearsal as a technique to remember the order of pictures.

Why didn't younger students rehearse the information? A number of possible explanations came to mind. One was called a **mediation deficiency** (Reese, 1962). This explanation held that even if children were forced to use a rehearsal strategy, it would not work—the strategy would not improve (or, in the language of learning theory, *mediate)* their performance. A second possibility is that children have a **production deficiency**—that is, they use and benefit by the strategy when made to use it, but they don't spontaneously think to use it.

A study by Keeney, Cannizzo, and Flavell (1967) tested these ideas. Using a similar procedure to Flavell et al. (1966), the researchers first identified 6- and 7-year-old "rehearsers" and "nonrehearsers." They found once again that rehearsers performed significantly better in recalling information than same-aged nonrehearsers. When the nonrehearsers were later trained to rehearse, their performance became indistinguishable from that of the initial "rehearsers." However, when left to their own devices, the initial "nonrehearsers" abandoned the rehearsal strategy. This seemed to constitute good evidence for a production deficiency explanation—younger children *can* make use of strategies but are much less likely to spontaneously think to use the strategies in the first place.

A third type of deficiency—called a **utilization deficiency**—was later identified (Miller, 1990). It is somewhat like a mixture of the two other deficiencies described above. It occurs in the early stages of a child learning a new strategy, when a child spontaneously produces and tries to use the new strategy but does not realize the gain in performance that other, experienced strategy users do. Put a little more simply, the idea is that when younger children first start using a new strategy, it doesn't work as smoothly or as efficiently as it does for children who've had more practice or experience with the strategy.

Figure 7.2 depicts the development of a strategy and its effect on recall. Initially, young children show no evidence of a strategy (Point A). The age at which this occurs depends on how sophisticated the strategy is—the more sophisticated the strategy, the later its first use occurs. Next, a child first spontaneously produces the strategy (Point B). This may actually cause a small decline in performance, as implementation of the strategy takes energy and attention, which are diverted away from the task at hand. Gradually, the child's continued use of the strategy becomes more efficient and more effective, which in turn results in higher performance (Points C, D, and E). Miller and Seier (1994) review evidence regarding utilization deficiencies in dozens of memory studies, although Schneider, Kron, Hünnerkopf, and Krajewski (2004) offer some critiques of Miller's ideas.

Tasks that require fewer strategic approaches typically are ones that show fewer developmental differences between older and younger children. Recognition memory tasks, for example, typically show fewer pronounced age differences than do recall memory tasks. If you have a younger sibling or you babysit, for example, you might have noticed that preschoolers can perform extremely well—as good or better than you, quite possibly—on memory games such as *Concentration* (Baker-Ward & Ornstein, 1988). Apparently, recognition memory for spatial location is especially good in preschoolers. (If you've forgotten this game, it works roughly like this. A special deck of cards is used that contains pairs of matching pictures—let's say, 24 pairs for a total of 48. These are shuffled and dealt across a table, face down. Player A selects two cards and turns them face up, showing the pictures. If they match, Player A takes them and keeps them. If not, the two cards are turned back over, and it becomes Player B's turn. The player who identifies the greatest number of pairs wins.)

Figure 7–2   Amount of recall as a function of level of development of a strategy. (A) No strategy; (B) initial strategy production; (C, D, E) later strategy production.

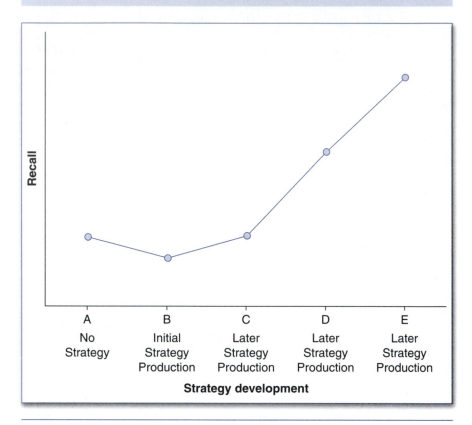

SOURCE: Miller & Seier (1994, p. 108).

Tasks that offer fewer cues are the ones that may require more strategies and are the ones for which preschoolers show poorer performance. Recalling unstructured lists of words is one example. There are several strategies adults bring to bear on some tasks. Rehearsal, as already discussed, is one. There are various kinds of rehearsal, actually, and the one we've described, where the learner repeats the stimuli several times, is typically called *maintenance rehearsal.*

Another strategy that can be used is called *organization.* To illustrate, imagine that I read you the following list of words: *tiger, apple, bicycle, grapes, train, orange, gorilla, sailboat, banana, giraffe, car, hippopotamus.* This list has 12 items, and it would typically be quite challenging, even

Photo 7.1   Playing memory games such as Concentration builds recognition memory for spatial locations.

for you, to remember 12 items if you weren't able to write them down. However, clever you have probably already noticed something about this list, namely, that it contains three different categories of things—fruits, animals, and vehicles. If you try to organize the items into these categories, it will make recalling the items easier, and you may even recall the entire list! Most preschoolers fail to use organization spontaneously but can use it effectively if prompted to do so sometimes. However, this strategy often shows a utilization deficiency when it first appears (Schneider & Bjorklund, 1998).

Event Memory and Scripts

Many of the experimental studies described above looked at young children's recall of disconnected pieces of information—words on a list or a sequence of pictures. In the real world, however, memory also occurs for connected information—such as information for events. When you remember, say, your 10-year-old birthday party, you remember it not just in terms of lists (who came, what presents you received, what games or other activities were played, what food was served) but rather in a more coherent and even story-like format known to cognitive psychologists as a script.

The pioneering work of developmental psychologist Katherine Nelson (1986; Nelson & Gruendel, 1981) showed that preschoolers form and use scripts to recall events, too. In fact, Nelson argued that children's scripts are the basic building blocks of children's mental representations and memories.

Nelson (1986) pointed out that children directly experience most of the events they know about. While older children and adults learn about the world through books, lectures, the Internet, and other sources, these are less available to younger children, especially those with limited literacy skills. Therefore, children's scripts seem a natural basis for them to use to store world knowledge and form memory traces.

So what are scripts? Nelson (1986) contrasted them with both abstract concepts (a kind of representation we will look at later in this chapter) and specific memories (such as the autobiographical memories we will turn to next). Scripts are a form of schemas, which are organized representations of knowledge that often contain both fixed and variable parts (Mandler, 1983; Rumelhart & Ortony, 1977).

Consider a schema for the concept of *chair.* The fixed part would include the information that a chair is a piece of furniture, has (typically) four legs, and is a place for people to sit; the variables would be things like color, or style (armchair, kitchen chair, desk chair, beanbag chair), or size (toy, child-sized, extra large, etc.). You might think of a schema as a sort of questionnaire with blanks to fill in. Labels next to the blanks indicate what sort of information to fill in (Just & Carpenter, 1987).

Scripts are schemas for events. Defined formally, a script is a "temporally and causally organized event representation constructed from experience in the real world that specifies appropriate action sequences in particular contexts" (Slackman, Hudson, & Fivush, 1986, pp. 48–49). They are best explained with another example. Stop for a moment and think about what happens when you go to McDonald's to eat. Your answer to this question constitutes your script for that event.

Here's my script for going to McDonald's: Enter, holding hand of 8-year-old daughter (as we've just crossed the parking lot with a lot of cars zooming through and she's short). Stand in line. Persuade daughter and son (aged 16) to tell me what they want before they run off to play video games with Ronald (daughter) or grab a newspaper section (son). Wait in line (at busy times), and when I get in front of cashier, give order. Pay, and move to the side while my order is assembled. Watch and count to be sure the right items are placed on the tray. Carry tray to table. Scold son for not coming to assist. Intervene in any ongoing dispute between daughter and son. Hand

Photo 7.2   Most American preschoolers have constructed a script for familiar events, such as eating out at a fast-food restaurant.

cups to son and request that he go to get drinks. Remind son *not* to fill my drink with some ungodly concoction. Remind son to also bring back ketchup and napkins and straws.

Hand out food items to daughter, son, and myself. Unwrap Happy Meal toy for daughter. Encourage daughter to eat something besides fries. Attempt to discuss the day's events with son. Encourage daughter to eat a little faster. Encourage son to stop wolfing his food. Eat my sandwich and salad. Steal a fry or two from daughter when she's paying attention to her Happy Meal toy. Clean up trash. Encourage daughter to eat a little faster. Attempt to stop son from picking fight with daughter over how slow she eats. Ignore son's rolled eyes and sarcastic remarks on this theme. Gather up purse and Happy Meal toy, find car keys, take daughter by hand, and leave.

Now, I expect that my script differs from yours in many different ways, as you do not have my two children accompanying you on your McDonald's trips (for this, you may be very grateful!). And, your local restaurant may not offer video games. So, one aspect of scripts is that they will vary from individual to individual, depending on circumstances. But I would wager a good sum of money that your McDonald's script also has episodes of ordering, paying, bringing food to a table, gathering supplies and getting drinks, eating, and cleaning up. I would further expect that my daughter's script would differ from mine (and yours) in that it would be much less likely to include episodes of ordering, paying, or cleaning up—she's rarely around for these transactions (being busy with video games or her Happy Meal toy).

Nelson and Gruendel (1981) studied the scripts of preschool children. They asked children to describe their knowledge of familiar routines, such as "What happens when you go to day care?" or "Tell me what happens when you make cookies." In response to the latter request, they obtained a variety of responses from children of different ages, ranging from "Well, you bake them and eat them" (a 3-year-old) to "First you need a bowl, a bowl, and you need about two eggs and chocolate chips and an egg beater! And then you gotta crack the egg open and put it in a bowl and ya gotta get the chips and mix it together. And put it in a stove for about 5 or 10 minutes, and then you have cookies. Then ya eat them!" (a child of 8 years, 8 months; p. 135).

Notice a few things here. First, clearly even 3-year-olds have some knowledge of this event. Second, notice how the children use temporal links from one step to another—for example, "*First* you do X, *then* you do Y, and *after that* you do Z." This use of temporal links is one way to distinguish scripts (event schemas) from other types of schemas.

One trend that appears with development is that the scripts become longer and more elaborate. Fivush and Slackman (1986) also showed that as children become more familiar with an event (e.g., if the event is "going to kindergarten" and children are tested repeatedly as the school year goes on), their scripts also become more complex, specifying more conditional information, such as "If it's raining, we play indoors" (Fivush, 1984). Children's organization becomes more hierarchical as they specify more options or choices for different activities (e.g., "I can play house, or I can draw, or I can read a book, until circle time"). Their organization also becomes more abstract, and when describing their script they mention fewer details specific to a certain day's activity. Table 7.1 provides examples of kindergarteners' scripts as the school year unfolds.

Nelson (1986) argued that scripts help support many cognitive activities, including comprehension, memory, and conversation. Scripts are said to provide the child with a "cognitive context" with which to interpret actions, events, and people in a situation. Especially because younger children appear to perform at their cognitive best only in certain contexts, it is important to learn which aspects of the context help or hinder them. Nelson believed that having a script is one important factor that helps children, especially preschool children, perform at their best.

Table 7–1   Kindergarteners' scripts on the second day of school and in the second, fourth, and tenth weeks of school

Kindergarteners' Scripts on the Second Day of School

"Play, Say hello to the teacher and then you do reading or something. You can do anything you want to… Clean up and then you play some more and then clean up and then play some more and then clean up. And then you do the gym or playground. And then you go home. Home your lunch and go home. You go out the school and you ride on the bus or train and go home."

"I just go to school. Then we do stuff. And then we have lunch or snack and then we go home… We play a little and then we go to the gym sometimes, or else we can go to the playground. And then we have snack and then, in an hour, we have lunch, And then we can draw a picture or read and then we go home."

Kindergarteners' Scripts During the Second Week of School

"We do art things. You go back in the class. Then we play. Then when the bell, we have a little bell in there, and when the bell rings, we go in the meeting. Like you sit in the square. Then we have snack. Then we go out to the minigym and then we come back. And we do some math. And then we have lunch. Then we play a little bit. We have nap. No, we don't, play a little. After lunch, we have nap. And then we get our stuff. Then we go on the bus or someone picks us up. But I always go on the bus."

"Well, we have to turn our name over. And then all you could do your handwriting, or something like that, or your could play games. But the really first thing, you have to turn your name over. I mean, the really first thing, you have to put your stuff in the locker. And then you have to turn your name over. That's the first thing. And then we could start playing, or doing our handwriting. And then after we do our handwriting we could play again. And then she tells us to clean up. And then we have to sit on the blue line [for meeting]. And then we have snack. And then we, after that, we can play again. And then after we play, you have to clean up and go to lunch. Then we could write stuff after that. And then we go to nap time. I mean, after that, we go to nap time. And then after we wake up, then we could play for a few minutes or play outside or something like that. And then our mothers take us home."

Kindergarteners' Scripts During the Fourth Week of School

"You have to put our stuff in the locker. And then we have to turn over our home. And then sometimes we can play. And then we have to sit on the blue line. And then we have, or we could do our handwriting. Then we have snack. Then after snack we can play again. At snack, we have to, the teacher reads us a story. And then after that, we play again. And then after that we eat lunch, and then after that we take a nap. And then we take our reading jobs. And then after that, we go home."

(Continued)

Table 7–1 (Continued)

"You have to put your things away. And then you can't play outside, you have to go inside. We have circle, and then we have reading jobs. Then we have free play time, and then snack time, and then minigym. Then lunchtime, then rest time. Then it's time to go downstairs [for after-school day-care]."

Kindergarteners' Scripts During the Tenth Week of School

"I turn over my name. I do my handwriting. If I have time I do my art project. Then we have meeting time. Then we have math time. Then we have another meeting with snack. Then sharing if it's Friday. If not, story with snack. And sharing if it's Friday. After snack and story, minigym. Go to the bathroom, have lunch, then you get a little play time. And then lunch, And then we have Ron's [science class] or nap."

"I put my things away. Play. And then I turn over my name. And then I go to an activity until the teacher comes in. Play, meeting, reading jobs, meeting again, math jobs, snack. Then after, then minigym. And then lunch. And then we have, then we go home."

SOURCE: Fivush & Slackman (1986, pp. 78, 82–83).

Autobiographical Memory

Another striking facet of memorial development in early childhood is the beginning of autobiographical memory—that is, memory of one's personal experiences and history—of "events that happened to *me*" (Howe, Courage, & Edison, 2003). We saw in Chapter 4 that infants can show good evidence of recognition memory, and there is even some suggestion of limited recall memory. But the emergence of what Howe (2000) calls "the cognitive self" happens during the preschool period and is marked by the first appearance of personally experienced event memories. Here, we are talking about children's recollection of a specific event, not their recall of what generally happens in a routine event (Nelson & Fivush, 2004).

Many researchers credit children's language development as enabling autobiographical memories to be encoded and retrieved (Schneider & Bjorklund, 1998). Others attribute the emergence of autobiographical memory to more general development in the cognitive spheres (Howe, 2000; Howe et al., 2003; Perner & Ruffman, 1995). Still others rest their explanations on the idea that autobiographical memories require social collaboration, especially talking about past events with others (Fivush & Haden, 2003; Nelson & Fivush, 2004). Those adopting this last stance tend to see the emergence of "true" autobiographical memories as coming later—say, at the latter part of the preschool period (Nelson, 2003).

One important factor in the development of autobiographical memory is the way parents (usually mothers) converse with their child to jointly recall a past event. Such collaborative conversations certainly show evidence of the Vygotskian idea of scaffolding, which we reviewed in Chapter 6. With very young children, parents have to do a lot of the work of remembering, offering a lot of prompts, cues, and specific queries to help point the child toward the correct memory trace. But the way in which parents talk with their children about past events varies quite a bit. One aspect of this variation is in the amount of *narrative structure* the parent provides. This has been called the degree of *elaborativeness* of the conversation.

To illustrate, consider the conversations shown in Table 7.2. Note that both the high-elaborative and low-elaborative mothers talk a lot to their

Table 7–2   Examples of high- and low-elaborative parents across early childhood

High-elaborative mother	Low-elaborative mother
40 months old	
Mother: What was near the ocean that you played with? *Child:* I don't know. *Mother:* Do you remember that we used to walk, we used to walk on the beach and... *Child:* Um hmm, Mommy. *Mother:* And what did we pick up? *Child:* I don't know. *Mother:* You don't remember? *Child:* You tell me. *Mother:* Remember we pick up sea... *Child:* Uh huh. *Mother:* ...shells. Remember all the seashells we collected?	*Mother:* Who else was with us? Think about who was in the car, when we went... *Child:* Tyler (younger brother). *Mother:* Did Tyler go with us? *Child:* Yeah. *Mother:* No, Tyler didn't go with us. Who else went? Did Daddy go? *Child:* Yeah. *Mother:* He did? Now think about who was in the car the day we went. *Child:* You and Daddy did. *Mother:* Daddy wasn't there. What was sitting up front with Mommy?
8 years old	
Mother: Do you remember any animals at that zoo that we don't have at our zoo?	*Mother:* Do you remember last summer When we were in Mount Eagle? *Child:* I think.

Table 7–2 (Continued)

High-elaborative mother	Low-elaborative mother
8 years old	
Child: Umm, cheetahs.	*Mother:* Well, Andrew and Emma and All of them were there.
Mother: Yeah. Oh, I remember one.	*Child:* Yeah.
Child: What?	*Mother:* And Lisa...
Mother: Kinda' big.	*Child:* Um hmm.
Child: Oh, white white tiger.	*Mother:* ...brought out some...
Mother: Yeah, that's right. They had white tigers... You know what? We may not have seen them now that I think about it. The hippos. Were the hippos out?	*Child:* Shaving cream. We had a shaving cream fight. I covered myself, but I...
Child: I don't think so. Oh, the kangaroos.	*Mother:* Tell me about that. How did you do all that?
Mother: Oh yeah! They had kangaroos, didn't they?	*Child:* You know, you were there.
Child: Um hmm.	*Mother:* Well, I wasn't down there. I was just watching.
Mother: I forgot about that.	*Child:* So, you were still there.

SOURCE: Nelson & Fivush (2004, p. 498).

children and ask a lot of questions. And, mothers of the younger children provide much more structure than do mothers of the older ones. What distinguishes the high- and low-elaborative conversations is the degree to which there is narrative, or story-like, structure:

Note that in the conversation between the highly elaborative mother and her child, there is a sense of story; with each conversational turn, this mother continues to tell another piece of the story until the entire episode is recollected, even though [for the 40-month-old child] the child contributes little to the emerging narrative. Contrast this with the low-elaborative mother. When her child does not recall any information, this mother repeats the same questions over and over and then simply switches topic. By the end of the preschool years [i.e., when the child is 8], the highly elaborative mother and her child coconstruct a rich story of a shared experience. Together they weave in details and embellishments about what occurred, creating a coherent and complex shared narrative. Again, in contrast, although the older child of the low-elaborative mother contributes to the reminiscing, the conversation takes place in a question-and-answer format, with little attention to creating a shared story of a shared past. (Nelson & Fivush, 2004, p. 498)

Mothers' elaborativeness turns out to be an important factor in the development of autobiographical memory. Reese, Haden, and Fivush (1993) conducted a longitudinal study of children when they were 40 months, 46 months, 58 months, and 70 months of age. At each point, the mothers of the children talked with them about three specific past shared experiences, and these conversations were coded for maternal elaborativeness and child recall. Both of these were defined as the degree to which the child or mother provided new information to the conversation. The authors correlated these measures over time, and the results are presented in Figure 7.3.

Figure 7–3   Significant correlations among maternal levels of elaboration and children's memory responses over time

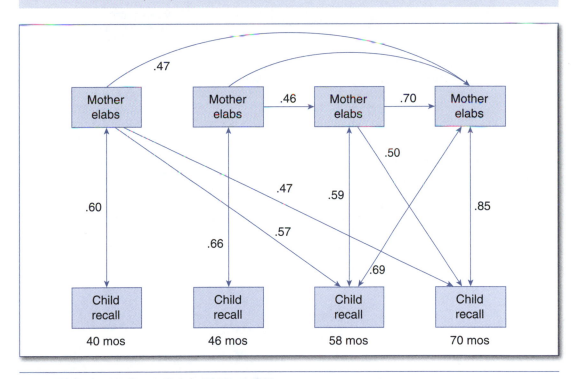

SOURCE: Reese, Haden, & Fivush (1993, p. 420).
NOTE: *elabs* = elaborations; *mos* = months.

Note that maternal elaboration and child recall are highly correlated at each time period (vertical arrows in the figure). The correlations range from .59 to .85. More important, the mothers' degree of elaboration when their children are 40 months old correlates moderately with the degree of child recall 18 to 30 months later! This means that the way mothers converse with their young children about events has a "long-standing relationship with the way in which children come to be able to recall their own past experience" (Reese et al., 1993, p. 424).

Nelson and Fivush (2004) present a more general model of the development of autobiographical memory, reproduced in Figure 7.4. It presents an

Figure 7–4 Hypothetical relations in developments from 1 to 5 years of age leading to the emergence of autobiographical memory. Larger arrows indicate more direct influences; double-headed arrows indicate reciprocal influences. Years (yr.) in the bottom scale indicate approximate ages when influences come into play on average in normal development. Areas above the center are presumed to be more endogenous and those below more exogenous as sources of development.

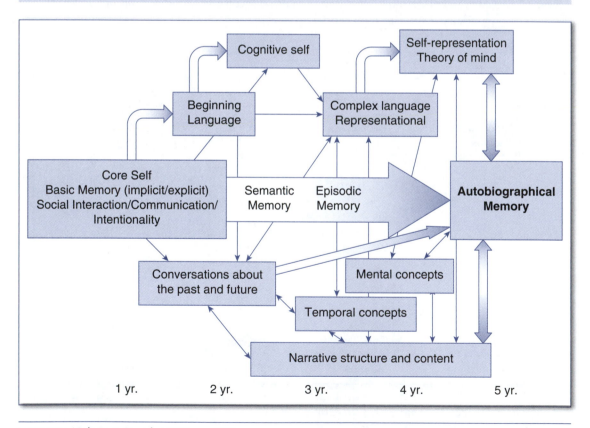

SOURCE: Nelson & Fivush (2004, p. 490).

overview of the emergence of different cognitive achievements, such as a sense of self, language skills, conversations, and some topics we have yet to talk about, such as semantic memory and theory of mind (we will talk about these topics later in the chapter and in Chapter 8, respectively). Arrows show influences, with bigger arrows indicating more direct influences. You can see from this diagram something that should have already become apparent: Autobiographical memory is a complex and multifaceted cognitive entity!

Eyewitness Memory

So far we've looked at how children remember information, including information about general events they've seen on television or heard about in books and events that they have personally experienced. We've seen that, though there are some disagreements over when autobiographical memory emerges, everyone agrees that older preschoolers do have some capacity for recollection of previously experienced events. This leads us to the question "How accurate and reliable are preschool children as eyewitnesses?" Given recent court cases, the issue of **eyewitness memory** is not a strictly academic one. We'll examine in this section how well preschool children are able to report on events they have witnessed and how much these reports are subject to intentional or accidental distortion.

A now-classic study, conducted by Lynne Baker-Ward and colleagues, examined preschool (and young school-aged) children's ability to report on what happened to them in an actual real-life event: a visit to their pediatrician (Baker-Ward, Gordon, Ornstein, Larus, & Clubb, 1993). Children aged 3, 5, and 7 years were asked to report on the pediatric visit immediately after the checkup and then either 1, 3, or 6 weeks later. An additional group of children (of the same ages) was questioned *only* after 3 weeks, to control for any possible effects of repeated interviewing. Although the specifics of each visit depended on the individual child, in general the events included in the visit were drawn from the lists presented in Table 7.3. You'll note in this list that the nurse took photographs of the children—this was done specifically for the study. Children with very atypical medical conditions (and who therefore may have had intervening pediatric visits) were excluded from the study.

In the memory interviews, children were initially asked a very general, open-ended question, such as "What happened during your checkup?" Interviewers probed children's responses and then asked somewhat more specific questions such as "What did the doctor [or nurse] do to check you?" Later in the interview came very specific questions such as "Did she [or he] check your eyes?" or "Did the doctor shine a light in your eyes?" Children were also asked about events that did not happen as well. For example, not all children

Table 7–3   Features of the physical examinations in the study reported by Baker-Ward et. al (1993)

Visit with nurse	Visit with doctor
Measure height	Check eyes
Measure weight	Check ears
Test vision	Check nose
Test hearing	Check mouth
Obtain urine sample	Check knees
Obtain blood sample	Check elbows
Measure blood pressure	Check wrists
Administer TB tine test	Check heels
Photograph child	Check bottoms of feet
…	Listen to chest (heart)
…	Listen to back (lungs)
…	Check genitalia
…	Observe backwards walk
…	Observe walk on tiptoes
…	Observe walk on heels
…	Ask child to clap hands
…	Ask child to touch nose
Administer inoculation(s)	
Distribute stickers	

SOURCE: Baker-Ward, Gordon, Ornstein, Larus & Clubb (1993, p. 1522).

received inoculations at their visit, but all were asked if they had received them. In addition, children were asked about events that never happened, such as "Did the doctor cut your hair?" or "Did the nurse sit on top of you?"

Photo 7.3   Studies on eyewitness testimony in children have used pediatric examinations as an event to interview young children about.

Each of the items listed in Table 7.3 was considered a potential feature of a child's pediatric visit. Based on parental and health care provider checklists, completed immediately after the visit, the investigators were able to determine which features had actually occurred during a particular visit. They then examined what proportion of features children accurately recalled, in response to either the open-ended or the specific questions. Results are presented in Figure 7.5.

It shows that there was very little difference in accuracy as a function of time delay. For example, children recalled about as much at 6 weeks after the visit as they did a week after or even immediately after. There were no differences between boys and girls either. There *were* differences as a function of age of the child, with older children recalling more than younger children overall, and especially in response to open-ended questions. That is, the 7-year-olds did not require lots of specific prompting the way the 3-year-olds did. There was also an interaction between age of the child and forgetting: Younger children forgot some information in as short as a week; older children showed very little forgetting even after 6 weeks. Of the 3-, 5-, and 7-year-olds, respectively 84%, 97%, and 100% recalled

Figure 7–5 Percent of features correctly reported in response to open-ended and specific probes by test conditions at ages 3 (Panel A), 5 (Panel B), and 7 (Panel C) years. Note that the data presented for the initial test are averaged across the three delay groups.

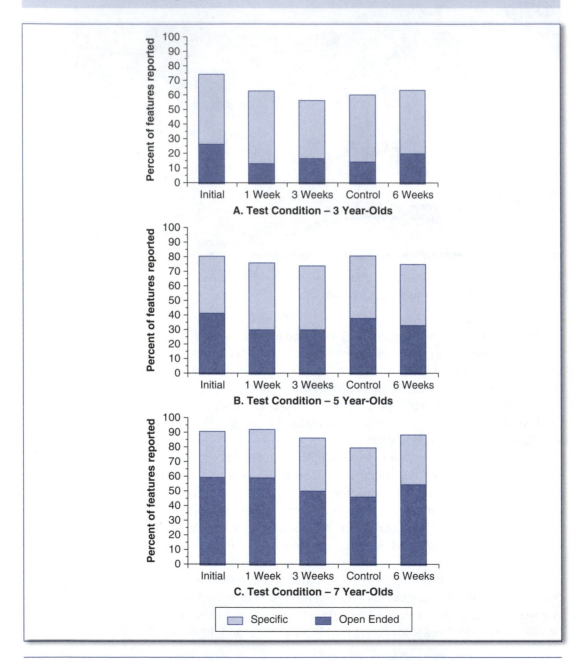

SOURCE: Baker-Ward, Gordon, Ornstein, Larus, & Clubb (1993, p. 1525).

having their picture taken (the incongruous event added to the pediatric exam just for this study).

The researchers also analyzed the children's responses to questions about absent features—parts of their physical exams that could have happened (and did happen for other children) but did not. The data showed that with age, correct responses (denials the events had happened) increased. The results were quite similar for the questions about events that did not happen (and do not typically happen during a physical exam), such as having their hair cut or having the doctor lick their knee. Three-year-olds showed fewer correct denials (averaging about 83% correct) than either 5-year-olds (who averaged around 95% correct) or 7-year-olds (who averaged 97% correct).

Based on the data, the investigators concluded that "young children's reports of personally experienced events can be extensive and accurate" (Baker-Ward et al., 1993, p. 1530). Even the 3-year-olds could remember much of what had gone on, even after delays of about 3 weeks. Of course, older children were better at this task than younger children and required less help, in the form of specific probes, to recall what had happened.

A related series of studies undertaken by Carole Peterson and her colleagues (Peterson, 1999; Peterson & Bell, 1996; Peterson & Whalen, 2001) yields a similar conclusion. The investigators interviewed children who had experienced a medical emergency (traumatic injury) and hospital emergency room treatment. The children were initially interviewed about a week after the injury and then 6 months, 1 year, 2 years, and 5 years later. Even 5 years later, children showed "excellent recall of their injury experience" with most recalling 80% or more of the central details of their injury (Peterson & Whalen, 2001, p. S7). Children who were 2 years old at the time of the injury were also able to provide some recall of the incident, although it was not quite as good as the recall of children who were older at the time of injury.

Quas and colleagues (1999) reported a study of children's memory of a painful medical procedure (a voiding cystourethrogram fluoroscopy, or VCUG, and a never-experienced procedure, a nose surgery). Children who were 4 years old or older at the time they received the VCUG tended to recall the procedure more accurately than children who were younger at the time of the procedure. Longer delays between the procedure and the interview led to less information recalled but little drop in accuracy for the information that was recalled.

Despite the data that young children are capable of giving accurate reports, there is also a large body of data suggesting that younger children are particularly vulnerable to suggestive questioning and distortion. For example, in the Quas et al. (1999) study described above, almost three quarters of the preschoolers (and half of the 6- to 8-year-olds) at some point in the interview agreed that they had experienced the nose surgery (the false event).

Michelle Leichtman and Stephen Ceci (1995) reported the now-famous "Sam Stone" study, in which children (aged 3 to 6 years) attending a day care center experienced a visit from "Sam Stone," a unfamiliar man. Sam Stone's visit to every classroom was described as follows:

> In each of the eight day-care classrooms, Sam Stone enacted the same scripted event. First, he entered the classroom and said hello to a teacher or aid [*sic*] who sat amidst the assembled children during a story-telling session and he was introduced by the teacher or aid [*sic*] to the children. Next, he commented on the story that was being read to the children by the teacher or aid [*sic*] ("I know that story; it's one of my favorites!") and strolled around the perimeter of the classroom. Finally he departed, waving goodbye to the children. In each case, the entire event was timed and lasted approximately 2 min. (Leichtman & Ceci, 1995, p. 570)

There were four conditions in the study. The children in the *control* condition simply experienced the Sam Stone visit, as described above. They were questioned about the visit once a week for 4 weeks after Sam's visit and also received a final forensic interview 10 weeks after the visit. A second condition, called the *stereotype* condition, had children who received a great deal of information about Sam Stone before he visited. Beginning about a month before Sam's visit, a research assistant (who happened to be visiting and playing with the children) presented three different scripted stories about Sam Stone. In each, Sam Stone was depicted as a "kind, well-meaning, but very clumsy and bumbling person" (Leichtman & Ceci, 1995, p. 570). Here is one example of such a story:

> You'll never guess who visited me last night. [pause] That's right. Sam Stone! And guess what he did this time? He asked to borrow my Barbie and when he was carrying her down the stairs, he accidentally tripped and fell and broke her arm. That Sam Stone is always getting into accidents and breaking things! But it's okay, because Sam Stone is very nice and he is getting my Barbie doll fixed for me. (Leichtman & Ceci, 1995, p. 570)

Children in the stereotype condition received the same kinds and frequency of interviews as did children in the control condition.

A third group of children was assigned to the *suggestion* condition. These children did not hear the stories about Sam Stone prior to his visit. However, during their interviews they were given two misleading suggestions about what had transpired during Sam Stone's visit—one that he had ripped a book and the other that he had soiled a teddy bear:

The exact questions about the events that occurred during Sam Stone's visit were different for this group of children during each of the interviews, but the same implications were embedded in each. For example, 1 week children were asked, "When Sam Stone got that bear dirty, did he do it on purpose or was it an accident?" and in the following interview session they were asked, "Was Sam Stone happy or sad that he got that bear dirty?" (Leichtman & Ceci, 1995, p. 571)

A fourth group of children received both the stereotyped information before Sam Stone's visits and the misleading suggestions. Finally, all children received a fifth interview, 10 weeks after the visit, conducted by a new interviewer who had not been present previously. The same questions were asked of all children. The script for that interview is presented in Table 7.4.

Data from the final interview were examined for accuracy. In particular, the researchers looked to see whether, in the initial free-response answers, children described a false event (e.g., Sam Stone ripping a book, soiling a bear, or something along those lines) spontaneously. Next, they examined whether the children asserted such an event in response to specific probes. Finally, they looked to see whether the children who *did* assert a false event continued to maintain that it really occurred when given the countersuggestions (i.e., Questions 6 and 7 in Table 7.4).

Figure 7.6 presents these results, broken down by condition. As you can see, children in the *control* condition did not make any false allegations. However, the results were quite different for children in the *stereotype* and *suggestion* groups. In both cases, a significant percentage (over 20%) of children indicated that Sam Stone either ripped a book or soiled a teddy bear, with children in the *suggestion* group making more false reports than children in the *stereotype* group. Upon hearing countersuggestions, many children in both groups recanted—only 10% or 12% continued to maintain that the false events had occurred.

The results were the most dramatic for the *stereotype plus suggestion* group. There, over 30% of the children spontaneously reported (in their open-ended responses) that Sam had committed one of the two acts; 72% claimed this in responding to specific probes, and even after countersuggestions, 44% continued to maintain that the false events had occurred. Younger preschoolers were more likely to be influenced by stereotypes or suggestions, especially the latter. Interestingly, adults who watched videotapes of the children's final interview were unable to discriminate between those children who were giving accurate reports and those who provided detailed narratives of events that had not happened. The researchers'

Table 7–4 Protocol and questions asked of all children in the final (fifth) interview of the "Sam Stone" study

With the cooperation of their teachers, children were taken out of the classroom individually by the interviewer, whom they were told wanted to ask them "some questions." Children chatted with the interviewer on the way to the interview room, and for up to several minutes once in the room, about pleasantries. Once in the room, children were seated comfortably on an upholstered chair facing the interviewer. The interviewer gained the child's attention and told him or her, "I have an important question for you." The following "free narrative" question was then asked:

1. "Remember that day that Sam Stone came to your classroom? Well, I wasn't there that day, and I'd like you to tell me everything that happened when he visited. Can you tell me what happened?"

Children were given time to tell as much about Sam Stone's visit as they could, and were asked, "Can you remember anything else?," followed by a chance to respond, until they indicated that they had nothing else to tell.

All children were then given the following specific "prompting" questions, unless they had referred specifically to the items mentioned in these questions in their free-narrative answers.

2. "I heard something about a book. Do you know anything about that?"

3. "I heard something about a teddy bear. Do you know anything about that?"

After both of these questions were posed, all children who indicated (either in response to the free narrative or the prompting) that Sam Stone did something to the book or the teddy bear during his visit were asked the following questions:

4. "Did you see him (action vis-a-vis the book, as noted by the child, inserted here; e.g., *rip the book*) with your own eyes?"

5. "Did you see him (action vis-a-vis the teddy bear, as noted by the child, inserted here; e.g., *put paint on the teddy bear*) with your own eyes?"

In the case of only those children who said that they saw Sam Stone commit the acts in question with their own eyes, countersuggestion questions were then posed:

6. "You didn't really see him (action vis-a-vis the book, as noted by the child, inserted here; e.g., *rip the book*), did you?"

7. "You didn't really see him (action vis-a-vis the teddy bear, as noted by the child, inserted here; e.g., *put paint on the teddy bear*), did you?"

SOURCE: Leichtman & Ceci (1995, p. 578).

Figure 7–6   Results by condition *(control, stereotype, suggestion,* and *stereotype plus suggestion)* for the "Sam Stone" study

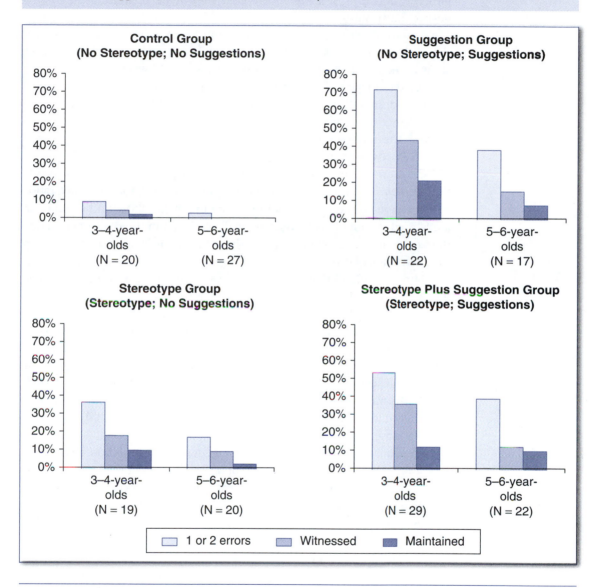

SOURCE: Leichtman & Ceci (1995, pp. 571–573).

NOTE: Each graph depicts the percentage of preschoolers' answers that were erroneous. Light colored bars indicate that the child asserted an incorrect event occurred. Medium colored bars indicate the child claimed to have witnessed this event. Dark colored bars indicate the child's insisting on having witnessed the event, despite mild attempt at dissuasion.

interpretation is that jurors or law enforcement officials might not be able to tell whether a long narrative from a preschool child is accurate or is either a reflection of a previously held stereotype or influenced by suggestive questioning.

A study by Principe, Kanaya, Ceci, and Singh (2006) sounds a similar theme. Four groups of preschoolers (aged 3 to 5 years) witnessed a magic show at their child care center. During the show, Magic Mumfry, the magician, tried but failed to pull a rabbit out of his hat. Immediately following the show, children in the *overheard* condition overheard a teacher talking to an unfamiliar adult confederate, saying that she had heard that the rabbit got loose in the school and was eating carrots in the target child's classroom (this event, by the way, never actually happened).

Children in the *classmate* condition were the classmates of children in the *overheard* condition. Children in the *witness* condition saw a live rabbit eating carrots in their classroom following the magic show, and a confederate labeled the rabbit as Mumfry's. Finally, children in the *control* condition did not witness a rabbit or overhear the staged conversation, nor were they the classmates of other children who overheard.

After a week, children were questioned in either a neutral or a suggestive manner. Both interviews started out the same way, with the following open-ended question: "Tell me everything that you remember about the day that Magic Mumfry visited your school. Don't guess or make anything up. Just tell me what you did or saw the time that Magic Mumfry came to your school" (Principe et al., 2006, p. 245). Specific follow-up questions came next. If the children failed to mention a loose rabbit, the interviewer asked, "Did anything happen to Mumfry's rabbit?" and the children were asked to elaborate if they mentioned the rabbit getting loose.

Additionally, children in the suggestive interview condition were asked four forced-choice questions that presupposed the event of the rabbit getting loose (e.g., "What did Mumfry's rabbit eat when he got loose in your school? Did he eat carrots or lettuce?"). The questions were consistent with what the *witness* group children had seen but were misleading for children in the other three groups.

Figure 7.7 presents the results. Look first at Panel A, which presents results from children who received the neutral interview. Notice that a few (10%) of the control children reported the rabbit had escaped, although none reported actually seeing it. In contrast, 100% of children in the witness condition (who did actually see the loose rabbit) reported the event, and reported actually seeing it. The striking results come from

Figure 7–7 Results from the "Magic Mumfry" study

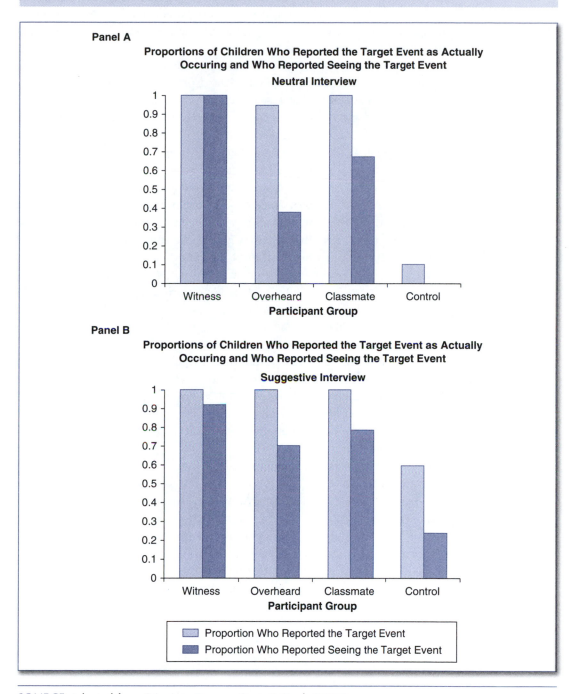

SOURCE: Adapted from Principe, Kanaya, Ceci, & Singh (2006).

children in the other two conditions. Close to 100% of children in both the *overheard* and the *classmate* conditions reported that the false event had occurred—that is, they reported an escaped rabbit when that never happened. A fairly substantial number of children actually reported witnessing this non-event as well.

Panel B shows an even more dramatic incidence of false reporting. This panel shows data from children who had experienced suggestive questioning. You can see that in that case, an even higher proportion of children in the *overheard* and *classmate* conditions reported actually seeing the loose rabbit, the incident that for them had not occurred.

Principe et al. (2006) conclude from their results that "overheard rumors discussed among peers can bias not only preschoolers' reports of an event, but also their beliefs about what they experienced" (p. 247)—even in the absence of suggestive questioning. These results replicated those found by Principe and Ceci (2002), who studied children's reports of a staged classroom event (an archaeological dig), where some children witnessed two target events but others only overheard their classmates talking about them. A fair proportion of children who heard classmates talking about the events but did not themselves see them *actually* reported seeing them, especially if exposed to suggestive questioning.

Some work suggests that preschool children are more susceptible to **source monitoring errors** in their recall of past events (Lindsay, 2007). Source monitoring errors are made when we confuse the origin of information we have in our memory. Suppose, for example, that you witness a car accident but do not witness the ambulance arriving and transporting the injured. Later you hear that one of the victims, a 7-year-old boy, suffered a broken arm. Upon being interviewed later, you report having *seen* the child with his arm broken. Essentially, you have confused what you yourself actually saw with reports you later heard about—making a classic source monitoring error.

Thierry and Spence (2002) gave preschoolers aged 3 and 4 years training in source monitoring. Children saw a puppet perform some actions live and others on videotape. They were asked to help a second puppet remember which actions the first puppet did "in real life" and which he did "on TV." They were also given training on detecting "trick" questions, such as those that presupposed something false. Results showed that children were able to transfer this training to their own eyewitness experience of live versus videotaped events. The authors concluded that preschoolers' failure to spontaneously use source monitoring strategies constituted a production deficiency, of the type described earlier in the chapter.

However, other studies suggest that getting preschoolers to actively monitor the sources of information does not always work (Leichtman, Morse, Dixon, & Spiegel, 2000).

The research on memory in preschool children, taken as a whole, suggests some fragile competence emerging. Preschoolers, relative to toddlers and infants, are gaining control of their memories and are able to deploy strategies under certain conditions. As they progress through the preschool years their memory for past events improves. At the same time, preschoolers are easily led astray by suggestive questioning. They do not always remember to use the strategies they have, and they don't always spontaneously keep straight what they actually witnessed from what they heard about later on (Klemfuss & Ceci, 2009; Pipe, Thierry, & Lamb, 2007).

CONCEPTUAL DEVELOPMENT

So far, we have focused on memory for events—both routine and specific. These would clearly fall under what Tulving (1972, 1989) called *episodic memory*. But as you'll recall from the beginning of this chapter, there is another kind of long-term memory, *semantic memory*, which is memory for information or memory for general knowledge. We are now going to turn our attention to this aspect of memory, namely, how preschoolers organize their knowledge bases, or their semantic memory.

The Knowledge Base

One obvious difference between preschoolers and older children or adults is in their knowledge base of most aspects of the world. For example, if you were to compare my knowledge base to that of my (rather smart) 8-year-old, you would find that I know much more about just about every topic. I have a larger vocabulary; I know more math facts; I know more about history, literature, science, popular culture, and education. I have many more scripts than she does—of faculty meetings, large lectures, and election days. There are probably one or two realms where she knows more than I (television shows such as *Handy Manny* or *Hannah Montana* come immediately to mind), but these are few and far between.

What specific difference might a larger knowledge base make? The answer to this question comes from a now-classic study by Chi and Koeske (1983).

Their sole participant was a four-and-a-half-year-old dinosaur aficionado. The investigators began by assessing the child's familiarity with and knowledge about different kinds of dinosaurs and divided 40 of these into two groups: those the child knew relatively more about and those the child knew relatively less about. The child was then presented on three different occasions with each list of 20 dinosaurs, at the rate of one dinosaur name every 3 seconds, and was then asked to recall the list. The child recalled significantly more of the "familiar" dinosaurs (about 9 out of 20) than the "unfamiliar" ones (about 4 out of 20).

Chi and Koeske (1983) argued from these and other results that part of the reason children may typically perform so poorly on memory (or presumably other cognitive) tasks is their relative lack of knowledge about or expertise with the information used in the tasks. Given the opportunity to perform the same tasks with materials they know well, their performance improves dramatically. Presumably, familiar materials require less cognitive effort to encode, retrieve relevant information about, notice novel features of, and so on. We'll now take a closer look at how knowledge is structured within this large repository of long-term memory.

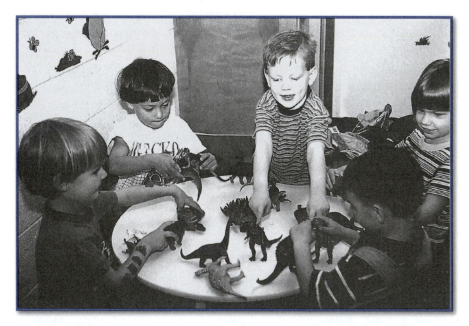

Photo 7.4 These dinosaur aficionados might do better on memory tests where the subject is dinosaurs rather than a subject with which they are less familiar.

Concepts and Categorization

We've already seen one kind of knowledge that young children possess—that for routine events. We've seen that many cognitive developmental psychologists argue that this knowledge is structured into *scripts*, with fixed and variable parts, that are adapted to specific instances.

What about knowledge of things other than routine events? For example, what about preschoolers' knowledge of animals, toys, letters and numbers, or furniture? Cognitive psychologists who study this kind of knowledge refer to the mental representation of these kinds of entities as concepts. They refer to the cognitive processes by which a stimulus is recognized or assigned to a concept as categorization.

Concepts can include more than mental representations of things, of course. They can also represent properties (e.g., being happy, being hungry, being colored orange), and they can represent abstract ideas (e.g., truth, power, justice). Concepts allow children to represent information efficiently. Instead of keeping track of each individual instance of a dog a child encounters, for example, she can group them all together under the general heading of *dog* and store common information about those instances (has four legs, has a tail, wags tail when happy, sniffs many things, eats things on the ground) under the general heading of dog (Gelman & Kalish, 2006).

Conceptual development requires revision of concepts. When we examine younger children's concept of a dog, for example, we may find it very sparse in relation to an adult's concept. Adults are much more likely to recognize different kinds of dogs (dachshunds, golden retrievers, Great Danes) and are more likely to recognize that dogs can serve different functions (family pet, guard dog, therapy dog, police dog, guide dog). Adults are likely to know much more about the biology of dogs and are more likely to draw correct inferences when it comes to determining whether a new instance is really a dog (as opposed to, say, a large cat or a small coyote).

From very early on, children's concepts, like those of adults, appear to be organized hierarchically, with a "basic" level of abstraction (Rosch, 1978; Rosch, Mervis, Gray, Johnson, & Boyes-Braem, 1976). For example, *dog* and *cat* are at the basic level, as are *chair* and *table*. There are more abstract or superordinate levels that include basic-level concepts (e.g., *animal, furniture*) as well as more specific, subordinate levels (e.g., *Labrador retriever, Persian cat, armchair, dining room table*).

Research shows that preschoolers are much more likely to learn basic-level terms before they learn superordinate or subordinate terms (Mervis & Crisafi, 1982), perhaps because when parents talk to young children, they are more likely to label objects at the basic level (e.g., "See the doggie?") than they are to label them at a different level (e.g., "See the animal?" or "See the Labrador retriever?"; Shipley, Kuhn, & Madden, 1983; but see Mandler, 2004, for some debate over this point). However, children with greater expertise in a domain are more likely to focus on subordinate-level categories (Johnson & Eilers, 1998). Thus, for example, we'd expect children who are dinosaur aficionados to use more subordinate terms in their language and their thinking about those extinct reptiles in comparison to their age-mates who have only a passing interest in the creatures.

Typically, adults use their conceptual knowledge to categorize newly encountered instances. Seeing an animal come toward them on the street, for instance, they use their conceptual knowledge to decide if it is a dog or a cat or a rat or maybe even an escaped elephant from the zoo. Children do this sort of thing as well. Susan Gelman and her colleagues (Gelman, 1988; Gelman & Markman, 1986) have centered their investigations on the question of how children make inferences about different kinds of things, given that they have some information about the category membership of those things.

Most of us know that although whales share a number of similarities with various kinds of fish (they swim, they live in water, they are often found in aquariums, and they have an overall shape that is fishlike), they are in fact mammals (whales are warm-blooded and bear live young). As adults, we know a whale must be categorized on the basis of something other than perceived features. The question is "Do children know this too?" Notice that the Piagetian view would predict that preschool children, being "perceptually bound," would probably perform the classification solely on the basis of how the thing to be classified looks.

In a series of studies, Gelman and Markman (1986) showed children sets of three pictures like the one shown in Figure 7.8. Each set was carefully constructed so that the third picture *looked* like one of the first two pictures but was really in the same category as the one it did not resemble. Note, for example, that in Figure 7.8 the owl *looks* more like the bat but is really (to a knowledgeable adult) in the same category as the flamingo (both the owl and the flamingo are birds; the bat is a mammal). Children were given information about the first two pictures in a set (e.g., "This bird's heart has a right aortic arch only" [as the experimenter points to a picture of the flamingo]; "This bat's heart has a left aortic arch only" [as the experimenter points to a picture of the bat]). While looking at the third picture (e.g., an owl shaped like the bat), the child was asked to predict what would be true of the owl's heart. Contrary to Piagetian predictions, even 4-year-old children based their inferences on category membership rather than on physical appearance (when the two were in conflict) approximately 68% of the time.

Figure 7–8   Stimuli from Gelman and Markman (1986)

SOURCE: Gelman & Markman (1986, p. 188).

In further work, Gelman (1988) investigated the constraints on children's inferences based on category membership. Preschoolers and second graders first learned presumably new facts about objects (e.g., "This apple has pectin inside") and then were asked whether these facts were true of other items of varying similarity (such as other apples, a banana, and a stereo). Gelman used two kinds of categories: natural kinds (naturally occurring objects, such as animals, plants, fruits, and other things not constructed by humans) and artifacts (objects constructed by people usually to perform a certain function, such as chairs, tools, and computers). Adults have been shown to treat these two kinds of concepts differently (Barton & Komatsu, 1989). The question was "Do children also treat these two kinds of concepts differently, and if they do, at what age do they start to make the distinction?"

Gelman (1988) found that preschool children (as well as second graders) consistently drew the inference that items in the same category shared the new property they had just learned about. For example, on being told that "apples have pectin," all the children were also likely to infer that a banana had pectin, too. They were much less likely to infer that a stereo had pectin. Apparently, then, even preschoolers use their knowledge of category membership to make inferences about what kinds of properties different things might have. It is interesting that second graders were sensitive to the natural-kind/artifact distinction and drew more inferences with natural-kind concepts. Preschoolers, in contrast, appeared relatively insensitive to the distinction. Gelman believed that this insensitivity resulted from their relative lack of deep knowledge about the objects being talked about (see also some recent studies by Brandone & Gelman, 2009, and Nelson, O'Neil, & Asher, 2008, looking at this issue).

Individual concepts are of course related to one another in some sort of organizational system, often referred to as ontology—a conception of the basic categories of existence (Keil, 1979). Each discipline has its own ontology—in physics, for example, concepts such as *force, velocity, mass,* and *energy* comprise that ontology, whereas in psychology such concepts as *beliefs, desires, thoughts,* and *theories* are the focus (Gelman & Kalish, 2006). One might inquire as to when preschool children begin to honor ontological distinctions. A full discussion of this rich topic is beyond our scope, so we will focus here on one important ontological category: animism.

Piagetian theory held that preoperational children have a great deal of trouble sorting out the properties and abilities of animate versus inanimate entities. Piaget used the term animism to refer to the tendency of preschoolers to grant human or biological properties to inanimate objects—believing that the sun shines because it is happy, that the wind blows because it intends to make leaves dance, or that rain means that the sky is sad (Flavell, 1963).

Later research called this view into some question. Massey and Gelman (1988) showed that 3- and 4-year-old children, given a number of photographs of unfamiliar items, were reliably able to identify which of the depicted objects could move by themselves and which could not. The color photographs depicted mammalian animals, nonmammalian animals, statues with animal-like forms and parts, wheeled vehicles, and multipart rigid objects. Figure 7.9 presents line drawings of the photographed objects and makes the point that the objects shown were unfamiliar and complex.

Children were shown a drawing of a hill. The experimenter first clarified that they understood what terms like *top, bottom, up,* and *down* meant. Then she explained that they would see pictures of "all kinds of things and she would ask them to help her figure out which ones could go up or down the hill by themselves and which needed help" (Massey & Gelman, 1988, p. 310). Overall, children correctly classified 83.5% of the photographs on their first attempt and often used category membership to justify their answers (e.g., "It can go by itself because it's an animal," or "It can't do anything 'cause it's just a toy"). This suggests in turn that preschoolers have at least a rudimentary understanding of animism and how that property applies to different things.

Some cognitive developmentalists would go further, to claim that some of the concepts preschool children possess have innate beginnings. Rochel Gelman (1990; Gelman & Williams, 1998), for example, holds that part of children's inborn mental equipment includes domain-specific principles that guide their behavior and their learning from the environment. These principles are not fully detailed but instead are skeletal—mere outlines of what their final form will be. Thus, Gelman would fall into the nativist theoretical camp when it comes to a description of how preschoolers acquire concepts.

Figure 7–9 Line drawing renditions of some of the photographed objects used in Massey and Gelman (1988). The samples shown here, starting in the top row and going left to right, are a displaying lizard, an echidna, a vessel made to look like a mythical creature, an insect-eyed figurine, an exercise device, and an old-fashioned two-wheeled bicycle. Note that line drawings were not used in the actual study.

Work by Rochel Gelman and Randy Gallistel (1978) with preschoolers in the United States demonstrated that even they know a great deal about counting. With small numbers (i.e., fewer than about five items), even 2- and 3-year-olds can count the number of items in a set. But what does it mean to count? Gelman and Gallistel offered this surprisingly complicated definition:

> [Counting] involves the coordinated use of several components: noticing the items in an array one after another; pairing each noticed item with a number name; using a conventional list of number names in the conventional order; and recognizing that the last name used represents the numerosity of the array. (p. 73)

Gelman and her colleagues observed the counting behavior of preschoolers and were able to identify several distinct "principles" of counting. These are described in the list shown in Table 7.5. A child might have some but not all of these principles at any stage of development. Nonetheless, even if her "counting" behavior doesn't exactly match that of an adult, she can be properly described as "counting" if her behavior shows evidence of honoring at least some of the principles. For example, a child aged 2 years and 6 months counted a plate containing three toy mice as follows: "One, two, six!" Asked by the experimenter to count the mice once again, the child happily complied: "Ya, one, two, six!" (Gelman & Gallistel, 1978, p. 91). This child shows

Table 7–5 The how-to-count principles

1. The One-One Principle. Each item in a to-be-counted array is "ticked" in such a way that one and only one distinct "tick" is assigned to each item.
2. The Stable-Order Principle. The tags (count words) assigned to each item must be chosen in a repeatable order.
3. The Cardinal Principle. When one is counting an array, the final tag represents the number of items in the set.
4. The Abstraction Principle. Any group of items, whether physical or not, whether of the same type or not, can be counted.
5. The Order-Irrelevance Principle. The order of enumeration (that is, which item is tagged "1," and which "2," and so on) of items in a set does not affect the number of items in the set or the counting procedure.

SOURCE: Gelman & Gallistel (1978).

clear evidence of respecting the one-one and stable-order principles and therefore really is counting, even though she uses a different count–word sequence than adults do.

Gelman (1990) believes that the skeletal principles underlying counting organize the preschool child's attention and therefore his learning. As he practices counting, presumably he becomes better at remembering the conventional list of number tags and becomes more skilled at remembering which of a set of items have been tagged (counted) and which remain to be tagged. This in turn frees up his attention to start noticing other things about counting—perhaps that counting two apples and adding three more always yields the same result as counting three apples and adding two more. Likewise, Gelman believes that young children's understanding of animism derives from underlying skeletal principles of whether or not things are capable of self-locomotion.

The general idea emerging from the research on preschool children's conceptual development is that preschoolers are not always bound by their perceptions, as Piagetian theory held. Instead, in some of the circumstances described above, children are able to distinguish between external appearances and internal, nonobservable, or even abstract properties. We'll talk more about this issue in Chapter 8 when we take up the topic of the child's ability to make the appearance–reality distinction.

SUMMARY

1. Memorial development during the preschool years involves increases in capacity, the use of more sophisticated strategies, and an ever-growing accumulation of knowledge about the world.

2. Working memory spans increase from about two for the average 2-year-old to four and a half for the average 5-year-old. Memory span size has been connected to children's executive functioning, with higher-span children more able to disengage their attention from one task and redeploy it to another. Working memory spans also predict children's later scholastic abilities.

3. Preschool children acquire and use more strategies as they develop. When younger preschoolers fail to use a memory strategy, it may be due to a *mediation deficiency* (the strategy won't work, even if used), a *production deficiency* (the strategy will work, but the child does not spontaneously think to use it), or a *utilization deficiency* (even if the child uses the strategy, it doesn't work as well initially as it will when the child has more experience with it).

4. Scripts are schemas for routine events. Evidence suggests that preschoolers are able to form scripts of the routine events they participate in—for example, going to day care, baking cookies, or visiting a fast-food restaurant. With development, scripts become more elaborate.

5. Parental discussions with their preschoolers are an important factor in children's development of autobiographical memory—memory for specific, personally experienced events. Another important hypothesized factor is language development.

6. Under some circumstances, preschoolers can reliably report on events they have witnessed. However, older preschoolers typically remember more than younger ones and require less specific prompting to recount what they have seen. Moreover, evidence suggests that especially younger preschoolers are very vulnerable to the effects of suggestive or manipulative questioning and that their eyewitness accounts can be rather easily distorted.

7. *Episodic memory* is the term used for memories of personal past events. *Semantic memory* is the term for memory for facts, concepts, schemas, scripts, and other pieces of knowledge that do not have an explicit connection to a person's specific history.

8. Concepts are mental representations of entities—objects, ideas, properties, and so forth. Categorization refers to the cognitive processes by which a person recognizes a stimulus as an instance of a concept.

9. Concepts appear to be organized hierarchically, with "basic" levels of abstraction. Preschool children typically learn basic-level terms (e.g., *chair, dog, tree*) before they learn subordinate terms (e.g., *rocking chair, beagle, evergreen*) or superordinate terms (e.g., *furniture, animal, plant*). However, children with expertise in a given domain do use more subordinate terms within their domain of expertise.

10. Some theorists believe that certain concepts have innate roots and that children are born with skeletal principles that become more elaborate as they gain experience in the world.

REVIEW QUESTIONS

1. Explain what a working memory span is and why it is of such importance to cognitive developmental psychologists.

2. Distinguish among mediation, production, and utilization deficiencies as they apply to preschoolers' memorial strategy use.

3. Give an example of a script that a young preschooler might have, and describe how that script would change as the preschooler developed.

4. Explain how parental conversations are thought to aid the development of preschool children's autobiographical memory.

5. Describe either the "Sam Stone" study (Leichtman & Ceci, 1995) or the "Magic Mumfry" study (Principe et al., 2006), and discuss the implications for the study of preschoolers' eyewitness memory.

6. Explain the episodic memory–semantic memory distinction and how it relates to preschoolers' memory and conceptual development.

7. Discuss the significance of the Chi and Koeske (1983) study of a child dinosaur expert.

8. Distinguish among basic, superordinate, and subordinate levels of concepts, providing examples.

9. What does Susan Gelman's research on preschoolers' conceptual development (e.g., Gelman, 1988; Gelman & Markman, 1986) reveal?

10. Describe the work by Rochel Gelman on preschoolers' counting abilities (e.g., Gelman & Gallistel, 1978), and describe the implications of that work.

KEY TERMS

Animism

Autobiographical Memory

Basic Level (of a concept)

Capacity

Concept

Eyewitness Memory

Mediation Deficiency (of a strategy)

Metacognition

Ontology

Production Deficiency (of a strategy)

Schema

Script

Source Monitoring Error

Subordinate Level (of a concept)

Superordinate Level (of a concept)

Utilization Deficiency (of a strategy)

CHAPTER 8

EARLY CHILDHOOD

Higher-Order and Social Cognition

In the last two chapters, we reviewed what might be called the "basic" cognitive processes—perception, attention, memory, and conceptual development—and how they progress during the preschool years. In this chapter, we will focus on what are sometimes called "higher-order" cognitive processes, including thinking, reasoning, and problem solving. These processes are thought to build on the basic cognitive processes, and allow the child more cognitive flexibility and power as he develops. We'll also look at social cognition—that is, a child's growing knowledge about his own personality and emotions and those of others. In a sense, this chapter is about seeing how the preschool-aged child puts his basic cognitive abilities to use in complex circumstances and contexts.

We'll begin with a look at Piagetian and Vygotskian perspectives on development in this realm. We will examine in detail the topic of play—the so-called "work" of the preschool child. We'll see that in the context of play, children exercise their creativity and imagination and begin to stretch themselves—physically, socially, and, as we will see, cognitively. We will then examine reasoning—preschool children's ability to draw inferences and conclusions from information they are given. Our focus will then shift to a recent phenomenon in cognitive development—the emergence of the child's **theory of mind**—or understanding of how her (and other people's) beliefs about the world come to be established and revised. We will conclude by examining the relationship between a child's theory of mind and her performance on other cognitive tasks.

THEORETICAL PERSPECTIVES

We begin by considering the foci of this chapter—higher-order cognition and social cognition. After a brief exposition of what these are, we'll turn to consider some relevant theoretical perspectives on these topics.

The Nature of Higher-Order and Social Cognition

The preschool years mark the clear emergence of **higher-order cognitive processes**. While some infancy researchers describe the precursors of such activities as goal setting, planning, or drawing inferences, most developmental psychologists would argue that higher-order processes don't become *unambiguously* evident before early childhood.

As the name suggests, higher-order cognitive processes are ones that make use of the functioning of more basic cognitive processes, such as perception, attention, and memory. Higher-order cognitive processes involve using and manipulating information, rather than acquiring it from the world, or storing it. Traditionally, activities such as thinking, problem solving, reasoning, and decision making have fallen under the umbrella of higher-order cognitive processes. There are others as well—creativity, setting goals and priorities, planning, and evaluating all come immediately to my mind.

Social cognition is another, related topic we will examine here. It has to do with a person's understanding of other people as well as of herself, with particular emphasis on mental life. The issues that fall under this general heading include a person's ability to take the role of another (either literally or mentally), to understand another's point of view, to predict and make allowances for differences between one's own view and that of another, and to predict and understand the goals and motivations of both oneself and another (Harris, 2006).

As we are about to see, theorists Piaget and Vygotsky had very different views of social cognition and its role in early childhood. Moreover, they differed in their view of how social cognition affects higher-order cognition. To explore these questions, let us turn now to a detailed look at the ideas of these important theorists.

A Piagetian View

We have already looked at several aspects of the Piagetian view of the preoperational period and seen that Piaget described the preschooler as being perceptually bound. But there are other characteristics of preoperational thought we need to explore more fully to round out the picture Piaget painted of the preoperational period.

Egocentrism

Recall from Chapter 6 that Piaget described preoperational children as *egocentric* in their thinking. By this he meant that children of this age have difficulty taking into account any viewpoint other than their own. For example, a 4-year-old coming home from nursery school might tell his mother, "Pascal did it," not explaining who Pascal is or what he did. According to Piaget, this egocentric language results from the child's inability to take his mother's perspective, to understand that his mother might not know who Pascal is. The 4-year-old assumes everyone knows what he knows, sees things as he does, and remembers what he remembers.

An experimental demonstration of egocentrism came from the work of Piaget and Inhelder (1956). They presented children with a three-dimensional model of three mountains. Arranged around the mountains were different objects, such as a small house and a cross, that were visible from some angles but not others. Preschool children were asked to describe whether an observer (a small wooden doll) on the other side of the table could see particular objects (see Figure 8.1). Children typically responded that the

Figure 8–1   Example of the stimulus apparatus for the three-mountain task

SOURCE: Galotti (2008, p. 507).

observer could see everything the child could see, failing to take into account the observer's different vantage point.

According to Piaget, preschool children's inability to "decenter" is responsible for cognitively "trapping" them in their own perspective. Preschoolers simply have an impossible time putting themselves in place of another—either physically, as their performance on the three-mountain task shows, or linguistically, as the example with Pascal demonstrates.

However, other researchers disputed this Piagetian interpretation. They showed that, at least on certain tasks, preschoolers can show ability to behave non-egocentrically. Borke (1975), for example, constructed a version of the three-mountain task using familiar landmarks and small toy animals and having the *Sesame Street* character Grover drive around the model. Given this task, even 3-year-olds could show good spatial perspective taking. Shatz and Gelman (1973) showed that 4-year-olds routinely adjusted their speech when they talked to 2-year-olds versus adults, suggesting at least some rudimentary ability to partially take the linguistic perspective of another. Epley, Morewedge, and Keysar (2004) have even argued that both adults and children make initial egocentric interpretations of information but that adults later subsequently correct them.

The Appearance–Reality Distinction

Another facet of preoperational children being bound by their perceptions, according to Piaget, is their inability to distinguish between appearance and reality. But the ability to make this distinction goes well beyond perception and into the realm of reasoning, which is why I chose to talk about this topic here.

To provide a concrete example of the phenomenon, take the experience of meeting characters dressed up in costume. Preschool children often have difficulty bearing in mind that the character is a person wearing a costume. Both of my children, as 3- or 4-year-olds, were scared of

Photo 8.1 Understanding that Minnie Mouse is really a person wearing a(n oversized) costume is a developing ability for preschoolers.

"bad guys" such as Captain Hook or Jafar when taken to Disney World. My son Tim, in fact, spent much of one memorable trip screaming and running away from any Disney character, even the cuddly ones like Winnie the Pooh or Minnie Mouse. (In Tim's defense, he was 3 years old at the time.) We had several discussions with him that day. In the calm of lunch he would thoughtfully repeat, "They're just people wearing a costume—like at Halloween," but this mantra seemed to leave his head when a character showed up!

Flavell, Green, and Flavell (1986) investigated children's ability to draw the **appearance–reality distinction** more systematically. First, the investigators made sure that children knew color and object names. Then they were shown a series of stimuli. Some were objects with a colored filter over them. So, for example, the child might have seen a red car and then watched while a green filter went over it, making the car appear black. Children were asked, "What color is this car? Is it red, or is it black?" They were also shown illusory objects such as an eraser with a Life Savers wrapper wrapped around it and were asked, "What is this? Is it candy or an eraser?" Most of the children (almost all 3-year-olds) had difficulty consistently answering these questions correctly. Flavell et al. embarked on a heroic series of training experiences to try to make the questions clearer to the children. Table 8.1 presents the training protocol used.

Table 8–1 Training protocol used by Flavell, Green, and Flavell (1986), Study 3

The experimenter introduced the child to a white lamb hand puppet and trained the child as follows.

Introduction. "Really and truly he is a white lamb. What color is his tummy? . . . his arms? . . . his back? That's right. Really and truly he is a white lamb. What color is he really and truly? That's right, really and truly he is a white lamb."

Opaque House. "He likes to play hiding games. He's going to hide behind this house [opaque]. Can you remember what color he is really and truly? That's right, really and truly he is white [puppet pops up]." If the child erred, the experimenter said, "Actually, really and truly he is white," showed the puppet, and then reasked the question.

Red Window. "Now he's going to hide his real color. This time he'll pretend to be a different color than he really and truly is. He'll hide behind a red window [made of red filter]. Really and truly he is a white lamb. But what color is he pretending to be right now? That's right/actually, he is pretending to be red right now. Right now he looks red but really and truly he's white [puppet peeks around window, then goes behind it again]."

Opaque Building. "Now he's going to hide behind the apartment building [opaque]. Can you remember what color this lamb is really and truly? That's right/actually..."

Blue Tent. "Now he will hide behind the blue tent. Really and truly he is a white lamb, but what color does he look right now? That's right/actually, right now he looks blue. This tent makes him look blue right now. But what color is he really and truly? That's right/actually, really and truly he is white [puppet pops up]. He just looks blue right now."

Green Bush. "Now he's going to hide his real color behind the green bush. What color is he really and truly—is he really and truly green or is he really and truly white? That's right/actually, he looks green right now, but really and truly he is white. Really and truly he is always white but he can look lots of different colors. This red window makes him look red [demonstrate]. This blue tent makes him look blue [demonstrate]. Why does he look green right now [lamb behind bush]? Because you are looking through the green bush. But really and truly he is white."

Powder Puff. "Now we'll play some more hiding games. I will hide some things so you can't see what color they are really and truly. Right now you can't see what color this powder puff is really and truly [pink powder puff behind blue filter]. How can you find out what color it is really and truly?" If the child does or says nothing or simply reports the apparent color, the experimenter says, "Can you move this to find out what color it is really and truly?" If the child does not say "pink" spontaneously after removing the filter, he is asked what color it is really and truly and, after answering, is told, "That's right, really and truly the powder puff is pink." Then while moving the powder puff slowly in and out from behind the blue filter, the experimenter says, "What color is the powder puff really and truly? That's right/actually really and truly it is pink. It just looks blue right now because of this thing [point to filter]."

Car. "Now I'm hiding a car [red car behind blue filter]. You find out what color the car is really and truly." If the child does not remove the filter, he or she is prompted to do so, and the car's real color is established, as above. "Now you use this [filter] to hide its real color. What color does the car look right now? That's right/actually, it looks black right now. But what color is it really and truly? That's right/actually, really and truly it is red. It just looks black right now."

SOURCE: Flavell, Green, & Flavell (1986, pp. 21–22).

As you can see, the investigators went to great lengths to explain to children what they meant by the distinction between what an object is (really and truly) and what it looks like (to the eye), and gave the children a lot of feedback and practice with appearance–reality questions. Despite this, only 1 child out of 16 showed substantial improvement as a result of the training.

From the results of the series of studies they conducted, Flavell, Green, and Flavell (1986) concluded that 3-year-olds really do not have a firm grasp of the appearance–reality distinction. In fact, this conclusion was consistent with a cross-cultural study carried out with 3-year-olds from China (Flavell, Zhang, Zou, Dong, & Qi, 1983). The authors speculated that 3-year-olds might form only one encoding or representation of a stimulus—and then report that representation for every question asked. You might note the similarity here to explanations DeLoache (1995) and her colleagues gave for two-and-a-half-year-olds' inability to use scale models—the inability to coordinate two different representations (we discussed this in Chapter 6).

Interestingly, 4- and 5-year-olds are much better at appearance–reality tasks (as they are also relatively quite proficient with scale models). What is it that causes this cognitive development? Presumably, neurological and experiential factors help. But it may also help to look at a context for preschoolers' activities to get some clues. As we are about to see, Vygotsky placed a lot more emphasis on the activities preschoolers engage in and the people they interact with than did Piaget. We turn next to these ideas.

A Vygotskian View

You may recall from Chapter 2 that theorist Lev Vygotsky developed what is known as the sociocultural approach to the study of cognitive development. In a nutshell, Vygotsky believed that the cultural context that surrounds a child is, in fact, inseparable from the child when studying development. Unlike Piaget, who saw cognitive development as an internal process, Vygotsky focused more on a child's social and cultural surroundings, seeing those as a vital force in how a child developed.

For Vygotsky, mental structures, such as those used in higher-order cognitive processing, were *co*-constructed by the child and his peers, parents, or teachers. That is, the mental structures emerged as a result of the activities the child engaged in. Thus, a child's level of cognitive development was not a specific point but rather a zone—the *zone of proximal development,* which we have already talked about in previous chapters. Said another way, a child's level of development would be at one point if he were working, unaided, on a task all by himself. But, if a more competent peer or adult was providing help or structured feedback (in a process known as *scaffolding*), that child's level of functioning would be higher. Neither level is more "correct" or true as a measure of the child's ability than the other—the entire zone represents the kind of performance a child is capable of giving, under a wide variety of different parameters.

For Piaget, cognitive development during early childhood largely equated to overcoming egocentrism and centration on one's own perceptions. For Vygotsky, in contrast, cognitive development during early childhood consisted of engaging in a wider variety of activities, including play, that make use of social relationships to develop and create new mental structures. We'll look at this idea in greater detail as we explore the topic of play.

The Role of Play

If you were to have visited my daughter's day care center 3 years ago at almost any time other than lunch or nap time, you would have found 20 or so children aged two and a half to five and a half engaged in free play. It's been said that the work of the child is play, and this explains why play influences so many realms of the preschooler's development. It is fairly self-evident how children learn important social skills during play—taking turns with a favorite toy or during a game; coordinating one's own vision of "house" with someone else's; figuring out how to enter or leave a group setting.

Perhaps less obvious are the many contributions that play can make to a child's cognitive development. Various theorists have taken different positions on the role of play in cognitive development. Some, such as Piaget, see play as a vehicle for a child to *express* his level of cognitive development. In other words, the complexity of play grows in tandem with the complexity of a child's level of cognitive functioning—older children play in more complex ways (role-playing a game of dinosaurs and kittens, for example) than do toddlers (who might stack blocks or bang a drum). Presumably, the more advanced underlying cognitive structures enable more sophisticated play (Fein, 1981).

Vygotsky, in contrast, saw play as *enabling* a zone of proximal development. In play, Vygotsky felt, children begin to use objects in a symbolic way: A branch becomes a horse to ride on, or a doll is treated as a baby, for example. In making these substitutions, children learn to separate an object's meaning from the object itself (Miller, 2011). The physical doll is no longer simply an object with arms and legs and a head but is treated as if it has needs and wants and perhaps even a personality. The doll is both a doll and a baby. Due to their use of symbolism in play, especially pretend play, children can operate at a higher level of cognitive functioning than they typically do outside the realm of play.

Pretense play (also known sometimes as pretend play, sociodramatic play, imaginative play, or fantasy play) is of particular relevance to Vygotsky's theory. In pretense play, children behave in a simulated, "as-if" manner (Fein, 1981). This kind of play emerges after a child's first birthday, when he may begin to show "pretend gestures," typically self-referenced ones. He may, for example, pretend to drink from a cup or pretend to sleep. By midway

Photo 8.2   Some theorists, such as Vygotsky, see children's play as enabling cognitive growth.

through the second year, the toddler may show other-referenced pretend behaviors—pretending to feed his mother or father. The use of dolls in pretend play increases during the years from 2 to 7, and by the time a child is 4, he can adopt different voices for the dolls, using "baby talk" to talk for them or to them (Fein, 1981).

At around age 3, children begin to engage in social pretense play. This is significant, for this kind of play requires a great deal of "metacommunication"— conversation about the ongoing game that is not part of the game. "How about if you have two cats and you don't like dogs?" one child might suggest to her play partner. Or, as my then 5-year-old daughter instructed a companion, "There *are* no kitties in a princess game, so you have to be something else." Children must build shared meaning in their pretend games, agreeing on who will play what role; determining what various objects in the game might represent; and developing scripts and dialogue (Howe, Petrakos, Rinaldi, & LeFebvre, 2005). And, to play their roles, they might need to adopt a different perspective or consider how an object or event would be experienced by someone else.

As children get a little older, the range of simulated identities they can assume becomes larger and more diverse. While 3-year-olds might restrict most of their pretense play to games of "house," with familiar roles of mommy and daddy and baby and dog, older preschoolers can play elaborate games of superheroes or rock stars (Fein, 1981). The pretend play of children aged 4 to 8 years has been shown to have a real narrative structure, much as the stories of children of this age would have, complete with protagonists, goals, events, episodes, and outcomes (Eckler & Weininger, 1989).

Pretense play is not the only kind of play thought to affect cognitive development. **Physical activity play**, sometimes called exercise play, involves children in games that are vigorous and can include running and chasing, play wrestling, jumping, tumbling, lifting, climbing, or the like (Pellegrini & Smith, 1998). This kind of play, which is typically seen as frequently as or even more frequently than pretense play, seems to increase from the toddler to the preschool period, peaking at around age 4 or 5 years. In addition to helping increase children's strength and physical endurance, it is also thought to provide several indirect benefits to cognitive processes. First, it can lead to heightened arousal, which might benefit cognitive performance on some tasks. Second, exercise play might provide necessary breaks from demanding cognitive tasks, and those breaks might allow better concentration and encoding when children go back to their cognitive work. Third, the lighthearted nature of exercise play might promote feelings of mastery, which might in turn enhance one's ability to confront complex cognitive challenges. This, in turn, might enable a preschooler to handle more higher-order cognitive tasks. As we shall see very soon, in fact, a playful context does enhance preschoolers' ability to reason.

REASONING

Standard Piagetian views of reasoning during the preschool period hold that these skills are unsystematic. Without concrete operations, preschoolers are completely unprepared to do any kind of abstract reasoning (a task requiring formal operations, which are held to emerge at or after puberty). And indeed, preschoolers' difficulty with conservation tasks (discussed in Chapter 6) or in perspective taking or separating appearance from reality seems to fit well with the Piagetian characterization of preschool cognitive incompetence.

Vygotskian theory grants preschoolers a little more competence. Under certain circumstances, with the appropriate amount of scaffolding, assistance, or a less complex version of a task, Vygotsky held, a child can show the beginnings of a fragile competence. And indeed, many researchers have come to reject the Piagetian views that preschoolers are, generally speaking, cognitively inept (Bjorklund & Green, 1992; Gelman, 1979).

In this section, we'll examine preschoolers' ability to reason and draw inferences, as well as make analogies. Before delving into the literature, a few definitions are in order. The term *reasoning* is often used interchangeably with the term *thinking*. Investigators who do make a distinction between reasoning and thinking see the first as a special case of the second. Specifically, the term *reasoning* indicates a specific kind of thinking: the kind done using certain principles of logic. At other times, the term *reasoning* is used more broadly, to cover instances of thinking in which people take certain information as input and, by making various inferences, either create new information or make implicit information explicit.

Cognitive psychologists distinguish between deductive and inductive reasoning (Galotti, 2008). There are several possible ways of drawing this distinction, but the one I think is clearest for our purposes is to say that deductive reasoning goes from the general to the specific or particular (e.g., "All kindergarteners like *Hannah Montana*. Kimmie is a kindergarten student. Therefore, Kimmie likes *Hannah Montana*"). Inductive reasoning, on the other hand, goes from the specific to the general (e.g., "Tim is a high school student. Tim likes mineral water. Therefore, all high school students like mineral water"). We'll take up the two different kinds of reasoning in turn.

Deductive Reasoning

In line with the Vygotskian perspective, Hawkins, Pea, Glick, and Scribner (1984) demonstrated that, under certain circumstances at least, preschoolers aged 4 and 5 years could draw deductive inferences. The authors began by constructing various deductive reasoning problems, examples of which are shown in Table 8.2. Their thinking was that one factor that might be a problem for preschoolers was isolating the premises from their preexisting real-world knowledge and reasoning only from the premises. In fact, adults have been found to have trouble with this isolation (Henle, 1962), as have individuals who have not received formal schooling (Cole & Scribner, 1974).

Table 8–2 Types of problems used by Hawkins, Pea, Glick, and Scribner (1984)

Model	Affirmative example	Negative example
A is B	Every banga is purple.	Bears have big teeth.
B is C	Purple animals always sneeze at people.	Animals with big teeth can't read books.
A is C	Do bangas sneeze at people?	Can bears read books?
***		
A has B	Pogs wear blue boots.	Rabbits never bite.
C is an A	Tom is a pog.	Cuddly is a rabbit.
C has B	Does Tom wear blue boots?	Does Cuddly bite?
***		
A does B when...	Glasses bounce when they fall.	Merds laugh when they're happy.
B is C	Everything that bounces is made of rubber.	Animals that laugh don't like mushrooms.
A has C	Are glasses made of rubber?	Do merds like mushrooms?

SOURCE: Adapted from Hawkins, Pea, Glick, & Scribner (1984, p. 585).

Hawkins et al. (1984) created three types of problems. The first consisted of premises that were congruent with the child's world knowledge—for example, "Bears have big teeth. Animals with big teeth can't read books. Can bears read books?" Note that whether a child actually reasoned from the premises or from her world knowledge of the general illiteracy of bears, she would have arrived at the deductively correct conclusion, "No." Preschoolers were expected to do particularly well on these problems, even if their scores overstated their true reasoning ability.

A second type of problem included information that was incongruent with the child's world knowledge—for example, "Glasses bounce when they fall. Everything that bounces is made of rubber. Are glasses made of rubber?" Here, the deductively correct answer is directly at odds with the answer a reasoner would derive from strictly reasoning from the premises to answer the question. Preschoolers were expected to do particularly poorly on these problems, as it was expected they would answer the questions using their world knowledge rather than use abstract reasoning to derive a valid conclusion.

The most theoretically interesting type of problem was one using so-called "fantasy" premises—for example, "Every banga is purple. Purple animals always sneeze at people. Do bangas sneeze at people?" Notice that in these problems, there is no relevant world knowledge for the child to call upon. Hawkins et al. (1984) believed, then, that fantasy problems would be the ones most likely to reveal whether or not preschool children could, in fact, use deductive reasoning.

The results were clear-cut. Children were presented with 8 problems of each kind. Overall, children gave correct responses to 7.5, 1.0, and 5.8 congruent, incongruent, and fantasy problems, respectively. A chance level of performance was 4, and thus children performed significantly better than chance on the fantasy (and congruent) problems. Thus, the authors concluded, preschool children, under limited circumstances, *can* reason deductively.

Hawkins et al. (1984) also looked at the kinds of justifications children provided for their answers. This helped distinguish children who were giving the correct answer, but for the wrong reason. One of the categories of justification was "theoretical," and children were credited with this type of justification *only* if they appeared to be reasoning strictly from the premises. Indeed, children provided a theoretical justification much more often on fantasy problems (1.64 out of 8) than they did on either congruent (0.83 out of 8) or incongruent (0.30 out of 8) problems.

Moreover, the order in which the problems were administered was crucially important. Children who reasoned with fantasy premises first tended to perform better on all problems, even the congruent and incongruent ones, than did the children who received congruent problems first, incongruent problems first, or problems in a jumbled order. Hawkins et al. (1984) argued that presenting fantasy problems first sets a context for children to help cue them as to how to correctly solve the problem. When congruent or incongruent problems were presented first, children mistakenly recruited their real-world knowledge to answer the questions, instead of relying strictly on the premises.

Inductive Reasoning

Another form of reasoning occurs more commonly in everyday life—**inductive reasoning**. We learned earlier that inductive reasoning goes from the specific to the general. What this means is that inductive conclusions can only have a probability of being true, unlike deductively valid conclusions, which are guaranteed to be true if the premises are true (Galotti, 1989). Examples of inductive reasoning include analogies, either verbal (e.g., father is to son as mother is to ____) or geometric, as shown in Figure 8.2. Inductive reasoning is also used in so-called *series completion problems* (e.g., fill in the letter that correctly fills the blank: a z b y c x d __).

Figure 8–2   Example of pictorial analogies

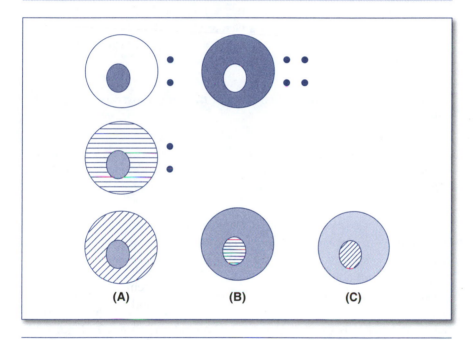

(A)   (B)   (C)

SOURCE: Galotti (2008, p. 432).

Inductive reasoning is also used in categorization, as the studies by Susan Gelman and her associates (reviewed in Chapter 7) showed. When reasoning about the internal organs possessed by a dog by generalizing from what he knows about a human or other animal, a child is drawing inferences that have inductive strength rather than deductive validity.

The study of children's (or adults') intuitive ideas about entities and processes in the biological world is known as **folk biology** (Waxman, Medin, & Ross, 2007). This area of investigation was energized by a landmark study conducted by Susan Carey in 1985. Carey invented something called a "projection" test. She interviewed children aged 4, 6, and 10 years and as adults and in the course of the interview told them about a presumably unfamiliar body part. Younger children were told about a spleen; 10-year-olds and adults about an *omentum* (which is a thin membrane that holds intestinal organs in place). Some of the participants were told that a person had the organ in question. Others were told that a dog had it. Still others were told that a bee had it. Carey (1985) used the following wording to teach the new term:

> I'm going to teach you a new word. Has anyone ever heard of a "spleen?" A spleen is round and green. Here's a picture of something that has a spleen. What is this a picture of? Good. I'm going to draw the spleen where it is found in the person's (or dog's or bee's) body. (p. 114)

Ten-year-olds and adults, first warned that the study was designed for younger children, were told:

> Omenta are yellowish in color, and are flat and thin. Here is a picture of something that has an omentum. I am going to draw one approximately where it is found in a person's (or dog's or bee's) body. (Carey, 1985, p. 115)

Next, respondents were asked whether other entities—people, dogs, birds, bugs, worms, flowers, the sun, a cloud, a harvester (farm machine)—would have a spleen (for the two youngest groups) or an omentum (for 10-year-olds and adults). All groups were likely to project the organ from people to other nonhuman animals, as shown in Figure 8.3. However, adults and older children were more differentiated in their projections from other animals than were younger children, as shown in Figure 8.4. Four-year-olds were more likely to project having a spleen to other animals if taught that a person had a spleen than if taught that a dog had a spleen. Even though arguably dogs are more similar to other mammals (such as aardvarks) than people, preschoolers were still less likely to generalize from dogs to aardvarks.

Carey's idea is that preschoolers have very limited intuitive ideas of biological properties and principles and that they reason instead based on an organism's similarity to a human being. In fact, Carey (1985) held that younger children don't adopt a mature intuitive notion of what living things are and what properties they have much before they reach their ninth or tenth birthday.

Figure 8–3 Patterns of projection from people. Spleen (4-year-olds, 6-year-olds); omentum (10-year-olds, adults)

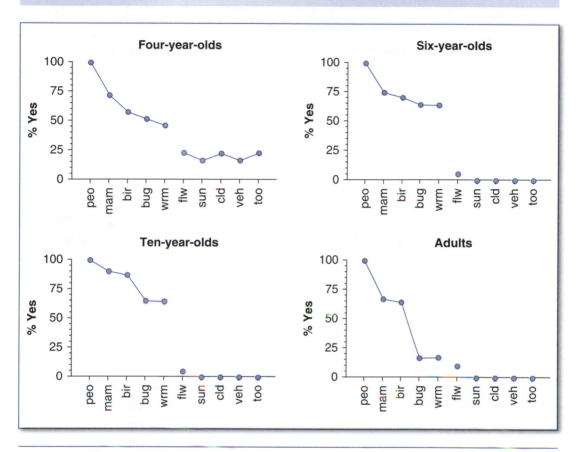

SOURCE: Carey (1985, p. 119).

More recent work has cast some doubt on Carey's claims, showing that at least some preschoolers have more biological knowledge than Carey described. Both Tarlowski (2006) and Waxman et al. (2007) showed that children who had more extensive exposure to biology—either because they were children of biologists or naturalists or because they lived in rural communities—were less likely than urban children of laypeople to make inductive inferences based on the similarity between a human being and another entity. In other words, children who had some expertise or background in biology showed more sophisticated biological inductive inferences.

Figure 8–4 Patterns of projection from people, dogs, and bees. Spleen (4-year-olds, 6-year-olds); omentum (10-year-olds, adults). ●———● taught on people; ☐·-·-☐ taught on dogs; ▲·····▲ taught on bees

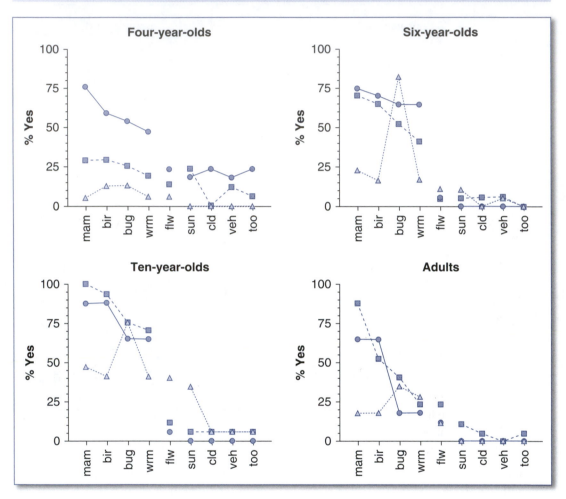

SOURCE: Carey (1985, p. 127).

Indeed, and more generally, many cognitive developmental psychologists see children's inductive reasoning as constrained by their limited knowledge bases. The reason that older children perform better on most inductive reasoning tasks is that older children, generally speaking, have more extensive knowledge and more expertise in more domains than do younger children. This expertise in turn is recruited when the child attempts to solve an analogy problem, discover a pattern, or project properties from one organism to another (Goswami, Leevers, Pressley, & Wheelwright, 1998; Richland, Morrison, & Holyoak, 2006). This conclusion seems to fit nicely with the conclusions about expertise and memory reached by Michele Chi, discussed in Chapter 7.

Reasoning About Number

Deductive and inductive reasoning are thought to be two very general forms of reasoning, applicable to a variety of topics or realms. That is, both are thought of as general-purpose cognitive mechanisms that children and adults can use in drawing conclusions in a wide range of domains. Some psychologists posit the existence of additional, *domain-specific* reasoning mechanisms—that is, ways of reasoning that only apply to one domain or a very limited number of domains. One example is reasoning about number.

We saw in Chapter 6 that preschool children typically fail the number conservation task (as well as several other kinds of conservation tasks for that matter). According to Piagetian theory, preschoolers fail a typical number conservation task because, lacking operations and being bound by their immediate perceptions, preschoolers confuse the appearance of the two rows of checkers, where the less dense one looks longer and appears to have more, with the reality that both rows of checkers have the same number. They fail to consider the fact that no numerically relevant transformation (e.g., addition or subtraction) has occurred and therefore that the numerosity of the row doesn't change when the row length is expanded or contracted.

Rochel Gelman (1969) argued that there is an alternative explanation for the child's responses. This explanation is based on the child's attention during the task. Notice that at the beginning of the conservation task the two rows of checkers are lined up in one-to-one correspondence. They are equal *not only* in the number of checkers *but also* in the length of the rows and in the density of the rows. Thus, even if the child were paying attention to length or density to answer the initial question of which row has more checkers, he would come to the correct answer that the two rows are the same. That is, even if the child were paying attention to the wrong cue (e.g., length or density) as opposed to the correct cue (numerosity), he would still give the correct response. Presumably, then, to help preschoolers become numerical conservers, experimenters needed to communicate more clearly to preschoolers what aspects of the stimulus display they should attend to.

Gelman (1969) tested this idea by presenting nonconserving preschoolers with discrimination training. These children were presented with sets of problems like those shown in Figure 8.5. They were asked either to show two rows that had the same number of things in them (on the number training trials) or to show two sticks that had the same length (on the length trials).

Figure 8–5 Schematic representation of intraproblem variations for length and number problems presented during training

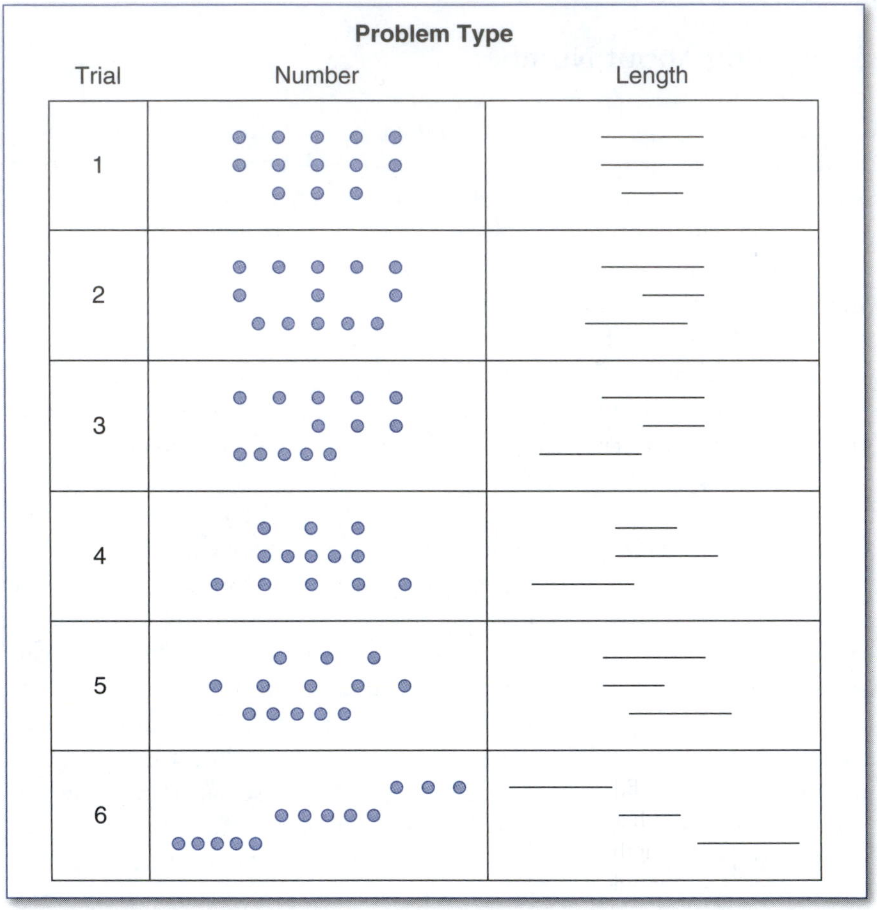

SOURCE: Gelman (1969, p. 174).

Children received 16 sets of number trials (where a set consisted of 6 trials as shown in Figure 8.5) and 16 sets of length trials. Each time children responded correctly they were given a small trinket as a prize.

The two sets of problems differed in color, size, and/or shape of the materials. Each set followed the sequences shown in Figure 8.5. Notice that, for the first problem shown, whether a child was paying attention to the length of rows, density of rows, or numerosity of rows (for the number trials), he would have been able to answer the question about number correctly. However, to answer correctly on Problems 2–5, the child would have had to attend specifically to numerosity, as that would be the only cue that would consistently lead to correct answers (and prizes!). The sixth trial could only be answered by using numerosity, as there were no rows matching in length or density.

Some children were given feedback on their performance after each trial, as described above. Other children, in a control condition, were not. Results showed that the first group of children, over trials, went from answering 60% of the problems correctly to answering 95% of the problems correctly. Children who did not receive feedback, in contrast, improved very little, answering only 70% correctly after 32 sets of problems. Gelman (1969) concluded that, with feedback, preschoolers quickly focused on the right cue, that of numerosity. Moreover, these previously nonconserving preschoolers answered a posttest of number and length conservation nearly perfectly (averaging around 95% correct on both). According to Gelman, then, at least some of the reason preschoolers fail standard Piagetian conservation tasks is because they are paying attention to the wrong cues.

Gelman (1972) followed up on this work with some classic studies that have come to be called "the magic experiments." Preschool children played games with an experimenter. Each game contained two white plates, each containing either two or three toy mice Velcroed into position. The plates were covered by white cans. The two plates differed in the number of mice and in either the length of the rows of mice or the density of the row of mice.

After a warm-up phase in which the experimenter played games with each child individually to establish rapport, the second phase began as follows:

[The experimenter, E,] picked up the cans covering the displays. The child saw two plates, each with a row of mice on it. The rows differed in number (three vs. two), and either length [of the row of mice] (8.8 cm vs. 5 cm) or density (2.5 cm vs. 6.2 cm between mice). *Without mentioning any of the differences between them,* the experimenter identified the three-mouse display and the two-mouse display the "winner" and "loser," respectively. The following instructions were given to the child:

Now, what do you see on the table in front of you [referring to the cans]? What do you think is under those cans? Take a look. Okay, now do you want me to tell you how we're going to play the game with those mice? We're going to try to find you the plate that wins you a prize. Do you like to win prizes? Good. Well, this is the winner [while pointing to the three-mouse display]. Whenever you find this under the can like this [covers, and uncovers], you get to pick a prize [E then covers the three-mouse display]. But this [E points to the two-mouse display] is the loser plate, and when you find it [covers, and uncovers], you never win a prize. Okay? [E then covers the two-mouse display.] Now remember, this [uncovers the three-mouse display] is the winner and this [uncovers the two-mouse display] is the loser. Are you ready to start playing the game? [E covers the plates and begins to mix the cans.] First, I'm going to mix up the cans all around and around. Now, where do you think the winner is? Okay, pick it up. Is that the winner? (Gelman, 1972, p. 78)

If the child uncovered a three-mouse display and correctly labeled it the winner plate, he was given a small trinket as a prize, and a new trial of hiding and mixing the plates ensued. If instead he initially uncovered a two-mouse display, the plate was covered, and with no further mixing, the child was invited to find the winner plate. (This was not a particularly hard task, and all the children succeeded at it.) When they identified it as the winner plate they won a prize.

This procedure continued for 10 or 11 trials of uncovering plates (11 if the 10th plate uncovered was a two-mouse plate). Then, surreptitiously, the game changed. While the child was playing with his pile of trinket prizes, the experimenter made a change to one of the displays. (Different changes were made for different children.) Some of these changes were number-relevant changes—for example, subtracting a mouse from the three-mouse display. Other changes were number-irrelevant—for example, changing the length and/or density of a row of mice on one of the plates. The question was what would happen after this surreptitious change, which appeared to the child to have come about "magically."

According to Piagetian theory, preschool children do not have a firm understanding of abstract concepts like number. Thus, they do not differentiate between transformations that affect numerosity (e.g., subtraction or addition) and those that do not (e.g., rearranging the spatial configuration of the mice on a plate). Thus, the children in the "magic" experiment should have reacted the same way to all kinds of changes.

Instead, children showed a great sensitivity to what kind of change was made. For the 48 children experiencing a number-relevant change, 92% showed clear signs of doubt that a winner plate existed after a mouse had been subtracted from the three-mouse plate. In contrast, 94% of the children experiencing a number-irrelevant change claimed that the rearranged mice still comprised a "winner" plate and that the game could go on. Gelman (1972) concluded that these data support the idea that very young children do, in fact, possess a rudimentary understanding of what number is and what kinds of transformations affect it.

THEORY OF MIND

There are many delightful cognitive developments to be seen during the preschool period. There are some consequences of those developments that are somewhat less than delightful. Specifically, I'm thinking here of the fact that my oldest child started to learn in this period how to lie effectively. My daughter, when she was in transition between the preschool period and middle childhood, still believed that I could tell when she was "fibbing" by looking her in the eyes. So when she lied, she shielded her eyes with her hand, which was a dead giveaway. However, older children figure out that if they keep a straight face and "look" honest, they can sometimes tell lies that go undetected.

We have moral prohibitions in our culture against lying, for the most part. It's not something we want children (or each other) to be good at. However, when looked at objectively, lying effectively is a pretty remarkable cognitive achievement. It requires the liar to model what she thinks the person being lied to knows and believes, and to frame the false message in believable terms. In short, it requires what developmental and comparative psychologists have called a *theory of mind* (Leslie, 1992; Premack & Woodruff, 1978; Wellman, 1992).

Theory of mind refers to more than just a list of how-tos on lying, of course. A person's theory of mind guides her beliefs and expectations about what another person is thinking, feeling, or expecting; it guides one's ability to predict accurately what another person's reaction will be to a specific set of circumstances (Flavell, Green, & Flavell, 1995). When I have been stressed out at home, for example, my preschool daughter often offered to let me hold her doll Bitty Baby (which, surprisingly, did not do for me what it did for her); my adolescent son, in contrast, sometimes cleaned up dinner dishes or picked his dirty socks up off the floor—actions that (somewhat inexplicably for him) made me feel noticeably better. My older child was showing his ability to predict what sorts of things provide me with comfort—while recognizing that what is important to me differed (at the time, drastically) from what was important to him.

Investigating Theory of Mind

One common task used to investigate preschool children's theory of mind is the so-called **false belief task** (Wimmer & Perner, 1983). For example, children might be told a story about a boy who puts a toy in a box and leaves the room. While he is away, his sister enters the room, takes the toy out of the box, plays with it, and puts it away in a different location. Children are then asked where the *boy* (who was not present in the room at the time the toy was moved) will think the toy is. In other words, can the children disentangle *their* own state of knowledge about the toy from the state of knowledge or belief of someone who lacks their information? Consistent with Piagetian theory, this ability develops slowly over the preschool period (Jenkins & Astington, 1996). Figure 8.6 provides a depiction of the task.

Figure 8–6 A depiction of the false belief task

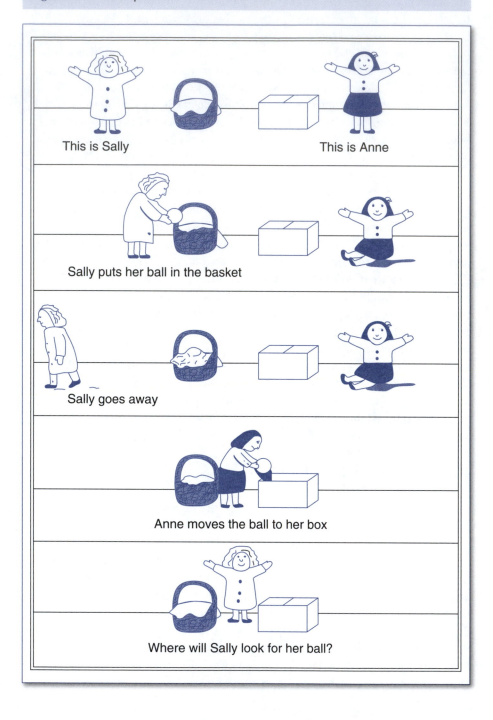

This is Sally   This is Anne

Sally puts her ball in the basket

Sally goes away

Anne moves the ball to her box

Where will Sally look for her ball?

Other theory of mind tasks include the *unexpected contents* task (Gopnik & Astington, 1988; Perner, Leekham, & Wimmer, 1987), in which a child is handed a box of, say, crayons but opens it to discover that the box really contains small candies. The child is then asked to predict what another child, who has no previous experience with the crayon box, will think is inside. Typically, children younger than about 4 years answer that they knew all along that the box contained candies rather than crayons, even though they initially answered "crayons" when asked what was in the box. Further, young preschoolers respond that someone else coming into the room later will think that the crayon box contains candies rather than crayons.

Notice that both the false belief and the unexpected contents tasks ask children to distinguish between reality and a person's beliefs about reality. As we saw earlier, distinguishing between reality and physical appearance is a task quite difficult for preschoolers younger than age 3. It may be that similar kinds of confusions hinder 3-year-olds' performance on theory of mind tasks.

A study by Mitchell and Lacohée (1991) is consistent with this view. They used a version of an unexpected contents task with a slight variation. Children were shown a tube of Smarties (a type of candy quite popular with the preschool set) and asked what they thought was inside the tube. Typically, the children responded that Smarties candies were in the Smarties tube. They were then asked to select a picture from among a set of four (depicting Lego toys, small toy people, crayons, and Smarties candies) and to "post" the picture into a mailbox. Next, the true (unexpected) contents of the Smarties tube was presented—it contained pencils. Next, the experimenters asked a very specific question of the children in the experimental condition: "When you posted your picture in the postbox, what did you think was inside this tube?" Children in the standard (control) condition were not asked to post a photo and were simply asked, "When you first saw the box, what did you think was inside it?"

Three-year-old children were tested. Of children who "posted" a picture, 71% answered the "what did you think was in the box" question correctly, compared with only 14% of similarly aged children in the control condition. However, the authors noted that the better performance of the first group of children might stem from the "posting" activity marking very specifically a moment in time from which children were asked to recall their beliefs. To rule out this possibility, Mitchell and Lacohée (1991) ran a control condition in which children were asked, after they first predicted the contents of the Smarties tube, to post an irrelevant picture (e.g., one of their favorite animal, food, color, or cartoon character). They then went on to open the tube and find the unexpected contents, and then they were asked, "When you posted your picture in the mailbox, what did you think was inside this tube?" In this control condition, only 36% of the 3-year-olds answered correctly.

Mitchell and Lacohée (1991) believe that the posting task helps endow children's initial (incorrect) belief with a physical embodiment (the posted card). It's as if posting makes a child's belief more concrete and, thus, more memorable. In turn, this physically enduring embodiment makes concrete for children that there is a difference between their current belief state and their original belief state.

Atance and O'Neill (2004) conducted a similar study. They first showed 3-year-olds a crayon box and asked them to predict the contents. Unsurprisingly, the children predicted crayons and went to get some paper to draw on. When they returned with the paper, the children were shown that the crayon box really contained candles. They were asked to say what they initially thought the box contained. Those children, unable to remember that they used to think it contained crayons, were unable to explain why they went to get paper. The authors argue that being able to simply remember a false belief is not enough to credit a child with a theory of mind. That crediting requires that a child be able to use her knowledge of false beliefs to explain actions.

You might be reminded in reading this section of similarities to children's confusion over the appearance–reality distinction. Indeed, there are many similarities. Children seem to acquire understanding of the appearance–reality distinction and master false belief tasks at about the same age (between 3 and 4 years old), and performance on the two tasks has been shown to be correlated (Gopnik & Astington, 1988; Melot, Houdé, Courtel, & Soenen, 1995; Slaughter & Gopnik, 1996). Moreover, Melot and Angeard (2003) report a fascinating study, in which they trained 3-year-olds (who had failed either an appearance–reality task pretest, a false belief pretest, or both) in either the appearance–reality distinction or the false belief task. Training worked in both cases to improve children's score on the task in which they were trained. More surprisingly, there were indirect benefits of training as well. Children trained, for example, on the appearance–reality distinction task showed improvement not only on those tasks but also on false belief tasks. Similarly, training on the false belief tasks led to better performance on both those tasks and appearance–reality distinction tasks.

Understanding Different Mental States

Having a theory of mind goes beyond simply understanding how to lie and deceive or how to predict what another's beliefs might be. Having a theory of mind entails understanding that people are psychological beings with different mental states—desires, beliefs, and intentions to name a few (Lillard & Flavell, 1990, 1992). In short, having a theory of mind means having what some theorists have called a folk psychology—a layperson's set of concepts and principles about how other people's minds appear to work (Churchland, 1988).

Understanding psychological states is a difficult task even for seasoned adults. After all, internal mental states do not reliably give rise to external indicators. When I want someone to do something, or when I believe that someone is not performing well, for example, there may be no physical or behavioral cues to my desire or belief. Indeed, part of becoming socialized as a functioning adult member of a community is learning to be polite, which sometimes means suppressing facial expressions or verbal requests or evaluations.

Lillard and Flavell (1990) found that 3-year-olds were somewhat more likely to choose to describe pictures in terms of a character's mental states (e.g., "She's looking for a toy") than in terms of an equally applicable behavioral description (e.g., "She's opening the toy box"). These findings suggest that 3-year-olds do reason, at least to some degree, about some mental states of others, even if the range of mental states they think about is limited.

In a later study, Lillard and Flavell (1992) found a developmental sequence to children's ability to understand that different mental states can differ from reality. First, children seem to understand that desires can differ from reality. Next, they understand that pretending that X is the case does not always mean that X is the case. Understanding a possible distinction between beliefs and reality came last.

Theory of Mind and Other Aspects of Cognitive Development

In the last three chapters we've examined several different aspects of cognitive development that (I hope) should seem quite interrelated. Specifically, the topics of executive functioning, working memory, conceptual development, understanding of the appearance–reality distinction, and development of theory of mind all seem to share common aspects. In this section, we will examine such interrelationships.

Hughes (1998) explored several of these interrelationships in a longitudinal study of preschoolers, who were tested twice over a period of 13 months beginning when they were 3 or 4 years old. Her main goal was to investigate the question "Does early performance on theory of mind tasks predict later executive functioning, or, conversely, does early executive functioning predict later theory of mind performance?"

To assess executive functioning, Hughes (1998) used two tasks. The first was a detour-reaching task. It involved the apparatus depicted in Figure 8.7. Inside, a marble sat on top of a trapdoor. The box was engineered with an infrared beam such that if one reached through the front window of the box to grab the marble, the beam activated a photoelectric circuit that opened the trapdoor, causing the marble to fall out of reach. The box had both a yellow and a green light mounted at the top of the front face. There was also a knob on the right-hand side of the box (which was attached, on the inside, to a lever and paddle). The yellow light, when lit, indicated that the knob could be used to knock the marble down a chute (this was called the "knob route" to retrieving the marble); when the green light was lit, in contrast, a switch on the left-hand side of the box could be used to deactivate the

Figure 8–7   The detour-reaching box

SOURCE: Hughes (1998, p. 1328).

circuit so that the child could reach directly into the box to retrieve the marble (called "the switch route").

After demonstrating that a direct reach into the box when the yellow light was lit resulted in the marble dropping out of sight, the experimenter gave the child the following instructions:

> "When the yellow light is on, you mustn't reach through the window for the marble. What you must do is to turn this knob here, like this." The experimenter then demonstrated the knob-route procedure for the child, and asked him or her to try to get the marble the same way. Once the child had succeeded on three consecutive knob-route trials, the next phase of the task, the switch-route trials, began. This change was effected by locking a small padlock across the lever paddle, such that the knob could no longer be used to reach the marble. The circuitry was arranged such that locking the padlock extinguished the yellow light and illuminated the green light—when the padlock was open, the lights were set in the opposite configuration.

> At this stage, the following instructions were given: "When the green light is on, you mustn't turn the knob any more, instead you have to push this switch down, and then reach with your hand for the marble." Having shown the child that the knob route was now blocked by the padlock, the experimenter demonstrated the switch-route procedure for the child, and asked him or her to try to get the marble the same way. (Hughes, 1998, p. 1329)

Hughes (1998) also used something called the hand game, invented by the Russian psychologist Alexander Luria, originally used to study executive deficits in inhibitory control shown by patients with lesions in the frontal lobe of the brain. The game is depicted in Figure 8.8. It has two conditions. In the imitative (control) condition (depicted in the top panel of Figure 8.8), the child is instructed to make the same hand shape (fist or pointed finger) that the experimenter does. In the conflict condition (depicted in the bottom panel of Figure 8.8), the child is instructed instead to make the opposite hand shape from the experimenter. Note that this latter task requires that the child inhibit a prepotent response—that is, an action that seems invited by the task. As we saw in Chapter 6, such inhibition is difficult for preschool children.

Hughes (1998) also used a version of the Dimensional Change Card Sort task described in Chapter 6 to measure executive functioning. In this version, children were shown a stuffed animal and a set of cards, of different shapes and colors (e.g., green circles and stars or orange circles and stars). Children were told that they had to help the experimenter figure out

Figure 8–8   The hand game

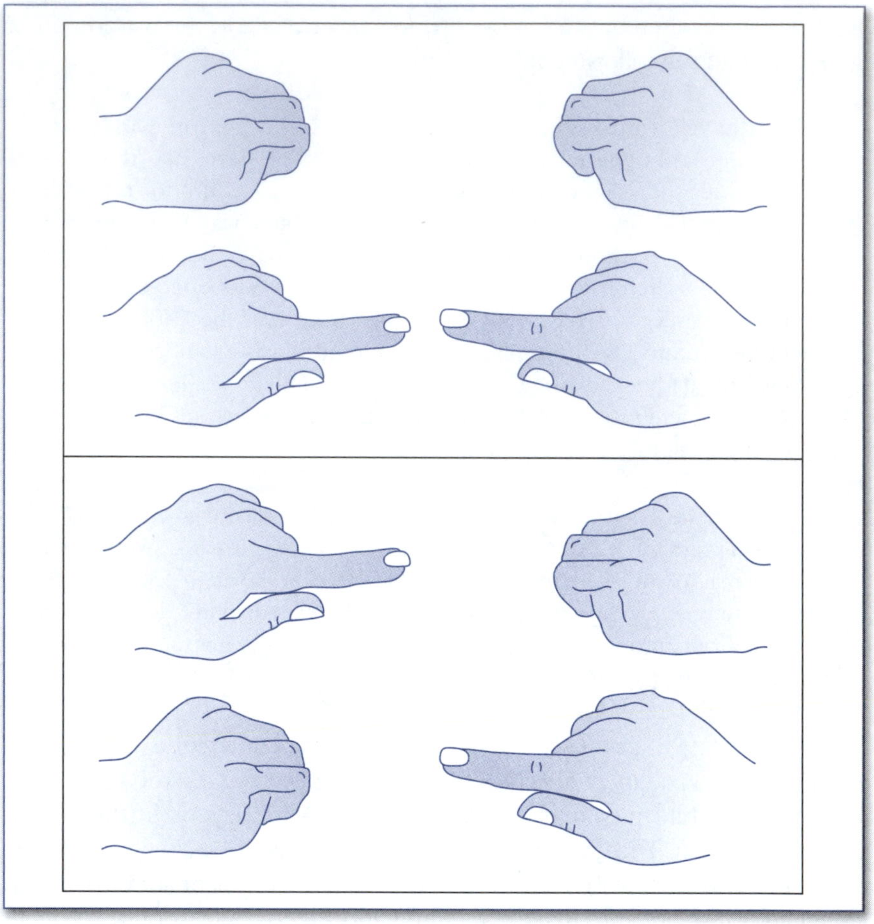

SOURCE: Hughes (1998, p. 1329).

which cards were "Teddy's favorites" and which cards "Teddy doesn't like at all" (Hughes, 1998, p. 1330). A different stuffed animal and a different deck of cards (e.g., Peter Rabbit and a deck with yellow moons and squares or pink moons or squares) were used to make it clear to the child when the rules were changing.

Finally, Hughes (1998) used a task of auditory memory called the "Noisy Book" task. A Little Red Riding Hood book with an array of nine pictures that produced sound effects when pressed was used. The experimenter first had the child name each of the nine pictures (to ensure that she and the child used the same terms to refer to a picture) and then introduced the task as follows: "I'm going to cover up the pictures and say the names of two things. Do you think you can push the pictures I've said? Try and do it just the way I say." After some practice trials, children were given three 2-item lists, three 3-item lists, and three 4-item lists. Testing continued until the child failed on two lists to push the buttons named in the correct sequence. The longest list length for which children succeeded was taken as a measure of their "spans." Previous work suggests that tasks like these provide a good measure of a child's working memory capacity.

At the second testing session, Hughes (1998) added to the above list of measures one of planning ability—a modified Tower of London task. The apparatus for this task, depicted in Figure 8.9, showed red,

Figure 8–9   An example of a four-move problem from the Tower of London. A: target arrangement; B: starting arrangement.

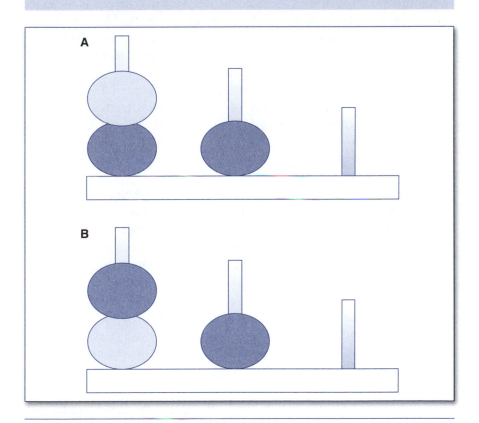

SOURCE: Hughes (1998, p. 1331).

green, and blue balls on three pegs. Children were instructed to arrange the balls into a particular pattern (e.g., the red, blue, and green balls all stacked up in that order on the largest peg), by moving one ball at a time from one peg to another. The patterns given to children required a minimum of either two, three, or four-move problems. Children received 2 points for every problem (three of each type) they solved with the minimum number of moves, or 1 point for every problem solved below the maximum number of moves, so their total score could range from 0 to 18.

Hughes (1998) also used a number of theory of mind tasks. Included were an unexpected contents task, a standard false belief task, and a more complex false belief task. From these she derived an overall theory of mind score.

The main findings from Hughes's (1998) study are presented in Table 8.3. It shows the correlations, both from the first testing period and from the second, among all of the measures described. Table 8.3 shows that children's overall theory of mind scores correlated significantly with several of the executive functioning tasks, both at Time 1 and even more strongly at Time 2. When Hughes statistically controlled for age and verbal ability (which she also measured at each testing session), correlations between theory of mind and executive functioning tasks were still significant.

Correlations, of course, tell us only about the degree of linear relationship between two variables. You probably know from your statistics course the old maxim, "Correlation does not mean causation." So these results alone do not tell us if theory of mind causes executive functioning, or the reverse, or if both are caused by a third underlying factor, or if the association is simply coincidence.

However, one approach to untangling these possibilities is to look at the pattern of correlations collected over time. If, for example, early executive functioning tasks correlate more strongly with later theory of mind scores than do early theory of mind scores with later executive functioning tasks, this suggests that executive functioning is more likely to play a causal role in theory of mind development. This is exactly what the correlations in Table 8.3 show. Similar studies conducted by other researchers have endorsed this general conclusion (Bialystok & Senman, 2004; Hasselhorn, Mahler, & Grube, 2005).

Why should executive functioning help in the development of theory of mind? On the face of it, they seem to be completely separate cognitive processes, aimed at different kinds of cognitive functioning. However, one could (and several psychologists did; see Hughes, 1998, for a sampling) make the argument that in order to effectively plan and regulate one's own behavior (activities at the core of executive functioning),

Table 8–3 Pearson's correlations between task scores

Measure	1	2	3	4	5	6	7	8	9	10	11	12	13	14	15	16	17
1. T1 age	—																
2. T1 vocabulary	.14	—															
3. T1 detour-reaching box (knob route)	.15	-.08	—														
4. T1 detour-reaching box (switch route)	.55**	.25	.08	—													
5. T1 hand game (imitation)	.05	.11	-.02	.16	—												
6. T1 hand game (conflict)	.60**	.13	-.03	.37**	.13	—											
7. T1 noisy book	.53**	.27	.13	.51**	.04	.18	—										
8. T1 set shifting	.24	.12	.14	.26	.03	.31*	.12	—									
9. T1 theory of mind	.56*	.41**	.05	.41**	.14	.37*	.49**	.04	—								
10. T2 detour-reaching box (knob route).	.04	.03	.30*	.24	.03	.14	.23	.07	.05	—							
11. T2 detour-reaching box (switch route)	.29*	.06	.01	.38**	-.09	.27	.13	.05	.16	.32*	—						
12. T2 hand game (imitation)	.21	.20	.15	.40**	.18	.25	.31	.12	.13	.62**	.38**	—					

(Continued)

Table 8–3 (Continued)

Measure	1	2	3	4	5	6	7	8	9	10	11	12	13	14	15	16	17
13. T2 hand game (conflict)	.31*	.29*	.02	.51**	-.12	.52**	.21	.39**	.26	.08	.27	.35*	—				
14. T2 noisy book	.40**	.29*	.10	.60**	.07	.38**	.44**	.34*	.33*	.23	.27	.34*	.33*	—			
15. T2 set shifting	.26	.13	.26	.34*	.00	.53**	.15	.44**	.21	.26	.30*	.25	.49**	.28*	—		
16. T2 Tower of London	.53**	.31*	.11	.69**	.18	.50**	.39**	.55**	.15	.27	.30*	.26	.66**	.49**	.43**	—	
17. T2 theory of mind	.46**	.33*	.11	.56**	.09	.41*	.40*	.27	.28*	.11	.30*	.18	.54**	.51**	.19	.61*	—

SOURCE: Hughes (1998, p.1335).

NOTE: Variables 3, 5, 10, and 12 are control conditions. $N > 45$ for all correlations. T1 = Time 1; T2 = Time 2.

$*p < .05$. $**p_1 < .01$.

one needs to understand one's own goals, beliefs, and desires. And, this argument goes, in order to understand one's goals, beliefs, and desires, one must have some sort of a theory of mind.

The last three chapters have provided us with a very detailed look at the cognitive changes occurring in the preschool period. We have seen that, in about 4 years, children undergo significant transformations in the way they approach cognitive tasks. Attention spans grow longer, perceptual processing becomes more analytic (at least in some circumstances), memory is deployed more strategically, and children acquire a great deal of knowledge about a great number of topics. They become better able to separate what things look like from what they really are. With some help and in some limited circumstances, their performance in drawing inferences can even be quite sophisticated.

However, preschool children do not have the degree of control over their cognition that older children do. They often need a lot more assistance than do school-aged children, and they are not as strategic, planful, or able to think about the long term as are their older siblings. We will see in the next few chapters how cognition continues to unfold during middle childhood.

SUMMARY

1. Piagetian theory holds that preoperational children are egocentric—they have difficulty adopting the physical or emotional point of view of another. Although more recent studies have shown that, under certain circumstances, preschoolers can take another's perspective, the more frequent finding is that preschoolers, especially those younger than age 4, have trouble with these types of tasks.

2. Piaget also described the difficulty preoperational children have in distinguishing between appearance and reality.

3. We've seen throughout the chapter that the context in which preschool children operate can have profound influences on their cognitive performance. Following Vygotskian theory, play is one context in which children can both exhibit and perhaps even stretch their cognitive muscles. Certainly, engaging preschoolers in a fantasy or narrative context has been shown to improve their ability to draw some deductive inferences.

4. We've seen as well that preschoolers have some, if limited, knowledge of the world that they draw upon when making inductive inferences. Children of biologists or children who live in rural communities seem to make biological inferences a little differently than do urban children of biological laypersons.

5. When we turn our attention to young children's knowledge about number concepts, we see once again that under the right circumstances, preschool children show a surprising amount of knowledge about the principles that underlie the skill of counting and basic arithmetic operations.

6. The theme here, of course, is that preschoolers' cognitive competence is often limited to very specific contexts and tasks. In Vygotskian terms, preschoolers need a lot of scaffolding— from the task itself, from competent others, and/or from the general context to display all of their cognitive abilities. Older children, in contrast, are more readily able to "show what they know" with less help, fewer clues, and fewer prompts.

7. We ended this chapter by taking a detailed look at the development of theory of mind. Over the course of the preschool years, young children develop a much more accurate, nuanced, and complex view of what other people know, believe, and expect. Moreover, we have seen that theory of mind relates to, and is likely at least in part a consequence of, development in other cognitive realms, specifically executive functioning.

REVIEW QUESTIONS

1. Discuss the concept of *egocentrism* as it pertains to cognition in early childhood. How does it fit in with other aspects of preoperational thought?

2. What is the appearance–reality distinction, and why does it figure so prominently in Piagetian descriptions of the preoperational period?

3. Compare and contrast Piagetian and Vygotskian views on the role of play in preschool children's cognitive development.

4. Describe the Hawkins et al. (1984) study of preschool children's ability to draw deductive inferences.

5. Summarize the different views over preschoolers' understanding of biology.

6. Evaluate the work on preschoolers' ability to reason about number concepts.

7. How important are the "magic" experiments in refuting Piagetian views of preschool children's understanding of number? Explain your view.

8. Describe and critique the methodology of tasks used to assess theory of mind.

9. Propose an explanation for why children's performance on appearance–reality tasks and their performance on theory of mind tasks are so strongly correlated.

10. Evaluate Hughes's (1998) study on the relationships among executive functioning measures and measures of children's theory of mind.

Appearance–Reality Distinction	Higher-Order Cognitive Processes
Deductive Reasoning	Inductive Reasoning
False Belief Task	Physical Activity Play
Folk Biology	Pretense Play
Folk Psychology	Theory of Mind

CHAPTER **9**

MIDDLE CHILDHOOD

Basic Cognitive Processes

Middle childhood is the period in which (in Western culture) a child begins formal schooling. The approximate age range for this developmental period is 6 to 11 years, although the cutoff ages are not absolute. In cultures that do not offer formal schooling, middle childhood is a time in which children begin apprenticing and learning the skills they will need for employment and survival in adulthood.

We begin the next set of chapters with another look at relevant theoretical frameworks of cognitive development. We also examine more explicitly the information-processing framework—a dominant approach in cognitive psychology—that provides a rather different description of what develops, cognitively, during this time frame. We then examine briefly some of the underlying neurological development occurring during middle childhood. These overviews of major developmental landmarks will serve as an important backdrop for all of the topics in Chapters 9 through 11.

In the remainder of this chapter, we begin our look at middle childhood by examining developments in basic cognitive processes—perception, attention, and working memory. We will see some discussion of how children become more skilled at focusing their cognition on selected stimuli, inhibiting their responses to others, and deploying their cognitive resources toward different tasks.

THEORETICAL PERSPECTIVES

By now, the theories of Piaget and Vygotsky ought to be quite familiar! The information-processing framework should also ring some bells, as we've talked about some of its assumptions and concepts in previous chapters. All three theoretical approaches share the goal of putting a particular period of cognitive development into a larger perspective—showing how the specific cognitive achievements might fit together and providing some description of what causes cognition to develop.

A Piagetian View of Middle Childhood

In Chapters 6 and 8 we reviewed Piagetian descriptions of the preoperational period. We reviewed the idea that much of this description was framed in terms of what preschool children *cannot* do, relative to their more cognitively competent older middle childhood siblings (Gelman, 1979). Children in middle childhood have achieved *concrete operations*, according to Piaget.

This means that they have internalized mental procedures that are organized into a coherent structure (Flavell, 1963; Inhelder & Piaget, 1964; Miller, 2011). It is highly appropriate here to consider some concrete examples!

Consider a *conservation of number* task first. I'll review this task very briefly in case you've forgotten it: Imagine a child sitting in front of two rows of nickels, laid out in one-to-one correspondence. The child first agrees that both rows have the same number of nickels and then watches while an experimenter spreads the nickels in one row farther apart, making it both longer and less dense. Although the preoperational child is likely to be fooled into thinking that the longer row "has more," the concrete operational child not only avoids making this error but can justify her answer in several different ways. She might focus on the *identity* of the number of nickels—arguing, "It's the same number—you just spread them apart." Here, she is noting that only addition or subtraction can transform the number of nickels in the row. Or, she might use the operation of *compensation,* arguing that while the transformed row is indeed now longer, it is also less dense or more widely spaced. Or, she might concentrate on the fact that the nickels could be easily moved back into their original position—demonstrating *reversible* thinking.

Consider a child **classifying** (i.e., systematically grouping) objects. To be concrete, imagine a 7-year-old boy sitting in front of a pile of wooden blocks. The blocks differ in color (red, blue, green, yellow), in shape (circle, triangle, square, oval, star, rectangle), and in size (small, medium, large). The child is instructed to "put together the things that go together." Although the preschool child might lay out a set of blocks to create a picture (making a house or a train) or might start by putting all the circles together but then suddenly add in all the yellow objects, the concrete operational child is able to choose and follow consistent sorting criteria. He may choose to sort by shape, putting all the circles, regardless of color or size, into one pile; all the squares in another pile; and so forth. Or he may sort on the basis of size or color. An older child may even succeed at a three-way classification, sorting simultaneously on all three dimensions!

Concrete operational children are also better at **seriation**, or putting in ascending (or descending) order a set of objects. For example, a child might

Photo 9.1 Being able to sort systematically is a skill that awaits concrete operations, according to Piaget.

arrange a set of apples in order from smallest to biggest, based on the circumference. Or she might line up her classmates in order of height, from tallest to shortest.

There are several other Piagetian tasks to illustrate cognitive operations, and the interested student can consult a good introductory source such as Flavell (1963). The important point to focus on is that Piaget saw concrete operations as being organized into a system. Each operation relates to other operations to form a coherent structure. An analogy to arithmetic operations might be useful here. Consider addition, subtraction, multiplication, and division. Each one coordinates with the others to form a whole. The meaning of any one operation derives from this structure and from other operations—subtraction, for example, is the inverse of addition (Miller, 2011).

Concrete operations are concrete, for Piaget, because the child cannot consider the operations separately from the objects the operations act upon. Thus, the concrete operational child can understand the arithmetic sentence "5 + 3 = 8" by referring to concrete instances of addition—if John has 5 apples and Mike gives him 3 more, then he has 8. However, children in the elementary years are not prepared to deal with the formal, abstract nature of addition as expressed by algebraic sentences such as "x + 2y = z," an ability that requires formal operations.

A View From the Information-Processing Framework

A different theoretical perspective on cognitive development in middle childhood comes from information-processing theory. We saw in Chapter 2 that information-processing theory provides a description of cognition that makes analogies to computer architecture. Figure 2.2 (see page 29) provides a general overview.

You might recall from Chapter 2 and Chapter 7 that information-processing theory posits the existence of various memory stores. One source of cognitive development this theory proposes is an increase in capacity of these stores. A second proposed cause of development is increased processing efficiency in transferring information from one store to another. We've also talked about increases in children's strategies and knowledge bases as contributors to their more sophisticated cognitive achievements.

Later in the chapter, we'll focus our attention on children's increasing attention span and ability to control and direct their attention. During middle childhood, this ability to direct attention and inhibit oneself from responding to distractions becomes increasingly important. A framework that describes this ability comes from the pioneering work of psychologist Alan Baddeley (1986, 1996, 2007) on working memory.

Baddeley used the term *working memory* as a contrast to an older term, *short-term memory*, which was held to be a storage area, limited to about seven or so slots, that held onto information for up to about a minute. Baddeley conceived of working memory as being a limited-capacity "work-space" that can be divided between storage and control processing.

Baddeley (1986, 1990, 2007) initially conceived of working memory as consisting of three components, as depicted in Figure 9.1. The first is the **central executive**. This component directs the flow of information, choosing which information will be processed, when it will be processed, and how it will be processed. In this sense, the central executive is thought to function more as an attentional system than a memory store (Baddeley, 1990), meaning that rather than dealing with the storage and retrieval of information, the central executive deals with the way resources are allocated to cognitive tasks. The central executive is also thought to coordinate information coming from the current environment with the retrieval of information about the past, to let people use this information to select options or form strategies. You can think of the central executive as the manager—it decides what tasks you should attend to and how much effort you should devote to each.

The two other components of Baddeley's model are concerned with the storage and temporary maintenance of information: the **phonological loop**, used to carry out subvocal rehearsal to maintain verbal material, and the

Figure 9–1   Baddeley's (1990) model of working memory

SOURCE: Galotti (2008, p. 170).

visuospatial sketch pad, used to maintain visual material through visualization. Researchers think the phonological loop plays an important role in such tasks as learning to read, comprehending language, and acquiring a vocabulary. It's the storage place for auditory material—it holds onto the sounds of what you've just heard or maybe just read. The visuospatial sketch pad involves the creation and use of mental images. If you imagine a mental map of your campus, for example, you are making use of the visuospatial sketch pad. We will return to talk about these two components of working memory later in the chapter.

A View From Cognitive Neuroscience

In Chapter 2 we had a brief introduction to different parts of the brain and, in particular, to cerebral structures and the four cerebral lobes: frontal, parietal, occipital, and temporal. You may want to review Figure 2.4 (see page 37), to see where each of these is located, and the section of Chapter 2 on cognitive neuroscience to remind yourself of what cognitive functions each lobe is associated with. You may recall that I said there that most brain growth is completed by the time a child turns 4 and that the brain typically attains adult weight when a child is between the ages of 5 and 10 (Caviness, Kennedy, Richelme, Rademacher, & Filipek, 1996; Reiss, Abrams, Singer, Ross, & Denckla, 1996).

Studies of brain development during childhood show that between about the ages of 5 and, say, 20, brains become about 10% larger in boys than in girls (De Bellis et al., 2001; Giedd et al., 1999; Reiss et al., 1996). One study examined the growth of both gray matter and white matter in children and adolescents aged 4 to 21 years (Giedd et al., 1999). Gray matter consists of the cell bodies and dendrites of the neurons in the brain, as well as glial cells, and mainly serves the function of routing sensory and motor information within the brain (Carlson, 2004). White matter, in contrast, consists of the axons of neurons in the brain, many of which have a fatty substance called myelin wrapped around them, which is white in color (Carlson, 2004).

Myelination, the process by which myelin wraps around the axons of neurons, is one of the most prolonged developmental changes in the human brain (Nagy, Westerberg, & Klingberg, 2004). Myelinated axons transmit information much more quickly than do unmyelinated ones. Thus, the brains of older children become much more efficient in comparison with those of younger children, because neural impulses are transmitted much more quickly.

Giedd et al. (1999) studied the growth of overall white matter, and gray matter in each of the four cerebral lobes, separately for males and females. Their results are presented in Figure 9.2. Notice that the growth of white

Figure 9–2   Predicted size with 95% confidence intervals for cortical gray matter in frontal, parietal, temporal, and occipital lobes for 243 scans from 89 males and 56 females, aged 4 to 22 years. The arrows indicate peaks of the curves.

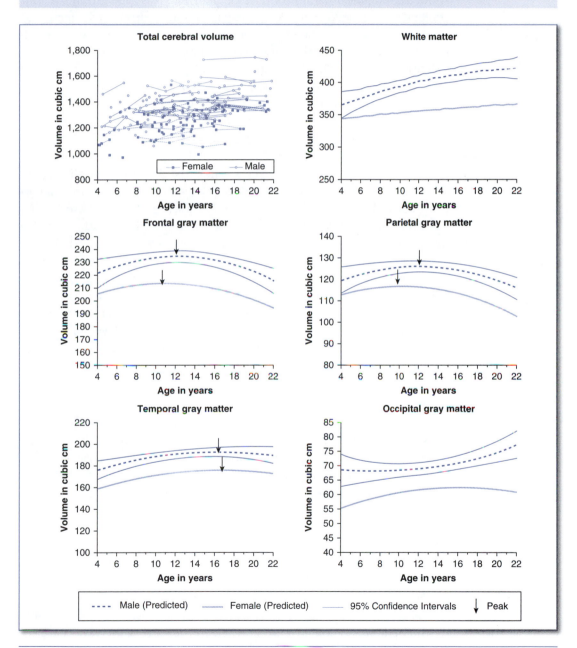

SOURCE: Giedd et al. (1999).

matter is fairly linear, showing a total increase of about 12%. The growth of white matter did not differ much in the different cerebral lobes.

The story is more complicated for the growth of gray matter, which showed a nonlinear pattern of development that was different in the four cerebral lobes (Giedd et al., 1999). Gray matter in the frontal lobe increased up until the age of about 12 years for males and 11 years for females, followed by a net decrease thereafter. Parietal lobe gray matter growth showed a similar trend, with slightly younger ages for peaks: 11.8 years for males and 10.2 years for females. Growth of gray matter in the temporal lobes peaked much later, at 16.5 years for males and 16.7 years for females, and showed only slight declines thereafter. Occipital gray matter showed linear increases with age and no peaks in the ages studied.

Reiss et al. (1996) correlated the size of different brain regions with IQ scores in children aged 5 to 17 years. They first divided the brain into 16 different regions. The authors found that the volume of the prefrontal cortex predicted about 20% of the variance in IQ scores. You might recall that the prefrontal cortex is that area of the brain associated with executive functioning—planning, making decisions, using strategies, and deploying working memory resources. We'll have more to say about executive functioning later in the chapter. Nagy et al. (2004) showed that working memory performance was positively correlated with increased myelination of the frontal lobe, while reading ability was correlated with myelination of the left temporal lobe. The important point for now is that the development and activity of specific brain regions give rise to very specific cognitive functions.

BECOMING MORE FOCUSED

We saw in Chapter 6 that there was a general suggestion that children's perceptual processing seemed to transition from a holistic to an analytic mode. Of course, there were some exceptions to this, notably in the area of face perception, a topic we will explore further here.

Perceptual Learning

Another factor that likely changes children's perceptual tendencies is the existence of perceptual learning (E. J. Gibson, 1969). A classic study by J. J. Gibson and E. J. Gibson (1955) illustrates this phenomenon. Participants (both children and adults) were first shown the card in the very center of Figure 9.3 by itself, for about 5 seconds. Next, they were shown a deck of cards, which included four copies of the original along with other cards that differed from the one originally shown. Their task was to identify any instances of the card originally shown in the deck. Participants received no feedback, but after seeing all the cards, they were shown the original card again for 5 seconds, and then they were shown the full deck of cards in a new order. This procedure continued until each person correctly identified all and only the four copies of the original.

Figure 9–3   Stimuli used by J. J. Gibson and E. J. Gibson (1955)

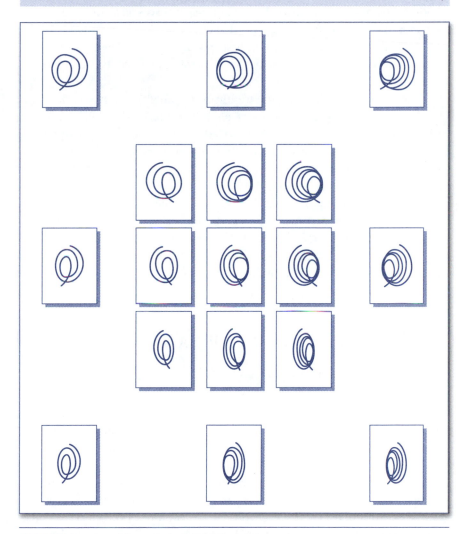

When J. J. Gibson and E. J. Gibson (1955) analyzed the errors participants made on this task, they found these errors were not random. Rather, the number of errors seemed to depend most on the number of similarities a stimulus shared with the original. Participants were more likely to falsely recognize a stimulus that had the same number of coils and was oriented in the same direction as the original than to falsely recognize a stimulus that only had the same number of coils.

Over time, participants seemed to notice more about the figures, responding to features of the stimuli they apparently had not noticed earlier. This explanation accords with other, everyday examples of perceptual learning. Children's learning of lowercase letters in English serves as a particularly relevant example. To the nonreader, the lowercase letters *b*, *d*, *p*, and *q* look awfully similar. Kindergarteners and first graders confuse these letters regularly. However, after about a year or two of reading practice, the letters come to look quite distinct.

What exactly is going on? Apparently, perceptually practiced individuals (such as children and adults who have already mastered the skill of reading) learn what aspects of the stimulus to attend to. They easily distinguish between different kinds of stimuli that might look very similar to the novice. Thus, although you might admit that *b* and *d* look very similar, the odds are very small that you ever confuse them now when you read.

Perceptual learning is something that occurs with experience and practice. As such, it is not so much a developmental effect as an expertise effect. However, when we remember that children in many ways are universal novices—that is, in almost every realm, they have much less experience and practice than do older children and adults—an expertise account can explain what looks to be a developmental effect.

Face Perception in Middle Childhood

In Chapter 6, we looked at some of the research on face recognition reported by Susan Carey. Recall that she proposed that children first process faces perceptually by focusing on individual features and then later switch to processing faces holistically. Carey (1996) made the argument that the change is caused by perceptual learning—as children acquire practice looking at faces, they become much better at extracting subtle information about different faces. In particular, older children pay attention to more points on the face than do younger children—so they encode more information about, say, the spacing between the eyebrows or between the bottom of the nose and the top of the upper lip. Older children (and adults) are therefore in a much better position to discriminate among similar faces, because they pick up on much more information when they look at faces.

Carey's general idea is that over the first 10 years of childhood, children learn to hone in on features that distinguish among faces, and become better able to distinguish between typical and atypical faces, a conclusion supported by other researchers (Tanaka, Kay, Grinnell, Stansfield, & Szechter, 1998). Carey notes that it takes children about 10 years to develop this competency, exactly the amount of time reported to develop perceptual expertise in other domains, such as becoming an expert judge for the American Kennel Club or an expert chess player.

A recent and very interesting study reports on the investigation of children's ability to recognize faces from their own racial group as well as from other racial groups. It is well known that adults are much better at recognizing faces from their own racial group (Meissner & Brigham, 2001). This phenomenon is most commonly explained in terms of differential practice or expertise—people generally have more practice looking at faces from their own racial group than they do looking at faces from a different racial group. If this explanation is correct, then we would expect that children younger than, say, 10 years would not show the own-race recognition advantage.

Goodman et al. (2007) tested children, adolescents, and adults from three countries (the United States, Norway, and South Africa) who were either Caucasian or biracial and ranged in age from 5 to 19 years. They saw photographs of 48 faces, 16 Caucasian (non-Hispanic), 16 Asian, and 16 African, half of which were male and half female. Study participants first viewed the faces and rated whether they were likely to be those of doctors, nurses, or teachers (a "cover story" to make them look carefully at the stimuli). Two days later, participants were given a surprise recognition task, where they saw 48 photos—12 "old" and 36 new—and were asked to say, after viewing each one, if it was one they had seen before.

In the youngest group (5- to 7-year-olds), children showed no difference in their ability to recognize faces as a function of race. Older children (ages 9 and 10), adolescents (ages 12 and 13), and undergraduates (mean age 19) were better, overall, at recognizing all faces than the youngest group. Moreover, these three groups showed a significant own-race recognition advantage. That is, they were better able to recognize faces from their own racial group than they were faces from another racial group. The same pattern of results held for biracial subjects as for Caucasian subjects (i.e., biracial children were better at identifying faces from either of their own racial groups than they were faces from other racial groups). The authors conclude that by late childhood (when children are aged 9–10) they develop sufficient expertise to both improve their face recognition and to be especially good at recognizing faces from their own racial group. However, in early middle childhood (e.g., at age 5 to age 7), they argue, children's face recognition is "plastic," and they are no better at recognizing faces from their own racial group than they are at recognizing faces from another one.

Global and Local Processing

Of course, children perceive lots of stimuli besides faces. We saw in Chapter 6 that one proposal, from Deborah Kemler Nelson, was that with cognitive development, children become more likely to process many stimuli analytically, focusing on features or parts, as opposed to holistically, although in certain circumstances even younger children can do both (Kemler, 1983).

Following up on that proposal, we will look here at the issue of perceptual organization, specifically the issue of global versus local processing. Figure 9.4 presents four stimuli that can be described either in terms of their overall, global shape (e.g., diamond, square, or circle) or in terms of the shapes of the smaller pieces or elements that make up the overall shape. Note, for instance, that the diamond shape is made up of eight small circles, the two circles are made up of small diamonds or squares, and the square is made up of small circles. When the stimulus is processed in terms of the large, overall shape we call that **global processing**, and when instead attention is directed to the smaller shapes we call that **local processing** (Burack, Enns, Iarocci, & Randolph, 2000; Porporino, Iarocci, Shore, & Burack, 2004).

Figure 9–4 Examples of stimuli that can be described by their overall shape or by their local elements

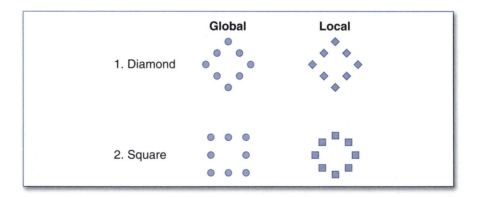

SOURCE: Porporino, Iarocci, Shore, & Burack (2004, p. 359).

Although Kemler Nelson's proposal might suggest that children change from a global to a local processing preference, more recent research suggests that global and local processing might involve separate mechanisms and, thus, might develop independently (Burack et al., 2000; Porporino et al., 2004).

In one experiment, Porporino et al. (2004) presented children aged 6, 8, 10, and 12 and adults with the stimuli shown in Figure 9.5. The participants had to respond either at the global or at the local level, saying whether the stimulus was a square or a diamond (in the global condition) or whether it was made up of diamonds or squares (with the global shape a circle) in the local condition. Some trials were presented without distraction, as illustrated in the top half of Figure 9.5. In others, the target stimulus (always presented in the middle) was flanked by two distractors, which were always circles made up of circles. The question was whether presentation of distractors would disrupt the participants' ability to respond, either slowing them down or causing them to make more errors.

The results, presented in Figure 9.6, show that, especially for the youngest two groups of children, distractors disrupt processing, particularly in the global condition. You can see that the older groups of children were faster in responding for all stimuli. Moreover, all age groups were usually faster in responding in the global condition than they were in the local condition. And, the presence of distractors slowed responses overall. However, the results showed that distractors were particularly disruptive for younger children (ages 6 and 8) in the global condition. For 10- and 12-year-olds and adults, the presence of distractors was similarly small for both global and

Figure 9–5   Examples of neutral distractor displays in which there were either no distractors (1) or distractors that contained no response-relevant information (2)

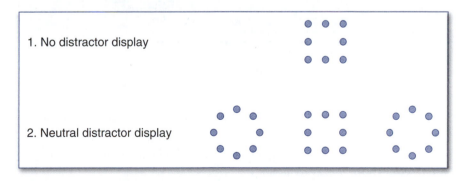

1. No distractor display

2. Neutral distractor display

SOURCE: Porporino, Iarocci, Shore, & Burack (2004, p. 359).

Figure 9–6 Reaction time and percentage errors for neutral distractor conditions plotted across age for global and local targets. The two-way interaction of target level by distractor presence is significant for the 6- and 8-year-olds and not for the older children and adults. Error bars represent the standard error of the mean between subjects.

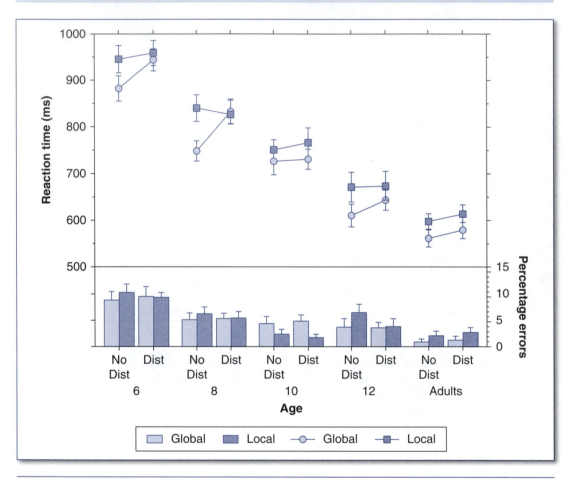

SOURCE: Porporino, Iarocci, Shore, & Burack (2004, p. 361).

NOTE: Dist = Distractor.

local processing. The researchers believe that global processing may be more vulnerable to the conditions of a perceptual task and, therefore, that attaining the adult-like efficiency of global processing may happen later, developmentally, than for local processing.

Let's pause here for a minute to sum up what we've seen about perceptual development during middle childhood. We've seen, first of all, that a great deal of perceptual learning occurs during this period. Especially as they acquire practice and experience encountering stimuli, children become more focused on certain aspects of those stimuli and thus more sensitive to certain nuances of difference. They are thus able to make many more discriminations among stimuli than are younger children, be those stimuli letters, faces, chairs, animals, or songs. Second, and relatedly, children in this age range are less likely to be distracted, or "thrown off" by unimportant aspects of a stimulus. In the case of letter recognition, for example, children in middle childhood pay less attention to the font, size, or color of the ink a letter is written in than do younger children. They are less likely to be fooled by a "disguise" of a hairstyle or hat in recognizing a face. Put very simply, children of this age are more perceptually focused on the important aspects of the stimuli they are perceiving than are younger children.

Selective Attention

We saw in Chapter 6 that, over the preschool years, children's attention spans become longer, especially on tasks that are not inherently interesting. At the same time, preschoolers show increasing inhibitory control over their actions—being better able to resist the temptation to act without asking permission, say, in a game of "Simon Says." Moreover, older preschoolers are better than younger ones at shifting their attention from one task to another.

Studies of selective attention in middle childhood indicate further development of the ability of children to concentrate on certain stimuli and ignore distractions. For example, Wetzel, Widmann, Berti, and Schröger (2006) conducted an auditory distraction experiment, using event-related potentials as their dependent measure. You may recall from Chapter 2 that an event-related potential, or ERP, measures an area of the brain's response to a specific event.

In the Wetzel et al. (2006) study, children aged 6 to 12 years and some young adults tried to discriminate between sounds of short and long duration. Most sounds were presented in one pitch, but occasionally sounds with a different pitch were presented. The changes in pitch were not relevant for the task but were distracting enough to impair the performance on the primary task of discriminating between short- and long-duration sounds. On other trials, participants watched a silent video as the same sounds were played, and they were told to ignore the sounds. (The idea here was to create a control condition where children heard sounds but were encouraged not to pay attention to them.)

Results showed that the pitch-changed sounds were, in fact, distracting for all participants: They caused longer reaction times and fewer correct responses than did the standard-pitched sounds. However, the magnitude of the distractability was larger for the youngest group of children (aged 6–8) relative to that for older children or adults.

Another ERP study of children aged 5 to 9 years showed that the ability to ignore irrelevant stimuli increases especially dramatically between the ages of 5 and 7 (Bartgis, Lilly, & Thomas, 2003). In particular, Bargtis et al. argue that 5-year-olds have an inability to select a relevant stimulus from other, irrelevant stimuli and perhaps also suffer from an inability to suppress incorrect responses. So, for example, a younger child will have a more difficult time focusing on a word written on a blackboard if there are other stray marks or drawings on that blackboard—7-year-olds will be better able to ignore the stray marks and doodles. Although 7-year-olds show a far superior ability to focus on relevant and ignore irrelevant stimuli, their performance is not yet perfect. However, the difference between the 7- and 9-year-olds was far less than the difference between the 5- and 7-year-olds.

Some of these results are endorsed enthusiastically by cognitive neuroscientist Michael Posner, who together with developmental psychologist Mary Rothbart (2007) has written about the development of attentional networks in infants and young children. Posner has identified three independent attentional networks, including the alerting network, which activates to bring the child into an aroused and alert state when a new stimulus is presented; the orienting network, which directs a child's focus toward a particular stimulus; and the executive network, which helps a child inhibit competing responses and maintain vigilance in the face of distraction. Figure 9.7 shows the brain areas that correspond to these distinct attentional networks. The important point for right now is that although orienting and alerting are pretty much fully functional sometime in infancy, Posner argues, the executive structures really begin to bloom in middle childhood.

Executive Functioning

Attention is but one component of a larger cognitive framework, however. We have previously encountered the idea of working memory. Here, we will examine that idea in a lot more detail. Specifically, we will be focusing on the development of the *central executive* component of working memory. Baddeley (1996) lists four main functions of the central executive. They are presented in Table 9.1.

Zoelch, Seitz, and Schumann-Hengsteler (2005) have investigated the development of the central executive by developing several measures that pertain to one or more of the four functions listed in Table 9.1. We'll look

Figure 9–7   Brain areas active for three attentional networks. The alerting network (squares) includes thalamic and cortical sites related to the brain's norepinephrine system. The orienting network (circles) is centered on parietal sites, and the executive network (triangles) includes the anterior cingulate and other frontal areas.

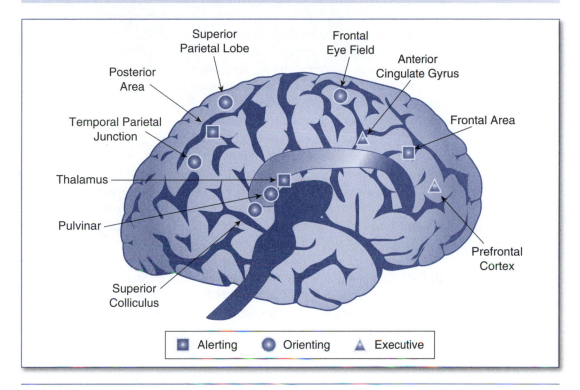

SOURCE: Posner & Rothbart (2007, p. 51).

Table 9–1   Functions of the central executive of working memory

1. The ability to coordinate performance on two separate tasks and to switch between them.
2. The ability to use retrieval strategies.
3. The ability to attend selectively to one stimulus and inhibit the disrupting effect(s) of others.
4. The ability to hold and manipulate information in long-term memory.

SOURCE: Baddeley (1996).

at these measures in a lot of detail, in order to get clearer on what the various functions of the central executive are. These measures include the following:

Generating a random series of digits. Participants were asked to generate a randomly ordered string of the digits 1, 2, 3, and 4. They generated strings of 60 digits, and the experimenters analyzed the strings generated for the degree of randomness they showed.

The Stroop task. Adapting a procedure used with adults by John Stroop (1935), the authors presented the participants with pictures of four vegetables and fruits. At first, the pictures depicted vegetables and fruits in congruent colors (e.g., a yellow lemon), and participants separately named the vegetables and fruits and then named the colors. Later, the pictures were presented in incongruous colors (e.g., a red lemon), and participating children were asked to name the *original* color—for example, yellow—as quickly as possible.

The color span backward task. Participants were shown a series of differently colored buttons and watched while the experimenter pressed different buttons. The first trial involved pressing two different buttons (e.g., blue-green), and the participants were asked to report the colors in a backward order (e.g., green-blue). They were given two trials with two colors. If they got at least one of these correct, the experimenter next presented two trials of three button presses (e.g., blue-red-green), and again, the participants had to report the buttons in reverse order (e.g., green-red-blue). The experimenter kept adding one to the length of the buttons displayed until each participant answered incorrectly on both trials. The longest color sequence recalled was recorded.

The visual decision span task. Participants viewed pictures of objects, one at a time, and had to decide if the object was edible or not. After all objects were shown, participants were asked to recall the objects in the order they had been presented.

The trail making task. Participants received a sheet of paper with yellow and green circles of different sizes placed randomly on it. They had to connect the circles as follows: smallest green, smallest yellow, next-smallest green, next-smallest yellow, and so forth. This task forces participants to switch tasks, between looking for circle color and looking for circle size.

The mental fusion task. This task is depicted in Figure 9.8. Participants saw two cards, one at a time, for 2 seconds each, alternating twice, and were asked to mentally fuse the two into a coherent picture. It was hypothesized that to mentally fuse two images, participants would need access to the contents of long-term memory, as well as the ability to manipulate that information.

Figure 9–8 Example of a mental fusion trial

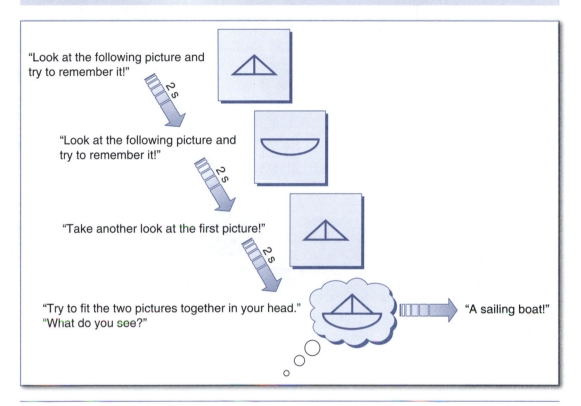

"Look at the following picture and try to remember it!"

2 s

"Look at the following picture and try to remember it!"

2 s

"Take another look at the first picture!"

2 s

"Try to fit the two pictures together in your head."
"What do you see?"

"A sailing boat!"

SOURCE: Zoelch, Seitz, & Schumann-Hengsteler (2005, p. 54).

The decision-making task. This task is depicted in Figure 9.9. It required selective attention to a specific criterion while concurrently inhibiting other responses. Participants were first given some criterion (e.g., a yellow ball). They were shown a series of pictures of children, some of whom had other colored balls, no balls, or yellow balls, and were instructed to respond "yes" only to the last group of pictures. Reaction times were recorded.

Figure 9.10 presents the performance data on each of the seven tasks used by Zoelch et al. (2005). As you can see, many of the tasks showed sharp breaks in performance between the kindergarteners and all the other age groups (i.e., the Stroop task, the mental fusion task, and the decision-making task). Others showed a more gradual change across age groups (i.e., the color span backward task, the visual decision span task, and the trail making task), while the random generation task showed few age differences (and therefore is not shown in Figure 9.10).

Figure 9–9   Example of a decision-making task

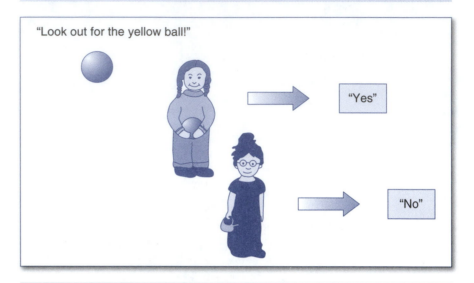

SOURCE: Zoelch, Seitz, & Schumann-Hengsteler (2005, p. 56).

Figure 9–10a   The Stroop Task: Age differences in solution times for naming color-incongruent objects

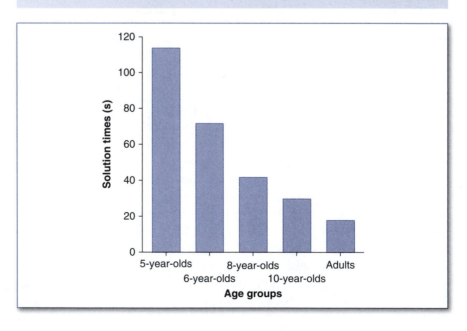

Figure 9–10b   Age differences for the color span backward task

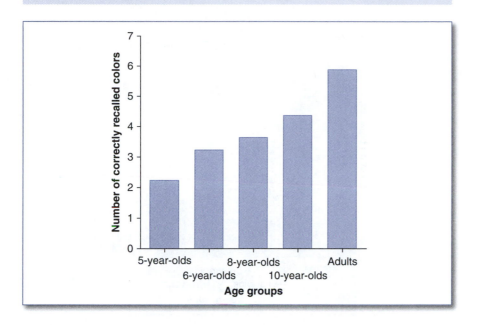

Figure 9–10c   Age differences in visual decision span

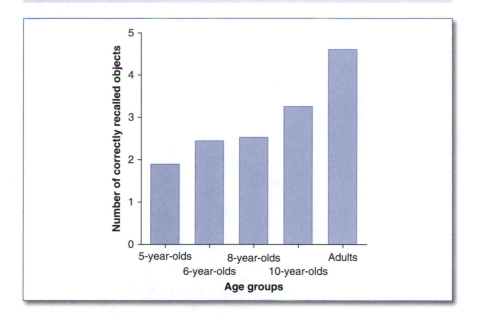

Figure 9–10d Age differences in the trail making task

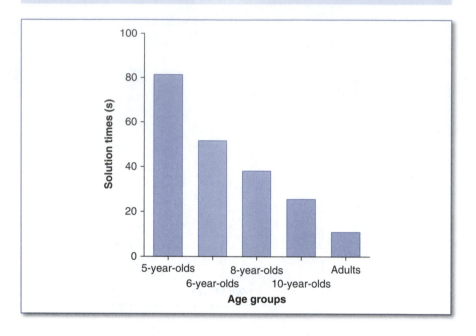

Figure 9–10e Age differences in the mental fusion task

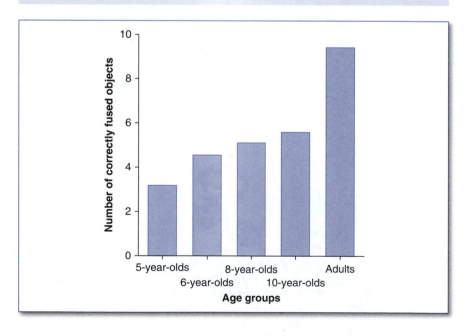

Figure 9–10f   Age differences in the decision-making task

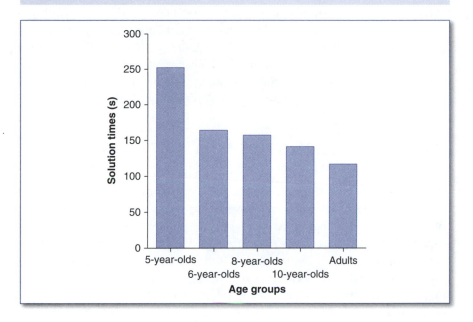

Zoelch et al. (2005) believe that these seven tasks tap into the central executive in various ways, as depicted in Figure 9.11. From their data, they

Figure 9–11   The relational pattern between different measurement tools and central executive processes

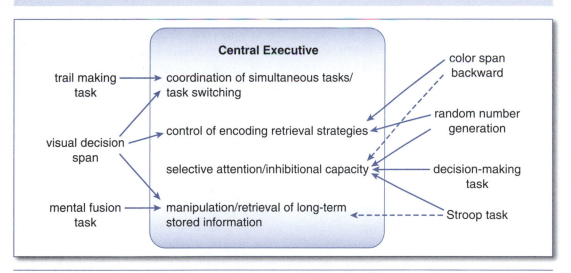

SOURCE: Zoelch, Seitz, & Schumann-Hengsteler (2005, p. 60).

surmise that the different aspects of the central executive presented earlier in this chapter undergo different developmental trends. Tasks that require complex processing, such as the visual decision span and color span backward tasks in particular, are not fully mastered until after age 10. Putting this finding together with the hypothesized relationships shown in Figure 9.10 in turn suggests that at least some aspects of selective attention, inhibitory control, and manipulation and retrieval of information in long-term memory are cognitive processes that continue to develop through adolescence.

INCREASING COGNITIVE CAPACITIES

We've previously looked at working memory, that part of our cognitive equipment that processes information that we are actively working on. When we talk of components of working memory—say, the phonological loop or the visuospatial sketch pad—we have so far not paid much attention to the fact that both are capacity-limited. We saw in Chapter 7 that preschoolers' working memory capacity was limited to about two (for younger children) to four (for older preschoolers) unrelated items. In the middle childhood years, that number grows until it approaches the adult level of capacity, often described by cognitive psychologists as the "magical number seven," plus or minus two (Miller, 1956).

We have seen previously in Chapter 7 that a larger working memory span seems to allow for all sorts of increased processing, which in turn allows for greater vocabulary and greater academic achievement. Gathercole, Pickering, Knight, and Stegmann (2004) demonstrated that these relationships continue in the middle childhood years. They studied British children aged 7 and 14, the ages at which national curriculum assessments are taken. Children were given a number of different working memory assessments, including a backward digit span task, a forward digit span task, and a listening recall task (children hear a series of sentences, make a true or false judgment about each one, and then recall the final word of each sentence). Some of these measures were aimed at measuring the capacity of the phonological loop; others were aimed at measuring the capacity of the central executive (the capacity of the visuospatial sketch pad had previously been shown not to predict differences in children's performance on national curriculum tests).

Children in both age groups were divided into low, average, and high performance groups, based on their performance on the national curriculum tests and the scores of each group on the phonological loop and central executive measures. Figure 9.12 presents these data for the younger (aged 7–8) group, with the left-hand set of bars showing grouping based on the English tests and the right-hand set of bars showing grouping based on the mathematics test.

Figure 9–12   Mean standard scores on phonological loop and central executive measures as a function of English and mathematics ability groups in the younger group, with standard error bars

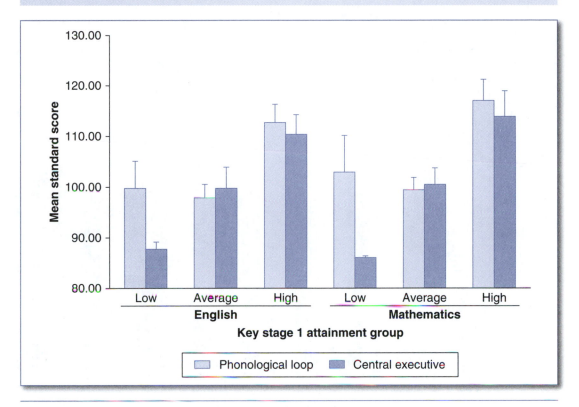

SOURCE: Gathercole, Pickering, Knight, & Stegmann (2004, p. 9).

As can be seen, children in the high-ability group have higher scores on the working memory measures, and this difference was shown to be statistically significant.

The older group, aged 14–15, took three standardized curriculum tests: one in English, one in mathematics, and one in science. These children, too, were grouped as low, average, or high for each subject based on their test results. Figure 9.13 presents these, and it shows a different pattern of results. Here, the working memory measures do not significantly distinguish among the groups based on the English test performance (see the leftmost set of bars in Figure 9.13). However, working memory scores (both phonological loop and central executive) differ significantly between the low-ability group and the others for both the mathematics and the science tests.

Figure 9–13 Mean standard scores on phonological loop and central executive measures as a function of English, mathematics, and science ability groups in the older group, with standard error bars

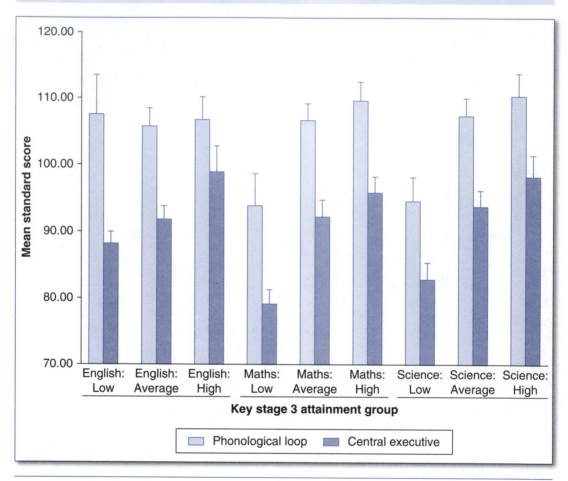

SOURCE: Gathercole, Pickering, Knight, & Stegmann (2004, p. 9).

These results suggest that working memory capacity continues to be important in academic achievement throughout the school years. However, the pattern of associations between working memory measures and academic achievement does change from early elementary to secondary school, as shown by the differences between Figures 9.12 and 9.13. What explains the development of increased working memory capacity? Several authors believe it has to do with maturation of the prefrontal cortex (Casey et al., 1995; Luna et al., 2001;

Nelson et al., 2000). In a study of auditory and visual working memory in Finnish children aged 6–10, Vuontela et al. (2003) found that performance on both tasks improved with age but that boys (especially the youngest boys) showed a larger degree of immaturity, showing more errors and faster reaction times.

Another important aspect of development concerning working memory may be children's increasing ability to inhibit distractions. We know that as children develop, they become increasingly able to inhibit their behaviors and to inhibit their responses to distracting stimuli (Bjorklund & Harnishfeger, 1995; Harnishfeger & Bjorklund, 1993). According to Harnishfeger and Bjorklund, elementary school-aged children also become more adept at inhibiting intrusive thoughts or associations as they work on a task. In all of these examples of inhibition, children become better able to keep distracting, irrelevant information out of working memory, thus freeing up more capacity to devote to the task at hand.

In this chapter we have examined theoretical perspectives on child development in middle childhood. We have also looked at cognitive processes that might be considered "basic" ones—perception, attention, and working memory. In Chapter 10, we will turn our attention to aspects of long-term memory, including the development of narrative memory and the knowledge base. We will see that many of these topics relate in fundamental ways to the basic cognitive processes described here, as well as to the theoretical perspectives we have just reviewed.

SUMMARY

1. Piagetian theory holds that concrete operational children are easily able to order (seriate), classify, and compare quantities. They have internalized mental procedures, called operations, that allow them to understand phenomena in the world in terms of coherent, stable structures. Their thinking is reversible, and they understand the difference between appearance and reality.

2. The information-processing framework describes human cognition in terms of different processes and storage mechanisms that acquire, hold, and transform information. This framework relies on analogies between human cognitive performance and the architecture and processing of computer systems. Cognitive development is thus described in terms of increases in storage capacity, processing speed, and/or increased or more efficient executive functioning. In this chapter, we focused on the development of working memory, a structure for immediate processing and temporary storage of information.

3. Developmentally, the brain reaches most of its adult weight before a child reaches middle childhood. However, during childhood, a process of myelination occurs in many of the neurons in the brain, resulting in faster transmission of neural impulses. White matter, which largely consists of myelinated axons, shows linear growth during childhood. Gray matter, consisting of the cells and dendrites of neurons, shows nonlinear patterns of growth that differ for the different cerebral lobes.

4. Growth of the prefrontal cortex has been shown to correlate with increased executive functioning and IQ scores.

5. One mechanism that may underlie other cognitive changes is perceptual learning. This is the phenomenon whereby as a child (or an adult) acquires experience in a domain, she becomes more sensitive to subtle differences among stimuli. Some psychologists explain, for example, children's increasing ability to discriminate among faces as a case of perceptual learning.

6. Research on perceptual processing suggests the existence of two independent systems. Global processing refers to perceptual identification of stimuli in terms of their large, overall characteristics, while local processing refers to the direction of attention to smaller features of a stimulus. Some work suggests that global processing attains adult-like efficiency somewhat later than does local processing.

7. Studies of selective attention in childhood suggest that children become increasingly able to ignore distractions. A dramatic increase in this ability happens between the ages of 5 and 7 years, although the ability continues to show some increases thereafter.

8. Working memory also shows development over the course of middle childhood, particularly the central executive. Inhibitory control seems to be almost mature by the time a child is 7 years old; complex processing seems to mature sometime after a child turns 10.

9. Research by Susan Gathercole and others suggests that the development of working memory, in particular the phonological loop and the central executive, is related to children's performance on standardized academic tests.

REVIEW QUESTIONS

1. Discuss the Piagetian description of concrete operations, in terms of both what the child gains, cognitively, from the preoperational period and what limitations he faces relative to an adolescent.

2. Review and discuss the information-processing approach to cognitive development in middle childhood.

3. Describe the major neurological developments of middle childhood.

4. Discuss the phenomenon of perceptual learning, and explain how it is thought to apply to children's increasing ability to recognize human faces.

5. Explain the distinction between global and local processing, and discuss evidence for the development of each.

6. Consider the development of selective attention during the middle childhood years. How might this relate to children's readiness for formal schooling or the beginning of an apprenticeship?

7. Describe and explain the workings of the major components of working memory.

8. Describe and critique the Zoelch et al. (2005) study on the development of the central executive.

KEY TERMS

Alerting Network

Attentional Network

Central Executive

Classification

Executive Network

Global Processing

Gray Matter

Local Processing

Myelination

Orienting Network

Perceptual Learning

Phonological Loop

Seriation

Visuospatial Sketch Pad

White Matter

CHAPTER **10**

MIDDLE CHILDHOOD

Long-Term Memory and the Knowledge Base

In the last chapter, we looked at "basic" cognitive processes—ones that arguably would be involved in most (if not all) cognitive tasks. Included among these were perception, attention, and working memory. In this chapter, we extend our survey of cognition in middle childhood by examining long-term memory processes—ones that rely on strategies, specialized knowledge, and one's own narrative memories of personal history. We will see that the theoretical frameworks introduced in Chapter 9 remain important for the topics we will discuss here. Indeed, many of the topics we'll cover here are tightly connected to the topics discussed in Chapter 9, and a large part of why coverage is separated into two chapters is simply to keep the information divided into manageable chunks.

THEORETICAL PERSPECTIVES

In Chapter 9, we focused on the topic of working memory—that part of our cognitive architecture that allows for the immediate processing of information. Here, we will concentrate on long-term memory. Information-processing theorists were the first to draw this distinction, so it is very appropriate to turn to a detailed look at that theoretical perspective.

A View From Information-Processing Theory

In the early days of cognitive psychology, working memory was called short-term memory (STM), to distinguish it from **long-term memory (LTM)**. This distinction actually goes back to psychologist William James (1890/1983), who used the terms *primary* and *secondary* memory to draw this distinction. Long-term memory was thought to have several characteristics quite different from those of short-term memory. Here are a few examples: STM was thought to have strong capacity limitations; LTM was thought to have either unlimited or at least vast amounts of capacity. Information in STM was thought to last up to about a minute, while information once transferred to LTM was thought to last either indefinitely or at least for a very long time.

In this chapter, we turn our focus to long-term memory. In doing so, we will need to review proposals of some cognitive psychologists to subdivide LTM into different parts. I hope you'll recall Endel Tulving's (1972) proposal for two separate memory systems within long-term memory. One system, *episodic memory*, holds memories of specific events in which you yourself somehow participated. The other system, *semantic memory*, holds information that has entered your general knowledge base: You can recall parts of that base, but the information recalled is generic—it doesn't have much to do with your personal experience. For example, your memory that Jean Piaget articulated a theory of cognitive development is presumably in your general knowledge base but divorced from your personal memories of what happened to you at a certain time. It's probable, actually, that you can't even remember when the fact about Piaget entered your memory.

Contrast this situation with when information about your first day of kindergarten or the 9/11 attacks on the World Trade Center and Pentagon entered your memory. For those instances you may recall not only the information itself but also the circumstances surrounding your acquisition of the information (where, when, why, how, and from whom you heard, saw, or otherwise acquired it, how you felt at the time, and maybe even what you were thinking at the time).

Traditional views of LTM emphasize the cognitive processes of both *encoding* and *retrieval*. Encoding is a process by which a memory trace is formed, or, to use a computer metaphor, by which input is entered into storage. Retrieval is a process by which a stored memory is accessed. Both processes benefit from the use of strategies, and, as was hinted at in Chapter 7, the use of strategies increases during middle childhood years. We will examine both processes in more developmental detail below.

DEVELOPMENT OF LONG-TERM MEMORY IN MIDDLE CHILDHOOD

We will begin our look at the development of LTM by focusing on parts of what Tulving (1983) would call the episodic system. We'll begin by looking at classic studies of children's encoding and retrieval. Next, we will look at narrative memory—memory for autobiographical events that the child recalls experiencing, witnessing, or participating in.

Encoding and Retrieval

Research on LTM in children goes back several decades. For example, Schneider and Pressley (1989) translated work by Brunswik, Goldscheider, and Pilek, published in 1932. These German authors studied memory in school-aged children, aged 6 to 18 years. The stimuli they presented were different for children of different ages (a methodological confound, which, unfortunately, clouds the interpretation of their results). Younger children received nonsense syllables, one-syllable words, and numbers; older children heard poems and word pairs. These authors reported that memory for meaningless materials peaked by about age 12 but that memory for meaningful material continued to develop past that point.

The most common strategy for encoding is *rehearsal*, and the study by Flavell, Beach, and Chinsky (1966), reviewed in Chapter 7, showed that very few kindergartener participants showed evidence of using rehearsal; a little more than half of the second graders and almost all of the fifth graders showed evidence of using rehearsal on a task requiring them to remember the order of pictures an experimenter pointed to (for details of the study, review Chapter 7).

Later studies showed that over the elementary school years, children develop increasing proficiency at rehearsal (Ornstein & Naus, 1985). During this period, children become less passive and more active when they rehearse. This conclusion was demonstrated dramatically in a study by Ornstein, Naus, and Liberty (1975), who presented children in Grades 3, 6, and 8 with lists of 18 unrelated words that they were asked to remember. Children were asked to rehearse each word aloud as it was presented, and then were asked to recall the words on the list in any order they chose.

A common finding in this kind of memory task is called the **serial position effect**, in which words at the beginning and the end of a list are more likely to be recalled than are words in the middle (Murdock, 1962). The elevated recall of words at the end of the list is called the **recency effect**, and it is thought to stem from the fact that the most recently presented items are still in working memory (Klatzky, 1980). The elevated recall of words from the beginning of the list is known as the **primacy effect**, and it is thought to arise because the first items are rehearsed more thoroughly than are any other items.

Figure 10.1 presents data from the study by Ornstein et al. (1975). In the first panel, you can see that students from all three grades showed both primacy and recency effects. Recency effects were the same for all three age groups tested, but primacy effects were larger for older students. This suggests that the oldest students were more likely to use rehearsal. In fact, third graders (aged 8) did not show much of a primacy effect; sixth and eighth graders (aged 11 and 13) did, with eighth graders showing a more pronounced effect than sixth graders.

The second panel of Figure 10.1 plots the number of different rehearsals (i.e., the number of repetitions) each child gave to each word, as a function of its position on the list. Note that items early on the list (e.g., the first or second serial position) received more repetitions than did subsequent items, even for the younger children. However, the number of repetitions does not track the eventual probability of recall (shown in the first panel of Figure 10.1).

Another analysis gave some insight into why rehearsal might have been more effective for older students. Table 10.1 shows a typical rehearsal protocol

Figure 10–1   Mean proportion of unrelated items recalled (Panel A), mean number of rehearsals of items (Panel B), and mean number of different items in each rehearsal set (Panel C) as a function of serial position for third-, sixth-, and eighth-grade subjects in Experiment 1

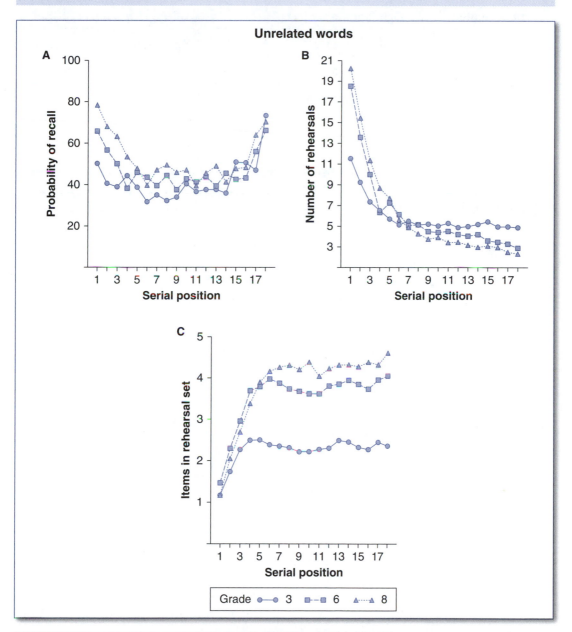

SOURCE: Ornstein, Naus, & Liberty (1975, p. 821).

Table 10–1 Typical rehearsal protocols (unrelated words), Experiment 1

Word presented	Rehearsal sets	
	Eighth-grade subject	Third-grade subject
1. Yard	Yard, yard, yard	Yard, yard, yard, yard, yard
2. Cat	Cat, yard, yard, cat	Cat, cat, cat, cat, yard
3. Man	Man, cat, yard, man, yard, cat	Many, many, many, many, many
4. Desk	Desk, man, yard, cat, man, desk, cat, yard	Desk, desk, desk, desk

SOURCE: Ornstein, Naus, & Liberty (1975, p. 822).

for an eighth grader and a third grader as they are read the first four words on the list. Notice that as the list is read, the older child incorporates more items into the rehearsal set (e.g., after the words *yard, cat, man,* and *desk* are read, the eighth grader rehearses all of them, saying "desk, man, yard, cat, man, desk, cat, yard," while the third grader instead only repeats the last word: "desk, desk, desk, desk"). The third grader can be said to be rehearsing more passively, while the eighth grader is making more connections among different words and actively trying to remember words presented earlier. The third panel of Figure 10.1 shows that, indeed, the number of items rehearsed together (in the above example, it would be four [*desk, man, yard, cat*] for the eighth grader and one [*desk*] for the third grader) was larger for older students.

What might explain why these different rehearsal strategies work differently? We've alluded already to one explanation—simply repeating a word over and over is a sort of passive, low-effort activity. In contrast, repeating the last several words on the list requires more of the learner—she must recall what the last few words were rather than just the last one. So, perhaps the older children put in more effort during the time of encoding, and that difference in effort led to a difference in the strength of the memory trace that was formed for each word.

A second explanation has to do with retrieval—the process(es) by which people bring material stored in long-term memory back into conscious awareness. Tulving and Thomson (1973) described a principle of retrieval known as the **encoding specificity principle**, which states that when material is first put into LTM, the way it is encoded depends on the context in which the material is learned. Put slightly differently, the manner of encoding is specific to a particular context. At the time of recall, it is a great advantage to have the same context information available, because aspects of that context function as **retrieval cues**—that is, stimuli that help one recall or recognize stored information.

For example, you may have had the experience of revisiting your old kindergarten classroom. As you walked around it, certain memories—for instance, the time the hamster escaped, the time you all made applesauce, or the day you celebrated the 100th day of school—seemed to spontaneously come back to you. Cognitive psychologists would say that some aspects of the classroom (maybe, seeing the art table, smelling the odor of the paint, or hearing a song the teacher played every day) served as retrieval cues. Those cues were originally present when the memory traces were formed, and were hooked onto the memories, such that when you encountered the cues again, they "brought back" the memories quite literally!

In the context of the Ornstein et al. (1975) study, rehearsing four words together, and changing which specific four words are rehearsed together, provides many more potential retrieval cues for each word. Thus, if you rehearse *yard, cat, man,* and *desk* together and then later are able to recall the word *yard,* it may become a retrieval cue for one or more of the other words it was rehearsed with originally. The encoding specificity principle would say that when you rehearse different words together, each one becomes a part of the learning context of each of the other words and, thus, becomes a possible retrieval cue for all the others.

Ornstein et al. (1975) conducted a second study, using different children of the same ages (students in Grades 3, 6, and 8) who were given lists of words that fell into four categories. For half of the children, the words were presented in random order; for the other half, all the words in one category were presented in a block, followed by all the words in a second category, and so forth. Results of this study are presented in Figure 10.2. The top two panels show that recall under blocked conditions was generally better than recall under the random word presentation, but age differences in performance seen in the last experiment occurred here as well.

The bottom two panels present the number of items children rehearsed in each set. Once again, older children rehearsed more words in a set than did younger children, especially in the blocked condition. There were also age-related differences in the way children recalled the words on these lists. Older children were more likely to recall words in category clusters than were younger children, particularly for the blocked condition.

Figure 10–2 Mean proportion of related items recalled under random (Panel A) and blocked (Panel B) conditions of presentation, and mean number of different items in each rehearsal set under random (Panel C) and blocked (Panel D) conditions of presentation, as a function of serial position, for third-, sixth-, and eighth-grade subjects in Experiment 2

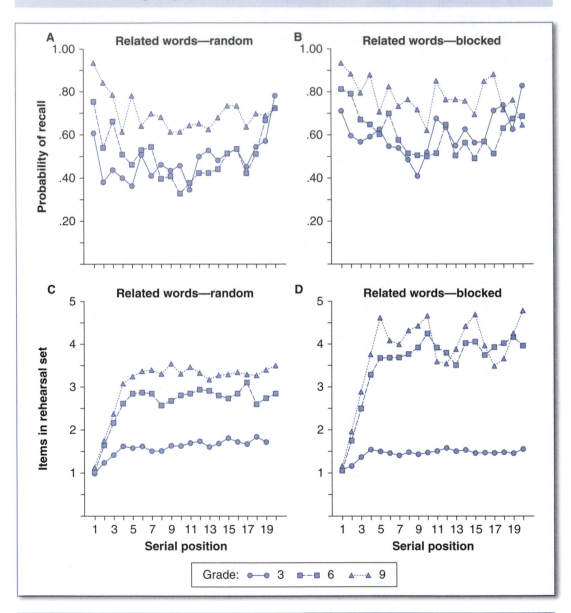

SOURCE: Ornstein, Naus, & Liberty (1975, p. 825).

This last finding brings us again to the topic of retrieval. Classic studies in cognitive psychology have shown that clustering during recall aids memory of word lists (Bousfield, 1953), perhaps because the categories themselves serve as a retrieval cue. Ornstein et al.'s (1975) findings suggest that older children may be more adept at noticing (either at the time of encoding, at the time of retrieval, or both) cues to help them efficiently search their memories for the desired information. Thus, they are more able to make use of a strategy known as *organization* to aid them in recalling words.

Thus, the Ornstein et al. (1975) study offers several possibilities for why older children remember more information than younger children. First, they might rehearse more actively and pay more attention as they are inputting the words into memory in the first place. Second, their rehearsal strategies might allow them to form more retrieval cues for target words on the to-be-remembered list. Third, older children might be more apt to notice and use retrieval cues, such as category names, as prompts to search for more items that were originally presented. All of these possibilities share the idea that older children are more in command of their memories, understand better how their memories work, and use information to help themselves perform well. Put in broader terms, older children show more evidence of *metacognition*, or knowledge of how their cognitive systems (in this case, their memory systems) work, and adapt their behavior to fit with this knowledge.

Event Memory

The studies we have considered so far in this chapter pertain to children's memory for experimental materials—lists of words or the order in which various pictures are pointed to by an experiment. But clearly, LTM holds much more than this. In particular, LTM holds lots of information about past events—both routine and extraordinary. We will look first at autobiographical memory—memory for events the child experienced and participated in. Next, we will look at memory for highly emotional, often surprising events, where the child remembers not just the event happening but what he was doing, whom he was with, how he received the information, and what he was thinking when he first received news of the event. These two topics will lead to a third—eyewitness memory, which we began to look at in Chapter 7.

Autobiographical Memory

We've seen already (in Chapters 4 and 7) that preschoolers have some autobiographical memories and that, under some circumstances, even toddlers show some ability to recall events. We also began our discussion of children's use of scripts—that is, schemas for events—in Chapter 7. You'll see shortly that those ideas will be drawn upon to understand what goes on during middle childhood as well.

Usher and Neisser (1993) reported a study of how adults recall childhood autobiographical memories. They surveyed college students about their memories of four specific life events: the birth of a younger sibling, a hospitalization, the death of a family member, and a family move from one residence to another. The authors' aim was to investigate the phenomenon of **childhood amnesia**, defined as the relative paucity of autobiographical memories dating from before the age of about 3 years (Neisser, 2004).

Usher and Neisser (1993) recruited college students who had experienced one or more of the above events at a known age in early childhood. Specifically, students at Emory University were recruited who had experienced any of the events when they were age 2, age 3, age 4, or age 5. The ages and events together defined 16 cells, and the investigators recruited at least 10–12 college students for each cell. In addition, two other cells were added of students who were 1 year of age during two events: the birth of a sibling and a family move (not enough participants were found who had experienced the other events at 1 year of age). Participants were asked to report only what they actually remembered, not what they recalled from family stories or other external sources such as scrapbooks or newspaper clippings.

Table 10.2 presents a list of questions that were asked of the "birth of a sibling" event participants. (For many of the participants, the researchers checked their responses against the recall of the participant's mother.) Figure 10.3 presents data on the proportion of participants in each cell who recalled enough about the target events to answer at least one (light bars) or at least three (dark bars) questions about the events. As can be seen, few autobiographical memories persisted from events that occurred when a child was 1 year old. When a child was 2 or 3, some autobiographical memories existed for some events, specifically birth of a younger sibling or a hospitalization; but little memory was available for the other events. But by the time a child reached age 4, some autobiographical memory seemed to persist for all of the events tested.

The authors explain that the birth of a sibling may be a very special type of event. Parents may talk about it well in advance, on numerous occasions, to prepare the child for the impending event. Afterward, they may be especially likely to tell and retell the "homecoming" story. Moreover, the hospitalization event may be particularly memorable for other reasons—due both to its unusualness and to the fact that it may have been experienced as a frightening occurrence. Usher and Neisser's (1993) participants were also

Table 10–2   Universal questions from the sibling birth questionnaire

Item no.	Universal question
1.	Who told you (that your mother was going to have a baby)?
2.	Where were you?
3.	What were you doing when this happened?
4.	What time of day was it?
5.	Who told you that your mother was leaving to go to the hospital?
6.	What were you doing when she left?
7.	Who went with her?
8.	What did you do right after your mother left?
9.	Who took care of you while your mother was in the hospital?
10.	How did you find out that the baby was a boy or girl?
11.	Where were you the first time you saw the baby?
12.	What was the baby wearing?
13.	What was the baby doing?
14.	Who picked your mother and the baby up from the hospital?
15.	What time of day was it when they came home?
16.	What did you do when they arrived home?
17.	Who was at home with you when they came home?

SOURCE: Usher & Neisser (1993, p. 157).

better at remembering birth of a sibling events than were participants in an earlier study of the same event type (Sheingold & Tenney, 1982), for reasons that are not quite clear. Nonetheless, the results suggest that, at least for some events and under some circumstances, children can form autobiographical memory traces from a very young age.

Of course, Usher and Neisser (1993) reported on retrospective memories—their adult participants recalled childhood memories, and the only standard

Figure 10–3 Proportions of subjects who answered at least one (light) or three (dark) question(s) about the target events

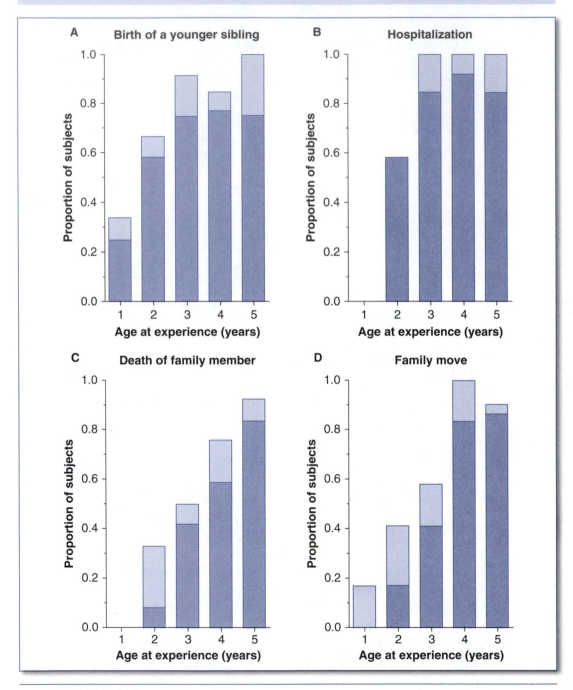

SOURCE: Usher & Neisser (1993, p. 158).

of accuracy available with which to check those memories was the (also retrospective) recall of the participants' mothers. Thus, there was no way to be sure that what a participant remembered of the original event was not, in fact, information he had learned subsequent to the event. Another study, this one by Judith Hudson and Robyn Fivush (1991), overcame this problem by comparing kindergarteners' immediate recall of a class field trip with their recall 6 years later.

Hudson and Fivush (1991) accompanied 16 kindergarten students on a 2-hour class field trip to a museum of archaeology. They interviewed each of the children the same day of the trip, 6 weeks later, 1 year later, and 6 years later. Thus, they had an original record of the event (which they themselves witnessed) as well as an immediate recall against which to compare all subsequent recall attempts.

Hudson and Fivush (1991) give the following account of the field trip:

> The investigators accompanied the kindergarten class on a 2-hour trip to the Jewish Museum, a museum of archaeology. They walked to the museum from the school. Once there, the group was introduced to a guide who told them a little of the history of the museum. They went upstairs, and the guide taught the children about archaeology—what archaeologists do, and the kinds of tools they use. Next, they went into a room where the children dug for "artifacts" hidden in a large box of sand using archaeological tools. Afterward, in another room, the children were asked to make clay models of the artifacts that they had found. Finally, with the children carrying their clay models, they walked back to school where they placed the models on a table to dry. (p. 349)

At the immediate and 6-week interviews, children were asked, "Can you tell me what happened when we went to the Jewish Museum?" No other cues were needed to prompt some sort of response. After this initial free response, children were shown six photographs (taken by the investigators the day of the field trip) depicting (a) walking to the museum, (b) going up the stairs, (c) talking with the guide, (d) digging for artifacts, (e) making clay models, and (f) the models drying on a table at the school. The pictures were presented in a predetermined random order, and children were asked if they could remember what was happening in each of the photos.

At the 1- and 6-year interviews, children were first given the open-ended prompt described above. If this did not prompt a reply, children received a second, more specific cue, namely, "Do you remember it was a museum of archaeology?" If this still did not elicit a recollection, the experimenter tried a third, more specific cue: "Do you remember there was a sandbox?" After the children responded with everything they could remember in response to these questions, they were shown the six photographs mentioned above, which served as very concrete cues. When viewing the photographs, children were required to do more than simply describe what was depicted; they had to provide evidence that they actually remembered some information not shown in the photographs.

Children's responses were coded into propositions, which the investigators defined as the number of statements with an argument and a predicate. Each proposition was coded as either an act (any action), a description (statements describing the physical environment), or an elaboration (repetitions of previously mentioned acts that included additional information). Figure 10.4 shows the number of acts, descriptions, and elaborations reported as a function of the recall trial—immediately, 6 weeks later, 1 year later, and 6 years later. You can see that the number of descriptions remains remarkably consistent over the 6 years studied, while the number of acts recalled drops. There was no significant difference between the number of elaborations recalled at 1 year versus the number recalled at 6 years, leading

Figure 10–4   Mean number of acts, descriptions, and elaborations recalled by children at each recall trial

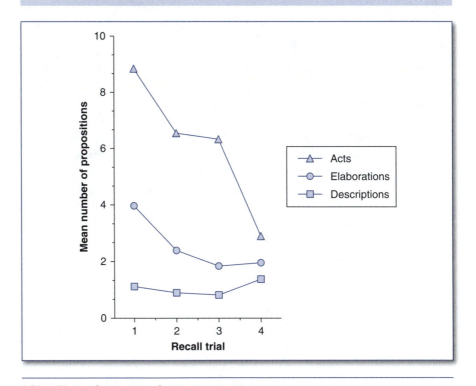

SOURCE: Hudson & Fivush (1991, p. 353).

Hudson and Fivush (1991) to conclude that what information was recalled at 6 years was recalled in as much detail as it was recalled earlier.

Recall that up to four different cues were used to elicit recollections, although the photographs had not been available for the immediate recall interview. Figure 10.5 presents the amount of information recalled in response to each of the four cues (Cue 1 is the most general question; Cue 4 is the photographs) at the 6-week, 1-year, and 6-year interviews. You can see that, over time, more specific cues are needed to elicit information. Responses to the most general cue (Cue 1: "What happened at the Jewish Museum?") were most plentiful at 6 weeks. That same cue elicited very little response at either the 1-year or the 6-year interview. Notice that the photographs (Cue 4) elicited a steady amount of information at each interview.

Figure 10–5 Mean amount of information children recalled to each cue at the 6-week, 1-year, and 6-year recall trials

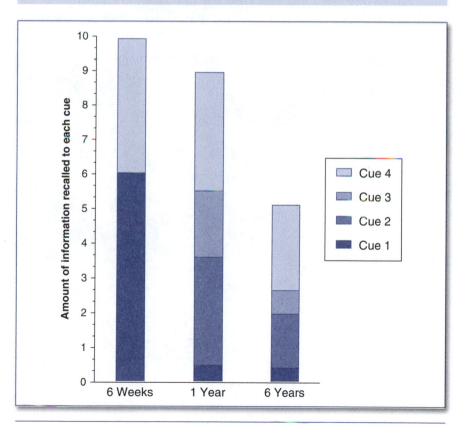

Hudson and Fivush (1991) also reported that, over time, children tended to forget aspects of the field trip that were not particularly distinctive to that particular trip (e.g., walking to the museum, climbing the stairs, or talking with the guide). More distinctive events, such as digging in the sand, using archaeology tools, or making models of artifacts with clay, tended to persist, even for as long as 6 years. This finding is quite consistent with studies of adult autobiographical memory (Linton, 1982).

A laboratory investigation of autobiographical memory conducted by Van Abbema and Bauer (2005) supports many of the conclusions Hudson and Fivush (1991) reported. Three-year-old children visited a psychological laboratory with a parent. While there, each child was given a box of animal crackers and asked to talk with the parent about six "relatively unique" events that had occurred in the child's recent past—three of these within 3 months and three that had occurred at least 6 months prior to the laboratory visit. The children revisited the laboratory once again, when they were aged 7, 8, or 9, and were asked to talk about four of the six events they had discussed at their first visit. The children recalled only about half of the four events, but those that they did recall were recalled accurately and in detail. Fivush and Schwarzmueller (1998)

Photo 10.1   Distinctive events, such as a special family vacation trip, may give rise to detailed event memories that persist for years.

reported similar kinds of results from a study of recall of naturally occurring events for children of similar ages.

Memory for Emotional or Traumatic Events

In the section above we looked at memory for routine and rather unremarkable events. But what of memory for extraordinary, surprising, and consequential events? Cognitive psychologists have long recognized the existence of so-called **flashbulb memories**, which are memories for one's personal circumstances upon receiving news that is often shocking and unexpected (Brown & Kulik, 1977). For example, many of us have very clear memories of hearing the news of the 9/11 attacks (Schmidt, 2004). Although at first flashbulb memories were thought to be "special" kinds of memories not subject to error or intrusions (Brown & Kulik, 1977), subsequent research indicated that, like other kinds of autobiographical memories, flashbulb memories are not always completely accurate (Greenberg, 2004; McCloskey, Wible, & Cohen, 1988; Neisser, 1982; Weaver, 1993).

Pillemer, Picariello, and Pruett (1994) reported one of the first studies of flashbulb memories of children. They interviewed preschoolers (age range 3–4 years) about an emergency preschool evacuation in response to a fire alarm. It was the first fire alarm the children had experienced at the preschool. Children were interviewed 2 weeks after the event and then again 7 years later.

The preschool divided children into two classrooms based on their age. Younger children were about 3 years old at the time of the evacuation; older children were about 4 or 5. All children were able to remember something about the event when questioned 2 weeks afterward, although the older children tended to answer more accurately and to understand more about why the evacuation had been necessary. This suggested to the investigators that older children had encoded the event more completely and with more understanding of what parts of the events caused other parts.

The 7-year interview took place at the preschool, which presumably afforded a variety of contextual cues to the children. Children were asked a variety of open-ended and forced-choice questions about the fire alarm (e.g., "Which room were you in when the alarm sounded?"; "What was your teacher's name?"). Only one child gave enough information in her response to open-ended questions that it was comparable to a typical adult flashbulb memory–type response. Children from the "older" group remembered more than children originally from the "younger" group, especially in their open-ended responses. Close to 33% of the "older" group produced a narrative account of the evacuation, 57% reported at least one fragmentary piece of information about the event, and 86% reported which classroom they had been in. The corresponding figures for children originally from the younger group are 0%, 18%, and 50%. Pillemer et al. (1994) concluded that the older group outperformed the younger group because its initial encoding of the event had been more complete.

Of course, the building evacuation event studied by Pillemer et al. (1994) is a far cry from the national events commonly studied in flashbulb memory research, which typically focus on presidential assassinations, terrorist attacks, and other events of national and historic significance. Warren and Swartwood (1992) studied such an event in their investigation of children's recall of the explosion of the space shuttle *Challenger* in 1986. This event might have been particularly relevant for children, as elementary teacher Christa McAuliffe was part of the crew for this mission, and many schools prepared lessons around the mission, to coordinate with her planned broadcasts from space. The accident occurred during the regular school day, at about noon eastern standard time, and some classrooms had the television on to watch the launch.

Warren and Swartwood (1992) interviewed a total of 347 children in kindergarten through eighth grade approximately 2 weeks and/or 2 months after the accident. Children were first asked to give a free (open-ended) narrative report of what they remembered about their first hearing of the *Challenger* explosion, and then cued with more specific questions if their narrative did not contain the information (e.g., "Where were you when you first heard about the space shuttle accident?" or "What were you doing?"). Many of the original participants were interviewed a third time in January 1988, 2 years after the original event, along with a new sample of children who had not previously been interviewed.

Warren and Swartwood (1992) examined responses to the open-ended question, "Please tell me everything you can remember about the first time you heard about the space shuttle exploding," by counting the number of words a child used in her response. They also examined the proportion of "canonical flashbulb" features (out of a possible six) that Brown and Kulik (1977) originally proposed as essential aspects of a flashbulb memory. This included source of the *Challenger* news, location, ongoing activity, the child's own emotional reaction, the emotional reaction of others present, and the aftermath—what happened after the news was broken. Table 10.3 presents these two measures as a function of a categorization of children into three age groups: young (kindergarten to second grade at the time of the explosion), middle (third to fifth grade at the time of the explosion), and older (sixth to eighth grade at the time of the explosion). As can be seen in the table, older children provided longer narratives than did the two younger groups, and reported more of the canonical flashbulb features in their responses. Over time, all age groups reported fewer canonical features.

Table 10–3   Means of content elaboration and report length over time by age groups

Grade	Time 1		Time 2		Time 3	
	Content*	Length†	Content	Length	Content	Length
K to 2nd (n = 37)	.42	49.80	.37	27.70	.23	21.50
3rd to 5th (n =44)	.40	34.50	.36	25.00	.30	23.40
6th to 8th (n = 30)	.67	75.50	.53	46.30	.54	39.40

SOURCE: Adapted from Warren & Swartwood (1992, p. 104).

NOTE: Only data from participants tested all three times are included.

*Content is the proportion of Brown and Kulik canonical features out of six possible reported in the recall narrative.

†Length is the number of words in the recall narrative.

Warren and Swartwood (1992) speculated that one factor that might account for the age differences in reports they found is a differing level of understanding of the original event. Other studies (reported by the authors) showed that younger students may not have fully comprehended what led the shuttle to explode, sometimes attributed animistic attributes to the explosion (e.g., "the rocket died"), and sometimes did not fully understand the implications of the tragedy (e.g., one child wondered if the space lessons would still be provided). Note here the connection to the Pillemer et al. (1994) study: Increased understanding of, or knowledge about, an event leads to a stronger and more elaborated retrospective memory of it.

Fivush, Sales, Goldberg, Bahrick, and Parker (2004) reported a study of children's long-term recall of Hurricane Andrew. Children who had experienced Hurricane Andrew were interviewed about their recollections of the event, both within a few months and 6 years later. All of the children were around 3 or 4 years old at the time of the hurricane. The authors divided them into three groups, depending on the stress the hurricane had caused them directly, as follows:

> Children in the high stress condition were at home with their families when their houses fell apart around them, including roofs caving in, trees coming into living areas, and window glass flying. Children in the moderate stress group also experienced a severe storm with winds knocking down trees, and water seeping into their homes, but the perimeters of their homes remained intact. Finally, families of children in the low stress group prepared for the

storm, but fortunately only experienced a heavy rainfall. Thus children in all three groups engaged in the same activities to prepare for the storm, but only children in the severe stress group experienced the full force of the storm. (p. 105)

All of the children were able to recall this event when interviewed 6 years after the hurricane struck. Indeed, they reported about twice as much information 6 years after the event than they did a few months after it occurred. Although at the initial interview, children in the high-stress group reported less information than children in the moderate-stress group, at the 6-year interview all children reported about the same amount of information. Children in the high-stress group required more prompting than did children from the other groups, but the information they did report was more consistent with what they had initially reported. The authors concluded that stressful events might be particularly well remembered over time (see Fivush, Hazzard, Sales, Sarfati, & Brown, 2003, for a comparison of children's ability to recall positive and negative events).

We see in these studies an echo of the conclusions from the studies on general autobiographical memory. Children form narrative memories for emotional events. They recall these events best when they have a good understanding of what the event is about at the time it occurs. Although memory fades over time, a good deal of what is retained is accurate.

Eyewitness Memory

We saw in Chapter 7 that preschool children have some fragile competence as eyewitnesses. That is, they can accurately recall some aspects of events they have witnessed, although they are very susceptible to suggestive questioning. In this section we continue to look at the ability to accurately report on witnessed events during middle childhood.

Roebers and Schneider (2000, 2002) have studied eyewitness memory in children in the relevant age group. In the 2002 study, they were interested in the question of how stable children's recollections were across events and how much their ability in one aspect of memory (e.g., giving a detailed account of a witnessed event) predicted their abilities in other events (e.g., resisting suggestive questioning).

Roebers and Schneider (2002) had three groups of children, aged 6, 8, and 10 years, watch two 7-minute videos ("Money Theft" and "Treasure Hunt") on two different occasions, 3 weeks apart. Children were later interviewed individually by a researcher. They first gave open-ended responses to general questions ("Tell everything you remember about the video") and then responded to a set of either unbiased or misleading specific questions about the video (assignment to unbiased or misleading question types was randomly determined at the beginning of the study). The children's free recall narratives were scored against a list of about 40 items that had been depicted in the videos. Their cued recall was measured by their responses to a subset of the specific questions they had been given.

Accuracy of the free recall narratives rose with age. Of the approximately 40 details of each video, the average overall percentage recalled was 9%, 23%, and 32% for the 6-, 8-, and 10-year-olds, respectively. The number of incorrectly recalled details in the free recall narratives was low and did not differ for the three age groups.

When cued recall was examined, there was again an age-related increase in accuracy for responses to the unbiased questions. There was likewise an age-related increase in accuracy for correct performance on the misleading questions (i.e., resisting the false suggestions). Moreover, the two younger groups of children performed significantly better on the unbiased than on the misleading questions; performance on the two types of questions was comparable for the 10-year-olds. Table 10.4 presents the mean proportion of

Table 10–4   Accuracy of cued recall as a function of age, question format (unbiased/misleading), and video (standard deviations are shown in parentheses)

	Money theft	Treasure hunt
6-year-olds		
Unbiased	.61 (.13)	.66 (.18)
Misleading	.26 (.30)	.27 (.26)
8-year-olds		
Unbiased	.75 (.15)	.70 (.15)
Misleading	.63 (.26)	.56 (.27)
10-year-olds		
Unbiased	.82 (.10)	.77 (.11)
Misleading	.82 (.11)	.73 (.21)

SOURCE: Roebers & Schneider (2002, p. 1093).

cued recall questions answered correctly as a function of age, question type, and the two videos shown.

More important, results showed some moderate correlation in the performance on different types of memory tasks. That is, being able to correctly recall details in the free recall narrative was significantly correlated (specific correlations ranged from .35 to .69) with ability to answer unbiased cued recall questions correctly. However, correlations were not as strong and were for the most part not statistically significant between being able to correctly recall details in the free recall narrative and answering misleading questions correctly (specific correlations ranged from .11 to .43).

Roebers and Schneider (2002) concluded that with increasing age, children in middle childhood become increasingly able to give elaborate recountings of events they have witnessed, and also become better able to provide correct answers to specific questions. However, like Bruck and Ceci (1999) before them, the authors concluded that younger children (below the age of 7, say) are especially vulnerable to suggestive or misleading questioning, with only about a third or fewer of the responses of 6-year-olds to misleading questions being correct. Indeed, work in forensic psychology suggests that a common forensic interviewing technique, repeating questions to assess the consistency (and therefore presumed accuracy) of a witness's report, may disproportionately affect younger children, who treat repeated questions from adults as suggestions that their first answer was not correct (Fivush, Peterson, & Schwarzmueller, 2002).

However, just as the literature in cognitive psychology demonstrates for adults, even older children are not immune to the effects of suggestive or misleading questioning (Bruck & Ceci, 2004). Moreover, older children (like adults) still make source monitoring errors, confusing information they heard about or saw on television with information they received through direct experience or witnessing (Lindsay, Johnson, & Kwon, 1991; Roberts, 2000a, 2000b; Roberts & Blades, 2000). The ability to discriminate between information that was witnessed or heard from that which was only imagined shows considerable improvement over middle childhood (Poole & Lindsay, 2002; Quas, Schaaf, Alexander, & Goodman, 2000).

Our look at memory in middle childhood reveals several themes. One is that, while children in middle childhood are more strategic and more intentional about their ability to recall information, they still are subject to the errors and confusions that affect preschoolers. Indeed, factors such as source monitoring errors and inability to discriminate among several similar events are things that hamper the memories of even experienced adults. But, as children get older, they come to understand more about events and other information and thus are often able to encode that information in memory more completely and more accessibly.

We noted earlier in the chapter a distinction between episodic and semantic memory. So far, we have limited our discussion to episodic memory. But it may be that part of the answer to what helps older children remember more about an event or a story or a television show has to do with their general world knowledge—in other words, their semantic memory. It is to that topic that we now turn.

DEVELOPING A WIDER AND DEEPER KNOWLEDGE BASE

As you may recall, semantic memory holds information in our knowledge base. Like episodic memory, semantic memory holds information that was previously learned. For example, your knowledge that a dollar is worth the same as 10 dimes or 20 nickels or 100 pennies is not innate—probably somewhere about the time when you were 5 or 6 years old you started to learn these facts. Unlike episodic memories, semantic memories don't seem to hold "time tags" or information about your personal circumstances of when you first learned the information. Thus, while you very likely could provide me with a narrative about where you were when you first heard about 9/11, you are very *unlikely* to provide such a narrative about where you were when you learned that a dime was worth two nickels.

One of the more noticeable aspects of cognitive development in middle childhood is the growth of the knowledge base. School-aged children in the United States learn an incredible amount of what adults would consider "basic" information—letters of the alphabet; how to read; addition, subtraction, multiplication, and division facts; historical and geographical facts; information about certain authors; and information about animals, planets, and machines, to take just a few examples from my children's elementary school's curriculum. Add to that knowledge of domains that aren't formally taught in schools—Pokémon characters, Webkinz Web site rules of operation, or characters from the *Captain Underpants* or *Harry Potter* book series or the *Hannah Montana* television shows are examples that come immediately to my mind, courtesy of my children.

When that much information is entering storage, issues immediately arise as to how it all gets organized. To understand this idea, consider the files on your personal computer. My bet is that, when you first started storing files on a computer, you may have created a folder called "My folder" on the hard drive and simply stuck all your files within it. When you have a reasonable number of individual files, such a system works just fine. But, over time, as you created more and more files, you probably had to develop a more complex system of filing, including the creation of different folders. Maybe you had one folder for all your school-related files, another one for all your photos, another one for all the letters you wrote, and so forth. But, over time, you likely found that an increasingly differentiated system was required. Finding a file called "Letter to Aunt Sarah" only works if you've written just one letter to her, ever. If you start a long correspondence with her, however, you'll need to differentiate file names and probably file all your letters to her in the same place for easy access.

Analogously, children need to find efficient ways of storing and representing all of the knowledge they acquire. How they do that is certainly a matter of active debate and discussion in the field (see S. Gelman & Kalish, 2006, for an overview). Here, we will focus on the development of concepts in middle childhood. As before, we will be continuing a discussion begun in Chapter 7 about conceptual development in the preschool years. There, we saw that children revise information about their concepts as they acquire more information, experience, and expertise in a domain. Young children sometimes group things together based on their perceptions (so a toddler might call a lion a "kitty" or a "doggie"), but when children have skeletal principles in a domain, they use those to reason about new instances they encounter in trying to figure out what the new instance is an instance of.

Understanding Class Inclusion

We've previously reviewed the Piagetian theory of concrete operations and looked in depth at children's performance on such "hallmark" tasks as the conservation task. Another famous Piagetian task thought to indicate the presence of concrete operations is the class inclusion task (Inhelder & Piaget, 1964). This task is depicted in Figure 10.6, which shows a line drawing of four roses and two daisies.

Figure 10–6 Depiction of stimuli for a Piagetian class inclusion task

In a typical Piagetian scenario, the child is asked to point first to all the roses, then to all the daisies, and then to all the flowers. Correct responses ensure that the child understands all the terms that will be used in the critical question and, further, understands the hierarchical nature of the concepts *rose, daisy,* and *flower.* That is, the child understands that the term *flower* encompasses other terms that name specific kinds of flowers.

Now the child is asked, "Who would have more, the person who had the flowers or the person who had the roses?" Typically, up until about the age of 8, the child will claim that there are more roses than flowers (McCabe, Siegel, Spence, & Wilkinson, 1982). This is so even though he previously agreed that roses are flowers! According to Piagetian theory, the child has trouble (until concrete operations are firmly established) keeping both the part (roses) and whole (flowers) classes in mind simultaneously. Although asked to compare two different levels of the hierarchy to each other, the child instead compares only entities at the same level of the hierarchy, and compares the roses to the less numerous daisies.

It would appear from these findings that younger children lack an important ability that older children readily display. But once again, Piaget's interpretation of children's performance on his original task was challenged by subsequent researchers. In particular, Ellen Markman (Markman, Horton, & McLanahan, 1980; Markman & Siebert, 1976) argued that younger children are more likely to understand **collections** and mentally impose this structure on class inclusion task stimuli.

What is a collection? According to Markman and Siebert (1976), a collection is a term such as *family* or *forest* or *pile* that describes not only a group of individuals (e.g., *people* or *trees* or *blocks*) but individuals who also have a specific organization in relation to each other. So, for example, one can presumably tell if something is a tree or not independently of its spatial relationship to other trees. However, one cannot tell if a tree is in a forest without knowing about these spatial relationships.

Markman et al. (1980) argued that collections are a psychologically more coherent principle of hierarchical organization than are classes and that children naturally impose a collection structure on class inclusion questions. And, indeed, kindergarteners and first graders tested by Markman and Siebert (1976) were much more able to answer a "collection" question (e.g., "Here is a family of frogs; this is the mother and this is the father frog, and these are the baby frogs, and this is the family. Who would have more pets, someone who owned the baby frogs or someone who owned the family?") than they were a typical class inclusion question (e.g., "Who would have more pets, someone who owned all the frogs or someone who owned the little frogs?").

In a follow-up study, Markman et al. (1980) found that, when information about the relationships among stimuli was ambiguous (the stimuli were line drawings of fictitious animals), children as old as 14 years tended to impose a collection, rather than a class, structure. How much the improvement is due to the greater psychological coherence of collections, relative to classes, is a matter of some debate (Hodges & French, 1988); however, the findings from Markman and Siebert (1976) regarding children's performance on class inclusion problems are generally replicable by other researchers.

This all implies that understanding the relationships among different concepts is not simple. It also implies that relationships among subordinate-level, basic-level, and superordinate-level concepts (identified by Eleanor Rosch and discussed in Chapter 7) might not be easy to see or automatically understood. It also suggests that certain complex cognitive skills such as reasoning (a topic we will take up in the next chapter) depend in complex ways on how knowledgeable children are about what is being reasoned about.

Developing New Theories

S. Gelman and Kalish (2006) divide the theoretical approaches conceptual developmental researchers take into three categories. The first is a nativist approach, which holds that some concepts are represented, at least in part, innately. For example, we have previously seen that some researchers (e.g., Spelke, 2000) believe that children are born into the world with concepts such as *animism* or *causation*; others such as Fodor (1983) have put forward the idea that just about any concept that has a name (e.g., *zebra, comb, airplane*) must have innate representation. R. Gelman's (2002) proposal on children's skeletal principles of counting (discussed in Chapter 7) would fall into this camp as well. There is debate among different researchers in this camp as to whether specific concepts (e.g., for *zebra*) are innate or whether simply the tendency to pay attention to certain stimuli and not others is innate.

A second theoretical camp shares an empiricist approach to cognitive development, arguing that concepts are acquired either through direct representations of one's sensory or perceptual experience or by combining information from different sensory or perceptual experiences. Empiricist approaches, in other words, focus on information that is learned, and ask questions about how children associate different experiences to form summary representations (S. Gelman & Kalish, 2006). For example, children are said to form concepts on the basis of similarity, grouping together instances on the basis of their overall surface appearance (e.g., Sloutsky, Kloos, & Fisher, 2007).

The third camp, the one that S. Gelman and Kalish (2006) advocate, is called the **naïve theory approach**. It holds that children construct common-sense understandings or theories that have individual concepts embedded in them, and that whatever concepts are acquired at any point in development are constrained by the existing knowledge base. Said another way, the idea is that children acquire concepts mainly by relating new knowledge to the knowledge they already have.

Susan Carey (1985, 2000b) offers an example of this third approach in talking about children's developing knowledge of biological concepts. We began looking at this topic in Chapter 7, when we discussed preschoolers' understanding of the concepts of *animate* and *inanimate* entities. Carey argues that children's understanding of what a living thing is undergoes tremendous change between the ages of 4 and 10:

> It seems unlikely that preschool children who insist that cars are alive could have the same concept of life as the adult and merely be mistaken about cars, and indeed, they do not. Rather, preschool children have constructed a very different theoretical framework from that held by adults in which they have embedded their understanding of animals, just as children of elementary school age have constructed a different framework theory in which they embed their understanding of the material world. These beliefs of young children are true beliefs, formulated over concepts that differ from those that underlie the intuitive or scientific theories that adults use to understand the world. (Carey, 2000b, p. 15)

Carey (1988, 2000b) argues that preschoolers have concepts of animals and people that are organized very differently from the way adolescents and adults organize these concepts. Preschoolers, Carey claims, understand what an animal is by making analogies to people. So, they make analogies and understand animal behavior, physiology, and relationships by invoking what they know about human behavior, physiology, and relationships. Mother animals take care of baby animals in similar ways used by human mommies toward their babies, in the children's minds. Animals are judged to have internal organs by projecting from what the child knows about a human's internal organs. Said a little more succinctly, Carey holds that preschoolers view humans as the prototypical animal.

Carey notes then that children face a challenge as they acquire biological information over the course of their elementary years. They must not only learn new information—they must reorganize their conceptual information, giving up the idea that humans are at the center of the biological universe!

The average 10-year-old, according to Carey (2000b), has constructed a new theory—putting animals and plants together into the category *living thing*—that does not place humans as the central prototype.

S. Gelman and Kalish (2006) point out that the naïve theory approach necessarily incorporates aspects of the two other theoretical camps. The approach assumes the existence of some innate framework (nativist approach) that gives infants and children some direction as they learn new information (empiricist approach) and form new concepts. The emphasis of the naïve theory approach, however, is that children revise their conceptual organization as they acquire more information. The analogy made is to scientists, who periodically need to reorganize their concepts and understandings as new revolutions in knowledge occur.

Waxman, Medin, and Ross (2007) conducted a study with roots in the naïve theory tradition, albeit one that differed from Carey's. They believe that children have skeletal biological principles (akin to the skeletal mathematical principles discussed in Chapter 7) that change as children acquire more information. In particular, they focused on children's understandings of how it is that an animal comes to be a member of one species rather than another.

Waxman et al. (2007) interviewed children (aged 4–10 years) and adults from four different communities: rural Native Americans (from the Menominee tribe in Wisconsin), members of the rural majority culture from the same part of Wisconsin, and members of suburban and urban North American communities. Participants were questioned about various inter-species adoption scenarios. These included the following pairs: turtle-toad, cow-pig, and pigeon-turkey. For each participant, the animal designated as the birth parent and adoptive parent was determined randomly. For example, the following scenario refers to a baby cow, adopted and raised by pigs. The scenario was presented to participants orally as follows:

> I'm going to tell you a story. One day a cow gave birth to a little baby. Here's a drawing of the cow that gave birth to the baby [drawing of cow is shown]. Right after the baby was born, the cow died without ever seeing the baby [drawing of cow is removed]. The baby was found and taken right away to live with pigs in a place where there are lots of pigs. Here's a drawing of the pig [drawing of the pig is shown] that took care of the baby the whole time that the baby was growing up [drawing of pig is removed]. The baby grew up with pigs and never saw another cow again. Now the baby is all grown up, and I'm going to ask some questions about what it's like as an adult. (Waxman et al., 2007, p. 298)

Interviewees were then asked about various traits or behaviors that the biological and adoptive mothers had and asked to predict what the baby would do or have when it was grown, as in "The cow mooed and the pig oinked. When the baby is all grown up, will it moo like a cow or oink like a pig?" and "The cow's heart got flatter when it sleeps, and the pig's heart got rounder when it sleeps. When the baby is all grown up, when it sleeps does its heart get flatter like the one of the cow or get rounder like the one of the pig?" (Waxman et al., 2007, p. 298). Table 10.5 presents a complete list of the behaviors, physical properties, and target animals included in the interview.

The results of the study showed that, among all four populations studied, interviewees believed that the baby would resemble the birth parent more than the adoptive parent. This tendency rose with age and was stronger for physical traits than for behaviors, especially for novel behaviors. Interviewees were also asked to say what kind of animal the baby was when

Table 10–5 Experiment 1: Properties associated with the cow-pig, pigeon-turkey, and turtle-toad scenarios

Target animal	Familiar behavior	Novel behavior[a]	Familiar physical	Novel physical[a]
Cow	Moos	Looks for sparrows	Straight tail	Heart gets flatter when it's sleeping
Pig	Oinks	Looks for cardinals	Curly tail	Heart gets rounder when it's sleeping
Pigeon	Very used to flying	Stops when it sees a maple tree	Short neck	Stomach gets harder when it's sleeping
Turkey	Very used to walking on the ground	Stops when it sees an oak tree	Long neck	Stomach gets softer when it's sleeping
Turtle	Walks slowly	Opens its eyes when it's afraid	Shell on its back	Blood becomes thick and sticky when it's sleeping
Toad	Hops	Closes its eyes when it's afraid	Warts on its back	Blood becomes thin and watery when it's sleeping

SOURCE: Waxman, Medin, & Ross (2007, p. 299).

NOTE: Novel behavioral and physical properties were counterbalanced across species.

it grew up—in our example, either a cow or a pig. Overwhelmingly, the interviewees chose the biological parent's species as the species of the baby.

Finally, interviewees were given a scenario of a blood transfusion, which was presented as follows:

> When the baby was growing up, it became sick. A doctor came and, with a needle, took out all of the old blood that the baby got from its mother [drawing of the birth parent is shown] when it was born. The doctor then went to the animal taking care of the baby [the drawing of the adoptive parent is shown] and took some of its blood to give to the baby. So the baby got all new blood like the blood of the pig. (Waxman et al., 2007, p. 299)

The purpose of presenting this scenario was to see whether participants believed that the mechanism of one's *kindhood*—that is, the species to which an animal belonged—would be seen as determined by its blood. Previous research had shown cross-cultural differences in response to such a scenario, with Mayan children and adults not regarding blood as providing the "essence" of species-hood (Atran et al., 2001) but Brazilian children thinking that a blood transfusion could affect the species to which an animal belonged (Sousa, Atran, & Medin, 2002). Indeed, the Menominee population studied by Waxman et al. (2007) was an interesting one to include because some tribal rights and membership were in fact based on blood quantum requirements (i.e., what percentage of "Menominee blood" an individual had was determined by the parental enrollment in a Menominee tribe).

Results showed that the Menominee children were indeed more likely to consider blood as a mechanism that established an animal's species. The authors argue that "in a community in which discourse about blood is salient, and in which issues concerning blood have strong consequences, children seize on blood as a candidate biological essence and consider its potential in the transmission of kindhood" (Waxman et al., 2007, p. 300). Adult Menominee respondents responded differently, and in line with the responses of the majority culture adults and children. The point here is that at least some children appear to form their theories of what instances (e.g., individual animals) belong in which categories (e.g., species) somewhat differently than do adults and that, as they acquire new information, those theories undergo change, sometimes change of a dramatic nature.

❖ ❖ ❖

In short, our brief look at conceptual change in childhood suggests that, during middle childhood, profound changes are taking place. Not only is a wealth of information being acquired, but new concepts and new organizations of those concepts are constructed. We will see some additional specific examples of concept acquisition and change in Chapter 11 when we discuss the acquisition of academic skills and knowledge.

SUMMARY

1. Cognitive developmental psychologists distinguish long-term memory from working memory based on several aspects, including length of storage of material, capacity limitations, and manner of coding.

2. Within long-term memory, many cognitive psychologists recognize a distinction between episodic memory, which holds memories of personally experienced events, and semantic memory, which holds information in a general knowledge base.

3. Empirical work in cognitive developmental psychology has established that during middle childhood, children become more likely to rehearse and organize information, and become both more intentional and more efficient in the way they rehearse and organize.

4. Research on childhood amnesia suggests that few memories are able to be retrieved by adults or older children that date from before the observer's first birthday. There are a few retrievable memories that date from the observer's age of 2 or 3 years and more that date from age 4 onward.

5. Studies of autobiographical memory in children show that, after children are about 3 or 4 years old, they can form long-lasting memories of significant events. Although not all events are remembered, those that are tend to be recalled in detail. Events that are particularly memorable tend to be ones that are unique.

6. Flashbulb memories are recollections of extraordinary, consequential, and often surprising events. Studies of flashbulb memories formed in middle childhood show that older children remember more than younger children, presumably because older children are better able to understand and encode the event.

7. Studies of eyewitness memory in children again suggest that older children are generally more accurate than younger children and better able to avoid source monitoring errors. However, children of all ages remain vulnerable to the effects of suggestive or misleading questioning (as do adults).

8. As children acquire more information and knowledge in several domains, their organization of that information becomes important to understand.

9. The Piagetian class inclusion task is one way to understand how children organize their knowledge about the way different concepts relate to one another.

10. Recent work suggests that in some domains (e.g., biology), children need to develop new theories and understandings as they acquire new information. However, the way theories are acquired and revised may depend in part on the cultural context in which children's lives are embedded.

REVIEW QUESTIONS

1. Explain why many cognitive developmental psychologists draw distinctions between working and long-term memory, and between episodic and semantic memory.

2. Describe the changes in rehearsal seen over the course of middle childhood, and explain the implications of these changes.

3. Discuss the Usher and Neisser (1993) study on childhood amnesia and the implications it has for the study of memory in children.

4. Describe studies of autobiographical memory in childhood and what results from these studies imply.

5. What do the studies of children's flashbulb memories tell us? Consider both the strengths and the limitations of this kind of research in your answer.

6. Given the research findings on children's eyewitness memory, what recommendations would you have for the judicial system when it comes to evaluating the accuracy of child witnesses?

7. Describe the Piagetian class inclusion task, and discuss the typical findings and what these do and do not imply.

8. Describe and critique the Waxman et al. (2007) study of children's knowledge of biological concepts.

KEY TERMS

Childhood Amnesia

Class Inclusion Task

Collection

Encoding Specificity Principle

Flashbulb Memory

Long-Term Memory (LTM)

Naïve Theory Approach (to conceptual development)

Narrative Memory

Primacy Effect

Recency Effect

Retrieval Cue

Serial Position Effect

CHAPTER 11

MIDDLE CHILDHOOD

Higher-Order and Complex Cognitive Skills

We've now caught up on developments in "basic" cognitive processes—such things as perception, attention, memory, and concept formation and representation. Cognitive psychologists often contrast these processes with "higher-order" cognitive processes, which are said to be ones that make use of the outputs from basic cognitive processes. Included in higher-order cognitive processes are thinking, reasoning, decision making, problem solving, and other related complex processes.

In this chapter we will examine cross-cultural differences in cognitive development. Specifically, we'll begin by looking at non-Western cultures in which schooling is not the major occupation of children in middle childhood. Instead, these children are typically apprenticing to their parents or other elders, learning a trade or vocation under the tutelage of an expert. We will contrast that kind of cognitive development with the kind experienced by children in Western cultures, focusing on the development of academic skills.

THEORETICAL PERSPECTIVES

We'll start this chapter, as we have in each of the previous chapters, by considering theoretical perspectives most relevant to the topics of this chapter, before we examine the specifics of development of higher-order cognitive processes, apprenticeships, and academic learning.

A Vygotskian View of Middle Childhood

In Chapter 9 we took a detailed look at Piagetian theory and its view of cognitive development in middle childhood. Recall that Piagetian theory sees cognitive development as occurring wholly *within* the individual child. While education, parental interaction, or media might *influence* the process, Piagetian theory holds that they are all external agents that are separate from the central cognitive changes that transpire within the child.

As we saw in Chapters 2 and 6, however, psychologist Lev Vygotsky took a very different view of cognitive development. For Vygotsky, the child cannot be isolated from the contextual surroundings, including the people and activities he interacts with. Together, the context, activities, background culture, and actors in an activity co-construct a child's mental structures at any given point of cognitive development.

We saw in Chapters 2 and 6 that Vygotsky created the concept of the *zone of proximal development*. By this he meant that the cognitive performance a child is capable of when working independently is at the bottom of a range of abilities of which she is capable. With the appropriate support and scaffolding (e.g., from a teacher or parent, or when interacting with more able peers) her cognitive abilities stretch a bit and show greater complexity and maturity.

Vygotsky was also a strong proponent of the idea that a culture and, specifically, the tools provided by a culture shape cognition and cognitive development. For example, in the United States most children in middle childhood go to school—formal educational settings that provide explicit instruction in sometimes abstract academic skills—literacy, arithmetic, and problem solving to take a few examples. However, not all cultures offer this kind of formal schooling to all children. Instead, in many of these settings, children serve **apprenticeships**, learning very specific job skills such as hunting, farming, or weaving under the tutelage of an elder (Rogoff, 1990). In such settings, there is much less emphasis on developing general-purpose skills, such as reading, that will apply potentially in a wide set of circumstances (e.g., reading a job application, reading a recipe, reading directions, reading a novel). Instead, the focus is on learning a very specific set of skills that will apply to a very limited realm.

According to Vygotsky, when children interact with either other children or adults, the products of the interaction become internalized into the child's mind. The Vygotskian slogan "the intermental constructs the intramental" is meant to capture this insight. Children experience more sophisticated problem solving in the context of a socially shared activity and eventually internalize this approach.

Another important insight of Vygotsky's is that the tools a culture provides or offers shape a child's intellectual functioning (Miller, 2011). By "tools" Vygotsky meant such things as language systems, writing systems, counting systems, and pictorial artifacts, in addition to the more commonly thought of tools such

Photo 11.1 An apprenticeship is a period in which novices learn very specific skills, such as weaving, under the guidance of an expert.

as computers, video games, cell phones, and iPods. Children in a nonliterate society, for example, don't have written texts and therefore will need to rely more heavily on auditory memory and oral means of information transmission. Children with access to television may have a very different set of quasi-educational experiences than children without. Tools, Vygotsky held, transform elementary mental functions—that is, mental abilities we share with other animals, such as recognition memory, auditory discrimination, and attention—into higher mental functions—ones that are uniquely human, such as abstract thinking or syntactic construction of utterances.

Language was a particularly important cultural tool for Vygotsky. When children learn to talk, they use language in at least two different ways. One of these ways is to communicate with others, of course. But a second way is to use something Vygotsky called *private speech*—what we might call "talking to oneself." Private speech is used to guide oneself through a challenging task. In fact, if you hang around preschoolers doing a puzzle, you'll be quite likely to observe them talking themselves through the process. In middle childhood, however, private speech becomes *inner* speech—that is, the children now begin to talk to themselves silently, a tendency that persists into adulthood.

A View From Learning Theory

We talked about learning theory, classical conditioning, and instrumental conditioning in Chapters 2, 3, and 5. Here, we will take a closer look at how instrumental (sometimes called operant) conditioning might apply to the learning that children in middle childhood engage in.

Learning theorist Edward Thorndike (1874–1949) pioneered basic concepts in instrumental conditioning that applied to animal learning. He was also known for his work in educational psychology, particularly in the study of how children learn arithmetic (Thorndike, 1925; R. Thorndike, 1991). Thorndike is most famous to introductory psychology students as the discoverer of the "law of effect"—the basic principle of instrumental conditioning, which states,

> Of several responses made to the same situation, those which are accompanied or closely followed by satisfaction to the animal will, other things being equal, be more firmly connected with the situation, so that, when it recurs, they will be more likely to recur; those which are accompanied or closely followed by discomfort to the animal will, other things being equal, have their connections with that situation weakened, so that, when it recurs, they will be less likely to occur. The greater the satisfaction or discomfort, the greater the strengthening or weakening of the bond. (Thorndike, 1911/2000, p. 244)

We see in this quote the idea that learning consists of the formation of bonds or connections that get strengthened through repetition and when they are followed by positive reinforcement. Thorndike brought these ideas to the study of how children learn arithmetic. For example, he believed in the idea that children learn associations between problems such as "8 + 7 = ?" and "15" through lots of repetition and practice. He advocated preparing realistic problems and giving children lots of opportunities to strengthen these bonds.

Similarly, in studying how best to teach children to read, Thorndike analyzed texts (books, magazines, newspapers) to see how frequently different words appeared. Again, the emphasis was on analyzing a complex task (such as reading) into component associations that needed to be learned, so that appropriate amounts of practice could be devoted to critical bonds or associations. We'll come back to many of these ideas when we talk about academic learning in a few more sections.

HIGHER-ORDER COGNITIVE SKILLS

"Higher-order" cognitive tasks typically include reasoning, decision making, problem solving, and thinking. In each of these tasks, the information that has been previously received, processed, and stored by basic cognitive processes gets used, combined, reformatted, or manipulated by higher-order cognitive processes. We will focus on just a few of the possible set of higher-order cognitive tasks, given space constraints on the book and time constraints on the student reader!

Reasoning

In Chapter 8 we saw that, at least under certain circumstances, preschoolers could reason, both deductively (drawing conclusions that go from the general to the specific) and inductively (going from the specific to the general). Specifically, young children performed better when asked to reason about information they were very familiar with, or else when the premises presented information about a fantasy world, which presumably cued the children not to rely on their world knowledge.

Deanna Kuhn (1977) performed one of the classic studies on reasoning in middle childhood. She worked with children aged 6 to 14 years, giving them a series of **conditional reasoning** problems. Conditional reasoning problems come in four basic forms, as shown in Table 11.1. Only a brief review of these is possible here, but any text in logic (e.g., Skyrms, 2000) would provide more details.

Table 11–1 Conditional reasoning problems

Modus ponens (valid)	Modus tollens (valid)	Denying the antecedent (fallacy)	Affirming the consequent (fallacy)
If p, then q	If p, then q	If p, then q	If p, then q
p	not q	not p	q
—— (therefore)	—— (therefore)	—— (therefore)	—— (therefore)
q	not p	not q	p

SOURCE: Skyrms (2000).

Conditional reasoning problems begin with *premises*, or given information that is assumed to be true. One premise common to all four forms is "If *p*, then *q*," often written symbolically as p → q. The symbol *p* in the expression "p → q" is called the *antecedent*, and *q* is called the *consequent* of that particular premise. According to propositional logic (Skyrms, 2000), "p → q" is true whenever the antecedent is false or the consequent is true. Alternatively, we could say that "p → q" is false only when *p* is true and *q* is false. Thus the sentence "If the second ice age started in 2000 A.D., then my dog is a poodle" is automatically true (even though all of my dogs have been Bernese mountain dogs), because the antecedent ("the second ice age started in 2000 A.D.") is false (I like poodles, though. Someday I think I'll get one).

Notice that in logic, no cause-and-effect relationship must be present, or is even implied. This contrasts with English, because we normally expect the antecedent (what precedes) to be related to the cause of the consequent (what follows) when we use the expression "If . . . , then . . ." Also, when using the English expression, we consider "If *p*, then *q*" to be false if *p* is false and *q* true (unlike in logic, where it would be considered true).

Two well-known rules of conditional reasoning are *modus ponens* and *modus tollens,* both shown in Table 11.1. Both are valid rules of reasoning, which basically means that if the premises are true the conclusions will also be true. Also shown in Table 11.1 are two other "rules" that turn out not to be valid; that is, they can produce conclusions that can be false even if the premises are true. "Rules" of this sort are called fallacies. Let's work through examples of why these rules are fallacies. Consider *affirming the consequent* as it applies to the following example: "If a person wears Birkenstock sandals, then he is a college professor. Roy is a college professor. Therefore, he wears Birkenstock sandals." Notice that the first premise ("If a person wears Birkenstock sandals, then he is a college professor") is not equivalent to the converse ("If a person is a college professor, then he wears Birkenstock sandals"). In fact, the first premise allows for the possibility of high-heeled professors (like some of my more fashionable colleagues), which contradicts the conclusion.

The second fallacy, *denying the antecedent*, is exemplified in the argument "p → q; ¬p, therefore ¬q." Using the example, these propositions would be instantiated as "If a person wears Birkenstock sandals, then she is a college professor. Mija does not wear Birkenstock sandals. Therefore, she is not a college professor." For the reason just given (namely, the possible existence of high-heeled college professors), this argument is also false.

And now back to Deanna Kuhn's (1977) investigation of how children perform conditional reasoning. To engage children's interest and make the task more comprehensible, Kuhn told her participants about a fictional far-away city called "Tundor," and played a game where she would give them one piece of information about Tundor (e.g., "John is tall, and Bob is short") and then ask questions (e.g., "Is Bob tall?") to which the child could respond "yes," "no," or "maybe." The pretest gave examples of questions that could be answered definitively as well as ones that could not, based on the given information. Only children who correctly answered both pretest questions were allowed to continue.

Next, Kuhn gave children each of the four conditional reasoning problems shown in Table 11.1. For example, a version of the *modus ponens* problem was "All of the people in Tundor are happy. Jean lives in Tundor. Is Jean happy?" (The correct, logically valid answer is yes.) A version of the *denying the antecedent* problem might have been something like "All people who live in Tundor own cats. Mike does not live in Tundor. Does he own a cat?" (Here, the correct answer is *maybe*, as no logically valid conclusion can be drawn.)

Some of the results from Kuhn's experiment are presented in Figure 11.1. You can see that on these problems, even the first graders show some reasoning ability, particularly on *modus ponens* problems. You can also see that children's performance varies dramatically as a function of the format of the problem (this is also true for adults; Markovits & Vachon, 1990). You might notice that with some problem forms there is a slight decline in performance for older students. Kuhn (1977) attributes this to the increased tendency for older children to respond "maybe" even when a more definitive answer could be made.

Kuhn's use of the "cover story" about the land of Tundor presumably made it easier for children to understand the task she was posing to them.

Figure 11–1   Average percent correct by grade and conditional reasoning problem

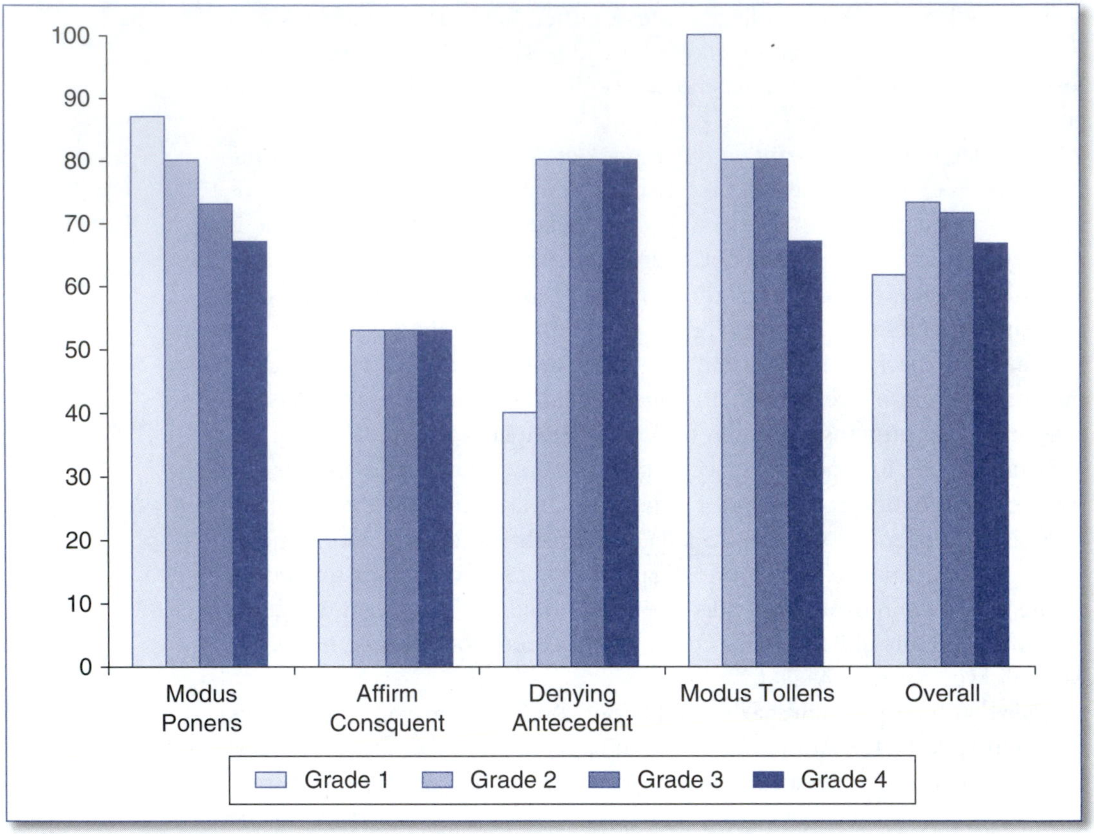

SOURCE: Adapted from Kuhn (1977, p. 346).

(You might recall from Chapter 8 that a study of deductive reasoning in preschoolers by Hawkins, Pea, Glick, & Scribner, 1984, used a similar technique.) Use of this cover story may account for the fact that children in her experiment performed much better than did children in earlier experiments given similarly structured problems with more abstract content (Byrnes & Overton, 1986; Ennis, 1975; Roberge & Paulus, 1971; Taplin, Staudenmayer, & Taddonio, 1974). Kuhn speculated that the ability to reason well with abstract formulations of these problems awaited attainment of the Piagetian stage of formal operations, an accomplishment typically seen in early adolescence.

Janveau-Brennan and Markovits (1999) round out this picture a little more. They worked with children aged 6 to 11 years, giving them conditional reasoning problems of the type depicted in Table 11.1. However, the content of the premises concerned so-called causal conditionals, statements that plausibly indicated a cause and effect. Some of the causal conditionals had relatively few easily imaginable alternative causes (the authors established this by having another group of children think of alternative causes). These included problems such as "If a person goes to sleep late, he will be tired" and "If the electricity goes off, the school will be closed," where it had been established children thought spontaneously of only a few alternative causes (e.g., other things that would cause the person to be tired or the school to be closed). They compared children's performance on these problems to their performance on problems where it was relatively easy to think of many alternative causes: "If a person breaks his arm, he will hurt" and "If a person drops a pot, there will be noise."

Table 11.2 presents the results by grade level of the children, both by the type of problem (again, refer to Table 11.1 for examples) and by the number of alternatives—few or many. It shows a consistent increase in correct responding (i.e., expressing uncertainty) to the two uncertain problems, affirming the consequent (AC) and denying the antecedent (DA). Somewhat paradoxically, there was a slight decline with age in responding correctly to the two forms that have valid conclusions, *modus ponens* (MP) and *modus tollens* (MT). The authors

Table 11–2 Percentage of correct responses to the four logical forms (MP, MT, AC, and DA) by grade level for premises with few possible alternatives and with many possible alternatives

	Logical form							
	MP		MT		AC		DA	
Grade	Few	Many	Few	Many	Few	Many	Few	Many
1	78.1	97.3	82.3	88.2	10.4	17.3	7.3	4.6
2	76.0	99.0	88.0	93.3	19.0	40.4	10.0	16.4
3	68.8	100.0	88.5	93.9	34.4	49.1	14.6	13.2
5	57.3	98.1	75.0	84.9	55.2	82.1	29.2	50.9
6	51.0	94.9	72.1	87.8	64.4	82.7	42.3	44.9

SOURCE: Janveau-Brennan & Markovits (1999, p. 907).

NOTE: MP = modus ponens; MT = modus tollens; AC = affirmation of the consequent; DA = denial of the antecedent.

believe that as children get older, they become more able to generate alternative causes and to imagine "disabling" conditions for a conclusion. Thus, given the problem "If the electricity goes off, the school will be closed" and "The electricity goes off," older children are more likely to think of possibilities such as the existence of emergency backup generators. This imagination, while normally serving the students well, does lead to incorrect performance in some cases.

As predicted, children performed better on problems where many alternative causes existed than they did on ones where few alternatives existed. This result replicated the findings of Cummins (1995) who had discovered this trend in adult participants. Janveau-Brennan and Markovits (1999) conclude that children are likely reasoning in ways fundamentally similar to the way adults reason, at least by the time they are in middle childhood, and when they are reasoning with the kind of concrete, specific content given in these particular problems.

The authors also looked at whether children's reasoning performance varied as a function of their ability to imagine alternatives. They had asked the children to generate as many alternatives as they could in 30 seconds to two other causal statements: "If someone takes a bath, then she will be wet" and "If someone plays the flute, then there will be music." In other words, for each of these two statements, children were given 30 seconds to think of and name alternative ways of getting wet or making music. The mean number of alternatives generated rose steadily with age, with 6-year-olds able to generate 6.43 and 11-year-olds able to generate 11.72. More important, children who generated more alternatives were the ones who performed the best on the reasoning tasks, particularly on the uncertain AC and DA problems.

Markovits, Fleury, Quinn, and Venet (1998) conclude on the basis of these results and others that the basic processes of reasoning that adults use are in place by middle childhood, especially by about second grade (see also Evans & Perry, 1995). What changes with development, then, is the efficiency and speed with which reasoning processes are executed—an idea we discussed at length in Chapter 8. Changes in the central executive mean that it requires less cognitive effort to draw conclusions, so they are drawn faster and more efficiently. In turn, this allows more resources to be devoted to other tasks, such as thinking of alternatives, which may allow reasoners to "catch" themselves from drawing a faulty conclusion.

Decision Making

The task of decision making requires assessing and choosing among alternatives in terms of their probability of occurrence and their expected value. This assessment and consideration may be explicit and complex or implicit and rapid, but without consideration of alternatives, no decision making can be said to have taken place. Many models of decision making exist; the one I will use includes five phases: setting goals, gathering information, structuring the decision (i.e., enumerating both options and criteria for deciding among those options), making a final choice, and evaluating the decision (Galotti, 2002). This model is depicted in Figure 11.2. The term *phases of decision making* is used to convey the idea that there may or may not be a set order to the tasks, that the performance of one task can overlap with the performance of another, that some tasks can be skipped, and that tasks can be done in different orders.

Goals are things that guide decision making and that especially influence the way a decision maker will appraise options or prioritize criteria. *Information gathering* refers to the processes by which a decision maker constructs lists of options, as well as possible criteria to use in making his choice. For complex decisions, with many alternatives and/or many criteria, decision makers need a way of organizing all their information. This phase of decision making, wherein the decision maker finds ways of organizing and comparing information, is known as *decision structuring*. After gathering all the information he is going to use, the decision maker needs to make a *selection or choice* from among the final set of options. This may involve

Figure 11–2   Phases of decision making

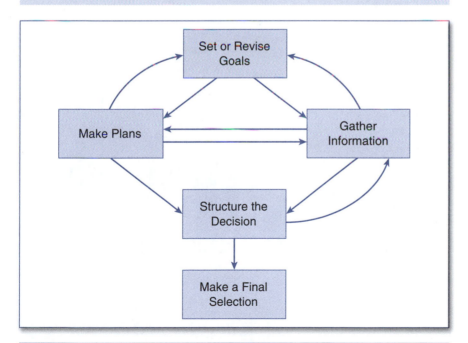

SOURCE: Galotti (2002, p. 97).

a procedure as simple as flipping a coin or throwing a dart at a wall, or it may be considerably more complex.

With that brief overview in mind, let's turn to an examination of how children make decisions. Let's first consider the phase of goal setting. This phase has been seen as a very important one for making good decisions. Byrnes (1998), for example, argues that "self-regulated" decision makers, those who make decisions that advance their own interests, are those who behave rationally. Or, as Miller and Byrnes (1997) put it: "A minimum requirement for being successful in life is knowing how to accomplish one's goals" (p. 814).

How does goal setting change with development during middle childhood? A few years ago, some students and I surveyed first, third, fifth, eighth, and twelfth graders, asking them to report on their goals for the upcoming day, week, month, year, and lifetime (Galotti, 2005). When the participants ran out of goals to list, we switched to cueing them by category of goal—for example, "Do you have any school- or camp-related [the data were gathered over the summer] goals? Any family-related goals? Any goals related to your friends?" We called the first kind of goal "time-cued" and the second kind of goal "category-cued." We found that, as shown in Figure 11.3, older students

Figure 11–3   Number of goals by cue and grade

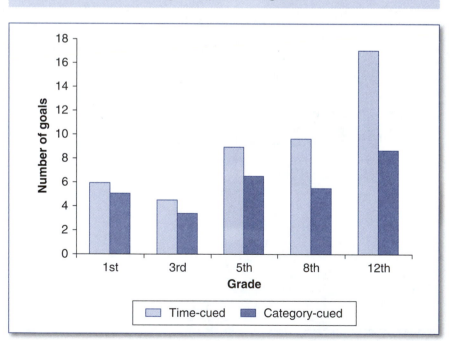

had more goals than younger students, particularly for the more open-ended "time-cued" goals. Moreover, older children reported a different "mix" of goals than younger children—goals related to hobbies and leisure activities became relatively less frequent, and goals relating both to school and camp and to chores and jobs became more frequent with age. Goals that pertained to either family or friends showed about the same proportion of use among all age groups, as shown in Figure 11.4.

Figure 11–4   Percentage of time-cued goals by category and grade

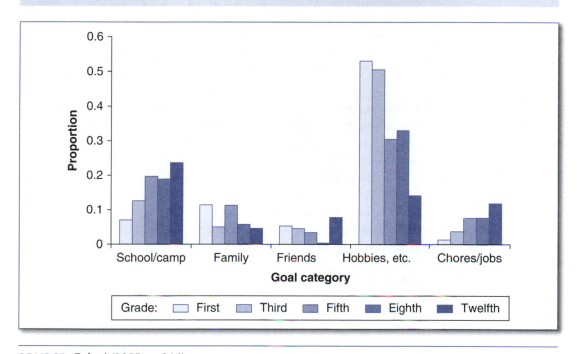

SOURCE: Galotti (2005, p. 316).

Research assistants rated each goal listed for complexity (having lots of parts or subgoals), difficulty (degree of effort required to achieve the goal), specificity (how clear it is when the goal has been achieved), controllability (degree to which the achievement of the goal is under the sole control of the participant), and realism (plausibility that the goal can be achieved). We found that rated complexity and difficulty rose with age but that specificity and realism ratings were unrelated to age. Controllability ratings rose with age for time-cued but not category-cued goals.

In sum, then, older children reported having more goals; a higher proportion of goals having to do with school, work, or chores; and more complex
and difficult goals than did younger children. One might assume that this
complexity would put more constraints on decision making, but that relationship has yet to be explored.

Planning is another aspect of decision making depicted in Figure 11.2.
This is a relatively understudied topic in developmental psychology, but
there are a few classic exceptions. A study by Mary Gauvain and Barbara
Rogoff (1989) provides one illustration. They defined planning as "the
process of devising and coordinating actions aimed at achieving a goal
and of monitoring the effectiveness of the actions for reaching the goal as
the plan is executed" (p. 140). To study this process, they devised an
errand-planning task in a model (roofless) grocery store. Inside this
(heavy cardboard) store were 160 grocery items depicted on 14 "shelves"
of groceries. Figure 11.5 provides a representation of the spatial layout of
the "store."

Children received "grocery lists" consisting of five items and were asked
to send a "shopper" (a small, plastic figurine) to travel through the "aisles" of
the store (without "flying" across the aisles) to fetch groceries. The shopper's
trip always had to begin and end at the "door" of the store, and children were
instructed to "help the shopper get the items on each list in the best way that
they could." Experimenters coded the children's responses to see if they
scanned the shelves in advance of moving the shopper through the aisles
and to see if they made any comments describing the "efficiency" of a route
through the store (e.g., reordering the list so as to minimize the number of
trips down aisles).

Older children (aged 9) showed more advanced scanning than did
5-year-olds. Younger children (aged 5) used routes that were 2.6 times the
length of the "optimal" route (determined in advance by the experimenters);
for the older children, their routes were only 1.5 times the length of the optimal one. The tendency to scan the store in advance correlated strongly with
the efficiency of the route planned.

In a subsequent study, Gauvain and Perez (2005) found that real-
world planning by children also undergoes development during the
period of middle childhood. They surveyed 140 children who were all
second graders at the start of the study, and followed them for 3 years,
examining how the children and their parents planned activities outside
of the school day. They included both organized activities (e.g., dance
lessons, choir, sports teams) and informal activities (e.g., watching television, playing video games, "hanging out"). They found that, as children
grew older, they participated more in planning these activities, although the
exact pattern of participation depended on the child's age, ethnicity, and
gender, as well as the type of activity and the expectations of the parents.

Figure 11–5   Map of grocery store used in Gauvain and Rogoff's (1989) study. Numbers and letters refer to "grocery list items" participants were asked to search for.

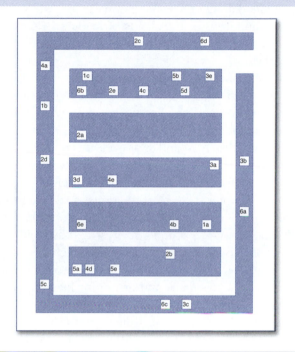

SOURCE: Gauvain & Rogoff (1989, p. 141).

Much more work has been done on children's "gathering information" phase of decision making. It has been shown in research on adult decision making that many adults use **heuristics** (shortcuts) and **biases** in their reasoning. For example, consider the following problem:

> Jim is buying a bicycle. Before buying it he gets information on different brands. A bicycle magazine says that most of their readers say the Zippo bike is best; however, he speaks to his neighbor and she says that the Whammo bike is best. Which bike should Jim buy? (Jacobs & Potenza, 1991, p. 169)

Psychologists Amos Tversky and Daniel Kahneman, in a series of landmark studies, showed that adults were likely to use something they called the *representativeness heuristic* to choose an answer, rather than going through the laborious calculations it would take to calculate exact probabilities. Kahneman and Tversky (1972, 1973) found, for example, that people typically ignored base rates—that is, responses collected from large samples—and instead disproportionately (and sometimes irrationally) paid too much attention to anecdotal information about one or two cases. Put in terms of the example above, adults would be more likely to ignore the recommendations of the bicycle magazine, which is based on the experience of hundreds or thousands of readers. Adults would instead give the majority of their attention to the recommendation of the one neighbor and her individual experience.

Jacobs and Potenza (1991) argued that in order to use the representativeness heuristic, children have to be able to compare information about a specific case (e.g., the neighbor's experience) with that of its representative category. They presented problems such as the one above to children in Grades 1, 3, and 6 as well as college students. The use of the representativeness heuristic rose with age. Younger children were more likely to offer idiosyncratic reasons for their choices or to "embellish" the stories with their own interpretations; sixth graders and college students were more likely to offer "textbook" representativeness explanations for their choices. Other studies suggest that as children get older, their estimates of base rates become more accurate and accessible (Jacobs, Greenwald, & Osgood, 1995). Relatedly, older children have acquired more social stereotypes and are more likely to use these when making decisions (Davidson, 1995).

Davidson (1991) devised a different way to examine how children gather information in making decisions. Figure 11.6 presents an information board, used in adult studies of decision making (Payne, 1976). In this particular example, the decision to be made was to choose an apartment from among five options—information about each option was displayed in columns. There were five different kinds of information shown—rent, size, number of closets, cleanliness, and kitchen facilities. Research participants turned over one card at a time (e.g., rent for Apartment A), and the experimenter monitored how much information they gathered and how systematically they gathered it.

Davidson (1991) also used information boards, but used bicycles instead of apartments. Table 11.3 shows the different kinds of decisions she presented and the information about each option in each decision. She found that second-grade participants examined more pieces of information than did older (fifth- and eighth-grade) children, but in a less systematic way, jumping from one dimension on one alternative to another dimension of information with another alternative. Older children were more likely to quickly eliminate alternatives (e.g., rejecting all bikes that cost "lots of money" or bikes that were too big or too small). In this respect, older children's performance was closer to that seen in adults (Payne, 1976), who are

Figure 11–6 Depiction of an information board

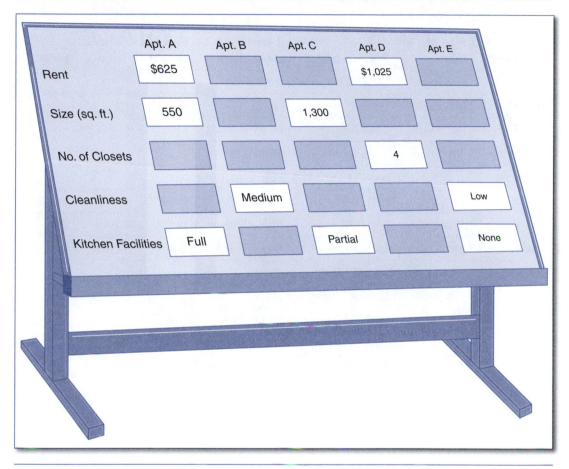

SOURCE: Galotti (2008, p. 487).

likely to adopt shortcuts that limit the amount of information they have to keep track of in making a decision.

At first blush, many of the above findings seem to be suggesting that younger children fall prey less often to decision-making biases, which might in turn imply that they are better decision makers. However, closer inspection of the results seems to suggest that younger children are less systematic, more idiosyncratic, and less analytic than older children, and that while they do not use common adult biases, they are not making

Table 11–3 Examples of 3 × 3, 3 × 6, 6 × 3 and 6 × 6 information boards used in the Davidson (1991) study

Dimensions	Size of bike	Price of bike	# Friends Have bike	Special features	Old/ new	Color
3 × 3						
Bike S	Just Right	Lots of Money	None			
Bike T	Just Right	Little Money	Many Friends			
Bike W	Too Small	Little Money	Many Friends			
3 × 6						
Bike P	Too Small	Little Money	Some Friends	Some	Old	White
Bike Q	Too Big	Some Money	Many Friends	Lots	New	Blue
Bike R	Just Right	Little Money	Many Friends	Lots	New	Red
6 × 3						
Bike G	Just Right	Lots of Money	None			
Bike H	Too Small	Little Money	Some Friends			
Bike I	Too Big	Little Money	Many Friends			
Bike J	Too Big	Some Money	Some Friends			
Bike K	Too Small	Lots of Money	None			
Bike L	Just Right	Little Money	Many Friends			
6 × 6						
Bike A	Just Right	Lots of Money	Many Friends	Some	New	White
Bike B	Just Right	Little Money	Many Friends	Lots	New	Red
Bike C	Just Right	Some Money	Some Friends	Some	New	Green
Bike D	Too Big	Little Money	None	Some	Old	Black
Bike E	Too Small	Lots of Money	None	None	Old	Blue
Bike F	Too Big	Little Money	Some Friends	None	New	Yellow

SOURCE: Galotti (2002, p. 107).

NOTE: The identical information was used to describe combs. From "Children's Decision-Making Examined With an Information-Board Procedure," by D. Davidson, 1991, *Cognitive Development, 6,* p. 81. Copyright 1991 by Elsevier Science. Reprinted with permission.

sound decisions. What changes with development seems to be the efficiency with which information is searched for and processed. Necessarily, that efficiency leads children to adopt time-saving shortcuts, such as heuristics. We'll discuss this idea in much more detail in Chapter 12 when we examine adolescent decision making.

APPRENTICESHIP AND GUIDED PARTICIPATION

Reasoning and decision making are two of the most easily recognized "higher-order" cognitive skills. And, as we will see in the next section of this chapter, these skills are important in many academic realms. But not all children in the world attend Western-type schools, and in this section, we'll take a look at how higher-order cognitive skills develop in non-Western cultures.

We've already looked at a theoretical perspective that provides an important framework for this topic—that of Lev Vygotsky. Recall that Vygotsky held that development is determined by many factors, including the tools available in a culture as well as the social milieu in which a child functions. Vygotsky described the *zone of proximal development,* arguing that children develop through participating in activities that are just slightly out of their cognitive reach. Through the guidance of skilled peers, parents, teachers, and others, children observe new skills and begin to internalize them (Guberman, 1996; Rogoff, 1990).

Consider, for example, a child learning an ordinary household task, such as folding laundry or making a bed. At first, the child has no idea what actions to take or how to carry them out. Typically, a child learns the sequence of steps by performing the chore with an older sibling or parent, who guides the child's actions either verbally ("No, take the sheet by the corner") or physically (e.g., by placing her hands over the child's hands). After a few sessions of practice, the young child learns how to do the chore and may even advance to the point of doing the entire task independently.

Rogoff (1990) introduced the term **guided participation** to describe this process. Her idea was that children acquire knowledge and skill about cognitive (and other) tasks when they both participate in the activities (as opposed to simply observing them) and receive guidance from a skilled practitioner. The guidance helps build a bridge from the child's beginning level of knowledge of the task to a more advanced one. The guidance is likely to be more explicit and physical at the start, and to fade as the child acquires more skill and understanding. Said another way, as the child gains

Photo 11.2 Learning to fold laundry under the watchful eyes of an adult is one example of guided participation.

practice and experience, she is granted increasing responsibility for carrying out the activity.

Rogoff and colleagues note a fundamental distinction between European American communities and others around the world when it comes to guided participation and apprenticeship. Many traditional communities do not segregate children from adults, affording children many opportunities throughout the day to observe and learn from adult activities (Mejia-Arauz, Rogoff, & Paradise, 2005; Morelli, Rogoff, & Angelillo, 2003). As a result, children can be regarded as *apprentices* to adults. They learn, not from explicit explanation and lecture, but instead from participating, with observation, guidance, and feedback from their more skilled adult mentor. Although there is guidance, it is more informal and implicit than is the overt control typically exhibited by a classroom teacher. Children collaborate cooperatively instead of working individually.

Chavajay and Rogoff (2002) report on a study of Guatemalan Mayan mothers constructing a puzzle with their children. Participants were formed into groups consisting of two or more mothers and three related children, aged 6 to 12 years. They constructed a three-dimensional jigsaw puzzle. Some of the groups included mothers with very little formal schooling (0–2 grades). Mothers in other groups had 6 to 9 grades of schooling, while mothers in the last group had 12 or more grades of schooling (i.e., they were high school graduates or more). Mayan mothers with more grades of schooling were much more likely to structure the task hierarchically, suggesting that labor be divided and that different children assume different responsibilities and work on different parts of the puzzle. Mayan mothers with less education were more likely to engage in a more collaborative, fluid, coordinated way, with all members of the group engaged in the same part of construction. The authors conclude that both forms of learning may be beneficial in the acquisition of new skills and understandings.

DEVELOPING ACADEMIC SKILLS

In the United States, middle childhood runs roughly from a child's first-grade (or perhaps kindergarten) year of school through fifth or sixth grade—a part of schooling we call "elementary" education (as opposed to middle school and high school, which comprise "secondary"). During the elementary years, the educational focus is on developing literacies of various sorts—learning to read, learning to write, and learning arithmetic. In addition, children are expected to master content in areas such as social studies, science, and perhaps health, art, and music. In this section, we will focus primarily on the "3Rs" (reading, 'riting, 'rithmetic).

Learning to Read

Learning to read is a task that consumes the bulk of the day in most kindergarten through second- or third-grade classrooms. The idea that spoken sounds correspond to written letters is often quite a concept to master, and the skills involved in the task of reading are many. In order to read a text, for example, a student must already understand how to hold a book or manuscript and which way the text goes (horizontally in English vs. vertically for Chinese, for example). She must also know the basic characters of the language and be able to decode letters into sounds. She must be able to recognize a number of "exception words" that do not follow the default spelling-sound rules of the language.

Jeanne Chall (1983) presented a stage theory of reading development, based on her work with children learning to read in the United States, and her reading of Piagetian theory of cognitive development. She accepts the idea of stages building hierarchically and progressively upon one another. She believes that interaction with the environment—at home, at school, and in the community—contributes to the progression through stages. As readers progress through the stages they become increasingly independent and intentional about their reading.

The first stage (Stage 0) is called "Prereading" and spans from roughly birth to age 6 years. During this time, the child develops the visual and auditory perceptual abilities that will later be used in reading (e.g., being able to discriminate between similar sounds), and might even begin to recognize certain letters or even certain words (e.g., the child's own name), assuming the child lives in a literate culture. Although I'm embarrassed to admit this, both of my children, when preschoolers, could recognize a variety of commercial logos—such as the ones for McDonald's, Applebee's, and (heaven help me) Chuck E. Cheese's. Chall would count all of this as a prereading activity. Prereading children may also engage in "pretend" reading, during which they hold a book and turn the pages, look at the pictures, and make up the "text" that goes along with the pictures (or recite the text from memory, in the case of a frequently read favorite).

Stage 1, "Initial Reading, or Decoding," occurs when most children are aged 6 or 7 and in first or second grade. It is during this stage when children learn the alphabet and the sounds corresponding to each letter or character. Chall (1983) calls this the "grunt and groan" or "barking at print" stage, because reading is a laborious task for young children, who expend most of their energy on just decoding. If you've ever listened to a first grader read aloud to you, you'll understand why Chall came up with these descriptive names! The 6-year-old in this stage reads laboriously, one word at a time, with long pauses between words, not a lot of fluency or inflection.

Elementary school teachers working with beginning readers often note a dramatic shift occurring in reading—where the child suddenly seems to "get it" and the reading becomes more fluent. At this point, the child has entered Stage 2, which Chall (1983) titles "Confirmation, Fluency, Ungluing From Print." It typically spans ages 7 and 8, Grades 2 and 3. During this stage, children consolidate gains from Stage 1, become more fluent and expressive in their reading, and gain what Chall calls "courage and skill" in reading.

The stage is a critical one; students whose reading skills are below average at the end of third grade are at risk for school failure in the future. Stage 2 also represents the point at which campaigns to foster adult literacy fail—although most adults who are illiterate can make it through Stage 1, if they falter the problem is likely to show up in Stage 2. According to Chall (1983), successful navigation of Stage 2 requires availability of familiar materials to read—most books, pamphlets, and newspapers require at least a Stage 3 reading level. Perhaps for this reason, reading skill gaps between high-socioeconomic-status and low-socioeconomic-status children widen during Stage 2. Presumably, wealthier families are more able to provide more readable materials to children in this crucial stage of reading development.

Stage 3, called "Reading for Learning the New: A First Step," corresponds to the later elementary and middle school years, Grades 4–8. It is during this stage that children start to read texts to get new information—that is, reading to learn instead of learning to read. Many so-called content areas of the curriculum (e.g., history, geography, health, and science) begin to be taught as separate subjects in the fourth grade, and from a reading perspective, this makes good sense. Much of the way students go about learning in these domains is through reading—textbooks or Web sites or workbooks. According to Chall (1983):

> The materials at the 4th-grade level and higher begin to go beyond the elemental, common experiences of the unschooled or barely schooled. To write out even the simplest informative materials—materials that present ideas that the reader does not already have—a readability level of at least Grade 4 is usually required. Materials at Grade 4 readability level begin to contain more unfamiliar, "bookish" abstract words (ones that are usually learned in school or from books) and a higher proportion of long and complex sentences. . . . While the learner is in the decoding (Stage 1) and confirming (Stage 2) stages, the task is to master the print; with Stage 3 the task becomes the mastering of ideas. (pp. 21–22)

Chall's (1983) final stages, Stage 4 and Stage 5, correspond to high school and college, respectively. Stage 4 has to do with reading a text from multiple points of view and dealing with layers of facts and concepts. Stage 5 concerns reading for one's own purpose—reading some texts closely and analytically, while skimming others only briefly.

Some controversy exists in the field of education over whether early reading should emphasize decoding (the so-called **phonics** approach) or instead focus mainly on meaning (the so-called **whole language** approach; Chall, 1992; Pressley, 1994; Pressley, Mohan, Raphael, & Fingeret, 2007). The debate centers on whether explicit instruction in decoding is required for at least some students to learn the skill and, further, whether explicit instruction in decoding will undercut students' motivation for, and enjoyment of, reading. Proponents of the whole language approach advocate for surrounding children with good literature that engages their imagination. They see reading as mainly involving higher-order cognitive processes such as making predictions and inferences, and assume that the lower-order decoding skills will naturally occur as children experience more literacy activities such as hearing stories, creating stories orally or in writing, and talking about stories.

Existing evidence in the psychological literature has not borne out these claims (Chall, 1992; Juel, 1988; Pressley, 1994). Indeed, one of the best predictors of reading achievement in the primary grades of school (Grades 1–3) is **phonemic awareness**, an ability to understand that words are composed of separable sounds. Typically, one important difference between good and poor readers at all age levels is that good readers have better phonemic awareness than do poor readers (Pressley, 1994), and are better able to categorize spoken words by their initial or ending sounds—that is, to find alliterating and rhyming words. Interestingly, a study by Evans, Fox, Cremaso, and McKinnon (2004) suggested that parents' lay views of reading were much more receptive to a phonics-based approach, while the teachers surveyed in this study were more likely to endorse a comprehension-based whole language approach.

Michael Pressley and his students (2007) performed an in-depth observational study of a public elementary school in Michigan, whose average scores on standardized tests of early literacy outperformed those of similar schools in the area and which was in the vicinity of the institution where Pressley worked. During the course of the yearlong project, the researchers interviewed the principal, teachers, and teaching interns and spent over 200 hours observing classrooms and staff meetings.

They found that a variety of factors were likely to have led to the school's success at promoting literacy. First, literacy was a core academic emphasis of the school, with many hours of teacher time devoted to it. The school was well stocked with books, and a variety of specialist teachers were available to supplement classroom teachers' efforts. Classroom teachers were committed to professional development and sought out opportunities to refine their skills in teaching reading and to better understand the structure and composition of the standardized tests. They incorporated phonics-based activities in many of their lessons in the lower grades, with increasing emphasis on sophisticated comprehension in the older grades. Children read aloud, with teachers listening, at least several times a week. Writing was also integrated into the literacy instruction from kindergarten. Pressley et al. (2007) concluded that, even in a suburban setting with relatively advantaged students, "great efforts may be required to produce high reading and writing achievement" (p. 221).

Learning to Write

Writing, like reading, is a complex skill. Early development of writing focuses on concrete issues, such as how to form letters correctly and conventionally when composing a message. We are all familiar with the handwriting charts such as the one shown in Figure 11.7. But teachers and researchers have described a number of stages that children's initial writing goes through before it reaches the maturity shown in Figure 11.7.

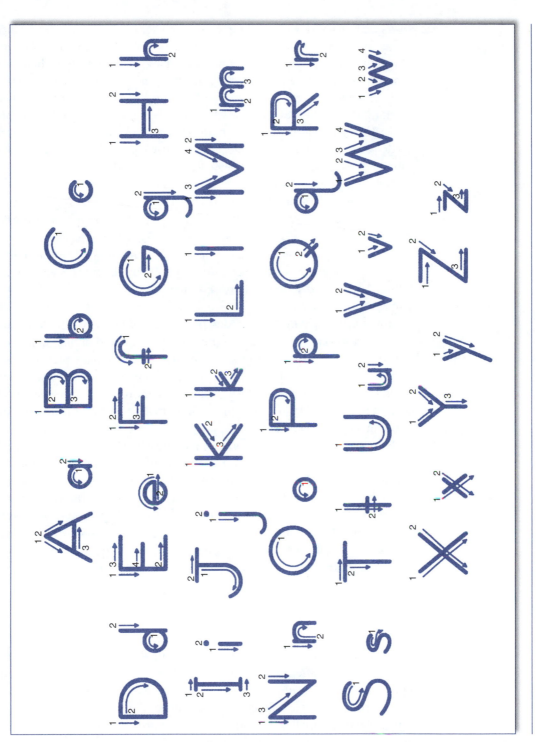

As we saw above with reading, writing is a subject children already know a great deal about by the time they get to school. Although they do not begin by writing words using the conventional spellings of the adults in their community, they still have a great deal of knowledge about what writing is. There is debate among early educators about how stage-like the early development of writing is, and the description below is an amalgamation of different proposals. The essential point is that children's unconventional attempts at writing do show structure and reflect their growing understanding of what writing is (Feldgus & Cardonick, 1999; Paul, 1976; Read, 1971; Richgels, 2001; Vukelich & Golden, 1984).

Most children begin writing by drawing and *picture writing*. Often the pictures are unrecognizable, but the child can, when prompted, describe what the picture depicts. Although you might want to argue that this is art and not writing, it does represent the earliest attempt to communicate thoughts and feelings by making marks on paper. By about age 3 years, many children make a distinction between drawing and writing (Dahl, 1985; Vukelich & Golden, 1984).

This stage of writing is succeeded by the *scribbling* stage. Children make random marks on the page, where the starting point and ending points can be anywhere on the page. Over time, children learn to make their marks in conventional directions (e.g., in U.S. culture, from left to right). Also occurring in the scribbling stage is the appearance of more recognizable shapes in pictures (e.g., stick figures of humans or animals, or a circle with lines surrounding it depicting a sun).

Next comes the *random letter* stage. An example of this is shown in Figure 11.8 and is the production of my daughter during preschool. The letters bear little relationship to conventional spelling, but there are recognizable letters of the alphabet in the writing. At this stage, the child may be capable of spelling her own name correctly, and the spelling may even be correct. (In my daughter Kimmie's case, however, she began by signing all her artwork "Emily," which greatly puzzled me until I learned that she was copying an older preschool friend, whom she sat next to every day during art time.)

Semiphonetic spelling comes next. Some letters in the writing match sounds, and especially the initial letters may be correctly placed, even when sounds corresponding to the middle and ends of words are not presented. Next comes *phonetic spelling,* where both beginning and ending sounds appear, some high-frequency words are correctly spelled, and often vowels appear (even if they aren't the correct ones). *Transitional spelling,* as the name implies, brings a child closer to the stage of conventional spelling and writing. Children spell by sounding out the words and spelling more high-frequency words correctly, and begin to leave spaces between words. They

Figure 11–8 An example of writing in the random letter stage. (The embedded names are not typical of this stage.)

may also begin to incorporate some punctuation. Figure 11.9 provides an example. Note that the misspelled word *gowing* actually makes phonetic sense—it indicates that the child is making an attempt to translate the sounds she hears in a word into letters. If you say the word *going* aloud, you may hear a *w* sound in the middle!

Eventually, likely in the later primary grades (2 or 3), most children settle into *conventional spelling,* where most words are spelled correctly,

Figure 11–9 An example of transitional spelling

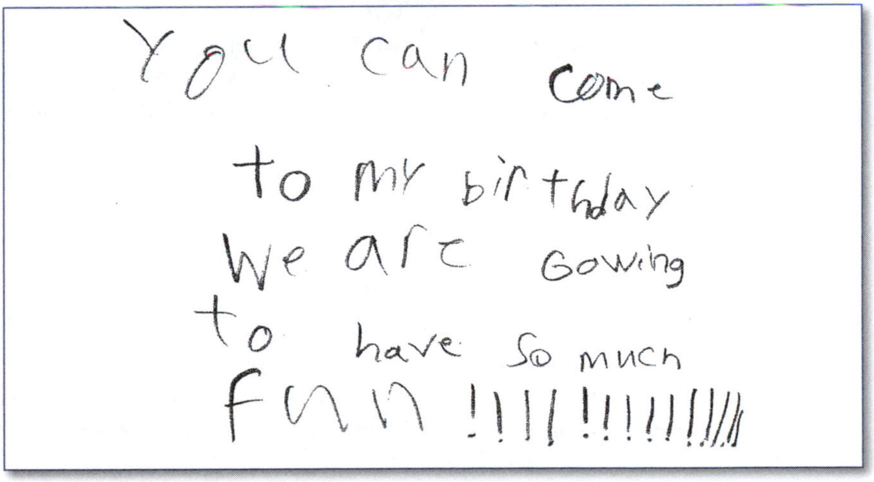

especially short or high-frequency ones. Children still revert to phonetic spelling for unfamiliar words. Capitalization and punctuation are used correctly, and the child systematically uses both capital and lowercase letters.

Writing is intimately connected with reading, leading many researchers to speak of emergent literacy as a general term involving both (Teale, 1987). Indeed, the claim is that the development of reading influences the development of writing and vice versa. It's easy to see how this principle might apply to early stages of spelling, for example. To write words phonetically, a child must be able to hear the different phonemes in the spoken versions of the word, and as we have seen, phonemic awareness is a critical reading skill.

Empirical research has demonstrated that young children's writing proficiency is significantly predicted by early reading skills such as letter awareness (Dunsmir & Blatchford, 2004). A longitudinal study following 54 at-risk students from first through fourth grade examined reading and writing performance each year (Juel, 1988). The correlation between writing skill and reading comprehension was .27 in first grade, .39 in second grade, .43 in third grade, and .42 in fourth grade. Reading performance was a stronger predictor of writing performance than the converse. Moreover, and frighteningly, "The probability that a child would remain a poor reader at the end of fourth grade if the child was a poor reader at the end of first grade was .88" (Juel, 1988, p. 437).

The above description of writing development focuses on early and concrete manifestations of writing—how marks are physically made and how children come to adopt standard ways of making them. But there is another, at least equally important component to writing—what Juel (1988) calls *ideation,* the ability to generate and organize ideas. This component has to do with how children create stories, essays, notes, memoirs, or other written products, focusing more on the text than on the spelling or penmanship.

We've seen already that young children know a lot about stories, even before they begin reading and writing. We saw in Chapter 7 the work by Katherine Nelson and her colleagues on children's scripts, which are organized schemas for representing event knowledge. We saw that children's scripts become more elaborate, organized, and hierarchical as they gain more experience with an event. Nelson (1986) saw scripts as the basis of children's autobiographical memories. Others have come to regard scripts as the basis of children's self-created stories (Mandler & Johnson, 1977).

Mandler and Johnson (1977) and Just and Carpenter (1987) are two sets of psychologists who developed the idea of *story grammars.* Story grammars are systems of rules that can "parse" a story into parts (just as a grammar for a language helps listeners and speakers parse the words into a known structure). Story grammars are similar to scripts in that both have variables or slots that are filled in differently for different stories. For example, different stories have different protagonists, settings, plots, conflicts, and resolutions. Story grammars are also similar to syntactic grammars in that they help identify the units (constituents) and the role each unit plays in the story (Just & Carpenter, 1987).

Like other schemata, story grammars provide the listener or reader with a framework with which to expect certain elements and sequences and to fill in with "default values" things that are not explicitly stated. For example, young children expect stories to begin with some sort of setting, say, "Once upon a time" or "A long time ago." One example of a story grammar is shown in Table 11.4 (Mandler & Johnson, 1977). It divides a story into several parts: settings, states, events, and so forth. Each of these parts may also have subparts; for example, settings may have location, characters, and time. Some parts may also have a number of different instances of certain subparts; for example, the plot may have several episodes. The asterisks in the table indicate that certain subparts (such as "state" in Rule 4) can be repeated an indefinite number of times. Parentheses around a subpart indicate the subpart is optional.

Children as young as 4 years of age have been found to recall stories better if those stories conform to a story grammar than if they do not (see Mandler, 1983), and, in retelling the stories they've heard, 4-year-olds tend to recount the elements of the story in the "correct" story grammar order. Research investigating children's production of stories shows that, with age, children produce more elaborated stories, with more details given to such aspects of the story as setting, character motivation, and complexity of plot (Mandler, 1983).

During the elementary years, children begin to focus less on the "secretarial" aspects of writing (e.g., handwriting and spelling) and more on the "compositional" aspects of it (generating ideas and organizing them; Wray, 1993). Lin, Monroe, and Troia (2007) studied second through eighth graders' views of what "good writing" is. They found that younger students focused more on the physical aspects of writing—things like punctuation, using cursive, and having good posture—while older students focused on higher-level aspects, such as audience, meaning, and communication. Second graders described the process of writing as "just think about it" before commencing—middle schoolers reported using more strategic planning activities, such as making outlines, or using story webs. Older students were also more likely to differentiate between different types of writing (e.g., narrative, expository, and persuasive writing), while younger students showed less understanding of these distinctions.

McCutchen (2006), drawing on the work of Hayes (1996; Hayes & Flower, 1980), describes three major cognitive processes involved in writing. The first is planning—which may involve making notes, thinking about goals, generating content, and organizing it. Younger children are less adept at planning than are adult expert writers. For example, young children are less likely

Table 11–4 Summary of rewrite rules for a simple story grammar[a]

FABLE → STORY AND MORAL

STORY → SETTING AND EVENT STRUCTURE

SETTING → $\begin{Bmatrix} \text{STATE* (AND EVENT*)} \\ \text{EVENT*} \end{Bmatrix}$

STATE* → STATE ((AND STATE))

EVENT* → EVENT $\left(\left(\begin{Bmatrix} \text{AND} \\ \text{THEN} \\ \text{CAUSE} \end{Bmatrix} \text{EVENT}\right)\right)$ ((AND STATE))

EVENT STRUCTURE → EPISODE ((THEN EPISODE))

EPISODE → BEGINNING CAUSE DEVELOPMENT CAUSE ENDING

BEGINNING → $\begin{Bmatrix} \text{EVENT*} \\ \text{EPISODE} \end{Bmatrix}$

DEVELOPMENT → $\begin{Bmatrix} \text{SIMPLE REACTION CAUSE ACTION} \\ \text{COMPLEX REACTION CAUSE GOAL PATH} \end{Bmatrix}$

SIMPLE REACTION → INTERNAL EVENT ((CAUSE INTERNAL EVENT)).

ACTION → EVENT

COMPLEX REACTION → SIMPLE REACTION CAUSE GOAL

GOAL → INTERNAL STATE

GOAL PATH → $\begin{Bmatrix} \text{ATTEMPT CAUSE OUTCOME} \\ \text{GOAL PATH (CAUSE GOAL PATH)} \end{Bmatrix}$

ATTEMPT → EVENT*

OUTCOME → $\begin{Bmatrix} \text{EVENT*} \\ \text{EPISODE} \end{Bmatrix}$

ENDING → $\begin{Bmatrix} \text{EVENT* (AND EMPHASIS)} \\ \text{EMPHASIS} \\ \text{EPISODE} \end{Bmatrix}$

EMPHASIS → STATE

SOURCE: Mandler & Johnson (1977, p. 117).

to make notes or revise the notes they do make when writing; they often begin a writing assignment by starting to write the text within a minute or two of receiving the assignment.

A second important cognitive process used in writing is text production—translating ideas into sentences and paragraphs (McCutchen, 2006). Essentially, children need to learn new schemas to generate text—they are used to creating spoken texts and now need to learn new schemas to generate written ones. In essence, children learning to write need to regard their written output as a kind of dialogue between themselves as writers and the reader(s) in their audience.

Finally, revision is crucially important, at least for good writing (as you already know from your college work!). Reviewing one's prose, reading it critically, and seeking feedback from others are all included here. Some work suggests that students with better writing skills focus their revision on issues of meaning and organization, while less skilled writers stay focused on the local level of individual sentences (McCutchen, 2006).

Writing is a complex skill that develops progressively over middle childhood and adolescence. According to Graham and Harris (2000; Graham, Harris, & Mason, 2005), it requires extensive self-regulation and attentional control—so that activities such as planning, generating sentences, and revising can be coordinated. As such, the executive functioning tasks we reviewed in Chapter 9 play an increasingly important role in writing as children progress through the elementary years.

Learning Math

In Chapter 8 we examined preschoolers' concepts about numbers and counting. We saw that, even before formal schooling begins, children have a number of implicit principles about how counting works. They know, for example, that each object or person to be counted should receive one count tag, that the same order of tags should be used on all occasions, and that the final tag represents the numerosity of the set of counted objects.

Children learn a lot more about math during elementary school. Not only does their counting become more conventional, but throughout the elementary school years, children learn facts about addition, subtraction, multiplication, and division. In the later elementary years (e.g., fourth through sixth grades), children begin to learn about complex arithmetic procedures, such as long division. In this section, we'll take a brief look at many of these academic achievements.

If you think back to your elementary math classes, you might recall a lot of "**drill and practice**," aimed at getting you to learn your basic math facts, including worksheets, computer games, flash cards, and "mad minute" tests such as that shown in Table 11.5. You might have wondered then (or you might wonder now) what the point of it all is. Why is it important to compute sums such as $3 + 5$ or 7×9 in seconds or fractions of seconds?

If you think back to what we've talked about with respect to working memory, you'll understand. The answer has to do with capacity. The more that arithmetic facts are practiced, the more automatic it becomes to retrieve them. The more automatic the retrieval, the less capacity is used. The less capacity that is used, the more that is left over for other tasks, or for more complicated tasks. Consider, for example, a complex procedure such as long division. A student

Table 11–5 Mad math minutes

Solve the following problems

11 + 1	17 + 8	20 − 6	18 + 3	20 + 18
5 + 3	9 + 0	12 + 3	16 + 6	12 −4
15 − 5	18 + 3	5 + 0	19 + 12	8 − 5
19 + 18	10 + 1	19 + 7	19 − 9	17 + 6

Check My Answers   Reset

learning this method for the first time is going to have a lot to think about and remember. Put in cognitive terms, the process requires a great deal of attentional capacity. If the student needs to stop to compute a fact such as 7×9 in the middle of trying to carry out long division, the whole process might collapse. On the other hand, if arithmetic facts have become automatized, then retrieval requires little effort and happens quickly (Resnick, 1989).

However, the "drill-and-practice" approach is not the only one adopted by elementary teachers. Another approach, sometimes called "meaningful learning" (Resnick & Ford, 1981) or the **number sense** (Resnick, 1989) approach, emphasizes conceptual understanding of mathematical principles. This kind of approach, for example, might stress fostering understanding among children that, if $5 + 3 = 8$, then $3 + 5 = 8$ and, as well, $8 - 3 = 5$ and $8 - 5 = 3$. The emphasis here would be on getting children to see the principles that underlie these relationships, instead of on speed of automatic retrieval. The argument is that children instructed with this approach will find it easier and more natural to apply their knowledge to new problems and situations.

Children's arithmetic strategies undergo a great deal of development during elementary school. Take, for example, addition. If you look at a typical 5-year-old trying to figure out what $3 + 5$ is, you might notice him counting on his fingers or perhaps putting up three fingers on one hand and five on another and counting the set. (This strategy runs into trouble, obviously, when one of the to-be-added numbers exceeds the number of fingers on one hand!) After entering school, most children are able to do "mental counting"—adding three and five by saying the count words without using fingers (Resnick, 1989). By around age 6 or 7, most children use a strategy psychologist Lauren Resnick (1989) calls "counting on." Given the problem $5 + 3$, the children

> behave as if they are setting a mental counter-in-the-head to one of the addends, and then count on by ones enough times to "add in" the second addend. Thus, to add 5 and 3, children might say to themselves, "5 . . . 6, 7, 8," giving the final count word as an answer. What is more, children do not always start with the first number given in a problem but will invert the addends to minimize the number of counts when necessary. Thus, in adding $3 + 5$, they perform exactly the same procedure as for adding $5 + 3$. Children's willingness, in a procedure they invent for themselves, to count *on*—without first counting *up* to the first number—demonstrates that they have come to appreciate that "a 5 is a 5 is a 5." . . . In addition, children's willingness to invert the addends shows that they implicitly appreciate the mathematical principle of *commutativity* of addition. It will be some time, however, before they will show knowledge of *commutativity* in a general way, across situations, across numbers, and above all, with an ability to *talk about* rather than just *apply* the principle. (pp. 164–165)

A study by Holmes and Adams (2006) of British children aged 7 to 11 years showed a number of statistically significant correlations among children's mathematics measures (assessing such things as number knowledge, counting, geometric knowledge, interpreting graphs, and performing mental arithmetic) and various measures of different components of working memory. Even when controlling for grade in school and age, there were several significant correlations between the visuospatial sketch pad, the central executive (discussed in Chapter 9), and the mathematical measures. The phonological loop was less effective as a predictor of children's performance on mathematical assessments.

Children's development of mathematical knowledge in elementary school also varies as a function of their culture, as studies by David Geary and his associates have shown (Geary, Bow-Thomas, Liu, & Siegler, 1996; Geary, Salthouse, Chen, & Fan, 1996). One's native language can be a powerful factor in learning to count. For example, in the English language, the numbers in the second decade (especially *eleven* and *twelve*) do not make transparent the base 10 system. In contrast, Chinese number words for 11, 12, and 13 can be translated as *ten one, ten two,* and *ten three,* respectively—making it more obvious that 11 means one *ten* unit and one single unit.

Moreover, the English names *eleven, twelve,* and so forth take longer to pronounce than do the corresponding Chinese count words. As a result, English-speaking children can say fewer digits in a short amount of time than can Chinese-speaking children. When digit spans are measured in children in the two cultures, Chinese-speaking children show a significant advantage over English-speaking children, with Chinese children's digit spans an average of two more slots larger than American children's.

Geary et al. (1996) use these findings to explain the fact that in their study, Chinese kindergarteners outperformed American kindergarteners on a test of simple addition problems in the fall of their first year of school. Moreover, by the end of that same year, the differences in performance grew greater. Similar patterns of initial difference followed by even greater subsequent difference were found for first, second, and third graders tested. The authors explain the greater gain for Chinese students in terms of the greater number of minutes specifically devoted to mathematics instruction in Chinese schools.

This research underscores the idea that academic skills such as arithmetic, reading, and writing are embedded in larger cultures, a very Vygotskian notion. The fact is that even supposedly abstract tasks such as addition take place in particular contexts, and aspects of those contexts, such as the language that is spoken, affect the way the task is carried out. Formal schooling is, of course, another important aspect of culture. As such, formal schooling has pervasive effects on the cognitive development of the children who attend.

We've covered a lot of ground in this chapter. We've talked a lot about different kinds of higher-order cognitive skills ranging from reasoning, to decision making, to planning, to problem-solving and a variety of academic skills such as reading, writing, and arithmetic. We have seen how the functioning of these higher-order skills can vary a great deal depending on the context in which these skills occur. We have seen that much of cognitive development during middle childhood, particularly increases in attentional focus and working memory capacity, enables the growth of higher-order skills.

We'll see in the remaining chapters that the refinement of higher-order cognitive skills comprises much of cognitive development in adolescence.

SUMMARY

1. Vygotskian theory holds that middle childhood is a time for either formal schooling (as is what happens in most of the United States) or *apprenticeships,* the acquisition of very specific job skills under the supervision of an expert elder. Vygotskian theory holds that cognitive development is very much a by-product of a culture and the tools that culture provides to its inhabitants.

2. Learning theorists such as Edward Thorndike believe that much of children's learning consists of the formation of bonds or connections that get strengthened through repetition and when they are followed by positive reinforcement. Thorndike applied these ideas to the study of educational psychology.

3. Higher-order cognitive tasks include reasoning, decision making, problem solving, and thinking, as well as academic skills such as reading, writing, and arithmetic.

4. Formal reasoning abilities show some development during the middle childhood years. With familiar, concrete content, most children can reason in ways that are typical for adults. One explanation is that this ability reflects a growing capacity for generating alternatives that are consistent with premises but that lead to different conclusions than the first one thought of. This may relate to growing capacity of the central executive, which enables reasoning processes to be carried out more quickly and efficiently.

5. The complex task of decision making can be divided into five phases: setting goals, gathering information, structuring the decision, making a final choice, and evaluating the process.

6. Although both older and younger children set goals for themselves, older students have more and a different mix of goals, with those relating to school or work becoming more frequent and those relating to leisure time or hobbies becoming less frequent with age. Studies of children's planning abilities suggest that they improve during middle childhood. Older children are reported to participate more in planning their own out-of-school activities than are younger children.

7. With increasing age, children gather information to make a decision in ways very similar to those used by adults. What seems to improve most is children's tendency to approach decisions systematically and efficiently.

8. Children in non-Western cultures who do not attend formal schooling tend to become "apprentices" to skilled adults during middle childhood. Through a process of guided participation, they learn how to participate in work activities and acquire more knowledge about particular tasks.

9. Learning to read is the dominant classroom activity for children in American schools from kindergarten to Grade 3. Jeanne Chall has created a stage theory of reading development, which includes the following stages: "Prereading" (ages 0–6), "Initial Reading, or Decoding" (ages 6–7), "Confirmation, Fluency, Ungluing From Print" (ages 7–8), and "Reading for Learning the New" (ages 9–13). (Other stages in her theory pertain more to high school– and college-level reading.)

10. Controversy has existed among elementary educators over whether a phonics or a whole language approach to reading instruction works most effectively. While both approaches have their strengths, empirical evidence underscores the importance of phonemic awareness in teaching children to read.

11. The development of children's writing abilities encompasses both concrete aspects, such as handwriting and spelling, and the ability to generate and organize ideas.

12. The development of writing in the early grades (up to about Grade 3) shows that children bring to school a large amount of knowledge about writing (as they also do about reading). Their early attempts at writing and spelling, while unconventional, reflect attempts of the child to communicate through written means.

13. In the upper elementary grades, children's writing development focuses more on composition, including planning ideas, generating text, and revising.

14. Children in elementary school also learn a lot about arithmetic. They begin by learning facts about addition, subtraction, multiplication, and division and progress to learning more complex procedures such as long division. Children acquire new strategies to use in performing these procedures as they progress through school.

15. Controversy exists among elementary educators over how much emphasis to place on drill and practice of basic facts versus instruction in underlying mathematical principles.

16. Cross-cultural differences in mathematics achievement among elementary school children indicate that arithmetic calculations can be influenced by language as well as the amount of instructional time devoted specifically to mathematics.

REVIEW QUESTIONS

1. Contrast a Vygotskian and a Thorndikian approach to the learning that typical children engage in during middle childhood.

2. Discuss typical research findings on performance with all four conditional reasoning argument types shown in Table 11.1 among elementary-aged children.

3. Contrast the findings of the Kuhn (1977) study with those from the Janveau-Brennan and Markovits (1999) study on children's conditional reasoning. What are the implications of each study?

4. Describe the phases of decision making. Which show(s) the most developmental differences and why? Justify your answer.

5. What do we know about the development of planning abilities in middle childhood? What important questions remain to be investigated? Make a case for your answer.

6. How well do the findings of Gauvain and Rogoff (1989) and Davidson (1991) fit together to describe developments in higher-order thinking in middle childhood?

7. Explain the concept of guided participation and how it might apply to a child not enrolled in formal schooling.

8. Describe, in detail, the first four stages of Chall's theory of reading development.

9. Contrast the phonics and whole language approaches to reading development. Assess what the existing empirical evidence supports.

10. Outline the various stages of the development of writing in the first few years of school. What underlying competencies does each stage reveal?

11. Why might learning to write stories (and other text) relate so heavily to both reading skill and development of the central executive?

12. Critique the drill-and-practice approach to teaching elementary school children basic arithmetic facts.

13. Describe and critique the cross-cultural studies by Geary and colleagues on children's arithmetical knowledge during the elementary school years in China and the United States.

KEY TERMS

Apprenticeship

Biases

Conditional Reasoning

Drill and Practice

Guided Participation

Heuristics

Number Sense

Phonemic Awareness

Phonics

Planning

Whole Language

CHAPTER **12**

ADOLESCENCE

Continuing Cognitive Development

As children transition into adolescence, many aspects of their life change. The physical and hormonal changes that comprise puberty are two very salient examples. But, as we will see in this chapter, much is changing in the cognitive and educational realms as well. Most adolescents in our culture see a change in schooling, for example, transitioning from the single classroom and teacher of elementary school to a more complex environment in junior high or middle school, with many teachers and classrooms. Expectations of working independently increase, both from teachers and parents and from the adolescents themselves.

We will begin this chapter with theoretical perspectives on adolescent cognitive development. We will then turn our attention to an examination of cognitive achievements in adolescence in basic cognitive processes, namely, perception, attention, and memory. We will next visit higher-order cognitive processes, including reasoning and decision making, where adolescents show an even more pronounced superiority to younger children.

THEORETICAL PERSPECTIVES

We begin, as we have in past chapters, with a theoretical overview. First we examine the Piagetian description of the final stage of cognitive development. We turn next to information-processing theory as an example of an alternative to Piagetian explanations. We then focus on some recent work in neuroscience on brain development in adolescence to round out the emerging picture of adolescent cognitive processing.

Piagetian Theory

Piaget (Piaget & Inhelder, 1969) named the final stage of cognitive development *formal operations*. This stage begins around puberty and is marked by an increase in systematic and abstract thinking. Piaget and Inhelder described the adolescent as being liberated from the confines of concrete thinking and able to think about possibilities beyond those that actually exist in the here and now. This leads to a very idealistic time and also a time when adolescents are able to think more broadly and more theoretically.

Systematic thinking is a hallmark of Piagetian formal operations. Consider an adolescent in a science laboratory, given a number of beakers containing different liquids and asked to determine how they can be mixed together to produce a liquid of a certain color. The typical adolescent will be able to do a number of things that a young child could or would not. First, she can generate all the possible combinations of liquids and often does this in a systematic way. She tests one combination at a time and accurately records the results. She understands the concepts of isolating variables and holding everything constant except one factor.

Abstractness is a second hallmark of formal operations. An adolescent can now deal with equations with variables and can understand the underlying concept. Given the statement x + y = c, where c is a constant, adolescents understand implications that hold for any number of combinations of x and y, where younger children often need to fill in the variables with specific numerical instances. Adolescents are, as a result, often much better at formal reasoning, as we will see below.

Another aspect of formal operations is the ability to now see reality as one of several possibilities. This allows the adolescent to be able to imagine other kinds of realities. This new liberation of thought has been described as one of the sources of adolescent idealism and political awakening. Now that they see that the existing rules are only one possible way of doing things, they can question the validity of the rules and propose alternatives (much to the consternation of parents and teachers!). Adolescents' awareness of different possibilities opens up for them many different possible paths to the future because they can think beyond old limits.

Photo 12.1   The ability to reason about abstract variables is a skill not typically seen until adolescence.

In one demonstration of formal operations, Piaget provided children and adolescents with flasks of colorless liquids. For ease of reference, let's refer to these flasks as A, B, C, D, and E. Suppose that the combination of the contents of Flasks A, C, and E produces a yellow liquid. Suppose further that Flask B contains a bleaching agent that, if added to the contents of Flasks A, C, and E, will mask the yellow color. Flask D contains water and won't change the color of any other mixture (Inhelder & Piaget, 1958). The child or adolescent subject watches as the experimenter takes a flask that already contains a mixture of liquid from A and C (although the participant doesn't know what's been mixed already) and adds drops of liquid from Flask E, turning the solution yellow. The participant is then given the five flasks and asked to figure out which mixture produces a yellow liquid.

Typically, a 7-year-old (i.e., a child in the stage of concrete operations) will combine, say, A with B, C with D, and A with E. He may or may not think of all the two-way combinations of liquids that are possible (there are 10, by the way: AB, AC, AD, AE, BC, BD, BE, CD, CE, DE). When none of those combinations produces the yellow-colored liquid, he is likely to try combining liquid from all five flasks (which won't work, due to the role of the bleaching agent).

The typical adolescent who has achieved formal operations looks very different. She is able to consider, systematically, what all the possible combinations of liquids are (i.e., five single liquids, 10 possible two-liquid mixtures, 10 possible three-way mixtures (namely, ABC, ABD, ABE, ACD, ACE, ADE, BCD, BCE, BDE, CDE), 5 possible four-way mixtures (i.e., ABCD, ABCE, ABDE, ACDE, BCDE), and one way of combining liquids from all five flasks). The adolescent is far less likely to overlook possible combinations. And, she is far more likely to notice and deduce the role of B and E in the mixtures, in part due to her superior ability to reason propositionally, a topic we will examine in more detail below.

Finally, formal operations entails a newly emerging ability Piaget (1968) called **reflective abstraction**. This ability allows adolescents, for the first time in their cognitive development, to acquire new knowledge and understanding simply from thinking about their own thoughts and abstracting from these reflections. By doing so, they may begin to notice inconsistencies in their beliefs. Reflective abstraction is also useful in other realms of thinking, notably those of social and moral thinking, and we'll take up these kinds of thinking in Chapter 13.

Adolescent thought has been described as having an advanced state of equilibrium, in Piagetian terms (Ginsburg & Opper, 1988). This means that adolescents are less likely to have their basic cognitive structures upset by new problems and situations that come their way than are younger children. Although 16-year-olds (the age at which Piaget thought formal operations became fully mature) still have a lot to learn, Piaget held that their basic cognitive structures are in place and fully operational.

Following the introduction of Piagetian theory, there was much debate over whether all adolescents ever reach the period of formal operations. Piaget (1972) maintained they do. However, he did not mean to suggest that they would always display their highest competence. Instead, his idea was that adolescents who acquire formal operations *have the ability* to think abstractly, systematically, and logically, even if they do not always do so (Ginsburg & Opper, 1988).

Information-Processing Theory

In Chapter 2 we first reviewed the information-processing framework of cognitive development. It may help to reexamine Figure 2.2 on page 29 to remind yourself of the basic premises of this paradigm; we'll take a briefer and more focused look here. Kail and Bisanz (1992) attempted to distill the core aspects of the information-processing approach into a list of some key assumptions. First and foremost is the idea that information can and is represented internally, and these mental representations undergo manipulation in real time. Again, the analogy most often used is that to the way computers operate.

A second assumption is that all cognitive activity stems from the operation of a relatively small number of elementary cognitive processes. That is, all the cognitive things we do—reading, solving problems, navigating through an area with a map, recognizing an old acquaintance—stem from the operation of a relatively small set of basic processes, which operated in concert. It's the goal of the information-processing approach to specify just what these processes are and how they interact.

Finally, the information-processing framework explains cognitive development in terms of the self-modification of the elementary processes. That is, the individual processes are assumed to modify themselves—increasing capacity, becoming faster or more efficient, becoming more elaborated. We discussed some of these proposals back in Chapters 4, 7, 9, and 10. Although the impetus for this self-modification may come from external sources (e.g., a child learns more information about a topic and thus has a larger and more integrated knowledge base about that topic), the final result is that internal processes undergo alteration.

Work by Robert Kail (reviewed in Kail & Bisanz, 1992) provides one illustration of a general information-processing approach to cognitive development. Consider Figure 12.1, which presents results from several different studies conducted by Kail. In each, children, adolescents, and young adults performed various cognitive tasks, such as mental addition, searching through memory, and attempting to mentally rotate a visually presented stimulus. Processing time in each task showed the same general exponential decline. These results suggested to Kail that not only were adults and adolescents

Figure 12–1 Developmental functions for rates of mental rotation, name retrieval, memory search, visual search, and mental addition. Data are taken from Kail, 1986, Experiments 1 and 2; Kail, 1988, Experiments 1 and 2.

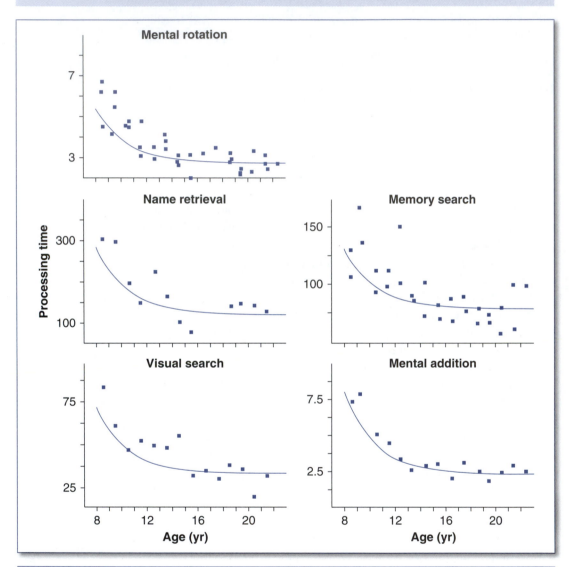

SOURCE: Kail & Bisanz (1992, p. 242).

NOTE: Rate of mental rotation is estimated by the slope of the function relating response time (RT) to the orientation of the stimulus. Name retrieval is estimated by the difference between times for name and physical matching. Visual search is estimated by the slope of the function relating RT to the size of the search set. Memory search is estimated by the slope of the function relating RT to the size of the study set. Retrieval of sums on the mental addition task is estimated from the slope of the function relating RT to the sum squared. The solid line depicts values derived from an exponential function in which the decay parameter, c, is the same for all five tasks.

faster than children at a variety of cognitive tasks, but the rate at which they got faster showed a very similar pattern. This in turn suggested that there was a common, general mechanism at work: speed of processing.

But increases in capacity and speed are not the only things information-processing theorists see developing. They also attribute increased performance to changes in the knowledge base. Adolescents, having more experience in the world than younger children, have much more knowledge in a number of realms. Thus, they have more knowledge to bring to bear on a wider variety of problems.

Moreover, adolescents may have different approaches or strategies to use on problems than do younger children. The research of psychologist Robert Siegler (1981, 1982) provides one example. He and his colleagues developed the **rule assessment approach** to the study of conceptual development in children and adolescents. The basic assumption is that some aspects of conceptual development are best characterized by "a sequence of increasingly powerful rules for solving problems" (Siegler, 1982, p. 272).

Consider, for example, balance scale problems, depicted in Figure 12.2. Children and adolescents are presented with the apparatus shown. Weights can be added to either side of the scale and can be placed either close to or farther away from the center point of the scale, called the fulcrum. Prediction of whether or not the scale will balance or tip toward one side depends on taking into account both the amount of weight and the distance from the fulcrum.

Siegler (1981) found that four different rules can be used to predict how children and adolescents will perform on balance scale problems. These are shown in Figure 12.3. Rule I is the simplest rule—it takes into account only information about one dimension (in this case, the amount of weight on each side of the fulcrum). Rule II adds onto this the idea that if the weight on both sides is equal, then the information on the subordinate dimension (in this case, distance from the fulcrum) is considered. Rules III and IV show increasing amounts of complexity in considering information.

To assess which rule a particular student might be using, Siegler (1981) designed six different types of problems, shown in Figure 12.4. This figure

Figure 12–2   Balance scale apparatus

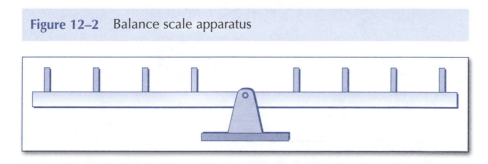

SOURCE: Siegler (1981, p. 7).

Figure 12–3   Modal rule models

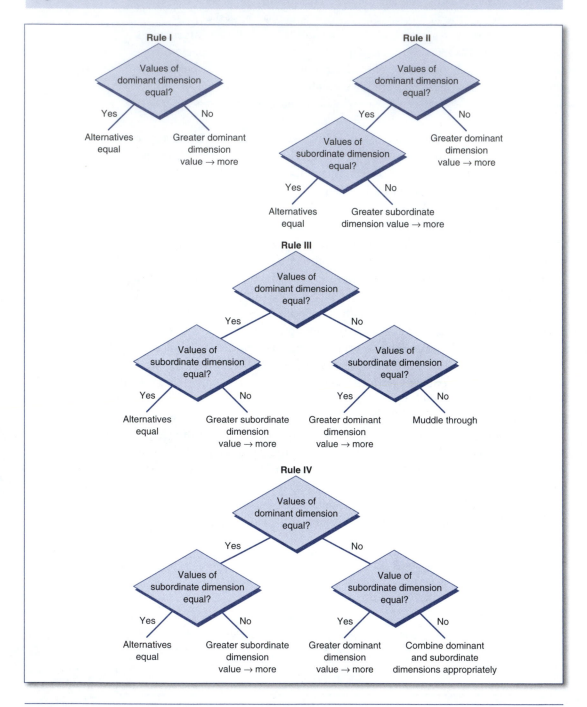

SOURCE: Siegler (1981, p. 6).

Figure 12–4   Predictions of percentage of correct answers and error patterns for children using Rules I–IV on balance scale task

Problem type	Rules			
	I	II	III	IV
Equal 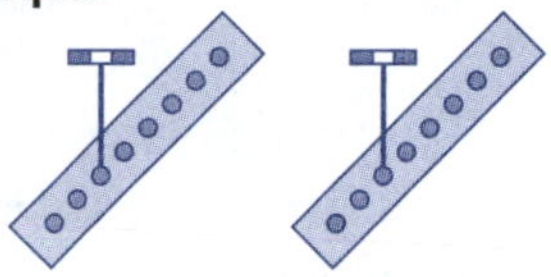	100	100	100	100
Dominant 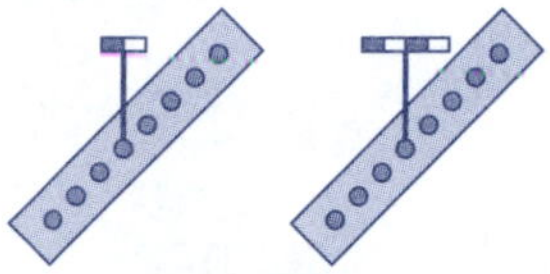	100	100	100	100
Subordinate 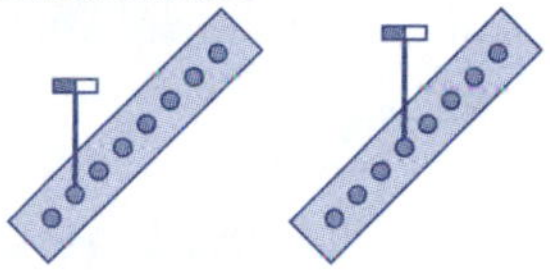	0 (should say "Equal")	100	100	100
Conflict-Dominant 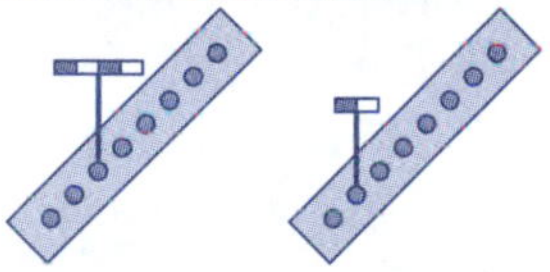	100	100	33 (chance responding)	100
Conflict-Subordinate 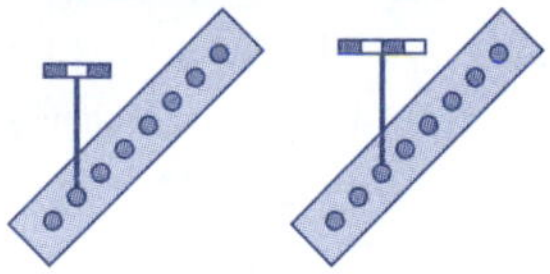	0 (should choose right side)	0 (should choose right side)	33	100
Conflict-Equal 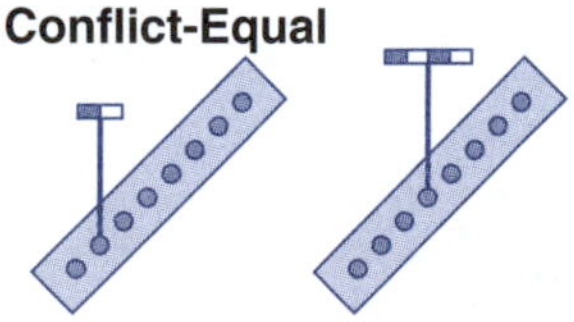	0 (should choose right side)	0 (should choose right side)	33 (chance responding)	100

SOURCE: Siegler (1981, p. 10).

shows that, if a student was using Rule I, she should correctly predict answers to Problem Types 1, 2, and 4, but not to any of the others. A student using Rule IV should make correct predictions on all problems.

As might be expected, Siegler (1981) found that younger children used less complex rules (on both the balance scale problems described here and other kinds of problems he investigated). Preschoolers overwhelmingly used either no discernable rule or Rule I. Eight-year-olds mostly used Rules II and III, with a few still using Rule I and a few using Rule IV. Most 12-year-olds used Rule III, with a few using Rules II or IV. The data for adults looked quite similar to the data for the 12-year-olds.

The general point to notice here is that Siegler's (1981) research attempts to specify, for any given domain, children's differing states of knowledge as they learn. Differing knowledge states predict different ways of solving problems and suggest differences in the way information about a problem will be encoded and used.

Neurological Development During Adolescence

We last looked at the topic of neurological development in Chapter 9. You may recall from that discussion that increasing myelination occurs throughout childhood and into adolescence (Nagy, Westerberg, & Klingberg, 2004). Myelination in certain regions of the brain, such as specific regions of the front lobes, is correlated with increases in working memory capacity. Nagy et al. argue that this increase in white matter of the brain underlies maturation of specific cognitive functions. You may recall from our earlier discussions of neurological development that myelination helps insulate transmission of messages along the axons of neurons—essentially making those neurons function more efficiently and quickly.

But growth is not the only neurological developmental process going on during adolescence. You may recall from Chapter 9 that gray matter has an inverted U-shaped pattern with age, showing decrements in adolescence (Casey, Galvan, & Hare, 2005). The loss of gray matter happens first in regions supporting the reception of sensory information and the initiation of motor responses (Amso & Casey, 2006). Next come losses of gray matter in the temporal and parietal lobes in regions associated with spatial attention and language. Last to mature and show losses of gray matter are regions including the prefrontal cortex thought to be involved in making higher-order associations and other aspects of executive functioning (Gogtay et al., 2004).

Why, you may be asking, would *losing* gray matter result in positive developmental change? The answer may have to do with streamlining communication in the brain. Amso and Casey (2006) describe this process as a "sculpting" of the immature brain. Synaptic connections between neurons that are not frequently used are "pruned" or "sculpted" away in a process known as **synaptic pruning**. This leaves fewer such connections in place, but plausibly ones that are stronger and operated more efficiently (Casey, Giedd, & Thomas, 2000; Kuhn, 2006). Thus, the view of some neuroscientists is that brain development underlying cognitive achievements in adolescence consists of improvement in existing capacities, rather than the acquisition of new abilities (Luna & Sweeney, 2001, 2004).

Another big development in the brain during adolescence occurs in the prefrontal cortex. Neuropsychologist Linda Spear (2000) describes a "remodeling" of this area taking place in the brains of adolescents of many species—humans and rats, to mention only two. As you may remember from our review in Chapter 2, the prefrontal cortex is implicated in executive functioning—that is, in planning, in goal-directed activities, and in the management of cognitive tasks and the allocation of cognitive resources to tasks. Luciana, Conklin, Hooper, and Yarger (2005) go further to argue that the prefrontal cortex development helps adolescents become adult-like, as it increases inhibitory control, the ability to integrate past knowledge with future goals, and being flexible with one's behavior. Spear (2000) uses the term *remodeling* to make the point that many different connections are made and lost among neurons in the prefrontal cortex during adolescence.

DEVELOPMENTS IN BASIC COGNITIVE PROCESSES

I hope by now you are quite clear on the distinction between basic and higher-order cognitive processes from earlier chapters. Just as a reminder, the basic processes include those relating to perception, attention, memory, and categorization. We saw in Chapters 9 and 10 that a great deal of cognitive development occurs in these processes during middle childhood. Thus, it may not be very surprising to find out that not much further change occurs in the basic cognitive processes in adolescence. However, there are some subtle refinements that take place, and we will review them in this section.

Perception

Plumert, Kearney, and Cremer (2007) performed a study of perceptual-motor development in late childhood and early adolescence that has a very applied focus—bicycling across traffic-filled roads. Specifically, they studied the gaps between cars that children and adolescents judged as being large enough for them to safely bicycle across an intersection within.

Participants in the study were aged 10 years, aged 12 years, and adults, and they rode an interactive bicycling simulator that is shown in Figure 12.5. The use of the simulator allowed the researchers to protect the safety of the research participants and control the traffic flow experimentally. Participants rode a bicycle mounted on a stationary frame in the middle of three large screens, onto which were projected high-resolution graphics depicting roads, buildings, and automobile traffic.

Participants encountered six different virtual intersections during their "ride" and had to cross these intersections without getting "hit." The simulated cross traffic traveled either at 25 miles per hour or at 35 miles per hour,

Figure 12–5   Adolescent riding a bicycle simulator

SOURCE: Plumert, Kearney, & Cremer (2007, p. 256).

with variably sized gaps between "cars." Although all age groups chose the same size gaps, children's behavior was less well suited to the gaps they chose. Younger children took more time to get started, leading to less time left between their bicycle and the approaching car. The authors concluded that the children were overestimating their physical abilities, something that could easily lead to severe injury in a real-life context.

The issue may simply be one of children not being as "ready" as are older adolescents or adults to synchronize their motor behaviors (pedaling) with their perceptual ones (the start of the gap). Or, it could be that younger children take longer than older ones to make the decision to attempt to cross the gap. Whatever the explanation, it is clear that there is still some perceptual room to grow in adolescence.

Attention and Executive Functioning

We saw earlier in the section on neurological development that many cognitive changes in adolescence are refinements of existing abilities, rather than the emergence of new ones (Luna & Sweeney, 2004). This principle applies especially to the developments in attention and executive functioning in adolescence. Younger children do have attentional abilities and have begun to master the ability to inhibit prepotent responses, as we saw in Chapter 9. In adolescence, these abilities show continued improvement.

A classic study by Comalli, Wapner, and Werner (1962) looked at the development of attentional control. They used a version of the **Stroop task**, a classic task in cognitive psychology. In this task, participants are presented with a list of words that are all color names. The ink in which the color names are printed changes for each item on the list and is never the same color as the word name. So, for example, the list might consist of the word *red* printed in yellow ink, the word *green* printed in blue ink, the word *red* printed in green ink, the word *blue* printed in red ink, and so forth. The participant is instructed to name the ink colors (so the correct responses to the list above would be yellow, blue, green, red, etc.). What makes the task hard is that it is much more "natural" or automatic to read the color names. To do the task, the participant needs to inhibit the prepotent response of reading the words, which is made all the more difficult because the words are names of colors that interfere with naming the colors of the ink.

Comalli et al. (1962) had participants aged 7 to 80 years old perform this task. Figure 12.6 displays their results. The line marked "Card A" refers to the

Figure 12–6 Changes in performance on Stroop color-word test from 7 to 80 years of age

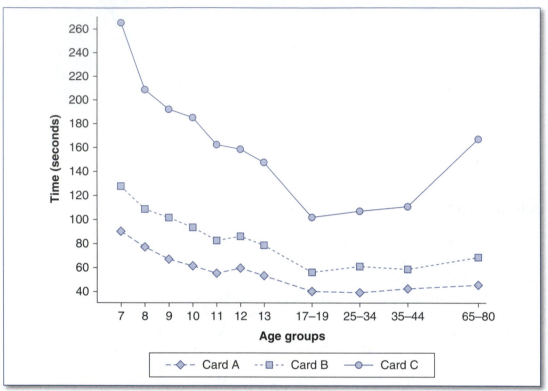

SOURCE: Comalli, Wapner, & Werner (1962, p. 49).

average amount of time it took participants to read a list of 100 color words printed in black ink. As you can see, this was the fastest task for all groups of participants. The line marked "Card B" refers to the average amount of time it took participants to name the colors of 100 randomly arranged rectangular patches of color (i.e., no reading was involved). The line marked "Card C" gives the results of the actual Stroop task. It shows that 7-year-olds are the slowest responders on this task and that response times gradually decrease across ages of participants until the group aged 17–19 (who would be considered older adolescents). It then remains fairly stable for other groups of young and middle-aged adults but rises again for elderly participants, aged 65–80.

The Stroop task is widely regarded as a test of executive functioning (Zelazo, Craik, & Booth, 2004). But it is certainly not the only task one can use. For another, very different example, let's turn our attention (!) to a study reported by Luna and Sweeney (2004). These researchers report on a very simple task called the **antisaccade task**. Participants are seated in front of a screen and asked to focus their eyes on a fixation point, typically placed in the center of the screen. As they fix their gaze on this point, other stimuli appear suddenly in the periphery. Sometimes (on so-called prosaccade trials), the fixation stimulus is green, and the participant is instructed to move her eyes to the newly appearing stimuli (making a sideways movement of her eyes, known as a "saccade"). Other times (on so-called antisaccade trials), the fixation stimulus is red, and the participant is instructed to avoid looking at the newly appearing stimuli. Figure 12.7 depicts the design of this experiment. Although children can, *on isolated trials*, inhibit their responses on the antisaccade trials, they are not able to do so as consistently as can adolescents. The ability to really control responses and inhibit eye movements increases with age and stabilizes in adolescence.

You might be wondering why the researchers used such a simple and artificial task to measure control of attention. After all, in real life there are very few occasions in which we have to keep our eyes from wandering to

Figure 12–7   Stimuli presented during antisaccade and prosaccade trials

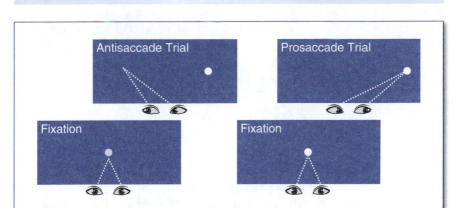

SOURCE: Luna & Sweeney (2004, p. 300).

look at a newly appearing object in our field of vision! Luna and Sweeney (2004) give two responses to this objection. First, the instructions for the task are simple and can easily be understood by participants of different ages and developmental levels. Second, the simplicity of the task means that the formulation of verbal strategies is both unnecessary and unhelpful. Thus, finding a developmental difference in the task, with (say) adolescents out-performing younger children, is more interpretable. Simply put, alternative explanations, such as the adolescents understanding the instructions better or using a different approach to the task, are made less plausible when such a simple task is used to investigate executive functioning.

Working Memory

Drawing a clear line between executive functioning generally and working memory specifically is not an easy task. As you may recall from earlier chapters, working memory is thought to be an important component of executive functioning. Even so, at least some researchers make a distinction between the subordinate systems of working memory (the phonological loop and the visuospatial sketch pad) and other executive functioning tasks that presumably are under the control of the central executive component or working memory. Since Baddeley's (1992) initial proposal about working memory, some neuropsychological evidence has been gathered that supports the distinction between the subordinate systems and the central executive (Luciana et al., 2005).

Luciana et al. (2005) studied the performance of children and adolescents aged 9–17 years on a variety of working memory tasks and compared it with the performance of a group of undergraduate students aged 18–20 years (considered "young adults"). The authors selected a variety of nonverbal working memory tasks that were thought to differ in their demands with respect to executive control. Table 12.1 presents a list and description of the tasks, as well as a list of the cognitive processes thought to be required to complete each task.

As can be seen, the tasks at the top of the table require fewer and less demanding cognitive processes to complete. The first task requires only recognition memory; the second, a delayed response task, requires inhibiting attention to distraction. The third and fourth tasks require a series of spatial locations to be remembered, but the fourth task (requiring backward responding) requires that the information in memory be manipulated. Finally, the last task on the list requires implementation of an organized search strategy.

Table 12–1   Nonverbal working memory tasks hierarchically organized by multitasking demand

Task	Paradigm	Processes required for success
Nonverbal face recognition memory	Delayed match to sample: Recognize single units of information (facial identities) after brief delays; categorical response; computerized	Attend to each stimulus when presented. Encode each stimulus according to facial identity. Remember each identity over a brief delay interval. Compare each face with a second one that is simultaneously presented. Select the face that is familiar.
Spatial delayed response	Delayed recall-guided response: Recall single units of spatial information after brief delays; execute a precise recall-guided response; computerized	Attend to each stimulus dot as it is presented. Encode the dot's location (vertical and horizontal coordinates) in extrapersonal space. Hold the location information in mind for delays of 0 ms, 500 ms, or 8 s. Inhibit shifting attention to internal or external distractors during the delay interval. When cued to respond, touch with precision the remembered location of the dot. Erase this information from short-term memory before the start of the next trial.
Spatial memory span: Forward	Sequential recall of multiple units of spatial information after brief delay; manual response; three-dimensional, noncomputerized display	Attend as the experimenter taps a sequence of locations. Encode and remember which locations were tapped. Encode and remember the order in which each location was tapped. Respond by reproducing the sequence in order.
Spatial memory span: Backward	Sequential recall plus manipulation of multiple units of spatial information; manual response; three-dimensional, noncomputerized display	Attend as the experimenter taps a sequence of locations. Encode and remember which locations were tapped. Encode and remember the order in which each location was tapped. Mentally reverse this order. Respond by reproducing the sequence in backward order.
Spatial self-ordered search	Recall plus manipulation of multiple units of information and strategic self-organization of that information; computerized	View an array of locations on screen. Touch locations one at a time to search for hidden tokens. If a token is not found, keep that location active as a possible response alternative. If a token is found, eliminate that location from possible response alternatives. Update this information as each token is found. Develop and execute an organized search strategy to minimize the task's mnemonic demands.

SOURCE: Luciana, Conklin, Hooper, & Yarger (2005, p. 700).

The results of the study are presented in Table 12.2. It shows no statistically significant age group differences in performance on the recognition memory task, suggesting that the processes used to perform this task have reached maturity by 9 years of age. On the spatial delayed response task, the oldest two groups were significantly better than the youngest three. For the memory span task, the oldest three age groups did not differ from one another but were better than the younger two age groups. The authors conclude that memory span continues to increase until about age 13–15, and this held for both forward and backward spans.

For the final task, the researchers examined the overall strategy sophistication. They found that the older two groups used better strategies than did the younger three groups (in Table 12.2, higher strategy scores correspond to poor use of strategies). The authors conclude that the ability to use a strategy to organize responses continues to develop until roughly age 16. Overall, the authors conclude that while the ability to maintain information in online memory has reached maturity before adolescence begins, the executive aspects of working memory continue to develop well into adolescence, a conclusion echoed by other researchers who used other kinds of working memory tasks (e.g., Brahmbhatt, McAuley, & Barch, 2008) as well as this group of researchers who subsequently investigated verbal working memory tasks (Conklin, Luciana, Hooper, & Yarger, 2007).

Long-Term Memory

Having covered the so-called online part of memory, we turn next to the offline storage part—long-term memory. You'll recall (I hope) from earlier chapters that long-term memory contains information that we are thought to not be currently processing or using. That is, long-term memory is thought to contain information we have stored but that we are not currently thinking about—a wealth of knowledge and recollections amassed over the course of our lives.

We saw in the section on working memory that much of the cognitive architecture that processes working memory has already reached full functional maturity by some point in adolescence. The storage functions of working memory seem to be "finished" developing first. So it will make some sense, I hope, to find out that the basic phenomena of long-term memory as well are largely in place by adolescence.

Fitzgerald (1981) presents one study demonstrating this claim. He compared younger adolescents (aged 12–15 years) to college students

Table 12–2 Cognitive task performance across age groups

	Ages 9–10	Ages 11–12	Ages 13–15	Ages 16–17	Ages 18–20
Recognition memory					
Face recognition (% correct)	76.5 (16.4)	74.8 (16.0)	74.9 (16.3)	79.3 (11.7)	83.8 (6.3)
Spatial delayed response Error scores (millimeters)					
No delay	2.67 (0.77)	2.35 (0.96)	2.27 (1.12)	1.62 (0.64)	1.42 (0.76)
500-ms delay	8.14 (2.92)	6.21 (2.54)	6.10 (1.97)	5.21 (2.10)	5.38 (1.84) .
8-s delay	12.84 (4.35)	9.31 (3.69)	8.30 (3.00)	7.75 (3.22)	7.79 (3.54)
Response latencies (milliseconds)					
No delay	1,722.14 (631.34)	1,504.53 (464.09)	1,557.72 (443.81)	1,622.83 (494.09)	1,789.51 (707.69)
500-ms delay	1,743.08 (515.29)	1,839.00 (455.33)	1,742.32 (367.02)	1,796.54 (412.83)	1,634.03 (395.77)
8-s delay	1,983.84 (429.98)	1,963.96 (523.41)	1,856.18 (392.94)	1,903.69 (438.14)	1,765.79 (460.04)
Memory span					
No. of spatial forward	5.08 (1.06)	5.77 (1.03)	6.57 (1.28)	6.48 (1.01)	6.93 (1.14)
No. of spatial backward	5.00 (0.83)	5.50 (1.36)	5.90 (1.00)	6.44 (1.08)	6.59 (1.25)
Spatial self-ordered search Forgetting errors					
3-location searches	0.12 (0.33)	0.04 (0.20)	0.07 (0.25)	0.08 (0.28)	0.04 (0.19)
4-location searches	1.20 (1.78)	0.68 (1.60)	0.47 (1.25)	0.38 (0.82)	0.26 (0.76)
6-location searches	13.20 (5.57)	10.20 (6.71)	4.30 (3.66)	2.25 (2.45)	3.81 (3.71)
8-location searches	27.36 (10.47)	23.88 (9.80)	15.63 (8.48)	9.71 (6.92)	9.30 (7.91)
Strategy score	36.16 (5.17)	35.64 (3.81)	33.10 (3.95)	28.67 (5.88)	29.89 (5.30)

SOURCE: Luciana, Conklin, Hooper, & Yarger (2005, p. 704).
NOTE: Values represent raw score means (± SDs).

(aged 17–21 years) in their performance on a modified free association task designed to elicit autobiographical memories. Experimenters chose three types of words from a longer list as prompts. Prompts could be *object* words, such as *desk* or *bell* or *river*; *action* words, such as *cut* or *fill* or *find*; or *affect* words, such as *surprised* or *angry* or *interested*. Each participant received 15 prompts, 5 from each category, and was asked to recall a specific memory relating to that word—the first one thought of. Participants were given some practice trials to ensure that they really thought of specific memories (e.g., "I remember my desk in first grade on the first day of school") as opposed to general ones (e.g., "I remember I sat at desks during elementary school"). Participants signaled when they had thought of a specific memory, and then were asked to write it down in enough detail so that "someone reading it would know what happened" (p. 70).

Fitzgerald (1981) had participants "date" the memories—as specifically as possible but at least with the month and year in which the event had occurred. One finding was that younger adolescents tended to report fairly recent memories—events that had occurred mainly within the past 6 months—for all three kinds of prompts. College students tended to recall "older" memories, dating back sometimes 2 or 3 years. However, the college students did recall significantly more recent memories for the affect words, with an average memory age of about 10 months for those. Fitzgerald wondered if the affect terms were less specific than the other words as prompts to elicit specific memories. He also speculated that perhaps adolescents' conceptual development, tending toward greater abstraction, might account for their larger time frame in recalling memories.

Yurgelun-Todd, Killgore, and Cintron (2003) studied relationships among certain brain structures and cognitive performance on various tasks among adolescents aged 12–17 years. They focused specifically on the **amygdala** and the hippocampus, two structures in the so-called limbic system of the forebrain, located in the temporal lobe. These two structures are diagrammed in Figure 12.8. The limbic system has long been thought to be involved in emotional responses and behavior (Zillmer & Spiers, 2001), but more recently, the hippocampus has been shown to play an important role in the encoding of episodic memories, and the amygdala in the formation of new learning (Yurgelun-Todd et al., 2003).

Yurgelun-Todd et al. (2003) gave adolescents an assessment battery of many cognitive tasks, including reading, spelling, and mathematics tests. The adolescents also received MRI tests from which the volume of various brain structures was measured. The size of the amygdala correlated

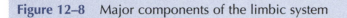

Figure 12–8 Major components of the limbic system

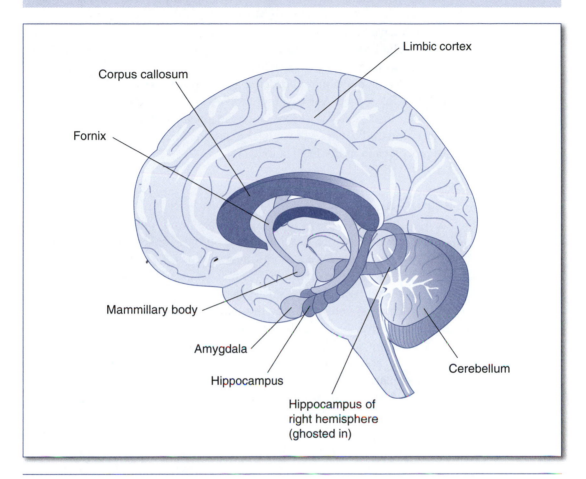

SOURCE: Carlson (2004, p. 86).

positively with age and with performance on a wide variety of cognitive tasks that drew upon long-term memory. Somewhat surprisingly, the size of the hippocampus did *not* correlate with age and showed only limited correlations with cognitive performance.

DEVELOPMENTS IN HIGHER-ORDER COGNITIVE PROCESSES

We've seen in the above sections that for many of the basic cognitive processes, adolescence marks a time of refinement of skills and abilities that are present from a much younger age. Said another way, the cognitive changes from childhood to adolescence simply aren't that dramatic in perception or attention or memory. Most of the rudiments of these aspects of cognition have been in place for quite a while before the adolescent reaches puberty. The changes that occur in adolescence typically involve more consistency, more efficiency, or perhaps more speed of execution.

Developments in higher-order cognitive processes are a little more dramatic in adolescence. As we will see, adolescents' abilities to solve problems, draw inferences, make decisions, and plan ahead all show big improvements when compared to those of younger children. We will examine these cognitive processes in more detail below.

Reasoning

One of my favorite developmental studies makes the point about a large change in adolescents' reasoning abilities. Osherson and Markman (1975) performed an experiment in which a research assistant showed children, adolescents, and adults small plastic poker chips in assorted solid colors. Participants were told that the experimenter would be saying some things about the chips and that they should indicate after each statement if it was true, if it was false, or if they "couldn't tell." Some of the statements were made about chips held visibly in the experimenter's open hand. Other, similar statements were made about chips hidden in the experimenter's closed hand. Among the statements used were logical *tautologies* (statements true by definition)—for example, "Either the chip in my hand is yellow, or it is not yellow"; logical *contradictions* (statements false by definition)—for example, "The chip in my hand is white, and it is not white"; and statements that were neither true nor false by definition but depended on the color of the chip.

Overall, the results showed that all of the children had difficulty distinguishing between statements that were empirically true or false (i.e., true in fact) and those that were logically true or false (i.e., true by necessity or definition). First, second, third, and even sixth graders did not respond correctly to tautologies and contradictions, especially in the hidden condition. They tended to believe, for example, that a statement such as "Either the chip in my hand is red, or it is not red" cannot be assessed unless the chip is visible. Tenth graders and adults, in contrast, were much more likely to respond that even when the chip couldn't be seen, if the statement was a tautology or contradiction, the statement about it could be evaluated on the basis of the syntactic form of the sentence. These results were consistent with Piaget's assertion that logical reasoning, particularly abstract, hypothetical reasoning, awaits the attainment of formal operations in adolescence.

Psychologist Henry Markovits (1993) adopted and elaborated on the Piagetian theory of the development of logical reasoning. Much of his research has investigated conditional reasoning—that is, reasoning involving some "if–then" relationship. You may recall that we examined the basic forms of conditional reasoning in Chapter 11 (a quick review of Table 11.1 [see page 340] may be in order here). You may also recall that Deanna Kuhn's research (also described in Chapter 11) showed that even first graders could draw correct inferences with *modus ponens* problems and that other problems were harder even for the oldest students tested (who were 14 years of age).

Markovits (1993; Markovits & Barrouillet, 2002) considered conditional reasoning in terms of a framework described initially by cognitive psychologist Phillip Johnson-Laird (1983), called the mental models approach to reasoning. In this view, adult reasoners are believed to construct mental scenarios of how premises in a reasoning problem can be interpreted. For example, imagine being asked to reason with the premises "If a customer buys an item on sale, the receipt will have a green star" and "The customer bought a DVD on sale." An effective reasoner would first imagine the scenario in which the customer bought a DVD on sale and received a green-starred receipt. He would find this scenario consistent with the premises. Next he might imagine a situation where the customer bought a DVD on sale and did not receive a green-starred receipt. A moment's reflection would inform him that this scenario is inconsistent with the premises. He might next consider scenarios where the customer bought a DVD at regular price—not on sale—and did or did not receive a green-starred receipt. He should discover, however, that both of these last scenarios are consistent with the premises originally given.

Markovits and Barrouillet (2002) believe that the mental models framework, developed to account for patterns of performance of adult reasoners, can also be applied to the reasoning of children and adolescents, and can offer an explanation of what underlies improved reasoning performance with development. What changes with development is the ability to consider a larger number of models simultaneously, and the efficiency with which a reasoner can retrieve information from long-term memory in building a model. Moreover, adolescents are assumed to have larger knowledge bases than younger children and, thus, to have more information that *can* be retrieved from long-term memory to use on a reasoning problem. Finally, adolescents are presumed to be better at inhibiting irrelevant information—especially in cases where the premises are empirically false—that might interfere with a

Figure 12–9   Teddy bear, with out and with accessories, used by Kuhn and Pease (2006)

SOURCE: Kuhn & Pease (2006, p. 282).

focus on the logical task (Simoneau & Markovits, 2003).

Markovits and Barrouillet (2002) thus predict that younger children (preschoolers and children in the first couple of elementary school grades) ought to reason competently with familiar premises, or with premises for which they can easily construct counterexamples. However, they should be less effective with unfamiliar or abstract premises, or premises for which they lack the knowledge to easily construct counterexamples. Older children and adolescents, in contrast, should be better able to deal with premises that require multiple models to consider. They should be better able to deal with a wider range of content in the premises and to generate models more quickly and efficiently.

In Markovits's work we see the idea that apparently small changes in basic cognitive processes, such as a small increase in working memory capacity or processing efficiency, can lead to bigger changes in the ability to perform higher-order cognitive tasks. This is a theme to which we will return when we consider adolescents' decision-making abilities.

Learning and Problem Solving

We saw above that adolescents typically outperform children on reasoning tasks, particularly if the reasoning tasks involve unfamiliar or abstract content. Presumably, adolescents have the edge over younger children in part because of differences in the knowledge base—older people have had more time to have more experiences and, thus, to encode and store more information.

Psychologist Deanna Kuhn took this idea one step further, in a study conducted with Maria Pease (2006). They compared the learning and hypothesis-testing abilities of young adolescents (aged 11–12 years) with those of young adults (age range late teens to late 20s) in a novel learning task, depicted in Figure 12.9. The task was designed to be equally novel for both groups of participants, and to be one that required the ability to integrate new information with existing understanding.

Participants were shown the teddy bear depicted in the top photo of Figure 12.9. They were told that a charity was giving away the bear as a promotion to raise money. The charity thought that donations might increase if the bear came with some accessories—seven different ones were shown. But, since the charity couldn't afford to give away bears with all seven accessories, participants were asked to select two that they thought would be most likely to increase donations and two others that they thought would not increase donations. For ease of reference, let's call the first two accessories selected a and b and the second two c and d.

Participants were then shown "data" from various accessory combinations and the resulting change in donations. Table 12.3 presents these (made

Table 12–3 "Data" presented to participants in the Kuhn and Pease (2006) study

Accessory combination	Percentage by which donations increase
abcd[1]	20
ab d	20
a d	10
ab	10
b d	20

SOURCE: Adapted from Kuhn & Pease (2006, pp. 283–284).

[1]abcd refers to the accessory combination worn by a particular bear—in this case, the bear wears all four of the accessories the participant selected, the two (a and b) she or he thought would increase donations, and the two (c and d) he or she thought would be least likely to increase donations.

up for the study) data. The question was how the participants would use these data. Notice that by making pair-wise comparisons in the table, one can assess how well each individual accessory worked in attracting donations. Comparing the first two cases, for example, shows that the increase in donations is the same, regardless of whether Accessory c is included. Thus, Accessory c is not very effective at raising donations. The c choice, recall, was an accessory the participant originally identified as not being effective, so these data serve to confirm the participant's initial idea.

Comparing the second and third case shows that Accessory b *is* effective in attracting more donations, which again supports the participant's initial idea (Accessory b was one of the options the participant initially selected). Comparing Cases 2 and 4, however, shows that Accessory d (which the participant initially thought would be ineffective) was in fact effective at raising donations, thus disconfirming the participant's initial idea. And, finally, comparing Cases 2 and 5 shows that Accessory a, initially thought to be effective, actually was not.

Case 5 actually shows the correct answer of which two accessories were the most effective in attracting increased donations. Only a minority (35%) of the younger group ever realized this (even after being prompted by the experimenter). The corresponding figure for young adults was 75%.

Kuhn and Pease (2006) interpret this result as follows: In this task, the participants had to integrate their initial beliefs with evidence. Kuhn and Pease believe that this integration required executive functioning of the type discussed earlier. To learn successfully, participants needed to be able to set aside some of their initial beliefs (e.g., that Accessory a would be effective and Accessory d wouldn't), while they assessed the empirical evidence presented to them. That is, they had to *inhibit* the effects that their initial beliefs would otherwise have had as they examined the data. They then had to coordinate the evidence with their initial beliefs to conclude that some of their initial beliefs were justified, while others were not. Cognitive development, specifically the development of executive functioning, allows this complex kind of learning to occur.

Other researchers support the idea of maturing executive functioning promoting the development of other higher-order cognitive processes. Asato, Sweeney, and Luna (2006) studied the development of planning in a task known as the Tower of London (TOL) task, a neuropsychological task often used to assess the functioning of the prefrontal cortex. Participants are asked to rearrange a set of three colored balls on three pegs. In the initial state (depicted in Figure 12.10), all of the balls are on one peg. The participant is shown a goal state (an example is also depicted in Figure 12.10) and asked to use the minimum number of moves (a move consists of transferring a single ball from one peg to another) to match the goal state.

Asato et al. (2006) gave participants aged 8–30 years the TOL task along with a number of other cognitive tasks. They found that the strongest predictor of planning performance on the TOL task was performance on an antisaccade task, similar to the one described earlier. They concluded that executive functioning, especially the ability to inhibit responses, is an important component of higher-order cognitive tasks that involve planning and problem solving.

Figure 12–10 Tower of London task—touch screen computer version. This figure shows a three-move problem, with the start state on the top, and the solution on the bottom in the order of selected ball movement. The balls were displayed in different colors.

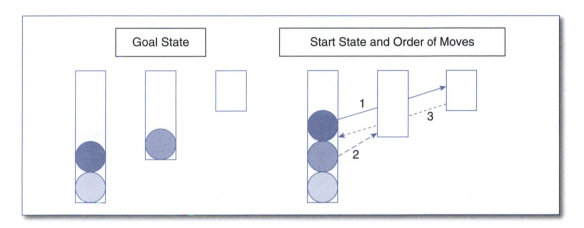

SOURCE: Asato, Sweeney, & Luna (2006, p. 2261).

Decision Making

You may recall that we looked at the task of decision making in detail in Chapter 11, dividing it into five phases, including setting goals, gathering information, structuring the decision, making a final choice, and evaluating the decision. Figure 11.2 (page 345) might help refresh the relevant memory traces! We saw that in the phases of information gathering and decision structuring, children are often idiosyncratic and less analytic than are adolescents and adults who perform the same or similar tasks. With cognitive development, children come to adopt time-saving shortcuts, which tends to make their decision making more efficient but possibly also more biased in specific directions.

Unfortunately, however, adults' performance on a variety of decision-making tasks is far from perfect. Many studies in the literature document the many ways in which the average adult makes irrational or impulsive decisions, gathers information in biased or distorted ways, fails to consider all of the relevant options or criteria, or otherwise goes awry (see Baron, 2008, for a comprehensive review of this literature). So, although adolescents are often better decision makers than are children, there is still a lot of room for improvement for both them and most adults!

Psychologist Paul Klaczynski (2001a, 2001b, 2005) has developed a model to try to account for these facts. He posits the existence of two independent information-processing systems that influence each other but develop separately. One he calls the "experiential" system, and the other the "analytic" system. We will take up each of these in turn.

The **experiential system** operates quickly and almost automatically. It makes use of judgments and heuristics that are acquired implicitly, through one's experience in the world. Once these heuristics are acquired, they are activated automatically by situational cues. This activation takes little effort and seems to yield intuitively correct "gut feelings" about how to proceed (Klaczynski, 2005). These gut feelings may turn out to be wrong, but much of the time they work out to yield an outcome that is "good enough."

Klaczynski (2001b) provides an example of an adolescent trying to decide whether to purchase a half keg of beer or a quarter keg of beer:

> [The] adolescent need not determine the number of people expected to attend a party, the number of drinks expected per attendee, or whether the extent to which the "Expected Attendance x Expected Average drinks/Attendee" product exceeds the number of drinks in a typical quarter keg. The judgment requires only a rough "more or less than a quarter keg" estimate: Calculating the precise number of drinks more (or less) than is provided in a quarter keg is cognitively wasteful, particularly given these uncertainties regarding multiplicands and the fact that kegs generally come in only two quantities, half and quarter. In such situations, decisions may reflect a trade-off between the motivation to conserve cognitive energy and the need for precision. (p. 292)

This quick and easy approach to cognitive processing is the one most people prefer to use, simply because it is easy and intuitive. It doesn't require a great amount of effort, it often yields outcomes that work, and it "feels" right for the situation. Thus, the experiential system is often the default one used in decision making.

The second information-processing system Klaczynski (2001a, 2001b, 2005) describes is called the **analytic system**. It is a more deliberate and explicit system than the experiential one. It takes effort to use and is consciously controlled. Analytic decision making might involve using pencil and paper to list pros and cons, to calculate expected costs, or to compute probabilities. Adolescents using analytic tools of decision making might make decisions that are normatively more rational; however, it is likely that this decision-making process won't inspire as much confidence as will use of the experiential system (Galotti, 2001). When you make a decision using your analytic system, you are aware of using it consciously to ponder the options.

Klaczynski is not the only one to describe two independent cognitive systems that operate in parallel (see Reyna & Farley, 2006; Stanovich & West, 2000). Reyna and Farley, in particular, use this idea to explain a well-known phenomenon in the study of adolescent decision making: their propensity to take risks.

Table 12.4 presents results of a survey conducted every 2 years by the Centers for Disease Control and Prevention, known as the Youth Risk Behavior Survey (YRBS). Ninth through 12th graders are asked to report on a number of risky behaviors they have engaged in, and do so confidentially and anonymously (Brener et al., 2004). Inspection of the table reveals, for example, that about one third of adolescents surveyed in 1991–2007 had ridden in a car with a driver who had been drinking alcohol; that about one quarter had smoked cigarettes within the past month; that a little fewer than half had had at least one drink of alcohol within the previous 30 days; and that about one fifth had used marijuana within the last 30 days.

One explanation for adolescents' risk taking was offered several decades ago by David Elkind (1967). A Piagetian theorist, Elkind believed that adolescents are subject to their own kind of egocentrism, which makes them see themselves as exquisitely unique and at the center of attention within their world. Elkind believed that adolescents construct something he called a "personal fable":

> [a] belief in personal uniqueness which becomes a conviction that he [the adolescent] will not die, that death will happen to others but not to him. This complex of beliefs in the uniqueness of his feelings and of his immortality might be called a *personal fable,* a story which he tells himself and which is not true. (p. 1031)

This personal fable, in turn, causes adolescents to tolerate more risk than would adults (or younger children, for that matter), because adolescents believe that bad outcomes can only happen to others.

However, subsequent work has not borne out Elkind's (1967) prediction. Beyth-Marom, Austin, Fischhoff, Palmgren, and Jacobs-Quadrel (1993) asked both adolescents and adults to list possible consequences, both positive and negative, of risky behaviors (e.g., drinking alcohol and driving, smoking marijuana, skipping school, driving without a license). Response patterns were similar for adults and adolescents, suggesting that adolescents show no special impediment to considering consequences. A related study conducted by Quadrel, Fischhoff, and Davis (1993) supported the idea that adolescents show no more "invulnerability" than do adults when considering risky behaviors.

Table 12-4 Trends in the prevalence of selected risk behaviors for all students (National YRBS: 1991–2007)

YRBSS

The national Youth Risk Behavior Survey (YRBS) monitors priority health risk behaviors that contribute to the leading causes of death, disability, and social problems among youth and adults in the United States. The national YRBS is conducted every two years during the spring semester and provides data representative of 9th through 12th grade students in public and private schools throughout the United States.

	1991	1993	1995	1997	1999	2001	2003	2005	2007	Changes from 1991–2007[1]	Change from 2005–2007[2]
Rarely or never wore a seat belt (When riding in a car driven by someone else.)											
	25.9 (20.8–31.7)[3]	19.1 (16.6–21.9)	21.7 (18.4–25.4)	19.3 (16.0–23.0)	16.4 (13.7–19.4)	14.1 (12.5–15.9)	18.2 (14.3–22.9)	10.2 (8.5–12.1)	11.1 (8.9–13.8)	Decreased, 1991–2007	No change
Rode with a driver who had been drinking alcohol (In a car or other vehicle one or more times during the 30 days before the survey.)											
	39.9 (37.7–42.2)	35.3 (32.7–38.1)	38.8 (35.0–42.7)	36.6 (34.4–38.8)	33.1 (30.8–35.4)	30.7 (28.7–32.8)	30.2 (28.1–32.5)	28.5 (26.5–30.5)	29.1 (27.2–31.2)	Decreased, 1991–2007	No change
Carried a weapon (For example, a gun, knife, or club on at least 1 day during the 30 days before the survey.)											
	26.1 (23.7–28.5)	22.1 (19.8–24.6)	20.0 (18.8–21.4)	18.3 (16.5–20.2)	17.3 (15.4–19.3)	17.4 (15.5–19.5)	17.1 (15.4–19.0)	18.5 (16.9–20.2)	18.0 (16.3–19.8)	Decreased, 1991–1999 No change, 1999–2007	No change
Did not go to school because they felt unsafe at school or on their way to or from school (On at least 1 day during the 30 days before the survey.)											
	NA[4]	4.4 (3.7–5.2)	4.5 (3.8–5.3)	4.0 (3.4–4.7)	5.2 (4.0–6.8)	6.6 (5.7–7.7)	5.4 (4.7–6.3)	6.0 (4.9–7.4)	5.5 (4.7–6.3)	Increased, 1993–2007	No change

	1991	1993	1995	1997	1999	2001	2003	2005	2007	Changes from 1991–2007[1]	Change from 2005–2007[2]
Attempted suicide (One or more times during the 12 months before the survey.)											
	7.3 (6.4–8.3)	8.6 (7.9–9.5)	8.7 (7.9–9.5)	7.7 (6.8–8.7)	8.3 (7.3–9.4)	8.8 (8.0–9.7)	8.5 (7.4–9.6)	8.4 (7.6–9.3)	6.9 (6.3–7.6)	No change, 1991–2001 Decreased, 2001–2007	Decreased
Current cigarette use (Smoked cigarettes on at least 1 day during the 30 days before the survey.)											
	27.5 (24.8–30.3)	30.5 (28.6–32.4)	34.8 (32.5–37.2)	36.4 (34.1–38.7)	34.8 (32.3–37.4)	28.5 (26.4–30.6)	21.9 (19.8–24.2)	23.0 (20.7–25.5)	20.0 (17.6–22.6)	Increased, 1991–1997 Decreased, 1997–2007	No change
Current alcohol use (Had at least one drink of alcohol on at least 1 day during the 30 days before the survey.)											
	50.8 (47.9–53.7)	48.0 (45.9–50.2)	51.6 (49.2–54.1)	50.8 (47.9–53.6)	50.0 (47.4–52.7)	47.1 (44.8–49.3)	44.9 (42.5–47.4)	43.3 (40.5–46.1)	44.7 (42.4–47.0)	No change, 1991–1999 Decreased, 1999–2007	No change
Current marijuana use (Used marijuana one or more times during the 30 days before the survey.)											
	14.7 (12.6–17.0)	17.7 (15.3–20.3)	25.3 (23.5–27.3)	26.2 (24.0–28.5)	26.7 (24.2–29.4)	23.9 (22.3–25.5)	22.4 (20.2–24.6)	20.2 (18.6–22.0)	19.7 (17.8–21.8)	Increased, 1991–1999 Decreased, 1999–2007	No change

(Continued)

Table 12–4 (Continued)

1991	1993	1995	1997	1999	2001	2003	2005	2007	Changes from 1991–2007[1]	Change from 2005–2007[2]
Lifetime methamphetamine use (Used methamphetamines [also called speed, crystal, crank, or ice] one or more times during their life.)										
NA	NA	NA	NA	9.1 (7.9–10.5)	9.8 (8.3–11.5)	7.6 (6.7–8.7)	6.2 (5.3–7.2)	4.4 (3.7–5.3)	No change, 1999–2001 Decreased, 2001–2007	Decreased
Ever had sexual intercourse										
54.1 (50.5–57.8)	53.0 (50.2–55.8)	53.1 (48.4–57.7)	48.4 (45.2–51.6)	49.9 (46.1–53.7)	45.6 (43.2–48.1)	46.7 (44.0–49.4)	46.8 (43.4–50.2)	47.8 (45.1–50.6)	Decreased, 1991–2007	No change
Had sexual intercourse with four or more persons during their life										
18.7 (16.6–21.0)	18.7 (16.8–20.9)	17.8 (15.2–20.7)	16.0 (14.6–17.5)	16.2 (13.7–19.0)	14.2 (13.0–15.6)	14.4 (12.9–16.1)	14.3 (12.8–15.8)	14.9 (13.4–16.5)	Decreased, 1991–2007	No change
Used a condom during last sexual intercourse (Among students who were currently sexually active.)										
46.2 (42.8–49.6)	52.8 (50.0–55.6)	54.4 (50.7–58.0)	56.8 (55.2–58.4)	58.0 (53.6–62.3)	57.9 (55.6–60.1)	63.0 (60.5–65.5)	62.8 (60.6–64.9)	61.5 (59.4–63.6)	Increased, 1991–2003 No change, 2003–2007	No change

	1991	1993	1995	1997	1999	2001	2003	2005	2007	Changes from 1991–2007[1]	Change from 2005–2007[2]
Ever taught in school about AIDS or HIV infection											
	83.3 (80.1–86.0)	86.1 (83.4–88.4)	86.3 (79.0–91.3)	91.5 (90.3–92.5)	90.6 (89.1–91.9)	89.0 (87.6–90.3)	87.9 (85.8–89.7)	87.9 (85.8–89.7)	89.5 (88.1–90.7)	Increased, 1991–1997 Decreased, 1997–2007	No change
Attended physical education classes daily (5 days in an average week when they were in school.)											
	41.6 (36.0–47.3)	34.3 (29.5–39.4)	25.4 (16.9–36.2)	27.4 (22.1–33.5)	29.1 (20.3–39.7)	32.2 (27.4–37.4)	28.4 (22.9–34.7)	33.0 (27.8–38.6)	30.3 (25.4–35.8)	Decreased, 1991–1995 No change, 1995–2007	No change
Were obese[5] (Students who were ≥ 95th percentile for body mass index, by age and sex, based on reference data.)											
	NA	NA	NA	NA	10.7 (9.6–12.0)	10.5 (9.5–11.5)	12.1 (10.8–13.6)	13.1 (12.2–14.0)	13.0 (11.9–14.1)	Increased, 1999–2007	No change

SOURCE: Centers for Disease Control and Prevention (2008).

[1]Based on trend analyses using a logistic regression model controlling for sex, race/ethnicity, and grade.

[2]Based on t-test analyses, p < .05.

[3]95% confidence interval.

[4]Not available.

[5]Previous YRBS fact sheets used the term "overweight" to describe those youth with a BMI >95th percentile for age and sex. However, this fact sheet uses the term "obese" rather than "overweight" in accordance with the 2007 recommendations from the Expert Committee on the Assessment, Prevention, and Treatment of Child and Adolescent Overweight and Obesity convened by the American Medical Association (AMA) and cofunded by AMA in collaboration with the Health Resources and Services Administration and CDC.

Reyna and Farley (2006) offer a different explanation for adolescent decision making. They agree that adolescents typically have an "optimistic bias," viewing their own risks as being less than those of their peers, but argue that this bias is characteristic of adult risk perception as well. The problem is not in adolescents' perception of risks, they claim, but rather in the adolescents' greater spontaneity, impulsiveness, and reactivity to immediate circumstances when making decisions to engage in risky behaviors. Neurological development in adolescence, particularly of the frontal lobe (which controls executive functioning, planning, reasoning, and impulse control), helps decrease risky decision making.

Reyna and Farley (2006) further argue for a so-called dual-process model of decision making much like the one proposed by Klaczynski (2001a, 2001b, 2005). That is, they believe in the existence of two independent systems that people call upon to make decisions. The analytic system continues to develop in adolescence, as Klaczynski and other theorists dating back to Piaget have claimed. Moreover, according to Reyna and Farley, the experiential system shows development as well. With development and experience, adolescents become better able to size up the *gist* of a decision-making situation and become better able to pick up on situational cues that might signal risk or danger. Thus, they become more likely to use their intuitive, fast-acting, experiential system to make quick but effective decisions by relying on tried-and-true gist-based maxims like "don't drink and drive" or "don't have sex without using protection."

The idea here is that cognitive development in decision making during adolescence consists of two changes. The first is in the increased ability to analyze situations deliberately and intentionally. An important second is in the acquisition of better intuitions and better abilities to size up the important cues in any specific situation. Thus, both the analytic *and* the experiential systems become more functional and operate better in adolescence, according to Reyna and Farley (2006).

Overall, then, the picture that emerges from work reviewed in this chapter is this: During the adolescent years, refinements are made to the basic cognitive processes, although no major changes or restructurings occur. Deeper and more obvious changes occur in higher-order processes, such as reasoning, problem solving, and decision making. Perhaps because of relatively small changes in basic cognitive processing, adolescents are better able to think of more possibilities, to overcome their initial hypotheses and biases, and to reason and analyze situations. There is also some suggestion that they become better able to "size up" situations quickly, with better intuitive responses.

We will see, in Chapter 13, how these adolescent abilities get applied to a broad set of circumstances. That is, we will examine how the cognitive abilities that have become solidified in adolescence are used to plan for the future, to reason about ethical dilemmas, and, even more generally, to develop a personal philosophy.

SUMMARY

1. Piaget named the final stage of cognitive development *formal operations*. It begins at around age 11 or 12 years and becomes solidified at about age 15 or 16. During formal operations, adolescents become more systematic and thorough in their thinking and become more able to reason abstractly. They are able to imagine alternative possibilities to reality and to reflect on their own thinking.

2. The information-processing view of cognitive development in adolescence locates much of the increased performance on a variety of cognitive tasks to the increased speed of cognitive processing adolescents have over younger children, as well as to general increases in the knowledge base.

3. Another factor commonly cited within an information-processing framework to explain the superiority of adolescents relative to younger children is the adoption and use of more sophisticated strategies. Robert Siegler developed the rule assessment approach to investigate the kinds of strategies children and adolescents bring to complex cognitive tasks.

4. Neurologically, adolescents are undergoing a number of profound changes, many of which are thought to underlie cognitive development. Among these are myelination in the frontal lobes, pruning of synaptic connections throughout the brain, and a remodeling of the prefrontal cortex.

5. Work by Plumert et al. (2007) shows that older adolescents make better decisions in a perceptual-motor task of traffic crossing using a bicycle simulator. The results suggest that, even though perceptual skills are largely developed before adolescence, there is still room for improvement during adolescence.

6. Work using the Stroop task and the antisaccade task has shown that adolescents show greater attentional control than do younger children. This means that they are better able to focus their mental energy and to ignore distraction.

7. Studies by Luciana and her colleagues show that working memory span increases until early to mid-adolescence but that the use of sophisticated strategies continues to show improvement until age 16.

8. Studies by Yurgelun-Todd and others suggest that the amygdala, thought to play a role in new learning, continues to grow into adolescence and correlates positively with a number of tasks that draw on long-term memory. In contrast, the hippocampus, a second brain structure thought to be involved in the formation of episodic memories, does not grow with age and does not correlate with performance on long-term memory tasks.

9. Adolescents' ability to reason abstractly is shown very clearly in studies of formal reasoning, where they are better able to recognize and reason with tautologies and contradictions.

10. Henry Markovits describes the improvement in reasoning in adolescence as a consequence of adolescents being better able to construct and manipulate a larger number of models simultaneously.

11. Kuhn and Pease believe that adolescents become better at integrating their initial beliefs with new evidence by being more willing to set aside some of their initial ideas and by analyzing which data support which beliefs and which do not. They believe that development of executive functioning is critical for this ability.

12. Recent theoretical work posits the existence of two, independent information-processing systems that are used in decision making and other cognitive tasks. The first is the experiential system, which is used to make quick, relatively effortless, intuitive decisions that respond to the overall gist of and specific cues given by a specific situation. The other is the analytic system, thought to require effort and intention. Both are thought to develop during adolescence, and both are thought to play an important role in decision making and other higher-order cognitive tasks.

REVIEW QUESTIONS

1. Describe the characteristic features of formal operations. Give specific examples to illustrate.

2. What are some explanations the information-processing framework offers to explain adolescents' superiority on a variety of cognitive tasks, in comparison with younger children?

3. Describe Siegler's rule assessment approach and its use in understanding a child or adolescent's performance on a complex cognitive task.

4. Describe the major neurological developments in adolescence, and explain how they might enable changes in cognitive processing.

5. Describe and critique the Plumert et al. (2007) study of perceptual motor development in childhood and adolescence.

6. Compare the Stroop and antisaccade tasks as measures of attentional control. What are the pros and cons of each?

7. Review and describe the cognitive developments in the working and long-term memory systems.

8. Explain how the findings of Osherson and Markman (1975) on reasoning with tautologies and contradictions support Piagetian descriptions of formal operations.

9. Explain how improvements in adolescent reasoning, a higher-order cognitive process, might be explained in terms of either basic neurological developments or developments in basic cognitive processes.

10. Describe and critique the Kuhn and Pease (2006) study of learning and problem solving in children and adolescents.

11. Compare and contrast the experiential and analytical information-processing systems, and describe the role each might play in adolescent decision making.

12. Review the arguments for why adolescents seem to take more risks than do children or adults, and explain how this can be accounted for by both the experiential and the analytic information-processing systems.

KEY TERMS

Amygdala

Analytic System (of decision making)

Antisaccade Task

Experiential System (of decision making)

Mental Models Approach (to reasoning)

Reflective Abstraction

Rule Assessment Approach

Stroop Task

Synaptic Pruning

Tower of London (TOL) Task

CHAPTER 13

ADOLESCENCE

Broader Impacts of Cognitive Development

I n the last chapter, we reviewed the cognitive changes that occur in adolescence in the major cognitive realms discussed throughout the book—perception, attention, memory, thinking, reasoning, and decision making. We saw that bigger changes occur during this developmental phase in the so-called higher-order cognitive processes than occur in the more basic ones. We focused the discussion, as we have throughout the book, on the typical adolescent, glossing over the fact that different adolescents often adopt different approaches to cognitive tasks.

In this chapter, we will briefly examine the idea of **individual differences** in cognition—stable variations among persons that frame the ways in which they perceive, acquire, and process information. We will distinguish between **ability differences**, which refer to differences in a capacity or skill, and stylistic differences, which refer to differences in a person's preference or habitual approach. As part of this discussion, we will also look at gender differences in cognition. We have not talked about individual differences before, so some of our discussion will reach back into middle childhood to examine individual differences there as well. All of these topics are broad ones and could easily take up a whole (and very rich) book, so we will necessarily only touch on some major themes.

We will next consider adolescent cognition in broader contexts—that is, how the cognitive skills of adolescents are used in wider domains. Adolescents use their cognitive abilities to reason about ethical and moral dilemmas. They develop general frameworks and theories about knowledge. And, they set goals and make plans for the future during this final phase of development before adulthood. These activities might be considered "cognition in action," so they are important topics to include in our discussion, and they serve as a fitting final chapter of the book. Again, as these are new topics for us to consider, we will include in our discussion a brief look at these processes as they emerge in middle childhood.

INDIVIDUAL DIFFERENCES IN COGNITION

So far, we have been assuming cognitive development proceeds in pretty much the same way for all children. Although we know that children often don't approach cognitive tasks exactly the way adults do, we have been making the assumption that with time, maturity, and perhaps education, they come to do so. In effect, we've been ignoring the fact that there may be reliable differences in children's capacities, their proclivities and preferences for cognitive tasks, or both. In this section, we'll examine three different kinds of proposals about individual differences.

Ability Differences

When we speak of ability differences among children, we have in mind such differences as working memory capacity, processing speed, strategy use and execution, and creativity. Many psychologists would use an umbrella term, *intelligence*, to capture these types of differences (e.g., Canivez, 2008; Flynn, 2007). Table 13.1, for example, lists the 10 subtests of the Wechsler Intelligence Scale for Children (WISC), a widely used intelligence test for school-aged children. You'll see in this table a wide variety of different intellectual abilities are being assessed.

Table 13–1 Subtests of the Wechsler Intelligence Scale for Children (WISC)

Information: On what continent is Argentina?

Arithmetic: If 4 toys cost 6 dollars, how much do 7 cost?

Vocabulary: What does "debilitating" mean?

Comprehension: Why are the streets usually numbered in order?

Picture Completion: Indicate the missing part from an incomplete picture.

Block Design: Use blocks to replicate a two-color design.

Object Assembly: Assemble puzzles depicting common objects.

Coding: Using a key, match symbols with shapes or numbers.

Picture Arrangement: Reorder a set of scrambled picture cards to tell a story.

Similarities: In what way are "dogs" and "rabbits" alike?

SOURCE: Adapted from Flynn (2007, p. 5).

Other psychologists would not *equate* cognitive abilities and intelligence, but most agree that people do vary in their intellectual (as well as several other important) abilities. Psychologists disagree over whether the best way to describe this variation is in terms of one general mental ability (called intelligence) or in terms of more numerous and varied intellectual abilities (Gardner, 1993).

Even psychologists who accept the idea of a general mental ability called intelligence debate just what the ability is. Some see it in terms of a capacity to learn efficiently; others in terms of a capacity to adapt to the environment. Other conceptions of intelligence include viewing it as mental speed, mental energy, or mental organization (Gardner, 1999; Sternberg, 1986). Many psychologists who study intelligence have looked at stable individual differences among various cognitive capacities to describe more general differences in people's performance on broader intellectual tasks.

Keating and Bobbitt (1978) report a now-classic study that adopts this framework. They studied third, seventh, and eleventh graders, including students of both average intelligence and above-average intelligence (as assessed with a nonverbal intelligence test). The experiments were all based on cognitive tasks previously used with adults. The investigators found that when they controlled for the effects of age (and presumably, therefore, for developmental level), ability differences still were apparent, especially on the more complicated cognitive tasks. For example, a very simple cognitive task was to ask participants to push a button as quickly as possible after a light appeared on a console. A slightly more complicated task required the participant to push one button as quickly as possible after a red light came on, and to push another button as quickly as possible when a green light appeared. This choice reaction task required the participant to make a quick decision before pressing a button.

Figure 13.1 presents the results, for participants of different ages and ability levels. Adolescents and older children had faster reaction times than younger children. Moreover, within each age group, high-ability students were faster than average-ability students, particularly on the more demanding choice reaction task.

Keating and Bobbitt (1978) believed that both age and ability differences result from the efficiency with which cognitive processes (such as perceiving a stimulus and making a decision) are carried out. Their view is that high-ability children (and high-ability adults) acquire, store, and manipulate information more rapidly and efficiently than do their same-age, normal-ability peers. An increase in speed and efficiency also comes with development. Tillman, Nyberg, and Bohlin (2008) elaborate on some of these ideas, arguing that various components of working memory make separate and independent contributions to intelligence in children and adolescents. In particular, they identify verbal and visual storage and verbal and visual executive functioning as being different predictors of overall intelligence.

Figure 13–1   Reaction time data from the Keating and Bobbitt (1978) study

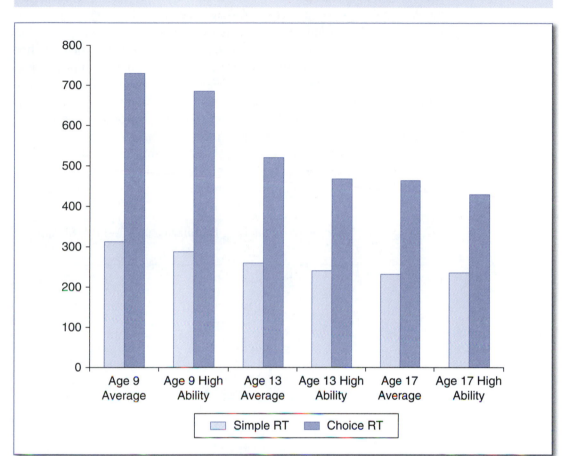

SOURCE: Adapted from Keating & Bobbitt (1978, p. 159).

Cognitive and Learning Styles

In addition to individual differences in cognitive abilities and capacities, cognitive psychologists have also identified stable, distinct patterns with which different people *use* their cognitive abilities or approach cognitive problems. These patterns are known as cognitive styles (Globerson & Zelnicker, 1989; Rayner & Riding, 1997). The term *cognitive style* is meant to imply certain personality and motivational factors that influence the way in which a person approaches a cognitive task (Sternberg, 1997).

One example of a cognitive style dimension that has been studied extensively by developmental psychologists is *cognitive tempo* (Kagan, Rosman, Day, Albert, & Phillips, 1964). It has to do with the degree to which a child or an adolescent will delay responding so that he can continue cognitively processing information. Some individuals seem to be prone to respond very quickly, after what seems to an outside observer to be only superficial thought or processing, in a wide variety of situations. Other individuals respond very slowly and very carefully, appearing to work very hard to avoid making mistakes or overlooking information. Children and adolescents in the former group are designated *impulsive*, while those in the latter group are called *reflective*.

Psychologists often use a test called the **Matching Familiar Figures Test (MFFT)** developed by psychologist Jerome Kagan and his associates (1964). Figure 13.2 provides an example item. The instructions given to children and

Figure 13–2   Example of a Matching Familiar Figures Test (MFFT) item

SOURCE: Kagan, Rosman, Day, Albert, & Phillips (1964, p. 22).

adolescents taking the test are to search through the six figures at the bottom to find the one that *exactly* matches the item shown at the top. Some children and adolescents respond very quickly on this test, choosing an answer after only a few seconds. Other individuals respond much more slowly. Some make very few errors, even on difficult items; others make a number of errors, even on easy items. Those individuals who respond rapidly and make many errors are said to be demonstrating an impulsive style, while those who respond slowly, with relatively few errors, are demonstrating a reflective style (Tyler, 1974).

Other theories offer other proposals for what specific cognitive styles exist. However, a common theme running through different proposals is the contrast between rational and intuitive approaches. The former connotes approaching a task objectively, unemotionally, analytically, and thoroughly; the latter connotes approaching a task personally, emotionally, holistically, and by drawing on one's feelings (Klaczynski, 2001a, 2001b; Stanovich & West, 2000).

Although you might be tempted to conclude that some adolescents (or adults) are rational and some are emotional in their approach to higher-order cognitive tasks, researchers such as Paul Klaczynski (2001a, 2001b) adopt a very different view, as we saw in Chapter 12. Adolescents (and adults), Klaczynski argues, are *both* rational and emotional in their cognition—at different times and under different circumstances. We saw in Chapter 12 that he advocates what is called **dual-process theory of cognition**, in which cognitive development is seen as progressing along two independent and unrelated trajectories. On the one hand, there is analytic cognition, which is effortful, under conscious control, and used to divorce the underlying structure of a problem from its superficial characteristics. On the other hand, people also develop a capacity for heuristic or experiential cognition, used rather effortlessly to make quick decisions or appraisals of information. Heuristic or experiential cognition is cued by features of a particular problem, or by the context in which an adolescent (or adult) starts to work on a problem. Klaczynski's major point is that the development of cognition is not a unitary process that becomes more rational over time. Instead, although rational processing becomes more *available* with development and education, heuristic processing remains available for use throughout a person's life.

The experiential processing system (Klaczynski, 2005) is one that functions automatically when activated by situational cues. Things like stereotypes are examples of experiential processing—these cognitive processes become triggered by some stimulus in the environment, and it takes more effort to stop the activation than to let the process proceed. Indeed, Klaczynski argues, sometimes we don't even know when an experiential cognitive process has been activated.

The analytic, more rational system, in contrast, does not operate automatically or without our awareness. When we are using this system, we are aware that we are using it, we are aware that we are expending mental effort, and we are deliberately intending to use these cognitive processes. Solving a logical puzzle and completing a Sudoku are two examples that come immediately to mind. Klaczynski (2005) argues that as analytic abilities develop, so too must an individual's motivation to make use of analytic cognitive processes. Put another way, it's not enough to have a *capacity* for rational thinking (for example); the individual has to also *want* to employ this mode of cognition.

Although in this view most adolescents and adults have the capacity for analytic or experiential processing, it may be that individual differences exist in the propensity to use either system. That is, there may be individuals who rely more frequently, or in a wider set of circumstances, on (say) their analytic processing system than do others. Much work remains to be done to fill in this proposal, and to understand how stable individual differences are across different circumstances in the uses of analytic and experiential processing.

Achievement Motivation

We've just seen that children and adolescents may differ in both their cognitive abilities and capacities and their preferences for approaching cognitive tasks in one way versus another. A third source of individual differences in cognition is known as **achievement motivation**. This term refers to an individual's beliefs about her own abilities and styles, and also has to do with the kind of goals she adopts when tackling cognitive challenges.

Psychologist Carol Dweck (2002) has conducted extensive research with children and adolescents with respect to achievement motivation. She believes that children's and adolescents' conceptions of their own abilities are critically important. During the later years of elementary school (fourth or fifth grade), and during middle school, adolescents begin to see their abilities as stable traits and to see connections among intellectual ability, effort, and performance. The "downside" to this maturing view of their own abilities is that older children and adolescents become more sensitive to external evaluation, such as grades or scores. Negative evaluations can hit especially hard.

Dweck's research shows that from as early as the preschool period, children have a sense of their abilities as an internal aspect of their personality. Moreover, when they fail at a task, they have the ability to connect that failure to their own views of their abilities (Dweck, 2002). Younger children tend to think about success and failure broadly—in terms of their overall goodness and badness. Older children (e.g., those in late elementary school) make distinctions in terms of realms of abilities—distinguishing, say, between being good at reading and being good at baseball or dancing.

Dweck (2002) sees children's ability conceptions as undergoing two periods of big developmental transformation—one when children are aged 7–8 (around second to third grade, in the United States) and another when they are aged 10–12 (fourth and fifth grade). Table 13.2 summarizes the ways

Table 13–2 Major changes in ability conceptions

Kindergarten	7–8 years	10–12 years
Definitions and nature of ability		
Mixed domains →	Domain-specific →	Can isolate ability from other variables
Skills and knowledge, mastery standard	More internal quality, more normative standard	Possibly capacity, mastery or normative standard
Not seen as predicting future performance	More stable, predictive	Seen as potentially highly stable and predictive
Impact of academic outcomes		
Do not affect ability estimates	Affect ability estimates but not motivation	Affect ability estimates and motivation
Social comparison		
Low interest and impact	High interest, some impact on ability evaluation	Strong impact on self-evaluation and motivation
Self-evaluations of ability		
High and inaccurate	Lower and more accurate; begin to affect expectations	Accurate, but some underestimatation, and more impact on motivation
Relation to other beliefs and to motivation		
Not related to other motivational beliefs and low impact on motivation	→	Coalesce with other motivational beliefs to have high impact on motivation

SOURCE: Dweck (2002, p. 63).

in which children conceive of cognitive abilities and how these conceptions are affected by various sorts of information.

A delightful aspect of children in preschool and early elementary school is their unbridled optimism. My daughter in kindergarten would describe most of her abilities—be they in reading, dancing, hitting a T-ball, or cleaning her room—as "awesome" or "great." As assistant coach of her T-ball team, I worried that her repeated failures to catch the ball would be upsetting, but, although she never caught a single hit ball all season, this did not seem to deter her optimism or view of her "awesome" catching ability. Fortunately for her self-esteem, perhaps, most of her teammates were similarly lacking in the coordination required to catch—and none of them seemed to make comparisons to the few children on their team (or opposing teams) who were more skilled. As Dweck (2002) would say, their self-evaluations of their abilities were "high and inaccurate."

At around age 7 or 8, when most children are in second or third grade, a shift occurs in children's perception of their abilities. For one

thing, they differentiate between ability in one domain (e.g., reading) and that in others (e.g., math or sports). Being good at reading is no longer subsumed under a general label of "goodness" but is seen as a distinct ability area. Children this age are beginning to understand that ability in a given area may be a fairly stable personal quality (Dweck, 2002). That is, 7- and 8-year-olds are beginning to understand that "good readers" are likely to stay good readers in the future.

Children's self-perceptions also become more accurate around this time. Their ratings of their academic abilities become more in line with the ratings of their teachers. They become less globally positive about their own abilities and less optimistic about the chances that they will be able to improve on their abilities in the future. Their spontaneous self-evaluations start to show more self-criticism. And, they begin to pay attention to social comparison feedback—that is, their relative standing among a group of peers (Ruble & Frey, 1991). So, children of this

Photo 13.1 Young children may overestimate their skills, both academic and athletic.

age begin to compare test scores, to know who's working on which addition facts levels, and to figure out that the "robins" reading group is the highest and the "blue-birds" the lowest, even if the classroom teacher takes pains to try to disguise this information.

A second shift in ability conceptions occurs when children reach the age of 10–12, in fourth through sixth grade. One big change is that children start reliably distinguishing between ability and effort, seeing these as two distinct contributors to performance (Dweck, 2002). Some of the trends that began in second and third grade become more solidified: Children see ability as an even more stable aspect than they previously did and become even more affected by social comparison information. Their own self-evaluations become even lower and even more accurate. Most important, children's perceptions of their academic abilities become more coordinated in a network with other beliefs, values, and goals. Children begin to value those things they perceive themselves to be skilled at, for example, and try to avoid those domains in which they believe themselves to be less skilled. Unfortunately for many adolescents, such avoidance is often directed at school (Eccles, 2008; Eccles, Wigfield, & Byrnes, 2003). Eccles and her coauthors report that between 15% and 30% of adolescents fail to complete high school—with many more experiencing a general disengagement with school, marked by declining grades.

As these networks of beliefs about ability begin to cohere, two major patterns of behavior that affect the ways children approach a broad range of academic tasks begin to emerge. Dweck labels these *mastery-oriented* (or *learning-oriented*) and *helpless* (or *performance*) patterns of goal orientation (Dweck, 1999; Dweck & Leggett, 1988). A brief description of each of these patterns is in order. Children (and adults) who adopt a mastery or learning orientation set goals to challenge themselves and therefore to increase their competence, understanding, or mastery of something new. These individuals persist when they encounter obstacles or difficulty. Often they also appear to enjoy putting in more effort when it is called for.

Photo 13.2   As they get older, children become more adept at interpreting feedback to figure out where they stand, relative to their peers, especially in the classroom.

In contrast, individuals with a helpless or performance orientation fail to set challenging goals and give up rather easily when "the going gets tough." They begin to see their performance as mostly reflecting some underlying and unchanging level of ability. Their aim is often (but not always) to prove to others that they have high ability, or else to avoid others coming to the conclusion that they lack a high level of ability (Urdan & Mestas, 2006). Tests and assessments, then, are merely occasions to demonstrate (or mask) true levels of ability.

In earlier work, Dweck uncovered gender differences in the ways boys and girls typically respond to challenges and feedback in elementary school, starting around fourth or fifth grade. A typical study Dweck and her colleagues ran to investigate mastery and helpless orientations worked as follows. Older elementary school–aged children were given a number of puzzles or similar problem-solving tasks. Often the tasks were set up to be unsolvable, and children were told they had failed to complete a particular task correctly.

In one study (Dweck & Bush, 1976), children received failure feedback from either a male or a female adult or peer. When the evaluator was an adult, and especially when the adult was female, girls tended to adopt a helpless strategy, attributing the cause of their failure to their own inability or lack of competence. Boys, in contrast, were likely in the same circumstances to attribute the failure to the evaluator's "fussiness."

Dweck, Davidson, Nelson, and Enna (1978) reported other findings that might explain why adults' feedback has such different effects on girls and boys. They examined the kind of feedback given to fourth- and fifth-grade girls and boys by classroom teachers. Every instance of feedback to children by the teacher was coded. The experimenters found that when looking at just the positive feedback given, for boys over 90% of it related to the intellectual quality of work but for girls the corresponding figure was less than 80%. The discrepancy for negative feedback was even stronger: For boys, only about a third of the feedback concerned intellectual quality (the rest tended to be about conduct, effort, neatness, or other such things), but well over two thirds of the negative feedback girls received had to do with intellectual aspects of their performance.

Dweck and Goetz (1978) concluded that girls, perhaps because of their greater compliance with adult demands, are seen by teachers as expending maximum effort and motivation. Therefore, girls come to believe that failure can be attributed only to their own lack of ability. Boys, in contrast, are more often seen by teachers as lacking in conduct or effort. Thus when boys' performance falls short of expectation, teachers are more likely (in fact, 8 times more likely) to attribute the problem to a lack of motivation than to a lack of ability. As a consequence, boys may be inadvertently taught both to be less devastated by criticism (because they receive so much) and to take it less personally (because so much of it has to do with nonintellectual aspects of work, and so much is directed to a perceived lack of motivation).

Girls, receiving less criticism, have less opportunity to learn how to handle it. Further, adult criticism of girls' work tends to focus on a perceived lack of competence or ability. In short, girls get the message that failure signals lack of ability (something there is little remedy for); boys, that failure signals a lack of effort (for which the remedy is obvious).

Children's type of goals become part of their larger views or theories of intelligence. In more recent work, Dweck (1999) has focused on children's, adolescents', and adults' theories of intelligence. She groups these theories into two categories. One she calls an *entity* theory of intelligence—the belief that intelligence is fixed at a certain level, and not subject to improvement or change with effort or further learning. Entity theorists of intelligence tend to hold performance goals and to believe that tests and assessments can do little more than reveal one's underlying level of ability.

In contrast, other children, adolescents, and adults adopt what Dweck (1999) calls an *incremental* theory of intelligence. Incremental theorists see intelligence as a malleable quality, one that can be increased with more effort or practice. Incremental theorists tend to adopt learning goals, and they see performance on a test or an assessment as only one of many opportunities to demonstrate competence, and as a possible means of redirecting effort.

Dweck (2002) argues that an incremental view is more common among younger children (who are also much more optimistic about their own future performance, and who are generally better able to cope with a failure experience). Failure on a specific task is more devastating for entity theorists (be they children, adolescents, or adults) because in an entity framework, there is little one can do to change one's ability. Incremental theorists, in contrast, are better able to handle setbacks, are more "hardy" in their own self-assessment, and show higher aspirations for the future (Ahmavaara & Houston, 2007; Butler, 1999). A recent study by Dweck and her colleagues (Blackwell, Trzeniewski, & Dweck, 2007) showed that seventh graders with an incremental intelligence theory showed an upward trajectory in their grades in mathematics courses, while their peers with an entity theory showed either a flat or a downward trend in their grades (when controlling for mathematical ability).

We've reviewed, in this section, three different proposals for ways in which individual children and adolescents might differ stylistically in their approach to cognitive tasks: They might differ in abilities present from birth, in their preference for certain approaches, or in their deeper goals or theories. These differences can have synergistic effects: Certain stylistic preferences, for example, could lead individuals to engage in certain kinds of tasks more than others and, as that happens, to get different amounts of practice with different sets of cognitive skills. In this view, two individuals with similar sets of cognitive abilities could end up with very different profiles of cognitive "habits" or expertise, simply due to differences in their underlying preferences for how to tackle cognitive challenges in their everyday lives.

REASONING ABOUT MORAL DILEMMAS

So far we have focused mostly on cognitive tasks in the academic realm—problems that are typically ones given in school, or in school-like contexts—divorced from personal goals, often self-contained, often with one correct answer, and with little personal interest or relevance. In another article (Galotti, 1989), I called these formal reasoning problems and contrasted them with everyday reasoning problems, ones that have personal relevance, are typically not self-contained, do not have all the premises neatly supplied, and so forth. Table 13.3 provides a summary of the distinction I drew between these two types of reasoning.

Table 13–3   Differences between formal and everyday reasoning tasks

Formal	Everyday
All premises are supplied.	Some premises are implicit, and some are not supplied at all.
Problems are self-contained.	Problems are not self-contained.
There is typically one correct answer.	There are typically several possible answers that vary in quality.
Established methods of inference that apply to the problem often exist.	There rarely exist established procedures for solving the problem.
It is typically unambiguous when the problem is solved.	It is often unclear whether the current "best" solution is good enough.
The content of the problem is often of limited, academic interest.	The content of the problem typically has potential personal relevance.
Problems are solved for their own sake.	Problems are often solved as a means of achieving other goals.

SOURCE: Galotti (1989, p. 335).

Much less is known about performance on everyday reasoning tasks, because everyday reasoning is harder to study. However, one aspect of everyday reasoning, reasoning about moral dilemmas, has given rise to a large and relevant literature in cognitive development, and we will pause here to survey that landscape.

Moral dilemmas are problems in which two or more principles or concerns come into conflict. At least some of these include some aspect of a person's sense of morality, which Krebs (2008) defines as involving thoughts and feelings about rights and duties, virtues and vices, and right or wrong motives or behaviors. Moral dilemmas center around standards of conduct—figuring out what the right thing to do is when different principles come into conflict. To whom is more obligation owed? Whose rights supersede whose, and why? When should rules be followed, and when should they not? What sorts of responsibilities does one have to others, and how are those to be balanced?

Kohlberg's Stages of Moral Development

Lawrence Kohlberg was a pioneering researcher of the development of moral reasoning. His work, which he labeled a "cognitive developmental approach," was grounded in Piagetian theory (Kohlberg, 1976). As such, it divided moral reasoning into six progressive stages, each one building both on the stage that came before and on Piagetian stages of concrete and formal operations.

Kohlberg (1976) originally proposed six moral stages, and a brief description of them is presented in Table 13.4. These six stages are grouped into three levels, with two stages at each level. The levels are given the labels preconventional, conventional, and postconventional (or principled) moral reasoning. For ease of exposition, I'll review only these three broad levels, leaving a more specific description of each stage within each level for the interested reader to peruse in Table 13.4.

Describing each level of moral reasoning will be much clearer if we first present a specific hypothetical moral dilemma used by Kohlberg in his research. This dilemma is only one of several that Kohlberg used but is the most famous, and it is known as the Heinz dilemma, after the protagonist:

In Europe, a woman was near death from a special kind of cancer. There was one drug that the doctors thought might save her. It was a form of radium that a druggist in the same town had recently discovered. The drug was expensive to make, but the druggist was charging 10 times what the drug cost him to make.

He paid $200 for the radium and charged $2,000 for a small dose of the drug. The sick woman's husband, Heinz, went to everyone he knew to borrow the money, but he could only get together about $1,000, which is half of what it cost. He told the druggist that his wife was dying and asked him to sell it cheaper or let him pay later. But the druggist said, "No, I discovered the drug and I'm going to make money from it." So Heinz gets desperate and considers breaking into the man's store to steal the drug for his wife. (Colby, Kohlberg, Gibbs, & Liberman, 1983, p. 77)

Table 13–4   The six moral stages of Kohlberg's theory

Content of stage			
Level and stage	**What is right**	**Reasons for doing right**	**Social perspective of stage**
LEVEL I— PRECONVENTIONAL Stage 1— Heteronomous Morality	To avoid breaking rules backed by punishment, obedience for its own sake, and avoiding physical damage to persons and property.	Avoidance of punishment, and the superior power of authorities.	*Egocentric point of view.* Doesn't consider the interests of others or recognize that they differ from the actor's; doesn't relate two points of view. Actions are considered physically rather than in terms of psychological interests of others. Confusion of authority's perspective with one's own.
Stage 2— Individualism, Instrumental Purpose, and Exchange	Following rules only when it is to someone's immediate interest; acting to meet one's own interests and needs and letting others do the same. Right is also what's fair, what's an equal exchange, a deal, an agreement.	To serve one's own needs or interests in a world where you have to recognize that other people have their interests, too.	*Concrete individualistic perspective.* Aware that everybody has his own interest to pursue and these conflict, so that right is relative (in the concrete individualistic sense).

Content of stage			
Level and stage	**What is right**	**Reasons for doing right**	**Social perspective of stage**
LEVEL II— CONVENTIONAL Stage 3—Mutual Interpersonal Expectations, Relationships, and Interpersonal Conformity	Living up to what is expected by people close to you or what people generally expect of people in your role as son, brother, friend, etc. "Being good" is important and means having good motives, showing concern about others. It also means keeping mutual relationships, such as trust, loyalty, respect and gratitude.	The need to be a good person in your own eyes and those of others. Your caring for others. Belief in the Golden Rule. Desire to maintain rules and authority which support stereotypical good behavior.	*Perspective of the individual in relationships with other individuals.* Aware of shared feelings, agreements, and expectations which take primacy over individual interests. Relates points of view through the concrete Golden Rule, putting yourself in the other guy's shoes. Does not yet consider generalized system perspective.
Stage 4—Social System and Conscience	Fulfilling the actual duties to which you have agreed. Laws are to be upheld except in extreme cases where they conflict with other fixed social duties. Right is also contributing to society, the group, or institution.	To keep the institution going as a whole, to avoid the breakdown in the system "if everyone did it," or the imperative of conscience to meet one's defined obligations. (Easily confused with Stage 3 belief in rules and authority; see text.)	*Differentiates societal point of view from interpersonal agreement or motives.* Takes the point of view of the system that defines roles and rules. Considers individual relations in terms of place in the system.
LEVEL III— POST- CONVENTIONAL, or PRINCIPLED Stage 5—Social Contract or Utility and Individual Rights	Being aware that people hold a variety of values and opinions, that most values and rules are relative to your group. These relative rules should usually be upheld, however, in the	A sense of obligation to law because of one's social contract to make and abide by laws for the welfare of all and for the protection of all people's rights. A feeling of contractual commitment, freely	*Prior-to-society perspective.* Perspective of a rational individual aware of values and rights prior to social attachments and contracts. Integrates perspectives by formal mechanisms

(Continued)

Table 13–4 (Continued)

Content of stage			
Level and stage	What is right	Reasons for doing right	Social perspective of stage
	interest of impartiality and because they are the social contract. Some nonrelative values and rights like *life* and *liberty*, however, must be upheld in any society and regardless of majority opinion.	entered upon, to family, friendship, trust, and work obligations. Concern that laws and duties be based on rational calculation of overall utility, "the greatest good for the greatest number."	of agreement, contract, objective impartiality, and due process. Considers moral and legal points of view; recognizes that they sometimes conflict and finds it difficult to integrate them.
Stage 6—Universal Ethical Principles	Following self-chosen ethical principles. Particular laws or social agreements are usually valid because they rest on such principles. When laws violate these principles, one acts in accordance with the principle. Principles are universal principles of justice: the equality of human rights and respect for the dignity of human beings as individual persons.	The belief as a rational person in the validity of universal moral principles, and a sense of personal commitment to them.	*Perspective of a moral point of view* from which social arrangements derive. Perspective is that of any rational individual recognizing the nature of morality or the fact that persons are ends in themselves and must be treated as such.

SOURCE: Kohlberg (1976, p. 34–35).

In the *preconventional* level, the individual adopts what Kohlberg (1976) calls a concrete individual perspective: a sort of "what's in it for me?"

approach to moral questions. The individual (typically an older child or a younger adolescent) seeks simply to avoid punishment for breaking rules or to gain favors for following rules. This individual sees society's rules and expectations for behavior as externally imposed.

The adolescent or adult reasoning at the *conventional* level of moral development has internalized the rules and expectations of authority. The individual reasoning at this level tries to live up to societal expectations, to be a "good" person in the eyes of others, and supports existing rules and authority in the interest of maintaining the social order for the greater good. In the second stage of this level (Social System and Conscience; see Table 13.4), the individual becomes more concerned with upholding his societal duties but sees the possibility, in very extreme circumstances, of breaking a law to uphold a higher-order principle.

The third, or *postconventional*, level of moral reasoning finds its reasoners (usually older adolescents or adults) being able to distinguish between self-chosen principles and the principles articulated by an authority (such as a government, a teacher, a minister, or a parent). Some values are seen as relative to a particular cultural context, but others are absolute.

Thus, a preconventional interviewee might focus on whether Heinz would get caught and go to jail or whether, if he let his wife die, he'd be left all alone with the housework. A conventional-level reasoner would focus instead on whether or not stealing a drug could ever be justified and, if it could, whether that might lead to a general breakdown in property rights or whether a marriage contract obligates a spouse to take any action necessary to save the other one from death. A postconventional reasoner, finally, might focus on the relative priorities of a right to property versus a right to life in deciding what Heinz should do. Throughout the stages, however, the important thing is how the reasoner arrives at his answer rather than what that answer is.

Kohlberg's original research followed a sample of males, who were originally aged 10, 13, or 16, for a period of about 20 years, testing them every 3 or 4 years (Colby et al., 1983). Figure 13.3 presents the frequency of usage of reasoning at each stage as a function of the age of the boys and men interviewed. You can see that the usage of Stage 1 and Stage 2 (preconventional) reasoning declines from age 10 on; the usage of Stage 3 and Stage 4 (conventional) reasoning increases from childhood to adolescence (with Stage 4 reasoning continuing to rise); and Stage 5 reasoning, never very common, increases after age 20–22. Stage 6 reasoning was not found very often in Kohlberg's interviews, although he argued that it could be seen, on occasion, in realms such as law, theology, and moral philosophy (Moshman, 2005).

Figure 13–3 Mean percentage of moral reasoning at each stage for each age group

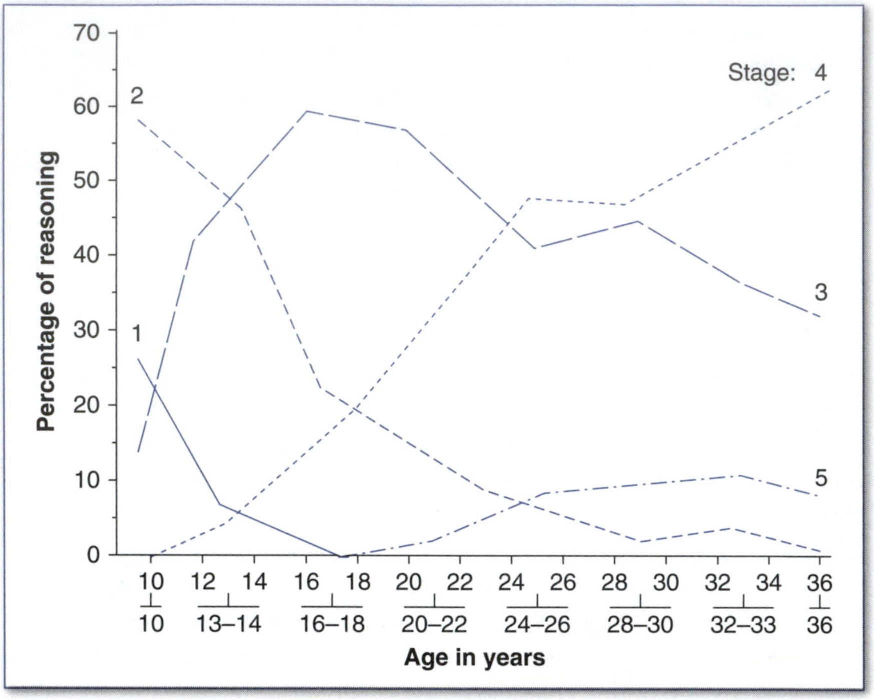

SOURCE: Colby, Kohlberg, Gibbs, & Liberman (1983, p. 46).

Kohlberg's work assumed a certain level of cognitive development as a prerequisite for moral development to occur. For example, an individual in the Piagetian concrete operations stage of cognitive development would be limited to the preconventional level of moral reasoning (Kohlberg, 1976). Likewise, an adolescent in early or emerging formal operations would not be able to reason higher than in the conventional level of moral reasoning. Said another way, cognitive development is necessary, but not sufficient, for a given level of moral development to occur. Another important ingredient of reasoning at an advanced moral level includes the ability to take another person's perspective—that is, to overcome one's own egocentrism.

Gilligan's Work on Gender Differences

Carol Gilligan, a onetime student and collaborator of Kohlberg's, began to question some of the methods and conclusions he had come to, while retaining others in her own proposal for a different scheme of stages of moral development. Gilligan (1977, 1979, 1982) objected to the exclusion of girls and women from Kohlberg's original sample, arguing persuasively that the theory meant to apply to human development ought to be formulated by hearing the responses of both genders. Although Gilligan agreed with Kohlberg's idea of progressive and hierarchical stages of moral reasoning, she rejected the idea that the stages could be fully specified by studying the responses of an all-male sample who reasoned only about hypothetical dilemmas revolving around issues of justice.

Gilligan (1977, 1982, 1988) argued that women were more likely than men to impose a "distinctive construction on moral problems, seeing moral dilemmas in terms of conflicting responsibilities" (1982, p. 105), rather than in terms of the abstract principles or competing rights that were typical of Kohlberg's hypothetical moral dilemmas. Gilligan believes women are more likely to reason about moral issues contextually, meaning that the "right" course of action to take will depend not on some absolute principle but rather on various aspects or features of a particular situation. In particular, Gilligan (1982) argued that women, more than men, were more likely to be concerned with issues of caring, responsibility for others, and the connection of themselves to other people and real-world dilemmas, while men's reasoning was more likely to focus on justice, rights, and prioritizing competing principles. Thus, Gilligan's argument went, to restrict study to an all-male sample was to exclude an important voice and an important focus.

Gilligan's (1982) methodology involved extensive interviews with 29 women who were considering an abortion. Gilligan's thinking was that, to investigate the moral reasoning of women in particular (a population that had been largely excluded from earlier research on moral reasoning), it made the most sense to choose a dilemma that women faced uniquely.

From these interviews, Gilligan (1982) identified different developmental levels of moral reasoning. Like Kohlberg, Gilligan constructed a stage theory of moral reasoning that comprised three levels. In the first stage or level, moral thinking is seen as being centered on the self and selfish needs. Moral dilemmas, then, arise only when two or more needs of the self are in conflict. For example, one of Gilligan's research participants, an 18-year-old, saw having a baby as providing "the perfect chance to get married and move away from home," but also as putting an obstacle in the way of her doing "a lot of things" (1982, p. 75).

In the second stage, Gilligan (1982) held that moral thinking centers on the issue of to whom the woman feels she owes responsibility. Dilemmas arise when one has competing obligations to others and someone has to be shortchanged. The problem for the reasoner, then, is figuring out whom to inflict the unavoidable hurt upon. Thus, in facing a decision about abortion, the woman at this stage of moral development tries to decide, for example, whether it is worse to abort the fetus or to disappoint her parents. In this stage, the woman is unlikely to place much weight on her own needs or desires, focusing instead on the needs and desires of others.

In the third and final stage of Gilligan's (1982) scheme of moral development, moral thinking involves balancing the needs of others with the needs of the self. In many ways this stage represents a combination of the two previous stages—but it represents, for Gilligan, a more complex way of thinking both about the self and about the nature of responsibility.

Kohlberg and associates (Colby et al., 1983) agreed with Gilligan that her research broadened in a useful way the definition of what moral reasoning is. Her research on real-life dilemmas added into the discussion a focus on issues of caring and responsibility to the issues of justice and principles Kohlberg had originally focused on. Other researchers (e.g., Ford & Lowery, 1986; Galotti, Kozberg, & Farmer, 1991; Walker, 1984), while reporting evidence of both kinds of issues in people's self-reported actual moral dilemmas, were not as likely to find large gender differences in reasoning as some readers of Gilligan had expected.

More Recent Work on Moral Development

Current work in the field of moral development has some interesting parallels with work on dual-process theories of cognition discussed earlier in the chapter. Psychologist Jonathan Haidt (2001, 2007, 2008) argues that moral reasoning actually stems from the operation of two independent systems. One yields quick and automatic judgments, even when the reasoner has difficulty explaining the basis for his reactions. Another, which operates more slowly, more intentionally, and more rationally, provides justification for one's moral judgments.

Haidt (2001) believes that the kind of moral reasoning studied by Kohlberg and Gilligan represents only a small portion of moral judgment. In his view, we arrive at many of the moral judgments we come to by a process more like perception. We simply "see" that something is wrong, even when we cannot articulate all the reasons to support our feelings. According to Haidt, the reasoning we do is often done after the fact to try to justify the intuition. Table 13.5 provides a list of the general features of the intuitive and the reasoning systems. You'll notice, I hope, a lot of overlap with the dual-process model of cognition advanced by Klaczynski (2001a, 2001b, 2005), discussed earlier. Here again, both processes of

Table 13–5 General features of intuitive and reasoning systems

The intuitive system	The reasoning system
Fast and effortless	Slow and effortful
Process is unintentional and runs automatically	Process is intentional and controllable
Process is inaccessible; only results enter awareness	Process is consciously accessible and viewable
Does not demand attentional resources	Demands attentional resources, which are limited
Parallel distributed processing	Serial processing
Pattern matching; thought is metaphorical, holistic	Symbol manipulation; thought is truth preserving, analytical
Common to all mammals	Unique to humans over age 2 and perhaps some language-trained apes
Context dependent	Context independent
Platform dependent (depends on the brain and body that houses it)	Platform independent (the process can be transported to any rule following organism or machine)

SOURCE: Haidt (2001, p. 818).

moral judgment are thought to operate independently and to possibly arrive at different conclusions.

Haidt (2001) notes that the reasoning system is likely to predominate only in very limited circumstances: when there is little time pressure, when the person is motivated to think objectively and thoroughly about an issue, or when she has no preexisting beliefs she feels a need to defend. Thus, Haidt would find Kohlberg's program of research one that did focus on the reasoning system. In contrast, in confronting real-life issues such as abortion or euthanasia (such as was the case in Gilligan's research), the intuitive system will come to predominate, and the reasoning system is "likely to be hired out like a lawyer by various motives, employed only to seek confirmation of preordained conclusions" (p. 822). Haidt argues, in fact, that in most real-life circumstances, moral intuitions are the "dog" and moral reasoning is the "tail" the dog wags. That is, Haidt believes that in many real-life circumstances in which people confront real moral dilemmas, they *first* experience an emotional reaction, are likely to react or make judgments based on this emotional reaction, and use reasoning, if at all, generally to confirm their initial reaction (Haidt, 2007; see also Murphy, Wilde, Ogden, Barnard, & Calder, 2009, for a relevant empirical investigation supporting this claim).

Haidt (2001) believes that moral judgment develops in ways analogous to the development of phonemic recognition and production, which we discussed in Chapter 5. You may recall that we saw there that infants seem to come into the world initially equipped to discriminate among, and produce, a wider variety of phonemes than they end up recognizing and producing by the time they are 2 or 3 years old. Presumably, exposure to their first language points them in the direction of making certain distinctions while ignoring other ones that are not used in their native language.

In much the same way, Haidt (2001), borrowing on work by cross-cultural and comparative psychologists, argues that children are born with a sense of certain moral intuitions such as sympathy and loyalty. However, different cultures emphasize certain moral issues over others, and a child's socialization into a particular culture causes him to pay more attention to those issues that his culture emphasizes, while paying less attention to those his particular culture glosses over. Thus, by the end of childhood, the intuitive moral system is largely in place.

What develops in adolescence, then, is the reasoning system. Although reasoning is often hijacked by the intuitive system, according to Haidt (2001, 2007), it sometimes *is* used to override initial intuitions. Adolescents and adults can and do make arguments that are used to persuade both others and themselves about the relative priority of different moral principles or issues. We saw in Chapter 12 that adolescents begin to be able to juggle multiple premises and to construct multiple mental models as they develop their reasoning abilities, and this in turn facilitates their reasoning to be more thorough, more efficient, more logical, and applicable to a wider set of circumstances. Moral judgment, it seems, provides yet another venue for reasoning.

EPISTEMOLOGICAL DEVELOPMENT

The focus of this chapter is on the broader impacts of adolescent cognitive development, so it is very appropriate that our penultimate substantive section of the chapter be centered on the topic of epistemological development—that is, the development of a theory of knowledge. As adolescents mature, they begin to develop a broad framework of knowledge—what it is, how it is acquired, how someone knows something, and how someone evaluates claims as being true, false, useful, or not useful.

Perry's Scheme

William Perry (1970, 1981) proposed an influential theory of epistemological development that applies mostly to middle and older adolescents. Like the work of Kohlberg, Perry's scheme is based on a Piagetian stage-like model of cognitive development. Thus, Perry sees qualitative differences in overall outlook among adolescents at different points in their epistemological development.

Perry (1970, 1981) created a scheme consisting of nine different positions of epistemological development that can be grouped into three major levels, which Perry termed dualism, multiplism, and relativism. Table 13.6 provides an overview of the positions. Space constraints prohibit a detailed examination of each position, so I will focus here instead on the three major levels.

Table 13–6   Scheme of cognitive and ethical development

Dualism modified	Position 1	Authorities know, and if we work hard, read every word, and learn Right Answers, all will be well.
	Transition	But what about those Others I hear about? And different opinions? And Uncertainties? Some of our own Authorities disagree with each other or don't seem to know, and some give us problems instead of Answers.
	Position 2	True Authorities must be Right, the others are frauds. We remain Right. Others must be different and Wrong. Good Authorities give us problems so we can learn to find the Right Answer by our own independent thought.
	Transition	But even Good Authorities admit they don't know all the answers *yet*!
	Position 3	Then some uncertainties and different opinions are real and legitimate *temporarily*, even for Authorities. They're working on them to get to the Truth.
	Transition	But there are *so many* things they don't know the Answers to! And they won't for a long time.

Table 13–6 (Continued)

Relativism discovered ↓	Position 4a	Where Authorities don't know the Right Answers, everyone has a right to his own opinion; no one is wrong!
	Transition *(and/or)*	But some of my friends ask me to support my opinions with facts and reasons.
	Transition	Then what right have They to grade us? About what?
	Position 4b	In certain courses Authorities are not asking for the Right Answer; They want us to *think* about things in a certain way, *supporting* opinion with data. That's what they grade us on.
	Transition	But this "way" seems to *work* in most courses, and even outside them.
	Position 5	Then *all* thinking must be like this, even for Them. Everything is relative but not equally valid. You have to understand how each context works. Theories are not Truth but metaphors to interpret data with. You have to think about your thinking.
	Transition	But if everything is relative, am I relative too? How can I know I'm making the Right Choice?
	Position 6	I see I'm going to have to make my own decisions in an uncertain world with no one to tell me I'm Right.
Commitments in Relativism developed ↓	Transition	I'm lost if I don't. When I decide on my career (or marriage or values) everything will straighten out.
	Position 7	Well, I've made my first Commitment!
	Transition	Why didn't that settle everything?
	Position 8	I've made several commitments. I've got to balance them—how many, how deep? How certain, how tentative?
	Transition	Things are getting contradictory. I can't make logical sense out of life's dilemmas.
	Position 9	This is how life will be. I must be wholehearted while tentative, fight for my values yet respect others, believe my deepest values right yet be ready to learn. I see that I shall be retracing this whole journey over and over—but, I hope, more wisely.

SOURCE: Perry (1981, p. 79).

Dualism is the first epistemological level. It draws its name from the fact that adolescents at this level see the world in terms of right and wrong, good and bad, and black and white. In terms of epistemology, students in dualism assume that right answers exist for every question and that hard work and effort are the key to finding these absolutely correct answers. The process of learning is seen somewhat as the collection of these right answers amassed from obediently completing every assignment given. Teaching is seen as the dispensation of right answers, perhaps sometimes in disguised ways, so that the students are forced to "find the right answers for themselves."

Especially when they get to college, however, students begin to notice that not everyone agrees on what the "right" answers are for certain issues. Smart, ethical, good people take different positions on questions such as whether gay marriage should be legal or whether euthanasia should be allowed in certain cases. Even in the classroom, this diversity of opinion sprouts up—students discussing *Hamlet,* say, have different interpretations of what his famous soliloquy means. At first, the student copes with this diversity by trying to distinguish between the "true" authorities and experts in a field and the "pretenders." The true authorities are the ones with the true right answers, and the student sees her job as sorting through the various opinions and other clues to figure out who the true authorities are.

Eventually, dualism gives way to *multiplism*, an epistemological position in which the student comes to see that there may be no right answers. At first, the student may see this state of affairs as a temporary one—for example, experts in English literature have not *yet* agreed on the true interpretation of Hamlet's soliloquy, but they will sometime in the future. Gradually, however, the student starts to see that time is *not* likely to tell—that, in fact, there are some instances in which right answers will never be known, because right answers do not exist. In many ways, this is a very liberating position! If no interpretation of a Shakespearean play can be declared to be correct, then, the student concludes, every interpretation is simply a matter of personal opinion. Thus, none is better or worse than any other—each one is equally useful for the person who believes it.

This democratic acceptance first becomes evident in fields such as literature and creative arts, spreading gradually to social studies. Fields like math and science are seen, initially, as bastions of right answers and true authorities. Some students cling to these disciplines, feeling an attraction to a realm of knowledge with certain facts that are either true or false. It's comforting at this point in development to have firm ground to stand on, to know that 2 plus 2 equals 4.

However, fairly soon, it becomes obvious that this arithmetic fact is true only in a certain framework (such as a particular base system). Even science and mathematics are shown to have a restricted number of absolute truths, and a study of the history of either discipline soon reveals that even these disciplines are full of different answers championed by different proponents. A particular fact or truth (e.g., the world is flat) can be discredited by further work. Uncertainty is unavoidable, even in the "hard science" disciplines.

But, if no absolute right answers exist for most questions, how is it that a teacher or professor can evaluate a student's academic work? If Kimmie writes a paper interpreting *Romeo and Juliet,* and in it she sincerely and grammatically expresses her opinion, how can a prof grade this response? Previously, the student expected grades to reflect how many right answers were in a paper, or perhaps how much effort and obedience the paper reflected. Now, however, the student sees a dilemma: There's no fair basis for a grade, since all interpretations of *Romeo and Juliet* are seen, by a student in the multiplism stage, as equally valid.

Students at this developmental moment can become cynical and alienated and actually get stuck in their epistemological journey. Perry (1970) calls this becoming "entrenched" in an "anything goes" mentality—if everything is simply a matter of opinion, and if opinions can't be challenged or assessed, then the student has as much right to his worldview as anyone and shouldn't have to "play" the "academic game" with profs who seem to be handing out wholly arbitrary grades.

Although not all students progress to the next level (unfortunately), the ones who do enter what Perry (1970, 1981) terms *relativism.* Students in this position start to realize that, although there may not be many absolute right answers, some ideas and interpretations are better than others. That is, the student comes to see that there are criteria—such things as coherence, explanatory power, or integrity—with which candidate ideas or interpretations can be assessed.

Moreover, students come to adopt this approach to thinking broadly— in many realms of their schooling—as well as to their own lives. As one example, students at my institution (Carleton College) spend their first 2 years exploring possibilities for their college major. (Carleton does not permit students to declare a major until spring of their sophomore year, and even among students who "know" their major when they arrive, many—perhaps as many as half—change their minds.) At some point many students have expressed to me a feeling of being almost overwhelmed by the possibilities in front of them—there are so many things they are interested in that it seems a shame to choose only one. But, as the time draws near, it has amazed me to see how many students start to think about how some of their interests take priority over others (Galotti, 1999b; Galotti et al., 2006). They stop thinking that there is one true, absolutely right major for them (which, in turn, takes a lot of pressure off the decision) and start to think about how to make trade-offs among their interests, their career plans, their time commitments, and other factors.

Perry (1970, 1981) describes the final positions of his scheme as being centered on the process of making commitments—to a value system, to a career, to a life partner, to a philosophical or political outlook. Mature commitments, according to Perry, can only be made when a student has achieved the level of relativism in epistemological development. That is, a student searching for the "right" career or "right" major or "right" person to marry is not in a position to make a mature commitment, because such a choice requires an understanding that few absolute right answers exist.

Women's Ways of Knowing

Perry's work has not been without its critics. The largest criticism parallels the one leveled by Carol Gilligan at Lawrence Kohlberg: Perry's original sample of students drew almost exclusively on the responses of male undergraduates at Harvard University in the classes of 1958 and 1963. Later researchers, including most prominently Mary Belenky, Blythe Clinchy, Nancy Goldberger, and Jill Tarule (1986; Goldberger, Tarule, Clinchy, & Belenky, 1996), argued that women sometimes chart a different course in their epistemological development. Belenky and collaborators argued that today's predominant culture, historically dominated by males, has come to prize rationality and objectivity over other, equally legitimate ways of understanding that may be more common among women and draw upon empathy or intuition.

Belenky et al. (1986) obtained their data from interviews of 135 women. Women were described by the investigators as seeking *connected knowing,* in which one discovers "truth" through a conscious process of trying to understand another's point of view. The kind of understanding sought involves discovery of a personal connection between the individual and the thing, event, person, or concept under consideration. It entails an acceptance and an appreciation for the thing, event, person, or concept on its own terms, within its own framework.

Photo 13.3   Choosing an undergraduate major can be a life-framing decision.

Another style of knowing these authors described, termed *separate knowing*, is perhaps more typical of males and also of women who are socialized in and successful in traditional male environments. This kind of knowing strives for objectivity and rigor, for the learner to "stand apart from" the thing, event, person, or concept being learned or understood. The orientation is toward impersonal rules or standards, and learning involves "mastery of" rather than "engagement with" the information to be learned.

Little has been done to assess how much the different responses articulated by Belenky et al.'s (1986) female participants are a function of gender, socioeconomic status, level of education, or other factors. Some work has replicated the existence of gender differences in separate and connected knowing, even among college undergraduates at an elite liberal arts college (Galotti, Clinchy, Ainsworth, Lavin, & Mansfield, 1999; Galotti, Drebus, & Reimer, 2001), yet much more remains to be done. More recent work has suggested that a person's "way of knowing" shifts with the context in which he is interacting, arguing against the idea that ways of knowing are stable tendencies (Ryan & David, 2003).

IDENTITY DEVELOPMENT

Perhaps the broadest impact of all in adolescent development is the development of a sense of identity—a reflective concept of the self, used to define who one is (Moshman, 2005). In brief, having an identity means having a mature sense of who you are and what your goals, values, and principles are. Moreover, having an identity means coming to see how your childhood experiences continue into the experiences of the adulthood yet to come—that is, to have a sense of your "life story" (Grovetant, 1993). Lifespan developmental psychologist Erik Erikson (1968) was the first to highlight the construction or discovery of identity as a major developmental task, typically first encountered during adolescence. Psychologist James Marcia (1966), however, is the one credited with operationalizing this idea and developing measures to study it.

Marcia (1966) saw identity development as proceeding through two or more phases, and these are depicted in Figure 13.4. His idea (which is quite consistent with some of the ideas William Perry articulated) was that a person's *identity status* was defined jointly by two factors: whether or not the person had made a definite choice or commitment (e.g., to a career, to a value system, to a romantic partner) and whether or not the person had gone through some sort of "crisis," or period of active doubt and exploration, in making that choice.

Figure 13–4   Marcia's identity statuses

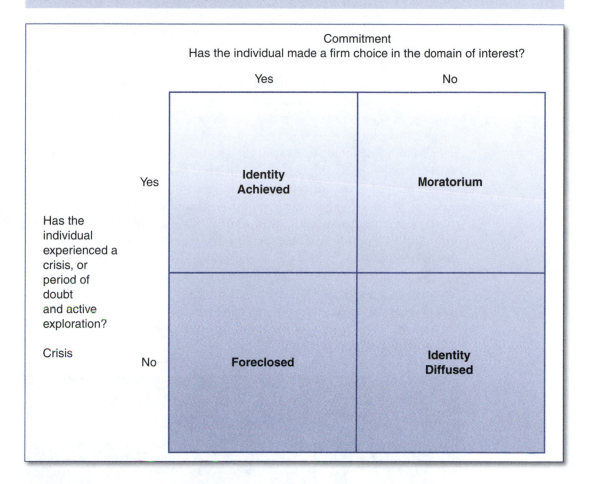

A teen in the *identity diffused* status has not made any commitments and has not developed a relevant set of values or principles with which to guide his goal setting and decision making in a given realm (e.g., career, education, political philosophy, religious affiliation). He has not experienced a period of crisis or doubt but, rather, either is in the early phase of identity development or is simply drifting along, with no set plan for the future.

An adolescent in the *foreclosure* status, in contrast, *is* very committed to a plan and/or to a set of values and principles. Similar to her identity diffused colleagues, however, she has never experienced a crisis or period of doubt. Typically, this indicates that she has adopted someone else's goals and plans, most often those of a parent or another significant adult figure.

Thus, adolescents in this status tend to have a very narrow vision for their future—and not much autonomy or power in making decisions. Students at my college who enter my office on their very first day of college, announcing they are "premed" or "prelaw" because both of their parents are doctors or lawyers and they've known since they were 5 what they'd be, tend to instantiate foreclosure.

The *moratorium* identity status is often typified by college students who "want to keep all their options open." They are actively exploring different options, experimenting and trying on for size the possibility of different majors, different careers, and different religious or political affiliations. The moratorium student is usually struggling and not in what others would call a "stable" state—that is, this individual is likely to remain in this period for only a brief period—a year or two (Moshman, 2005). Moratorium is a period of delay, in which the individual knows that a commitment must soon be made but is not yet ready to make it. Individuals in this status usually either resolve this crisis in a positive way, moving into the identity achieved status, or, in less successful cases, retreat into identity diffusion.

Marcia (1966) held that only individuals who experienced moratorium could move into the best outcome—the *identity achieved* status. The individual here has made one or more personal commitments, after having struggled to find his own path toward that decision. He has considered alternative options and weighed both the pros and the cons. This status is

Photo 13.4 Involvement in an activity such as theater may help high school or college students explore their identities.

seen as marking a successful end to adolescent development, as a bridge has been built from one's childhood to one's future adulthood. Accompanying identity achievement are increases in self-acceptance.

Marcia's (1966) proposal has been an influential one that has spawned much research, though it is not without critics (Bosma & Kunnen, 2008; Kroger, 2000; McLean & Breen, 2009; Njus & Johnson, 2008; Waterman, 2007). Many theorists find it a useful analogy for understanding one major realm of adolescent development (Moshman, 2005). Interestingly, it ties together some of the work we have previously reviewed on moral and epistemological development. Identity encompasses one's value system as well as one's view of knowledge and oneself as a learner and an agent in the world.

❖ ❖ ❖

And so, we come to the end of this chapter and, also, the end of this book. I've tried to convey in these chapters the idea that cognition changes dramatically over the first 2 decades of life. In particular, the cognitive challenges that individuals routinely face become more numerous and more complex as development proceeds. However, the cognitive skills, capacities, and strategies grow along with the challenges faced.

Cognition has captivated my attention and energy over the last three and a half decades, first as an undergraduate research assistant, then as a graduate student and faculty member, and these days as a parent and a teacher who plans curriculum and writes textbooks. My hope for you, the reader, is that at least some parts of this book have sparked your interest and curiosity and that, long after your course in cognitive development ends, you will continue to wonder about and be amazed by the flexible and multifaceted nature of cognitive development.

SUMMARY

1. Individuals differ in the way they approach many cognitive tasks. Some of these differences stem from variation in cognitive capacities—such things as working memory size, processing speed, and the use and efficiency of strategies. These are called ability differences.

2. Work comparing ability and developmental differences in approaches to cognition suggests that both stem at least partially from differences in the efficiency with which basic cognitive processes (such as recognizing a letter) are carried out. Higher-ability children and adults are faster than their lower-ability counterparts at performing these basic cognitive tasks. Moreover, with development, everyone grows more efficient at processing information.

3. Cognitive styles are stable distinct patterns with which people approach cognitive tasks. They often reflect a personal or motivational preference for dealing with information in one particular way rather than other, equally effective possible ways.

4. Klaczynski argues for the existence of two independent systems of cognition—a so-called dual-process theory. One, the analytic system, is effortful and under conscious control and focuses on the underlying structure of a problem, rather than its superficial characteristics. In contrast, the heuristic, or experiential, system functions automatically and is triggered by cues from the immediate environment.

5. Work on achievement motivation suggests that children, adolescents, and adults differ in their beliefs about their own abilities and styles, which in turn affects the goals they set for themselves when they approach cognitive, and specifically academic, tasks.

6. Reasoning about moral dilemmas is one kind of everyday reasoning, a form of thinking that involves personal relevance and is open-ended. Moral reasoning specifically involves thinking about principles involving rights, duties, virtue, justice, and care.

7. Lawrence Kohlberg constructed a theory of moral development that involves six changes, organized at three levels, based on extensive longitudinal studies. At each level, the complexity and depth of thinking grows. Each level requires a prerequisite degree of cognitive development as well as some social interaction.

8. Carol Gilligan proposed a somewhat different developmental scheme of moral development for women, arguing that Kohlberg's reliance on hypothetical moral dilemmas and his initial use of a largely male sample restricted his data to a narrow focus. Gilligan's work, involving interviews with women actually confronting moral dilemmas in their own lives, added another dimension to the study of moral development.

9. Jonathan Haidt argues that the reasoning we do with moral dilemmas engages only one of our two moral systems. The other, intuitive, system reacts more immediately and emotionally and often engages the reasoning system afterward to construct plausible reasons to justify the conclusions it has already reached.

10. Epistemological development is the development of a theory of knowledge—coming to an understanding of how information can be assessed, how theories relate to data, and how claims can be tested or proven. William Perry, studying male undergraduates at Harvard, advanced a stage-like theory of how college students develop epistemologically. More recent work by Belenky et al. has supplemented this view and challenged parts of it by focusing on the responses of women.

11. Identity development is the progressive construction of a sense of self that incorporates one's values, goals, and plans for the future. Following Erikson's (1968) description of the identity crisis in adolescence, James Marcia (1966) described four distinct identity statuses, which adolescents could be classified into. These statuses are jointly defined by whether or not an adolescent has experienced an active period of doubt and exploration (e.g., "crisis")

and whether or not she has made a firm commitment to a goal, plan, or set of values. The most mature status, identity achievement, can only be attained if the adolescent has experienced both a crisis and a commitment.

REVIEW QUESTIONS

1. Choose one individual difference that pertains to cognitive ability. Show how differences in that ability might affect performance on a complex cognitive task of your choice.

2. Describe the Keating and Bobbitt (1978) study and evaluate what their findings reveal about ability and developmental differences in cognition.

3. Explain the differences between cognitive abilities and cognitive styles.

4. Describe the distinction between analytic and experiential cognition, and explain how these two systems are thought to work together.

5. Give some examples of how children's beliefs about their abilities change with their level of development.

6. Describe the differences between a mastery-oriented and a helpless pattern of goal setting, and explore how these might relate to other ability and stylistic individual differences.

7. Compare and contrast Lawrence Kohlberg's and Carol Gilligan's developmental theories of moral reasoning.

8. Compare and contrast Klaczynski's dual-process theory of cognition with Haidt's proposal for two autonomous systems of moral thought.

9. Describe each of the levels of Perry's scheme of epistemological development.

10. Review each of Marcia's (1966) identity statuses, and consider what implications (if any) a person's identity status might have for her level of either moral or epistemological development.

KEY TERMS

Ability Differences

Achievement Motivation

Cognitive Styles

Dual-Process Theory of Cognition

Epistemological Development

Identity Development

Individual Differences

Matching Familiar Figures Test (MFFT)

Moral Dilemmas

GLOSSARY

Ability Differences   Individual differences stemming from difference in cognitive capacity, speed of processing, or strategy use or from some other basic intellectual difference.

Academic Skills   Skills and abilities that develop in formal educational settings, typically including reading, writing, and arithmetic.

Accommodation   In Piagetian theory, the change in mental structures that is elicited by new stimuli or experiences.

Achievement Motivation   An individual's beliefs about his or her own abilities and preferences and the kind of goals he or she adopts when tackling cognitive challenges.

Adaptation   In Piagetian theory, changes in reflexes or mental structures through assimilation and accommodation.

Alerting Network   An attentional network that activates to bring the child into an aroused and alert state when a new stimulus is presented.

Amygdala   A brain structure thought to be involved with formation of new memories, especially emotional memories.

Analytic Cognition   Cognition focused on individual features or aspects of a stimulus, rather than on the whole context.

Analytical System (of decision making)   An effortful and intentionally used system to process information and make rational decisions.

Animism   The concept of being alive or having biological properties.

Antisaccade Task   An experimental task used to measure the ability to control responses, in which a person is asked to fixate her eyes on a certain point and to avoid moving them to look at a newly appearing stimulus.

Appearance–Reality Distinction   Understanding that the way an object, a person, or an event might superficially appear can be different from the way that object, person, or event truly is.

Apprenticeship   A period of learning a specific set of job skills, acquired by closely observing a skilled practitioner and receiving specific feedback from that practitioner.

Assimilation   In Piagetian theory, the application of an existing mental structure to a new stimulus or experience.

Attention   The ability to allocate mental resources to certain tasks.

Attention Span   The duration for which an individual can focus mental energy on a task.

Attentional Inertia   The inability of young children to shift their focus from one task to another, or from one aspect of a task to another.

Attentional Network   An organized system of attention, specialized in function and localized in a certain area of the brain.

Auditory Perception   The interpretation or classification of sound stimuli.

Autobiographical Memory   Memory for specific, personally experienced events.

Automatic Processes   Cognitive processes that are carried out with minimal mental resources.

Babbling   The production of random syllables.

Basic Level (of a concept)   A level of abstraction thought to be psychologically most fundamental or simple.

Between-Subjects Design   A research paradigm in which different participants participate in different conditions.

Biases   Tendencies to think in a certain way or follow certain procedures regardless of the specific circumstances.

Brain Imaging   The construction of pictures of the anatomy and functioning of intact brains, through techniques such as MRI, CAT scans, or PET scans.

Capacity   The total amount of cognitive resources available at a given time.

CAT Scan   A computerized axial tomography imaging technique in which a focused beam of X-rays is passed through the body from many different angles.

Categorical Perception   The classification of sounds that vary on an acoustic dimension continuously into discrete categories.

Categorization   The organization of information into meaningful, coherent groups.

Central Executive The proposed component of working memory responsible for directing the flow of information and selecting what information to work with.

Cerebral Cortex The surface of the cerebrum, the largest structure of the brain.

Childhood Amnesia The relative paucity of autobiographical memories dating from before the age of about 3 years.

Circular Reaction In Piagetian theory, repeated behavioral patterns.

Class Inclusion Task A task developed by Piaget in which a young child is shown a set of objects (e.g., four toy cars and two toy trucks). The child is asked to compare the entire set (e.g., vehicles) with one of the subsets (e.g., toy cars).

Classical Conditioning A learning technique that builds acquired or learned reflexive responses on top of existing, hardwired reflexes.

Classification A task used by Piaget in which a young child is given a number of objects (e.g., wooden blocks) and asked to consistently sort them into groups.

Clinical Interviews A research paradigm in which an investigator begins by asking a series of open-ended questions but follows up with specific questions prepared in advance.

Cognition The processes by which an individual acquires, stores, manipulates, retrieves, and uses information.

Cognitive Development The study of how cognition changes in predictable, age-related ways over the course of infancy through adolescence.

Cognitive Styles Habitual and/or preferred means of approaching a cognitive task.

Cohort Effects The influence(s) of being born in a certain time and place.

Collection A term such as *family* or *forest* or *pile* that describes not only a group of individuals (e.g., *people* or *trees* or *blocks*) but also a specific organization of individuals in relation to each other.

Concept A mental representation of a category.

Concrete Operations A Piagetian stage of middle childhood marked by the acquisition of certain mental operations such as conservation, classification, and seriation.

Conditional Reasoning   A kind of logical reasoning problem with the first premise in the form "If p, then q" and the second premise either "p," "q," "not p," or "not q."

Conservation   A task developed by Piaget in which a young child is shown two stimuli that are equivalent in some respect (e.g., number or amount). The child watches while the experimenter makes a particular transformation (e.g., spreads apart a row of checkers or pours liquid from a short, wide glass into a thin, narrow glass) and is asked whether the original aspect of the two stimuli now differs.

Constancies (perceptual)   The lack of change in perceptual interpretation as a stimulus undergoes objective change as a function of the viewer's changing angle of vision. Examples include size constancy and shape constancy.

Cooing   The production of vowel sounds in early infancy.

Correlation   The degree of linear relationship between two variables, measured on a scale from −1 to +1 with higher absolute values indicating stronger linear relationships.

Correlational Studies   Research paradigms that make use of correlations as the main method of data analysis.

Critical Period   A developmental period during which an infant or a child is particularly sensitive to environmental input and must develop a structure or an ability if it is ever going to emerge.

Cross-Sectional Comparisons   Contrasts between different individuals at different ages.

Decision Making   The cognitive process(es) by which an individual selects one course of action from among alternatives.

Deductive Reasoning   Drawing logically necessary conclusions from premises.

Deferred Imitation   Sequences of behavior that are reproduced after some time interval, usually of days or weeks.

Discourse Knowledge   Understanding the mechanics of how a conversation should work.

Divided Attention   The ways in which a person allocates mental focus or energy to two or more tasks simultaneously.

Drill and Practice   An approach to teaching basic arithmetic facts involving lots of repetition and emphasizing automatic retrieval of facts.

Dual-Process Theory of Cognition   A view that cognitive development progresses along two independent trajectories: (a) analytic and (b) experiential or heuristic.

Dual Representation   The idea that a symbol can have two meanings—as an object and as a marker referring to another object.

Ecological Validity   A property of research such that the focus of study is something that occurs naturally outside an experimental laboratory.

Egocentrism   A concept in Piagetian theory pertaining to a child's inability to take the point of view of another person.

Elicited Imitation Task   An experimental paradigm in which infants are shown an unusual sequence of actions performed on novel objects and asked to demonstrate their memory of the sequence sometime in the future.

Empiricism   A philosophical position emphasizing the role of experience in the acquisition of knowledge.

Encapsulation   The degree to which the mechanisms that deal with a particular cognitive process are specialized only for that process.

Encoding   The cognitive process(es) by which information is translated into a mental or an internal representation and stored.

Encoding Specificity Principle   A principle of retrieval specifying that when information is first encoded, it incorporates information from its original context such that, at the time of recall, it is more easily retrieved in its original context.

Episodic Memory   A portion of long-term memory thought to store memory of specific events.

Epistemological Development   The development of a theory of knowledge.

Equilibration   In Piagetian theory, stability of cognitive structures.

Event-Related Potentials (ERPs)   An electrical recording technique to measure the response of the brain to various stimulus events.

Executive Functioning   Cognition including planning, implementation of strategies, inhibiting inappropriate responses, resisting distraction, and using working memory to process information.

Executive Network   An attentional network that helps a child inhibit competing responses and maintain vigilance in the face of distraction.

Experiential System (of decision making)   An automatic system to process information and make intuitive decisions.

Experiment   A test of a scientific theory in which the researcher controls and manipulates the independent variable(s).

Experimental Studies   Research designs based on experiments.

Explicit Memory   Consciously recalled or recollected memory.

Extended Mapping   The processes by which children learn all the dimensions of meaning and nuances of usage of a word.

Eyewitness Memory   A narrative memory of a personally witnessed event.

False Belief Tasks   Tasks that require a reasoner to distinguish between his own knowledge and that of another.

Fast Mapping   The processes by which young children quickly learn some aspects of the meaning of a new word after one or very few exposures to that word.

Flashbulb Memory   A phenomenon in which people recall their personal circumstances (e.g., where they were, whom they were with, what they were doing) at the time they heard of or witnessed an unexpected and very significant event.

fMRI (functional magnetic resonance imaging)   A brain imaging technique that uses MRI equipment to examine blood flow in different regions of the brain.

Folk Biology   A non-expert layperson's understanding of the principles of biology.

Folk Psychology   A non-expert layperson's understanding of the principles of psychology.

Forebrain   The part of the brain containing the cerebral cortex, as well as the thalamus, hypothalamus, amygdala, and hippocampus.

Formal Education   Education with an explicit curriculum, designed to teach general-purpose skills that are thought to have wide generalizability.

Formal Operations   A Piagetian stage of adolescence marked by the acquisition of the ability to reason abstractly and hypothetically.

Frontal Lobe   A division of the cerebral cortex located just behind the forehead, containing the motor cortex, frontal cortex, and prefrontal cortex.

Global Processing   Perceptual processing that concentrates on the larger features or aspects of a stimulus.

Grammar   A system of linguistic rules that produces well-formed or "legal" entities such as sentences.

Gray Matter   Substance in the cerebral hemispheres consisting of the cell bodies and dendrites of the neurons in the brain, as well as glial cells, and mainly serving the function of routing sensory and motor information within the brain.

Guided Participation   Learning to perform a task by interaction with a skilled practitioner who provides scaffolding of the to-be-learned task.

Habituation   In learning theory, the lack of response to a stimulus after repeated or prolonged exposure to it.

Heuristics   A shortcut method of thinking or problem solving.

Higher-Order Cognitive Process   A cognitive process that makes use of the functioning of more basic cognitive processes and/or involves using and manipulating information, rather than acquiring or storing it.

Hindbrain   The part of the brain containing the most evolutionary primary structures that maintain life support and balance, and transmit information to the spinal cord.

Hippocampus   A structure of the brain, located in the medial temporal lobe, thought to be involved in the formation and storage of memories.

Holistic Cognition   Cognition focused on the context surrounding a stimulus, including environmental, cultural, and philosophical influences.

Identity Development   The formation of a reflective concept of the self, used to define who one is and what one's goals, values, and principles are.

Implicit Memory   Memory that is not deliberate or conscious.

Impossible/Possible Events Task   An experimental paradigm in which infants are shown sequences of actions that either violate or do not violate laws of physics.

Individual Differences   Stable patterns of performance that differ qualitatively and/or quantitatively across different people.

Inductive Reasoning   Drawing conclusions from premises that are suggested but not necessarily true.

Infancy   The period of development from birth to about 12–24 months.

Infant-Directed Speech (IDS)   Speech by adults to infants, marked by the following characteristics: lots of repetition, higher average pitch, a more extreme range of pitch, more stress on content words, shorter utterances, and longer pauses.

Informal Education   Education that is modeled on an "apprenticeship" system, with the student acquiring very specific skills relevant to a trade or practice.

Information-Processing Theory   An approach to cognition that uses a computer metaphor to describe the way information is acquired, stored, processed, and transmitted.

Instrumental Conditioning   A branch of learning theory describing the acquisition of voluntary (nonreflexive) behaviors, emphasizing the contingency between an organism's responses and the consequences of those responses.

Intersubjectivity   Sharing mental control, acting together, and sharing experience in harmony with other people.

Knowledge Base   Stored information including all general knowledge possessed by an individual (sometimes known also as semantic memory).

Knowledge Representation   The mental depiction, storage, and organization of information.

Language   A system of communication that is governed by a system of rules (a grammar) that allows an infinite number of ideas to be expressed.

Language Acquisition Device (LAD)   A theoretically postulated "organ," thought by nativist theorists to exist at birth to aid children in acquiring a sophisticated system of language.

Lexical Development   The growth of the set of words one produces and/or understands.

Lexicon   A mental store thought to hold an individual's knowledge of words, including their pronunciation, definition, and part of speech.

Local Processing   Perceptual processing that focuses on smaller features or aspects of a stimulus.

Longitudinal Comparisons   Contrasts between the same individual at different ages.

Long-Term Memory (LTM) A memory store thought to have a large, possibly infinite, capacity that holds onto incoming information for long periods, perhaps permanently.

Matching Familiar Figures Test (MFFT) An experimental task used to measure cognitive tempo, or the degree to which an individual is impulsive or reflective.

Mediation Deficiency (of a strategy) Failure of a strategy to work effectively, even when the child thinks to use it.

Memory The cognitive processes underlying the storage, retention, and retrieval of information.

Mental Models Approach (to reasoning) Constructing different mental scenarios to depict possible conclusions consistent with premises.

Mental Representation An internal depiction of information.

Metacognition Knowledge or awareness about one's own cognitive processes and functioning.

Midbrain The part of the brain containing structures that are involved in relaying information between other brain regions or in regulating levels of alertness.

Moral Dilemma Hypothetical problems in which two or more ethical principles or concerns come into conflict.

Morpheme The smallest unit of meaning in a word.

MRI A brain and body imaging technique that surrounds the region to be scanned with a strong magnetic field to produce a composite three-dimensional image.

Multitasking Performing more than one cognitive task at a time.

Mutual Exclusivity Principle During the early phases of word learning in toddlerhood, the idea that toddlers will map a new word onto an object or event that they do not yet have an existing word for.

Myelin A layer of fatty insulation that wraps around the axons of certain neurons and helps speed neuronal transmission.

Myelination A process of brain development in which myelin becomes wrapped around the axons of neurons, speeding transmission of neural impulses.

Naïve Theory Approach (to conceptual development)   A theoretical framework for conceptual development that holds that children construct commonsense understandings or theories that have individual concepts embedded in them and that whatever concepts are acquired at any point in development are constrained by the existing knowledge base.

Narrative Memory   Memory for autobiographical events that the child recalls experiencing, witnessing, or participating in.

Nativism   A philosophical position emphasizing the role of innate structures in the acquisition of knowledge.

Neo-Piagetians   A group of developmental psychologists, heavily influenced by some aspects of Piaget's theory, who add additional postulates to Piaget's theory.

Neurons   Basic cells of the nervous system that transmit electrical signals and communicate with each other by means of chemical neurotransmitter substances.

Number Sense   An approach to teaching mathematics that emphasizes deep conceptual understanding of underlying principles.

Object Coherence   The knowledge that a partially occluded object has unity as a single entity.

Object Identity   The knowledge that an object that reappears in view is the same one that was previously encountered.

Object Permanence   In Piagetian theory, the understanding that objects and other people continue to exist even when the infant is not in sensory or motor contact with them.

Observational Studies   Research investigations that record behaviors and responses that occur in naturalistic settings.

Occipital Lobe   A division of the cerebral cortex located at the back of the head that is involved in the processing of visual information.

Ontology   A conception of the basic categories of existence.

Orienting Network   An attentional network that directs a child's focus toward a particular stimulus.

Overextension   The tendency for toddlers to use a word to refer to a wider range of things than would an adult (e.g., using *doggie* for all animals).

Parietal Lobe   A division of the cerebral cortex located at the top rear part of the head that integrates sensory information from different modalities.

Perception   The cognitive processes involved in interpretation of sensory information to yield a meaningful understanding.

Perceptual Learning   The phenomenon whereby as a child (or an adult) acquires experience in a domain, she becomes more sensitive to subtle differences among stimuli.

PET Scan   A positron emission tomography brain imaging technique that shows which areas of the brain are most active at a given point in time.

Phone   A sound of speech.

Phoneme   A unit of sound that makes a meaningful difference in a language.

Phonemic Awareness   An ability to understand that words are composed of separable sounds; this predicts later literacy abilities.

Phonics   An approach to reading instruction emphasizing the relationship between spoken and written language.

Phonological Loop   The proposed component of working memory responsible for storing auditory information for brief periods.

Physical Activity Play   Play involving exercise or vigorous movement.

Planning   Devising and coordinating actions aimed at achieving a goal and at monitoring the effectiveness of the actions for reaching the goal.

Poverty of the Stimulus Argument   The idea that the environment does not provide enough structure to support empirical learning of language in the amount of time that children typically require.

Practice Effect   The decrease in the amount of mental effort required to complete a task after many repetitions.

Pragmatic Knowledge   Knowledge of the communicative functions of language.

Prefrontal Cortex   A region of the frontal lobe involved in executive functioning.

Preoperational Stage   A Piagetian stage of early childhood marked by the acquisition of mental representation and symbolic functions.

Prepotent Response   A default or readily activated behavior that must be inhibited in order to exhibit an alternative behavior.

Pretense Play   Play involving fantasy, imagination, and behaving "as if" a different world were true.

Primacy Effect   The improvement in retention of information learned at the beginning of a task.

Production Deficiency (of a strategy)   Failure to think to use a strategy that would have been effective.

Productivity   The property of language that allows an infinite number of sentences to be constructed from a finite number of elements.

Quasi-Experimental Design   An empirical study that lacks full experimental control, for example, through nonrandom assignment of participants to conditions.

Reasoning   The cognitive processes used in drawing inferences from given information to generate conclusions.

Recall Memory   The retrieval of information in which the individual must generate most of the information without prompts or cues.

Recency Effect   The improvement in retention of information learned at the end of a task.

Recognition Memory   The retrieval of information in which the individual must decide if the presented information has been previously encountered.

Reflective Abstraction   An ability proposed by Piaget to emerge during adolescence, in which new knowledge and understanding is acquired simply from thinking about one's own thoughts and noticing general patterns or contradictions.

Regularity   The property of language that requires that sentences follow a system of rules, called a grammar.

Rehearsal   A memory strategy of repeating information (either aloud or silently) to facilitate retention and later retrieval.

Research Methods   The design of empirical studies and the techniques used to measure dependent variables in those empirical studies.

Retrieval   The processes by which stored information is brought back to conscious awareness.

Retrieval Cue   A stimulus that helps a person recall or recognize stored information.

Rule Assessment Approach   An analysis of performance on a cognitive task in terms of a nested series of rules that predict performance.

Scaffolding   Assistance (either physical or verbal) provided by a competent peer or adult to a younger child or novice as he or she learns to complete a task. As the novice gains proficiency, the assistance is gradually faded out.

Schema   Organized representation of knowledge that often contains both fixed and variable parts.

Script   A schema for routine events.

Selective Attention   Focusing mental energy on one task to the exclusion of others.

Semantic Memory   A portion of long-term memory thought to store general knowledge.

Sensorimotor Stage   A Piagetian stage of infancy marked by the absence of the capacity for mental representation.

Sequential Touching Task   An experimental paradigm in which infants are presented with objects from two (or more) different categories and the order in which the infant touches the objects is recorded.

Serial Position Effect   The phenomenon that items at the beginning or end of a list are more easily recalled than items from the middle of the list.

Seriation   A task used by Piaget in which a young child is given a number of objects (e.g., cups or sticks) and asked to consistently order them along one dimension (e.g., size or length).

Shape Constancy   The perception that an object retains its shape even when the observer's angle of view with respect to that object changes.

Size Constancy   The perception that an object retains its size even when the observer moves closer to or farther away from that object.

Social Cognition   The cognitive processes involved in processing information about other people and social situations.

Sociolinguistic Knowledge   Understanding how language use differs as a function of the social class or status of a conversational partner, the formality of the setting, or other relevant contextual factors.

Source Monitoring Error   Confusing the original source of information in memory.

Stage Theory   Theories of development that posit qualitatively different periods (stages).

Strategies   Deliberate plans or routines used to carry out particular cognitive tasks.

Stroop Task   A task invented by J. R. Stroop in which a participant sees a list of words (color terms) printed in an ink color that differs from the word printed (e.g., *green* printed in blue ink). The participant is asked to name the ink colors of the words in the list, and demonstrates great difficulty in doing so when the words on the list are actual color names.

Subordinate Level (of a concept)   A level of abstraction that makes more distinctions among exemplars than does a basic level or superordinate level.

Superordinate Level (of a concept)   A level of abstraction that makes fewer distinctions among exemplars than does a basic or subordinate level.

Synapses   Gaps, or junctions between neurons, through which chemical neurotransmitters are sent.

Synaptic Pruning   The elimination of synaptic connections that are infrequently used.

Syntax   The structure of words within a sentence.

Taxonomic Principle   During the early phases of word learning in toddlerhood, the idea that when children have a word for an object, they generalize that word to other objects that are of the same kind as the one they know about.

Temporal Lobe   A division of the cerebral cortex located on the side of the head, involved in the processing of auditory information and in some aspects of memory.

Theory of Mind   An understanding of what another person might be thinking, feeling, believing, or expecting or what her reaction might be to a specific set of circumstances.

Thinking   The cognitive process(es) used in transforming or manipulating information.

Tower of London (TOL) Task   A neuropsychological task often used to assess the functioning of the prefrontal cortex. Participants are asked to rearrange a set of three colored balls on three pegs by moving one ball at a time using the minimum number of moves.

Underextension   The tendency of a toddler to use a new word to refer only to a subset of the things that an adult would use the same word to refer to.

Utilization Deficiency (of a strategy) Failure of a strategy to work effectively when it is first adopted.

Visual Cliff An experimental apparatus used to study depth perception in infants, consisting of a sheet of glass with a patterned cloth under it, to simulate the appearance of a cliff.

Visual Paired Comparison (VPC) Task An experimental paradigm in which infants are shown one stimulus for familiarization, followed by presentation of the old stimulus alongside a new one, and observers record which stimulus the infant looks at.

Visual Preference Paradigm An experimental paradigm in which infants are shown two stimuli, and their reliably attending more to one than the other is taken as evidence that they discriminate between them.

Visuospatial Sketch Pad The proposed component of working memory responsible for storing visual or spatial information for brief periods.

White Matter Substance in the cerebral hemispheres consisting of the axons of neurons in the brain, many of which have a fatty substance called myelin wrapped around them, which is white in color.

Whole Language An approach to reading instruction emphasizing meaning and understanding of the text and involving higher-order cognitive processes such as making predictions and inferences.

Whole Object Assumption The assumption made by toddlers during the early years of word learning that new words name single whole objects.

Within-Subjects Design A research paradigm in which the same participants participate in all conditions of a study.

Working Memory (WM) A memory structure described as consisting of a limited capacity work space that can be allocated, somewhat flexibly, into storage space and control processing.

Zone of Proximal Development A term developed by Vygotsky to refer to the range of what a learner is able to do with and without help or scaffolding.

REFERENCES

Ahmavaara, A., & Houston, D. M. (2007). The effects of selective schooling and self-concept on adolescents' academic aspiration: An examination of Dweck's self-theory. *British Journal of Educational Psychology, 77,* 613–632.

Akshoomoff, N. (2002). Selective attention and active engagement in young children. *Developmental Neuropsychology, 22,* 625–642.

Alloway, T. P., & Gathercole, S. E. (2005). Working memory and short-term sentence recall in young children. *European Journal of Cognitive Psychology, 17,* 207–220.

Alloway, T. P., Gathercole, S. E., Willis, C., & Adams, A.-M. (2004). A structural analysis of working memory and related cognitive skills in young children. *Journal of Experimental Child Psychology, 87,* 85–106.

Amso, D., & Casey, B. J. (2006). Beyond what develops when: Neuroimaging may inform how cognition changes with development. *Current Directions in Psychological Science, 15,* 24–29.

Anderson, D. R., Bryant, J., Wilder, A., Santomero, A., Williams, M., & Crawley, A. M. (2000). Researching *Blue's Clues:* Viewing behavior and impact. *Media Psychology, 2,* 179–194.

Anderson, D. R., Huston, A. C., Schmitt, K. L., Linebarger, D. L., & Wright, J. C. (2001). Early childhood television viewing and adolescent behavior: The recontact study. *Monographs of the Society for Research in Child Development, 66*(Serial No. 264), vii–147.

Anderson, D. R., & Pempek, T. A. (2005). Television and very young children. *American Behavioral Scientist, 48,* 505–522.

Anglin, J. M. (1993). Vocabulary development: A morphological analysis. *Monographs of the Society for Research in Child Development, 58*(10), v–165.

Asato, M. R., Sweeney, J. A., & Luna, B. (2006). Cognitive processes in the development of TOL performance. *Neuropsychologia, 44,* 2259–2269.

Aslin, R. N., Jusczyk, P. W., & Pisoni, D. B. (1998). Speech and auditory processing during infancy: Constraints on and precursors to language. In W. Damon (Series Ed.) and D. Kuhn & R. S. Siegler (Vol. Eds.), *Handbook of child psychology* (5th ed., Vol. 2, pp. 147–198). New York: Wiley.

Atance, C. M., & O'Neill, D. K. (2004). Acting and planning on the basis of a false belief: Its effects on 3-year-old children's reasoning about their own false beliefs. *Developmental Psychology, 40,* 953–964.

Atkinson, R. C., & Shiffrin, R. M. (1968). Human memory: A proposed system and its control processes. In K. W. Spence & J. T. Spence (Eds.), *The psychology of learning and motivation: Advances in research and theory* (Vol. 2, pp. 89–195). New York: Academic Press.

Atran, S., Medin, D., Lynch, E., Vapnarsky, V., Ucan Ek', E., & Sousa, P. (2001). Folkbiology doesn't come from folkpsychology: Evidence from Yukatec Maya in cross-cultural perspective. *Journal of Cognition and Culture, 1,* 3–42.

Baddeley, A. (1992). Working memory. *Science, 255,* 556–559.

Baddeley, A. (2007). *Working memory, thought, and action.* New York: Oxford University Press.

Baddeley, A. D. (1966). The influence of acoustic and semantic similarity on long-term memory for word sequences. *The Quarterly Journal of Experimental Psychology, 18,* 302–309.

Baddeley, A. D. (1986). *Working memory.* New York: Oxford University Press.

Baddeley, A. D. (1990). *Human memory: Theory and practice.* Boston: Allyn & Bacon.

Baddeley, A. D. (1996). Exploring the central executive. *The Quarterly Journal of Experimental Psychology, 49,* 5–28.

Baddeley, A. D., Gathercole, S. E., & Papagano, C. (1998). The phonological loop as a language learning device. *Psychological Review, 105,* 158–173.

Baillargeon, R. (1986). Representing the existence and the location of hidden objects: Object permanence in 6- and 8-month-old infants. *Cognition, 23,* 21–41.

Baillargeon, R. (1999). Young infants' expectations about hidden objects: A reply to three challenges. *Developmental Science, 2,* 115–132.

Baillargeon, R. (2008). Innate ideas revisited: For a principle of persistence in infants' physical reasoning. *Perspectives on Psychological Science, 3,* 2–13.

Baillargeon, R., & DeVos, J. (1991). Object permanence in young infants: Further evidence. *Child Development, 62,* 1227–1246.

Baillargeon, R., & Graber, M. (1987). Where's the rabbit? 5.5 month-old infants' representation of the height of a hidden object. *Cognitive Development, 2,* 375–392.

Baker-Ward, L., Gordon, B. N., Ornstein, P. A., Larus, D. M., & Clubb, P. A. (1993). Young children's long-term retention of a pediatric examination. *Child Development, 64,* 1519–1533.

Baker-Ward, L., & Ornstein, P. A. (1988). Age differences in visual-spatial memory performance: Do children really out-perform adults when playing *Concentration? Bulletin of the Psychonomic Society, 26,* 331–332.

Baldwin, D. A., Markman, E. M., & Melartin, R. L. (1993). Infants' ability to draw inferences about nonobvious object properties: Evidence from exploratory play. *Child Development, 64,* 711–728.

Banich, M. T. (2004). *Cognitive neuroscience and* neuropsychology (2nd ed.). Boston: Houghton Mifflin.

Baron, J. (2008). *Thinking and deciding* (4th ed). New York: Cambridge University Press.

Barr, R., Muentener, P., & Garcia, A. (2007). Age-related changes in deferred imitation from television by 6- to 18-month-olds. *Developmental Science, 10,* 910–921.

Bartgis, J., Lilly, A. R., & Thomas, D. G. (2003). Event-related potential and behavioral measures of attention in 5-, 7-, and 9-year-olds. *Journal of General Psychology, 130,* 311–335.

Barton, M. E., & Komatsu, L. K. (1989). Defining features of natural kinds and artifacts. *Journal of Psycholinguistic Research, 18,* 433–447.

Bauer, L., & Nation, P. (1993). Word families. *International Journal of Lexicography, 6,* 253–279.

Bauer, P. J. (2002a). Building toward a past: Construction of a reliable long-term recall memory system. In N. L. Stein, P. J. Bauer, & M. Rabinowitz (Eds.), *Representation, memory, and development: Essays in honor of Jean Mandler* (pp. 17–42). Mahwah, NJ: Erlbaum.

Bauer, P. J. (2002b). Long-term recall memory: Behavioral and neuro-developmental changes in the first 2 years of life. *Current Directions in Psychological Science, 11,* 137–141.

Bauer, P. J. (2006). Constructing a past in infancy: A neuro-developmental account. *Trends in Cognitive Science, 10,* 175–181.

Bauer, P. J. (2007). Recall in infancy: A neurodevelopmental account. *Current Directions in Psychological Science, 16,* 142–146.

Bauer, P. J., Wenner, J. A., Dropik, P. L., & Werweka, S. S. (2000). Parameters of remembering and forgetting in the transition from infancy to early childhood. *Monographs of the Society for Research in Child Development, 65*(4, Serial No. 263), v–204.

Bauer, P. J., Wiebe, S. A., Carver, L. J., Waters, J. M., & Nelson, C. A. (2003). Developments in long-term explicit memory late in the first year of life: Behavioral and electrophysiological indices. *Psychological Science, 14,* 629–635.

Behme, C., & Deacon, S. H. (2008). Language learning in infancy: Does the empirical evidence support a domain specific language acquisition device? *Philosophical Psychology, 21,* 641–671.

Belenky, M. F., Clinchy, B. McV., Goldberger, N. R., & Tarule, J. M. (1986). *Women's ways of knowing: The development of self, voice, and mind.* New York: Basic Books.

Berko, J. (1958). The child's learning of English morphology. *Word, 14,* 150–177.

Bernstein, D. M., Atance, C., Loftus, G. R., & Meltzoff, A. N. (2004). We saw it all along: Visual hindsight bias in children and adults. *Psychological Science, 15,* 264–267.

Bernstein, D. M., Loftus, G. R., & Meltzoff, A. N. (2005). Object identification in preschool children and adults. *Developmental Science, 8,* 151–161.

Beyth-Marom, R., Austin, L., Fischhoff, B., Palmgren, C., & Jacobs-Quadrel, M. (1993). Perceived consequences of risky behaviors: Adults and adolescents. *Developmental Psychology, 29,* 549–563.

Bialystok, E., & Senman, L. (2004). Executive processes in appearance-reality tasks: The role of inhibition of attention and symbolic representation. *Child Development, 75,* 562–579.

Bjorklund, D. F., & Green, B. L. (1992). The adaptive nature of cognitive immaturity. *American Psychologist, 47,* 46–54.

Bjorklund, D. F., & Harnishfeger, K. K. (1995). The evolution of inhibition mechanisms and their role in human cognition and behavior. In F. N. Dempster &

C. J. Brainerd (Eds.), *Interference and inhibition in cognition* (pp. 141–173). San Diego, CA: Academic Press.

Blackwell, L. S., Trzeniewski, K. H., & Dweck, C. S. (2007). Implicit theories of intelligence predict achievement across an adolescent transition: A longitudinal study and an intervention. *Child Development, 78,* 246–263.

Bloom, L. (1998). Language acquisition in its developmental context. In W. Damon (Series Ed.) and D. Kuhn & R. S. Siegler (Vol. Eds.), *Handbook of child psychology* (5th ed., Vol. 2, pp. 309–370). New York: Wiley.

Bloom, P. (2000). *How children learn the meanings of words.* Cambridge, MA: MIT Press.

Booth, A. E. (2008). The cause of infant categorization? *Cognition, 106,* 984–993.

Borke, H. (1975). Piaget's mountains revisited: Changes in the egocentric landscape. *Developmental Psychology, 11,* 240–243.

Bornstein, M. H., Kessen, W., & Weiskopf, S. (1976). Color vision and hue categorization in young infants. *Journal of Experimental Psychology: Human Perception and Performance, 2,* 115–129.

Bosma, H. A., & Kunnen, E. S. (2008). Identity-in-context is not yet identity development-in-context. *Journal of Adolescence, 31,* 281–289.

Bousfield, W. A. (1953). The occurrence of clustering in the recall of randomly arranged associates. *Journal of General Psychology, 49,* 229–240.

Bower, T. G. (1966a). Slant perception and shape constancy in infants. *Science, 151,* 832–834.

Bower, T. G. (1966b). The visual world of infants. *Scientific American, 215,* 80–92.

Bowerman, M. (1973). Structural relationships in children's utterances: Syntactic or semantic? In T. E. Moore (Ed.), *Cognitive development and the acquisition of language* (pp. 197–213). New York: Academic Press.

Brahmbhatt, S. B., McAuley, T., & Barch, D. M. (2008). Functional developmental similarities and differences in the neural correlates of verbal and nonverbal working memory tasks. *Neuropsychologia, 46,* 1020–1031.

Braine, M. D. S. (1963). The ontogeny of English phrase structure: The first phase. *Language, 39,* 1–13.

Brandone, A. C., & Gelman, S. A. (2009). Differences in preschoolers' and adults' use of generics about novel animals and artifacts: A window onto a conceptual divide. *Cognition, 110,* 1–22.

Bremner, J. G. (2001). Cognitive development: Knowledge of the physical world. In G. Bremner & A. Fogel (Eds.), *Blackwell handbook of infant development* (pp. 99–138). Malden, MA: Blackwell.

Brener, N. D., Kann, L., Kinchen, S. A., Grunbaum, J. A., Whalen, L., Eaton, D., et al. (2004, September 24). Methodology of the Youth Risk Behavior Surveillance System, 53(RR12), 1–13. Atlanta, GA: Centers for Disease Control and Prevention. Retrieved February 19, 2010, from http://www.cdc.gov/mmwr/preview/mmwrhtml/rr5312a1.htm

Brooks, P. J., Hanauer, J. B., Padowska, B., & Rosman, H. (2003). The role of selective attention in preschoolers' rule use in a novel dimensional card sort. *Cognitive Development, 18,* 195–215.

Brown, R. (1973). *A first language: The early stages.* Cambridge, MA: Harvard University Press.

Brown, R., & Kulik, J. (1977). Flashbulb memories. *Cognition, 5,* 73–99.

Brown, R. W. (1957). Linguistic determinism and the part of speech. *Journal of Abnormal and Social Psychology, 55,* 1–5.

Bruck, M., & Ceci, S. J. (1999). The suggestibility of children's memory. *Annual Review of Psychology, 50,* 419–439.

Bruck, M., & Ceci, S. (2004). Forensic developmental psychology: Unveiling four common misconceptions. *Current Directions in Psychological Science, 13,* 229–232.

Burack, J. A., Enns, J. T., Iarocci, G., & Randolph, B. (2000). Age differences in visual search for compound patterns: Long- versus short-range grouping. *Developmental Psychology, 36,* 731–740.

Bushnell, I. W. R. (2001). Mother's face recognition in newborn infants: Learning and memory. *Infant and Child Development, 10,* 67–74.

Butler, R. (1999). Information seeking and achievement motivation in middle childhood and adolescence: The role of conceptions of ability. *Developmental Psychology, 35,* 146–163.

Byrnes, J. P. (1998). *The nature and development of decision-making: A self-regulation model.* Mahwah, NJ: Erlbaum.

Byrnes, J. P., & Overton, W. F. (1986). Reasoning about certainty and uncertainty in concrete, causal, and propositional contexts. *Developmental Psychology, 22,* 793–799.

Camaioni, L. (2001). Early language. In G. Bremner & A. Fogel (Eds.), *Blackwell handbook of infant development* (pp. 404–426). Malden, MA: Blackwell.

Campbell, D. T., & Stanley, J. C. (1963). *Experimental and quasi-experimental designs for research.* Chicago: Rand McNally.

Canivez, G. L. (2008). Orthogonal higher order factor structure of the Stanford-Binet intelligence scales—fifth edition for children and adolescents. *School Psychology Quarterly, 23,* 533–541.

Carey, S. (1978). The child as word learner. In J. Bresnan, G. Miller, & M. Halle (Eds.), *Linguistic theory and psychological reality* (pp. 264–293). Cambridge, MA: MIT Press.

Carey, S. (1985). *Conceptual change in childhood.* Cambridge, MA: Bradford Books.

Carey, S. (1988). Conceptual differences between children and adults. *Mind and Language, 3,* 167–181.

Carey, S. (1996). Perceptual classification and expertise. In R. Gelman & T. Au (Eds.), *Perceptual and cognitive development* (pp. 49–69). San Diego, CA: Academic Press.

Carey, S. (2000a). The origin of concepts. *Journal of Cognition and Development, 1,* 37–41.

Carey, S. (2000b). Science education as conceptual change. *Journal of Applied Developmental Psychology, 21,* 13–19.

Carey, S., & Diamond, R. (1977). From piecemeal to configurational representation of faces. *Science, 195,* 312–313.

Carey, S., & Diamond, R. (1994). Are faces perceived as configurations more by adults than by children? *Visual Cognition, 1,* 253–274.

Carey, S., & Xu, F. (2001). Infants' knowledge of objects: Beyond object files and object tracking. *Cognition, 80,* 179–213.

Carlson, N. R. (2004). *Physiology of behavior* (8th ed). Boston: Allyn & Bacon.

Carraher, T. N., Carraher, D. W., & Schliemann, A. D. (1985). Mathematics in the streets and in the schools. *British Journal of Developmental Psychology, 3,* 21–29.

Carver, L. J., & Bauer, P. J. (2001). The dawning of a past: The emergence of long-term explicit memory in infancy. *Journal of Experimental Psychology, 130,* 726–745.

Casey, B. J., Cohen, J. D., Jezzard, P., Turner, R., Noll, D. C., Trainor, R. J., et al. (1995). Activation of prefrontal cortex in children during a nonspatial working memory task with functional MRI. *NeuroImage, 2,* 221–229.

Casey, B. J., Galvan, A., & Hare, T. A. (2005). Changes in cerebral functional organization during cognitive development. *Current Opinions in Neurobiology, 15,* 239–244.

Casey, B. J., Giedd, J. N., & Thomas, K. M. (2000). Structural and functional brain development and its relation to cognitive development. *Biological Psychology, 54,* 241–257.

Caviness, V. S., Jr., Kennedy, D. N., Richelme, C., Rademacher, J., & Filipek, P. A. (1996). The human brain age 7–11 years: A volumetric analysis based on magnetic resonance images. *Cerebral Cortex, 6,* 726–736.

Centers for Disease Control and Prevention. (2008). *National trends in risk behaviors.* National Center for Chronic Disease Prevention and Health Promotion, Division of Adolescent and School Health, October 16 (updated February 17, 2009). Retrieved December 30, 2008, from www.cdc.gov/healthyyouth/yrbs/trends.htm

Chall, J. (1992). The new reading debates: Evidence from science, art, and ideology. *Teachers College Record, 94,* 315–328.

Chall, J. S. (1983). *Stages of reading development.* New York: McGraw-Hill.

Chavajay, P., & Rogoff, B. (2002). Schooling and traditional collaborative social organization of problem solving by Mayan mothers and children. *Developmental Psychology, 38,* 55–66.

Cherry, E. C. (1953). Some experiments on the recognition of speech, with one and two ears. *Journal of the Acoustical Society of America, 25,* 975–979.

Chi, M. T. H., & Koeske, R. D. (1983). Network representation of a child's dinosaur knowledge. *Developmental Psychology, 19,* 29–39.

Chomsky, N. (1968). *Language and mind.* New York: Harcourt, Brace, & World.

Chomsky, N. (1977). *Essays on form and interpretation.* Amsterdam: North-Holland/Elsevier.

Chomsky, N. (1988). *Language and the problems of knowledge.* Cambridge, MA: MIT Press.

Chomsky, N. (1993). On the nature, use, and acquisition of language. In A. I. Goldman (Ed.), *Readings in philosophy and cognitive science* (Vol. C, pp. 511–534). Cambridge, MA: MIT Press.

Christakis, D. A., Zimmerman, F. J., DiGiuseppe, D. L., & McCarthy, C. A. (2004). Early television exposure and subsequent attentional problems in children. *Pediatrics, 113,* 708–713.

Churchland, P. M. (1988). *Matter and consciousness.* Cambridge, MA: MIT Press.

Clark, E. V. (1993). *The lexicon in acquisition.* New York: Cambridge University Press.

Cohen, L. B. (1991). Infant attention: An information processing approach. In M. J. S. Weiss & P. R. Zelazo (Eds.), *Newborn attention: Biological constraints and the influence of experience* (pp. 1–21). Westport, CT: Ablex.

Cohen, L. B., & Cashon, C. H. (2001a). Do 7-month-old infants process independent features or facial configurations? *Infant and Child Development, 10,* 83–92.

Cohen, L. B., & Cashon, C. H. (2001b). Infant object segregation implies information integration. *Journal of Experimental Child Psychology, 78,* 75–83.

Cohen, L. B., & Cashon, C. H. (2003). Infant perception and cognition. In R. M. Lerner, M. A. Easterbrooks, & J. Mistry (Eds.), *Handbook of psychology: Developmental psychology* (Vol. 6, pp. 65–89). New York: Wiley.

Colby, A., Kohlberg, L., Gibbs, J., & Liberman, M. (1983). A longitudinal study of moral judgment. *Monographs of the Society for Research in Child Development, 48*(1–2, Serial No. 200), 1–96.

Cole, M., Cole, S. R., & Lightfoot, C. (2005). *The development of children* (5th ed.). New York: Worth.

Cole, M., & Scribner, S. (1974). *Culture and thought: A psychological introduction.* New York: Wiley.

Colombo, J. (2002). Infant attention grows up: The emergence of a developmental cognitive neuroscience perspective. *Current Directions in Psychological Science, 11,* 196–200.

Colombo, J., Richman, W. A., Shaddy, D. J., Greenhoot, A. F., & Maikranz, J. M. (2001). Heart rate-defined phases of attention, look duration, and infant performance in the paired-comparison paradigm. *Child Development, 72,* 1605–1616.

Comalli, P. E., Wapner, S., & Werner, H. (1962). Interference effects of Stroop color-word test in childhood, adulthood, and aging. *Journal of Genetic Psychology, 100,* 47–53.

Conklin, H. M., Luciana, M., Hooper, C. J., & Yarger, R. S. (2007). Working memory performance in typically developing children and adolescents: Behavioral evidence of protracted frontal lobe development. *Developmental Neuropsychology, 31,* 103–128.

Cooley, E. L., & Morris, R. D. (1990). Attention in children: A neuropsychologically based model for assessment. *Developmental Neuropsychology, 6,* 239–274.

Couperus, J. W., & Nelson, C. A. (2006). Early brain development and plasticity. In K. McCartney & D. Phillips (Eds.), *Blackwell handbook of early childhood development* (pp. 85–105). Malden, MA: Blackwell.

Courage, M. L., & Setliff, A. E. (2009). Debating the impact of television and video material on very young children: Attention, learning, and the developing brain. *Child Development Perspectives, 3,* 72–78.

Craik, F. I. M., & Lockhart, R. S. (1972). Levels of processing: A framework for memory research. *Journal of Verbal Learning and Verbal Behavior, 11,* 671–684.

Crawley, A. M., Anderson, D. R., Wilder, A., Williams, M., & Santomero, A. (1999). Effects of repeated exposures to a single episode of the television program *Blue's Clues* on the viewing behaviors and comprehension of preschool children. *Journal of Educational Psychology, 91,* 630–637.

Cummins, D. D. (1995). Native theories and causal deduction. *Memory & Cognition, 23,* 646–658.

Curtiss, S. (1977). *Genie: A psycholinguistic study of a modern-day "wild child."* New York: Academic Press.

Dahl, K. (1985). Research on writing development: Insights from the work of Harste and Graves. *The Volta Review, 87,* 35–46.

Davidson, D. (1991). Children's decision-making examined with an information-board procedure. *Cognitive Development, 6,* 77–90.

Davidson, D. (1995). The representativeness heuristic and the conjunction fallacy effect in children's decision making. *Merrill-Palmer Quarterly, 41,* 328–346.

De Bellis, M. D., Keshavan, M. S., Beers, S. R., Hall, J., Frustaci, K., Masalehdan, A., et al. (2001). Sex differences in brain maturation during childhood and adolescence. *Cerebral Cortex, 11,* 552–557.

DeLoache, J. S. (1987). Rapid change in the symbolic functioning of very young children. *Science, 238,* 1556–1557.

DeLoache, J. S. (1995). Early understanding and use of symbols: The Model model. *Current Directions in Psychological Science, 4,* 109–113.

DeLoache, J. S., Miller, K. F., & Rosengren, K. S. (1997). The credible shrinking room: Very young children's performance with symbolic and nonsymbolic relations. *Psychological Science, 8,* 308–313.

DeLoache, J. S., & Smith, C. M. (1999). Early symbolic representation. In I. E. Siegel, (Ed.), *Development of mental representation: Theories and applications* (pp. 61–86). Mahwah, NJ: Erlbaum.

DeLoache, J. S., Uttal, D. H., & Rosengren, K. S. (2004). Scale errors offer evidence for a perception-action dissociation early in life. *Science, 304,* 1027–1029.

Dempster, F. N. (1981). Memory span: Sources of individual and developmental differences. *Psychological Bulletin, 89,* 63–100.

Dunsmir, S., & Blatchford, P. (2004). Predictors of writing competence in 4- to 7-year-old children. *British Journal of Educational Psychology, 74,* 461–483.

Dweck, C. S. (1999). *Self-theories: Their role in motivation, personality, and development.* Philadelphia: Psychology Press.

Dweck, C. S. (2002). The development of ability conceptions. In A. Wigfield & J. Eccles (Eds.), *Development of achievement motivation* (pp. 57–88). San Diego, CA: Academic Press.

Dweck, C. S., & Bush, E. S. (1976). Sex differences in learned helplessness: I. Differential debilitation with peer and adult evaluators. *Developmental Psychology, 12,* 147–156.

Dweck, C. S., Davidson, W., Nelson, S., & Enna, B. (1978). Sex differences in learned helplessness: II. The contingencies of evaluative feedback in the classroom, and III. An experimental analysis. *Developmental Psychology, 14,* 268–276.

Dweck, C. S., & Goetz, T. E. (1978). Attributions and learned helplessness. In J. H. Harvey, W. J. Ickes, & R. F. Kidd (Eds.), *New directions in attribution research* (Vol. 2, pp. 157–179). Hillsdale, NJ: Erlbaum.

Dweck, C. S., & Leggett, E. L. (1988). A social-cognitive approach to motivation and personality. *Psychological Review, 95,* 256–273.

Eccles, J. S. (2008). The value of an off-diagonal approach. *Journal of Social Issues, 64,* 227–232.

Eccles, J. S., Wigfield, A., & Byrnes, J. (2003). Cognitive development in adolescence. In R. M. Lerner, M. A. Easterbrooks, & J. Mistry (Vol. Eds.) and I. B. Weiner (Ed.-in-Chief), *Handbook of psychology: Developmental psychology* (Vol. 6, pp. 325–350). Hoboken, NJ: Wiley.

Eckler, J. A., & Weininger, O. (1989). Structural parallels between pretend play and narratives. *Developmental Psychology, 25,* 736–743.

Eimas, P. D., & Quinn, P. C. (1994). Studies of the formation of perceptually based basic-level categories in young infants. *Child Development, 65,* 903–917.

Eimas, P. D., Siqueland, E. R., Jusczyk, P., & Vigorito, J. (1971). Speech perception in infants. *Science, 171,* 303–306.

Elkind, D. (1967). Egocentrism in adolescence. *Child Development, 38,* 1025–1034.

Ennis, R. H. (1975). Children's ability to handle Piaget's propositional logic: A conceptual critique. *Review of Educational Research, 45,* 1–41.

Epley, N., Morewedge, C. K., & Keysar, B. (2004). Perspective taking in children and adults: Equivalent egocentrism but differential correction. *Journal of Experimental Social Psychology, 40,* 760–768.

Erikson, E. H. (1968). *Identity: Youth and crisis.* New York: Norton.

Espy, K. A., & Bull, R. (2005). Inhibitory processes in young children and individual variation in short-term memory. *Developmental Neuropsychology, 28,* 669–688.

Evans, J. S. B. T., & Perry, T. S. (1995). Belief bias in children's reasoning. *Current Psychology of Cognition, 14,* 103–115.

Evans, M. A., Fox, M., Cremaso, L., & McKinnon, L. (2004). Beginning reading: The views of parents and teachers of young children. *Journal of Educational Psychology, 96,* 130–141.

Fagan, J. F. (1973). Infants' delayed recognition memory and forgetting. *Journal of Experimental Child Psychology, 16,* 424–450.

Fantz, R. L. (1958). Pattern vision in young infants. *The Psychological Record, 8,* 43–47.

Fantz, R. L. (1961). A method for studying depth perception in infants under six months of age. *The Psychological Record, 11,* 27–32.

Fantz, R. L. (1963). Pattern vision in newborn infants. *Science, 140,* 296–297.

Fantz, R. L. (1964). Visual experience in infants: Decreased attention to familiar patterns relative to novel ones. *Science, 146*(Whole No. 3644), 668–670.

Fantz, R. L., & Fagan, J. F. (1975). Visual attention to size and number of pattern details by term and preterm infants during the first six months. *Child Development, 46,* 3–18.

Fantz, R. L., & Ordy, J. M. (1959). A visual acuity test for infants under six months of age. *The Psychological Record, 9,* 159–164.

Fein, G. G. (1981). Pretend play in childhood: An integrative review. *Child Development, 52,* 1095–1118.

Feldgus, E. G., & Cardonick, I. (1999). *Kid writing: A systematic approach to phonics, journals, and writing workshop* (2nd ed.). Bothell, WA: Wright Group McGraw-Hill.

Fernald, A. (2001). Hearing, listening, and understanding: Auditory development in infancy. In G. Bremner & A. Fogel (Eds.), *Blackwell handbook of infant development* (pp. 35–70). Malden, MA: Blackwell.

Fisch, S. M. (2004). *Children's learning from educational television:* Sesame Street *and beyond.* Mahwah, NJ: Erlbaum.

Fisch, S. M., Truglio, R. T., & Cole, C. F. (1999). The impact of *Sesame Street* on preschool children: A review and synthesis of 30 years' research. *Media Psychology, 1,* 165–190.

Fitzgerald, J. M. (1981). Autobiographical memory: Reports in adolescence. *Canadian Journal of Psychology, 35,* 69–73.

Fivush, R. (1984). Learning about school: The development of kindergarteners' school scripts. *Child Development, 55,* 1697–1709.

Fivush, R., & Haden, C. A. (2003). Introduction: Autobiographical memory, narrative and self. In R. Fivush & C. A. Haden (Eds.), *Autobiographical memory and the construction of a narrative self* (pp. vii–xiv). Mahwah, NJ: Erlbaum.

Fivush, R., Hazzard, A., Sales, J. M., Sarfati, D., & Brown, T. (2003). Creating coherence out of chaos? Children's narratives of emotionally positive and negative events. *Applied Cognitive Psychology, 17,* 1–19.

Fivush, R., Peterson, C., & Schwarzmueller, A. (2002). Questions and answers: The credibility of child witnesses in the context of specific questioning techniques. In M. L. Eisen, J. A. Quas, & G. S. Goodman (Eds.), *Memory and suggestibility in the forensic interview* (pp. 331–354). Mahwah, NJ: Erlbaum.

Fivush, R., Sales, J. M., Goldberg, A., Bahrick, L., & Parker, J. (2004). Weathering the storm: Children's long-term recall of Hurricane Andrew. *Memory, 12,* 104–118.

Fivush, R., & Schwarzmueller, A. (1998). Children remember childhood: Implications for childhood amnesia. *Applied Cognitive Psychology, 12,* 455–473.

Fivush, R., & Slackman, E. A. (1986). The acquisition and development of scripts. In K. Nelson (Ed.), *Event knowledge: Structure and function in development* (pp. 71–96). Hillsdale, NJ: Erlbaum.

Flavell, J. H. (1963). *The developmental psychology of Jean Piaget.* New York: Van Nostrand.

Flavell, J. H., Beach, D. R., & Chinsky, J. M. (1966). Spontaneous verbal rehearsal in a memory task as a function of age. *Child Development, 37,* 283–299.

Flavell, J. H., Green, F. L., & Flavell, E. R. (1986). Development of knowledge about the appearance-reality distinction. *Monographs of the Society for Research in Child Development, 51*(Serial No. 212), 1–69.

Flavell, J. H., Green, F. L., & Flavell, E. R. (1995). Young children's knowledge about thinking. *Monographs of the Society for Research in Child Development, 60*(Serial No. 243), 1–96.

Flavell, J. H., Miller, P. H., & Miller, S. A. (1993). *Cognitive development* (3rd ed.). Englewood Cliffs, NJ: Prentice Hall.

Flavell, J. H., Zhang, X.-D., Zou, H., Dong, Q., & Qi, S. (1983). A comparison between the development of the appearance-reality distinction in the People's Republic of China and the United States. *Cognitive Psychology, 15,* 459–466.

Flynn, J. R. (2007). *What is intelligence? Beyond the Flynn effect.* Cambridge, England: Cambridge University Press.

Fodor, J. A. (1983). *Modularity of mind.* Cambridge, MA: MIT Press.

Fogel, A. (2001). *Infancy: Infant, family, and society* (4th ed.). Belmont, CA: Wadsworth.

Ford, M. R., & Lowery, C. R. (1986). Gender differences in moral reasoning: A comparison of the use of justice and care orientations. *Journal of Personality and Social Psychology, 50,* 777–783.

Frye, D., Zelazo, P. D., & Palfai, T. (1995). Theory of mind and rule-based reasoning. *Cognitive Development, 10,* 483–527.

Galotti, K. M. (1989). Approaches to studying formal and everyday reasoning. *Psychological Bulletin, 105,* 331–351.

Galotti, K. M. (1999a). *Cognitive psychology in and out of the laboratory* (2nd ed). Pacific Grove, CA: Brooks/Cole.

Galotti, K. M. (1999b). Making a "major" real-life decision: College students choosing an academic major. *Journal of Educational Psychology, 91,* 379–387.

Galotti, K. M. (2001). Helps and hindrances for adolescents making important real-life decisions. *Journal of Applied Developmental Psychology, 22,* 275–287.

Galotti, K. M. (2002). *Making decisions that matter: How people face important life choices.* Mahwah, NJ: Erlbaum.

Galotti, K. M. (2005). Setting goals and making plans: How children and adolescents frame their decisions. In J. E. Jacobs & P. A. Klaczynski (Eds.), *The development of judgment and decision making in children and adolescents* (pp. 303–326). Mahwah, NJ: Erlbaum.

Galotti, K. M. (2008). *Cognitive psychology in and out of the laboratory* (4th ed.). Belmont, CA: Thomson/Wadsworth.

Galotti, K. M., Ciner, E., Altenbaumer, H. E., Geerts, H. J., Rupp, A., & Woulfe, J. (2006). Decision-making styles in a real-life decision: Choosing a college major. *Personality and Individual Differences, 41,* 629–639.

Galotti, K. M., Clinchy, B. McV., Ainsworth, K. H., Lavin, B., & Mansfield, A. F. (1999). A new way of assessing ways of knowing: The Attitudes Toward Thinking and Learning Survey (ATTLS). *Sex Roles, 40,* 745–766.

Galotti, K. M., Drebus, D. W., & Reimer, R. L. (2001). Ways of knowing as learning styles: Learning MAGIC with a partner. *Sex Roles, 44,* 419–436.

Galotti, K. M., Kozberg, S. F., & Farmer, M. C. (1991). Gender and developmental differences in adolescents' conceptions of moral reasoning. *Journal of Youth and Adolescence, 20,* 13–30.

Gardner, H. (1993). *Multiple intelligences: The theory in practice.* New York: Basic Books.

Gardner, H. (1999). *Intelligence reframed: Multiple intelligences for the 21st century.* New York: Basic Books.

Garrett, B. (2009). *Brain and behavior: An introduction to biological psychology* (2nd ed.). Thousand Oaks, CA: Sage.

Gathercole, S. E., Pickering, S. J., Knight, C., & Stegmann, Z. (2004). Working memory skills and national curriculum assessments at 7 and 14 years of age. *Applied Cognitive Psychology, 18,* 9.

Gauvain, M., & Perez, S. M. (2005). Parent-child participation in planning children's activities outside of school in European American and Latino families. *Child Development, 76,* 371–383.

Gauvain, M., & Rogoff, B. (1989). Collaborative problem solving and children's planning skills. *Developmental Psychology, 25,* 139–151.

Geary, D. C., Bow-Thomas, C. C., Liu, F., & Siegler, R. S. (1996). Development of arithmetical competencies in Chinese and American children: Influence of age, language, and schooling. *Child Development, 67,* 2022–2044.

Geary, D. C., Salthouse, T. A., Chen, G.-P., & Fan, L. (1996). Are East Asian versus American differences in arithmetical ability a recent phenomenon? *Developmental Psychology, 32,* 254–262.

Gelman, R. (1969). Conservation acquisition: A problem of learning to attend to relevant attributes. *Journal of Experimental Child Psychology, 7,* 167–187.

Gelman, R. (1972). Logical capacity of very young children: Number invariance rules. *Child Development, 43,* 75–90.

Gelman, R. (1979). Preschool thought. *American Psychologist, 34,* 900–905.

Gelman, R. (1990). First principles organize attention to and learning about relevant data: Number and the animate-inanimate distinction as examples. *Cognitive Science, 14,* 79–106.

Gelman, R. (2002). Cognitive development. In H. Pashler & D. Medin (Eds.), *Steven's handbook of experimental psychology* (3rd ed., Vol. 2, pp. 533–559). Hoboken, NJ: Wiley.

Gelman, R., & Baillargeon, R. (1983). A review of some Piagetian concepts. In P. H. Mussen (Series Ed.) and J. H. Flavell & E. M. Markman (Vol. Eds.), *Handbook of child psychology* (4th ed., Vol. 3, pp. 167–230). New York: Wiley.

Gelman, R., & Gallistel, C. R. (1978). *The child's understanding of number.* Cambridge, MA: Harvard University Press.

Gelman, R., & Meck, E. (1983). Preschoolers' counting: Principles before skill. *Cognition, 13,* 343–359.

Gelman, R., & Williams, E. M. (1998). Enabling constraints for cognitive development and learning: Domain specificity and epigenesis. In W. Damon (Series Ed.) and D. Kuhn & R. S. Siegler (Vol. Eds.), *Handbook of child psychology* (5th ed., Vol. 2, pp. 575–630). New York: Wiley.

Gelman, S. A. (1988). The development of induction within natural kind and artifact categories. *Cognitive Psychology, 20,* 65–95.

Gelman, S. A., & Kalish, C. W. (2006). Conceptual development. In W. Damon & R. M. Lerner (Series Eds.) and D. Kuhn & R. S. Siegler (Vol. Eds.), *Handbook of child psychology* (6th ed., Vol. 2, pp. 687–733). Hoboken, NJ: Wiley.

Gelman, S. A., & Markman, E. M. (1985). Implicit contrast in adjectives versus nouns: Implications for word-learning in preschoolers. *Journal of Child Language, 12,* 125–143.

Gelman, S. A., & Markman, E. M. (1986). Categories and induction in young children. *Cognition, 23,* 183–209.

Gibson, E. J. (1969). *Principles of perceptual learning and development.* New York: Appleton-Century-Crofts.

Gibson, E. J. (2000). Commentary on perceptual and conceptual processes in infancy. *Journal of Cognition and Development, 1,* 43–48.

Gibson, E. J., & Walk, R. D. (1960). The "visual cliff." *Scientific American, 202,* 67–71.

Gibson, J. J., & Gibson, E. J. (1955). Perceptual learning: Differentiation or enrichment? *Psychological Review, 62,* 32–41.

Giedd, J. N., Blumenthal, J., Jeffries, N. O., Castellanos, F. X., Liu, H., Zijdenbos, A., et al. (1999). Brain development during childhood and adolescence: A longitudinal MRI study. *Nature Neuroscience, 2,* 861–863.

Gilligan, C. (1977). In a different voice: Women's conceptions of self and morality. *Harvard Educational Review, 47,* 481–517.

Gilligan, C. (1979). Woman's place in man's life cycle. *Harvard Educational Review, 49,* 431–446.

Gilligan, C. (1982). *In a different voice: Psychological theory and women's development.* Cambridge, MA: Harvard University Press.

Gilligan, C. (1988). Remapping the moral domain: New images of self in relationship. In C. Gilligan, J. V. Ward, J. M. Taylor, & B. Bardige (Eds.), *Mapping the moral domain: A contribution of women's thinking to psychological theory and education* (pp. 1–19). Cambridge, MA: Harvard University Press.

Ginsburg, H. P., & Opper, S. (1988). *Piaget's theory of intellectual development* (3rd ed.). Englewood Cliffs, NJ: Prentice Hall.

Gleitman, H., Fridlund, A. J., & Reisberg, D. (2004). *Psychology* (6th ed.). New York: Norton.

Globerson, T., & Zelnicker, T. (Eds.). (1989). *Human development* (Vol. 3). Northwood, NJ: Ablex.

Gogtay, N., Giedd, J. N., Lusk, L., Hayashi, K. M., Greenstein, D., Vaituzis, A. C., et al. (2004). Dynamic mapping of human cortical development during childhood through early adulthood. *Proceedings of the National Academy of Science, 101,* 8174–8179.

Goldberger, N. R., Tarule, J. M., Clinchy, B. McV., & Belenky, M. F. (Eds.). (1996). *Knowledge, difference, and power: Essays inspired by women's ways of knowing.* New York: Basic Books.

Golinkoff, R. M., & Alioto, A. (1995). Infant-directed speech facilitates lexical learning in adults hearing Chinese: Implications for language acquisition. *Journal of Child Language, 22,* 703–726.

Goodman, G. S., Sayfan, L., Lee, J. S., Sandhie, M., Walle-Olsen, A., Magnussen, S., et al. (2007). The development of memory for own- and other-race faces. *Journal of Experimental Child Psychology, 98,* 233–242.

Gopnik, A., & Astington, J. W. (1988). Children's understanding of representational change and its relation to the understanding of false belief and the appearance-reality distinction. *Child Development, 59,* 26–37.

Goswami, U., Leevers, H., Pressley, S., & Wheelwright, S. (1998). Causal reasoning about pairs of relations and analogical reasoning in young children. *British Journal of Developmental Psychology, 16,* 553–569.

Graham, S., & Harris, K. R. (2000). The role of self-regulation and transcription skills in writing and writing development. *Educational Psychologist, 35,* 3–12.

Graham, S., Harris, K. R., & Mason, L. (2005). Improving the writing performance, knowledge, and self-efficacy of struggling young writers: The effects of self-regulated strategy development. *Contemporary Educational Psychology, 30,* 207–241.

Greenberg, D. L. (2004). President Bush's false "flashbulb" memory of 9/11/01. *Applied Cognitive Psychology, 18,* 363–370.

Greenough, W. T., Black, J. E., & Wallace, C. S. (1987). Experience and brain development. *Child Development, 58,* 539–559.

Grice, H. P. (1975). Logic and conversation. In P. Cole & J. L. Morgan (Eds.), *Syntax and semantics* (Vol. 3, pp. 41–58). New York: Academic Press.

Grovetant, H. D. (1993). The integrative nature of identity: Bringing the soloists to sing in the choir. In J. Kroger (Ed.), *Discussions of ego identity* (pp. 121–146). Hillsdale, NJ: Erlbaum.

Guberman, S. R. (1996). The development of everyday mathematics in Brazilian children with limited formal education. *Child Development, 67,* 1609–1623.

Haidt, J. (2001). The emotional dog and its rational tail: A social intuitionist approach to moral judgment. *Psychological Review, 108,* 814–834.

Haidt, J. (2007). The new synthesis in moral psychology. *Science, 316,* 998–1002.

Haidt, J. (2008). Morality. *Perspectives on Psychological Science, 3,* 65–72.

Haith, M. M., & Benson, J. B. (1998). Infant cognition. In W. Damon (Series Ed.) and D. Kuhn & R. S. Siegler (Vol. Eds.), *Handbook of child psychology* (5th ed., Vol. 2, pp. 199–254). New York: Wiley.

Hanauer, J. B., & Brooks, P. J. (2005). Contributions of response set and semantic relatedness to cross-model Stroop-like picture-word interference in children and adults. *Journal of Experimental Child Psychology, 90,* 21–47.

Harnishfeger, K. K., & Bjorklund, D. F. (1993). The ontogeny of inhibition mechanisms: A renewed approach to cognitive development. In M. L. Howe & R. Pasnak (Eds.), *Emerging themes in cognitive development* (Vol. I, pp. 28–49). New York: Springer-Verlag.

Harris, M., Barrett, M., Jones, D., & Brookes, S. (1988). Linguistic input and early word meaning. *Journal of Child Language, 15,* 77–94.

Harris, P. L. (2006). Social cognition. In W. Damon & R. M. Lerner (Series Eds.) and D. Kuhn & R. S. Siegler (Vol. Eds.), *Handbook of child psychology* (6th ed., Vol. 2, pp. 811–858). Hoboken, NJ: Wiley.

Hartshorn, K., & Rovee-Collier, C. (1997). Infant learning and long-term memory at 6 months: A confirming analysis. *Developmental Psychobiology, 30,* 71–85.

Hasselhorn, M., Mahler, C., & Grube, D. (2005). Theory of mind, working memory, and verbal ability in preschool children: The proposal of a relay race model of the developmental dependencies. In W. Schneider, R. Schumann-Hengsteler, & B. Sodian (Eds.), *Young children's cognitive development: Interrelationships among executive functioning, working memory, verbal ability, and theory of mind* (pp. 219–237). Mahwah, NJ: Erlbaum.

Hawkins, J., Pea, R. D., Glick, J., & Scribner, S. (1984). "Merds that laugh don't like mushrooms": Evidence for deductive reasoning by preschoolers. *Developmental Psychology, 20,* 584–594.

Hayes, J. R. (1996). A new framework for understanding cognition and affect in writing. In C. M. Levy & S. Ransdell (Eds.), *The science of writing: Theories, methods, individual differences, and applications* (pp. 1–27). Mahwah, NJ: Erlbaum.

Hayes, J. R., & Flower, L. S. (1980). Identifying the organization of writing processes. In L. W. Gregg & E. R. Steinberg (Eds.), *Cognitive processes in writing* (pp. 3–30). Hillsdale, NJ: Erlbaum.

Hayne, H. (2004). Infant memory development: Implications for childhood amnesia. *Developmental Review, 24,* 33–73.

Henle, M. (1962). On the relation between logic and thinking. *Psychological Review, 69,* 366–378.

Hodges, R. M., & French, L. A. (1988). The effect of class and collection labels on cardinality, class-inclusion, and number conservation tasks. *Child Development, 59,* 1387–1396.

Hoff, E. (2005). *Language development* (3rd ed.). Belmont, CA: Wadsworth.

Holmes, J., & Adams, J. W. (2006). Working memory and children's mathematical skills: Implications for mathematical development and mathematics curricula. *Educational Psychology, 26,* 339–366.

Howe, M. L. (2000). Memory development during the preschool years. In M. L. Howe (Ed.), *The fate of early memories: Developmental science and the retention of childhood experiences* (pp. 35–57). Washington, DC: American Psychological Association.

Howe, M. L., Courage, M. L., & Edison, S. C. (2003). When autobiographical memory begins. *Developmental Review, 23,* 471–494.

Howe, N., Petrakos, H., Rinaldi, C. M., & LeFebvre, R. (2005). "This is a bad dog, you know . . .": Constructing shared meanings during sibling pretend play. *Child Development, 76,* 783–794.

Hudson, J. A., & Fivush, R. (1991). As time goes by: Sixth graders remember a kindergarten experience. *Applied Cognitive Psychology, 5,* 347–360.

Hughes, C. (1998). Finding your marbles: Does preschoolers' strategic behavior predict later understanding of mind? *Developmental Psychology, 34,* 1326–1339.

Huston, A. C., Bickham, D. S., Lee, J. H., & Wright, J. C. (2007). From attention to comprehension: How children watch and learn from television. In N. Pecora, J. P. Murray, & E. A. Wartella (Eds.), *Children and television: Fifty years of research* (pp. 41–63). Mahwah, NJ: Erlbaum.

Huston, A. C., & Wright, J. C. (1998). Mass media and children's development. In W. Damon (Series Ed.) and I. E. Sigel & K. A. Renninger (Vol. Eds.), *Handbook of child psychology* (5th ed., Vol. 4, pp. 999–1058). New York: Wiley.

Huston, A. C., Wright, J. C., Marquis, J., & Green, S. B. (1999). How young children spend their time: Television and other activities. *Developmental Psychology, 35,* 912–925.

Huttenlocher, P. R. (1990). Morphometric study of human cerebral cortex development. *Neuropsychologia, 28,* 517–527.

Ingram, D. (1989). *First language acquisition: Method, description, and explanation.* Cambridge, England: Cambridge University Press.

Inhelder, B., & Piaget, J. (1958). *The growth of logical thinking from childhood to adolescence* (A. Parsons & S. Milgram, Trans.). New York: Basic Books.

Inhelder, B., & Piaget, J. (1964). *The early growth of logic in the child.* New York: Harper & Row.

Istomina, Z. M. (1982). The development of voluntary memory in children of preschool age. In. U. Neisser (Ed.), *Memory observed: Remembering in natural contexts* (pp. 349–365). San Francisco: W. H. Freeman.

Jackendoff, R. (1994). Patterns in the mind: Language and human nature. New York: Basic Books.

Jacobs, J. E., Greenwald, J. P., & Osgood, D. W. (1995). Developmental differences in baserate estimates of social behaviors and attitudes. *Social Development, 4,* 165–181.

Jacobs, J. E., & Potenza, M. (1991). The use of judgment heuristics to make social and object decisions: A developmental perspective. *Child Development, 62,* 166–178.

Jacoby, L. L. (1998). Invariance in automatic influences in memory: Toward a user's guide for the process-dissociation procedure. *Journal of Experimental Psychology: Learning, Memory, and Cognition, 24,* 3–26.

James, W. (1983). *The principles of psychology.* Cambridge, MA: Harvard University Press. (Original work published 1890)

Janveau-Brennan, G., & Markovits, H. (1999). The development of reasoning with causal conditionals. *Developmental Psychology, 35,* 904–911.

Jenkins, J. M., & Astington, J W. (1996). Cognitive factors and family structure associated with theory of mind development in young children. *Developmental Psychology, 32,* 70–78.

Johnson, K. E., & Eilers, A. T. (1998). Effects of knowledge and development on subordinate level categorization. *Cognitive Development, 13,* 515–545.

Johnson, M. H. (1998). The neural basis of cognitive development. In W. Damon (Series Ed.) and D. Kuhn & R. S. Siegler (Vol. Eds.), *Handbook of child psychology* (5th ed., Vol. 2, pp. 1–49). New York: Wiley.

Johnson, M. H. (2001). Functional brain development during infancy. In G. Bremner & A. Fogel (Eds.), *Blackwell handbook of infant development* (pp. 169–190). Malden, MA: Blackwell.

Johnson, M. H., Munakata, Y., & Gilmore, R. O. (Eds.). (2002). *Brain development and cognition: A reader* (2nd ed.). Oxford, England: Blackwell.

Johnson-Laird, P. N. (1983). *Mental models.* Cambridge, MA: Harvard University Press.

Juel, C. (1988). Learning to read and write: A longitudinal study of 54 children from first through fourth grades. *Journal of Educational Psychology, 80,* 437–447.

Just, M. A., & Carpenter, P. A. (1987). *The psychology of reading and language comprehension.* Boston: Allyn & Bacon.

Kagan, J., Rosman, B. L., Day, D., Albert, J., & Phillips, W. (1964). Information processing in the child: Significance of analytic and reflective attitudes. *Psychological Monographs, 78*(1, Whole No. 578).

Kahneman, D., & Tversky, A. (1972). Subjective probability: A judgment of representativeness. *Cognitive Psychology, 3,* 430–454.

Kahneman, D., & Tversky, A. (1973). On the psychology of prediction. *Psychological Review, 80,* 237–251.

Kail, R., & Bisanz, J. (1992). The information-processing perspective on cognitive development in childhood and adolescence. In R. J. Sternberg & C. A. Berg (Eds.), *Intellectual development* (pp. 229–260). New York: Cambridge University Press.

Kalat, J. W. (2002). *Introduction to psychology* (6th ed.). Pacific Grove, CA: Wadsworth/Thomson.

Keating, D. P., & Bobbitt, B. L. (1978). Individual and developmental differences in cognitive-processing components of mental ability. *Child Development, 49,* 155–167.

Keeney, T. J., Cannizzo, S. R., & Flavell, J. H. (1967). Spontaneous and induced verbal rehearsal in a recall task. *Child Development, 38,* 953–966.

Keil, F. C. (1979). *Semantic and conceptual development: An ontological perspective.* Cambridge, MA: Harvard University Press.

Kellman, P. J., & Arterberry, M. E. (2006). Infant visual perception. In W. Damon & R. M. Lerner (Series Eds.) and D. Kuhn & R. S. Siegler (Vol. Eds.), *Handbook of child psychology* (6th ed., Vol. 2, pp. 109–160). New York: Wiley.

Kellman, P. J., & Spelke, E. S. (1983). Perception of partly occluded objects in infancy. *Cognitive Psychology, 15,* 483–524.

Kemler, D. G. (1983). Holistic and analytic modes in perceptual and cognitive development. In T. J. Tighe & B. E. Shepp (Eds.), *Perception, cognition, and development: Interactional analyses* (pp. 77–102). Hillsdale, NJ: Erlbaum.

Kirkham, N. Z., Cruess, L., & Diamond, A. (2003). Helping children apply their knowledge to their behavior on a dimension-switching task. *Developmental Science, 6,* 449–476.

Kirkorian, H. L., Wartella, E. A., & Anderson, D. R. (2008). Media and young children's learning. *Future of Children, 18,* 39–61.

Klaczynski, P. A. (2001a). Analytic and heuristic processing influences on adolescent reasoning and decision-making. *Child Development, 72,* 844–861.

Klaczynski, P. A. (2001b). Framing effects on adolescent task representations, analytic and heuristic processing, and decision making: Implications for the normative/descriptive gap. *Journal of Applied Developmental Psychology, 22,* 289–309.

Klaczynski, P. A. (2005). Metacognition and cognitive variability: A dual-process model of decision-making and its development. In J. E. Jacobs & P. A. Klaczynski (Eds.), *The development of judgment and decision making in children and adolescents* (pp. 39–76). Mahwah, NJ: Erlbaum.

Klatzky, R. L. (1980). *Human memory: Structure and processes* (2nd ed.). San Francisco: W. H. Freeman.

Klemfuss, J. Z., & Ceci, S. J. (2009). Normative memory and the child witness. In K. Kuehnle & M. Connell (Eds.), *The evaluation of child sexual abuse allegations: A comprehensive guide to assessment and testimony* (pp. 153–180). Hoboken, NJ: Wiley.

Kohlberg, L. (1976). Moral stages and moralization: The cognitive-developmental approach. In T. Lickona (Ed.), *Moral development and behavior: Theory, research, and social issues* (pp. 31–53). New York: Holt, Rinehart, & Winston.

Kovack-Lesh, K. A., & Oakes, L. M. (2007). Hold your horses: How exposure to different items influences infant categorization. *Journal of Experimental Child Psychology, 98,* 69–93.

Krebs, D. L. (2008). Morality: An evolutionary account. *Perspectives on Psychological Science, 3,* 149–172.

Kroger, J. (2000). *Identity development: Adolescence through adulthood.* Thousand Oaks, CA: Sage.

Kuhn, D. (1977). Conditional reasoning in children. *Developmental Psychology, 13,* 342–353.

Kuhn, D. (2006). Do cognitive changes accompany developments in the adolescent brain? *Perspectives on Psychological Science, 1,* 59–67.

Kuhn, D., & Pease, M. (2006). Do children and adults learn differently? *Journal of Cognition and Development, 7,* 279–283.

Lane, H. (1976). *The wild boy of Aveyron.* Cambridge, MA: Harvard University Press.

Leichtman, M. D., & Ceci, S. J. (1995). The effects of stereotypes and suggestions on preschoolers' reports. *Developmental Psychology, 31,* 568–578.

Leichtman, M. D., Morse, M. B., Dixon, A., & Spiegel, R. (2000). Source monitoring and suggestibility: An individual differences approach. In K. P. Roberts & M. Blades (Eds.), *Children's source monitoring* (pp. 257–287). Mahwah, NJ: Erlbaum.

Lenneberg, E. H. (1967). *Biological foundations of language.* New York: Wiley.

Leslie, A. M. (1992). Pretense, autism, and the theory-of-mind module. *Current Directions in Psychological Science, 1,* 18–21.

Lightfoot, C., Cole, M., & Cole, S. R. (2009). *The development of children* (6th ed.). New York: Worth.

Lillard, A. S., & Flavell, J. H. (1990). Young children's preference for mental state versus behavioral descriptions of human action. *Child Development, 61,* 731–741.

Lillard, A. S., & Flavell, J. H. (1992). Young children's understanding of different mental states. *Developmental Psychology, 28,* 626–634.

Lin, S. C., Monroe, B. W., & Troia, G. A. (2007). Development of writing knowledge in grades 2–8: A comparison of typically developing writers and their struggling peers. *Reading & Writing Quarterly, 23,* 207–230.

Lindsay, D. S. (2007). Autobiographical memory, eyewitness reports, and public policy. *Canadian Psychology, 48,* 57–66.

Lindsay, D. S., Johnson, M. K., & Kwon, P. (1991). Developmental changes in memory source monitoring. *Journal of Experimental Child Psychology, 52,* 297–318.

Linton, M. (1982). Transformations of memory in everyday life. In U. Neisser (Ed.), *Memory observed* (pp. 77–92). San Francisco: W. H. Freeman.

Lisker, L., & Abramson, A. (1970). The voicing dimension: Some experiments in comparative phonetics. *Proceedings of the Sixth International Congress of Phonetic Sciences,* Prague, 1967 (pp. 563–567). Prague, Czechoslovakia: Academia.

Littschwager, J. C., & Markman, E. M. (1994). Sixteen- and 24-month-olds' use of mutual exclusivity as a default assumption in second-label learning. *Developmental Psychology, 30,* 955–968.

Lock, A. (2001). Preverbal communication. In G. Bremner & A. Fogel (Eds.), *Blackwell handbook of infant development* (pp. 379–403). Malden, MA: Blackwell.

Luciana, M., Conklin, H. M., Hooper, C. J., & Yarger, R. S. (2005). The development of nonverbal working memory and executive control processes in adolescents. *Child Development, 76,* 697–712.

Luck, S. J. (2005). *An introduction to the event-related potential technique.* Cambridge, MA: MIT Press.

Luna, B., & Sweeney, J. A. (2001). Studies of brain and cognitive maturation through childhood and adolescence: A strategy for testing neurodevelopmental hypotheses. *Schizophrenia Bulletin, 27,* 443–455.

Luna, B., & Sweeney, J. A. (2004). The emergence of collaborative brain function: fMRI studies of the development of response inhibition. In R. E. Dahl & L. P. Spear (Eds.), *Adolescent brain development: Vulnerabilities and opportunities* (pp. 296–309). New York: New York Academy of Sciences.

Luna, B., Thulborn, K. R., Munoz, D. P., Merriam, E. P., Garver, K. E., Minshew, N. J., et al. (2001). Maturation of widely distributed brain function subserves cognitive development. *NeuroImage, 13,* 786–793.

Mandler, J. M. (1983). Representation. In P. H. Mussen (Series Ed.) and J. H. Flavell & E. M. Markman (Vol. Eds.), *Handbook of child psychology* (4th ed., Vol. 3, pp. 420–494). New York: Wiley.

Mandler, J. M. (2000). Perceptual and conceptual processes in infancy. *Journal of Cognition and Development, 1,* 3–36.

Mandler, J. M. (2004). A synopsis of *The foundations of mind: Origins of conceptual thought (2004).* New York: Oxford University Press. *Developmental Science, 7,* 499–505.

Mandler, J. M., & Bauer, P. J. (1988). The cradle of categorization: Is the basic level basic? *Cognitive Development, 3,* 247–264.

Mandler, J. M., Bauer, P. J., & McDonough, L. (1991). Separating the sheep from the goats: Differentiating global categories. *Cognitive Psychology, 23,* 263–268.

Mandler, J. M., & Johnson, N. S. (1977). Remembrance of things parsed: Story structure and recall. *Cognitive Psychology, 9,* 111–151.

Mandler, J. M., & McDonough, L. (1993). Concept formation in infancy. *Cognitive Development, 8,* 291–318.

Mandler, J. M., & McDonough, L. (2000). Advancing downward to the basic level. *Journal of Cognition and Development, 1,* 379–403.

Maratsos, M. (1998). The acquisition of grammar. In W. Damon (Series Ed.) and D. Kuhn & R. S. Siegler (Vol. Eds.), *Handbook of child psychology* (5th ed., Vol. 2, pp. 421–466). New York: Wiley.

Marcia, J. E. (1966). Development and validation of ego-identity status. *Journal of Personality and Social Psychology, 3,* 551–558.

Markman, E. M. (1989). *Categorization and naming in children: Problems of induction.* Cambridge, MA: MIT Press.

Markman, E. M., Horton, M. S., & McLanahan, A. G. (1980). Classes and collections: Principles of organization in the learning of hierarchical relations. *Cognition, 8,* 227–241.

Markman, E. M., & Hutchinson, J. E. (1984). Children's sensitivity to constraints on word meaning: Taxonomic versus thematic relations. *Cognitive Psychology, 16,* 1–27.

Markman, E. M., & Siebert, J. (1976). Classes and collections: Internal organization and resulting holistic properties. *Cognitive Psychology, 8,* 561–577.

Markovits, H. (1993). The development of conditional reasoning: A Piagetian reformulation of mental models theory. *Merrill-Palmer Quarterly, 39,* 131–158.

Markovits, H., & Barrouillet, P. (2002). The development of conditional reasoning: A mental model account. *Developmental Review, 22,* 5–36.

Markovits, H., Fleury, M. L., Quinn, S., & Venet, M. (1998). The development of conditional reasoning and the structure of semantic memory. *Child Development, 69,* 742–755.

Markovits, H., & Vachon, R. (1990). Conditional reasoning, representation, and level of abstraction. *Developmental Psychology, 26,* 942–951.

Marzolf, D. P., DeLoache, J. S., & Kolstad, V. (1999). The role of relational similarity in young children's use of a scale model. *Developmental Science, 2,* 296–305.

Massey, C. M., & Gelman, R. (1988). Preschoolers' ability to decide whether a photographed unfamiliar object can move itself. *Developmental Psychology, 24,* 307–317.

Matlin, M. W. (2004). *Cognition* (6th ed.). New York: Wiley.

Maurer, D., & Salapatek, P. (1976). Developmental changes in the scanning of faces by young infants. *Child Development, 47,* 523–527.

McCabe, A. E., Siegel, L. S., Spence, I., & Wilkinson, A. (1982). Class-inclusion reasoning: Patterns of performance from three to eight years. *Child Development, 53,* 780–785.

McCloskey, M., Wible, C. G., & Cohen, N. J. (1988). Is there a special flashbulb-memory mechanism? *Journal of Experimental Psychology: General, 117,* 336–338.

McCutchen, D. (2006). Cognitive factors in the development of children's writing. In C. A. MacArthur, S. Graham, & J. Fitzgerald (Eds.), *Handbook of writing research* (pp. 115–130). New York: Guilford Press.

McLean, K. C., & Breen, A. V. (2009). Processes and content of narrative identity development in adolescence: Gender and well-being. *Developmental Psychology, 45,* 702–710.

Meissner, C. A., & Brigham, J. C. (2001). Thirty years of investigating the own-race bias in memory for faces: A meta-analytic review. *Psychology, Public Policy, and Law, 7,* 3–35.

Mejia-Arauz, R., Rogoff, B., & Paradise, R. (2005). Culture variation in children's observation during a demonstration. *International Journal of Behavioral Development, 29,* 282–291.

Melot, A.-M., & Angeard, N. (2003). Theory of mind: Is training contagious? *Developmental Science, 6,* 178–184.

Melot, A.-M., Houdé, O., Courtel, S., & Soenen, L. (1995). False beliefs attribution, distinction between appearance and reality and visual perspective taking: Do they develop simultaneously? *The Genetic Epistemologist, 23,* 12.

Mervis, C. B., & Crisafi, M. A. (1982). Order of acquisition of subordinate-, basic-, and superordinate-level categories. *Child Development, 53,* 258–266.

Miller, D. C., & Byrnes, J. P. (1997). The role of contextual and personal factors in children's risk taking. *Developmental Psychology, 33,* 814–823.

Miller, G. A. (1956). The magical number seven, plus or minus two: Some limits on our capacity for processing information. *Psychological Review, 63,* 81–97.

Miller, J. L. (1990). Speech perception. In D. N. Osherson & H. Lasnik (Eds.), *An invitation to cognitive science* (Vol. 1, pp. 69–93). Cambridge, MA: MIT Press.

Miller, P. H. (1990). The development of strategies of selective attention. In D. F. Bjorklund (Ed.), *Children's strategies: Contemporary views of cognitive development* (pp. 157–184). Hillsdale, NJ: Erlbaum.

Miller, P. H. (2011). *Theories of developmental psychology* (5th ed.). New York: Worth.

Miller, P. H., & Seier, W. L. (1994). Strategy utilization deficiencies in children: When, where, and why. In H. W. Reese (Ed.), *Advances in child development and behavior* (Vol. 25, pp. 108–156). San Diego, CA: Academic Press.

Miller, S. A. (2007). *Developmental research methods* (3rd ed.). Thousand Oaks, CA: Sage.

Mitchell, P., & Lacohée, H. (1991). Children's early understanding of false belief. *Cognition, 39,* 107–127.

Morelli, G. A., Rogoff, B., & Angelillo, C. (2003). Cultural variation in young children's access to work or involvement in specialised child-focused activities. *International Journal of Behavioral Development, 27,* 264–274.

Morrongiello, B. A., Fenwick, K. D., Hillier, L., & Chance, G. (1994). Sound localization in newborn human infants. *Developmental Psychobiology, 27,* 519–538.

Moshman, D. (2005). *Adolescent psychological development: Rationality, morality, and identity* (2nd ed.). Mahwah, NJ: Erlbaum.

Murdock, B. B., Jr. (1962). The serial position effect of free recall. *Journal of Experimental Psychology, 64,* 482–488.

Murphy, F. C., Wilde, G., Ogden, N., Barnard, P. J., & Calder, A. J. (2009). Assessing the automaticity of moral processing: Efficient coding of moral information during narrative comprehension. *The Quarterly Journal of Experimental Psychology, 62,* 41–49.

Nagy, Z., Westerberg, H., & Klingberg, T. (2004). Maturation of white matter is associated with the development of cognitive functions during childhood. *Journal of Cognitive Neuroscience, 16,* 1227–1233.

Nazzi, T., Bertocini, J., & Mehler, J. (1998). Language discrimination by newborns: Towards an understanding of the role of rhythm. *Journal of Experimental Psychology, 24,* 756–766.

Neisser, U. (1982). Snapshots or benchmarks? In U. Neisser (Ed.), *Memory observed: Remembering in natural contexts* (pp. 43–48). San Francisco: W. H. Freeman.

Neisser, U. (2004). Memory development: New questions and old. *Developmental Review, 24,* 154–158.

Nelson, C. A., Monk, C. S., Lin, J., Carver, L. J., Thomas, K. M., & Truwit, C. L. (2000). Functional neuroanatomy of spatial working memory in children. *Developmental Psychology, 36,* 109–116.

Nelson, C. A., Moulson, M. C., & Richmond, J. (2006). How does neuroscience inform the study of cognitive development? *Human Development, 49,* 260–272.

Nelson, D. G. K., O'Neil, K. A., & Asher, Y. M. (2008). A mutually facilitative relationship between learning names and learning concepts in preschool children: The case of artifacts. *Journal of Cognition and Development, 9,* 171–193.

Nelson, K. (1973). Structure and strategy in learning to talk. *Monographs of the Society for Research in Child Development, 38*(1–2, Serial No. 149), 1–136.

Nelson, K. (1986). Event knowledge and cognitive development. In K. Nelson (Ed.), *Event knowledge: Structure and function in development.* (pp. 1–19). Hillsdale, NJ: Erlbaum.

Nelson, K. (2000). Global and functional: Mandler's perceptual and conceptual processes in infancy. *Journal of Cognition and Development, 1,* 49–54.

Nelson, K. (2003). Narrative and self, myth and memory: Emergence of the cultural self. In R. Fivush & C. A. Haden (Eds.), *Autobiographical memory and the construction of a narrative self: Developmental and cultural perspectives* (pp. 3–28). Mahwah, NJ: Erlbaum.

Nelson, K., & Fivush, R. (2004). The emergence of autobiographical memory: A social cultural developmental theory. *Psychological Review, 111,* 486–511.

Nelson, K., & Gruendel, J. M. (1981). Generalized event representation: Basic building blocks of cognitive development. In A. Brown & M. Lamb (Eds.), *Advances in developmental psychology* (Vol. 1, pp. 131–158). Hillsdale, NJ: Erlbaum.

Newport, E. L., Gleitman, H., & Gleitman, L. R. (1977). Mother, I'd rather do it myself: Some effects and noneffects of maternal speech style. In C. E. Snow & C. A. Ferguson (Eds.), *Talking to children: Language input and acquisition* (pp. 109–150). Cambridge, England: Cambridge University Press.

Nisbett, R. E., Choi, I., Peng, K., & Norenzayan, A. (2001). Culture and systems of thought: Holistic versus analytic cognition. *Psychological Review, 108,* 291–310.

Njus, D., & Johnson, D. R. (2008). Need for cognition as a predictor of psychosocial identity development. *Journal of Psychology: Interdisciplinary and Applied, 142,* 645–655.

Nolte, J. (2009). *The human brain: An introduction to its functional anatomy* (6th ed.). Philadelphia: Mosby/Elsevier.

Oakes, L. M., Horst, J. S., Kovack-Lesh, K. A., & Perone, S. (2009). How infants learn categories. In A. Woodward & A. Needham (Eds.), *Learning and the infant mind* (pp. 144–171). Oxford, England: Oxford University Press.

Ornstein, P. A., & Naus, M. J. (1985). Effects of the knowledge base on children's memory strategies. In H. Reese (Ed.), *Advances in Child Development and Behavior, 19,* 113–148.

Ornstein, P. A., Naus, M. J., & Liberty, C. (1975). Rehearsal and organizational processes in children's memory. *Child Development, 4,* 818–830.

Osherson, D. N., & Markman, E. (1975). Language and the ability to evaluate contradictions and tautologies. *Cognition, 3,* 213–226.

Pascalis, O., & De Schoen, S. (1994). Recognition memory in 3- to 4-day-old human neonates. *Neuro Report, 5,* 1721–1724.

Pascalis, O., & De Haan, M. (2003). Recognition memory and novelty preference: What model? In H. Hayne & J. W. Fagen (Eds.), *Progress in infancy research* (Vol. 3, pp. 95–119). Mahwah, NJ: Erlbaum.

Paul, R. (1976). Invented spelling in kindergarten. *Young Children, 31,* 195–200.

Payne, J. W. (1976). Task complexity and contingent processing in decision making: An information search and protocol analysis. *Organizational Behavior and Human Performance, 16,* 366–387.

Pellegrini, A. D., & Smith, P. K. (1998). Physical activity play: The nature and function of a neglected aspect of play. *Child Development, 69,* 577–598.

Pellicano, E., & Rhodes, G. (2003). Holistic processing of faces in preschool children and adults. *Psychological Science, 14,* 618–622.

Pellicano, E., Rhodes, G., & Peters, M. (2006). Are preschoolers sensitive to configural information in faces? *Developmental Science, 9,* 270–277.

Perner, J., Leekham, S. R., & Wimmer, H. (1987). Three-year-olds' difficulty with false belief: The case for a conceptual deficit. *British Journal of Developmental Psychology, 5,* 125–137.

Perner, J., & Ruffman, T. (1995). Episodic memory and autonoetic consciousness: Developmental evidence and a theory of childhood amnesia. *Journal of Experimental Child Psychology, 59,* 516–548.

Perry, W. G. (1970). *Forms of intellectual and ethical development in the college years: A scheme.* New York: Holt, Rinehart, & Winston.

Perry, W. G. (1981). Cognitive and ethical growth: The making of meaning. In A. W. Chickering (Ed.), *The modern American college* (pp. 76–116). San Francisco: Jossey-Bass.

Peters, K. M., & Blumberg, F. C. (2002). Cartoon violence: Is it as detrimental to preschoolers as we think? *Early Childhood Education Journal, 29,* 143–148.

Peterson, C. (1999). Children's memory for medical emergencies: 2 years later. *Developmental Psychology, 35,* 1493–1506.

Peterson, C., & Bell, M. (1996). Children's memory for traumatic injury. *Child Development, 67,* 3045–3070.

Peterson, C., & Whalen, N. (2001). Five years later: Children's memory for medical emergencies. *Applied Cognitive Psychology, 15,* S7–S24.

Piaget, J. (1952). *The origins of intelligence in children* (M. Cook, Trans.). New York: Norton.

Piaget, J. (1968). *Six psychological studies* (D. Elkind & A. Tenzer, Trans.; D. Elkind, Ed.). New York: Vintage Books.

Piaget, J. (1972). Intellectual evolution from adolescence to adulthood. *Human Development, 15,* 1–12.

Piaget, J. (1983). Piaget's theory. In P. H. Mussen (Series Ed.) and W. Kessen (Vol. Ed.), *Manual of child psychology* (4th ed., Vol. 1, pp. 103–132). New York: Wiley. (Original work published 1970)

Piaget, J., & Inhelder, B. (1956). *The child's conception of space.* London: Routledge & Kegan Paul.

Piaget, J., & Inhelder, B. (1969). *The psychology of the child* (H. Weaver, Trans.). New York: Basic Books.

Pillemer, D. B., Picariello, M. L., & Pruett, J. C. (1994). Very long-term memories of a salient preschool event. *Applied Cognitive Psychology, 8,* 95–106.

Pinker, S., & Jackendoff, R. (2005). The faculty of language: What's special about it? *Cognition, 95,* 201–236.

Pipe, M., Thierry, K. L., & Lamb, M. E. (2007). The development of event memory: Implications for child witness testimony. In M. P. Toglia, J. D. Read, D. F. Ross, &

R. C. L. Lindsay (Eds.), *The handbook of eyewitness psychology* (Vol. 1, pp. 453–478). Mahwah, NJ: Erlbaum.

Plude, D. J., Enns, J. T., & Brodeur, D. (1994). The development of selective attention: A life-span overview. *Acta Psychologica, 86,* 227–272.

Plumert, J. M., Kearney, J. K., & Cremer, J. F. (2007). Children's road crossing: A window into perceptual-motor development. *Current Directions in Psychological Science, 16,* 255–258.

Poole, D. A., & Lindsay, D. S. (2002). Reducing child witnesses' false reports of misinformation from parents. *Journal of Experimental Child Psychology, 81,* 117–140.

Porporino, M., Iarocci, G., Shore, D. I., & Burack, J. A. (2004). A developmental change in selective attention and global form perception. *International Journal of Behavioral Development, 28,* 358–364.

Posner, M. I., & Rothbart, M. K. (2007). *Educating the human brain.* Washington, DC: American Psychological Association.

Premack, D., & Woodruff, G. (1978). Does the chimpanzee have a theory of mind? *Behavioral and Brain Sciences, 1,* 515–526.

Pressley, M. (1994). State-of-the-science primary-grades reading instruction or whole language? *Educational Psychologist, 29,* 211–215.

Pressley, M., Mohan, L., Raphael, L. M., & Fingeret, L. (2007). How does Bennett Woods Elementary School produce such high reading and writing achievement? *Journal of Educational Psychology, 99,* 221–240.

Principe, G. F., & Ceci, S. J. (2002). "I saw it with my own ears": The influence of peer conversations and suggestive questions on preschoolers' event memory. *Journal of Experimental Child Psychology, 83,* 1–25.

Principe, G. F., Kanaya, T., Ceci, S. J., & Singh, M. (2006). Believing is seeing: How rumors can engender false memories in preschoolers. *Psychological Science, 17,* 243–248.

Quadrel, M. J., Fischhoff, B., & Davis, W. (1993). Adolescent (in)vulnerability. *American Psychologist, 48,* 102–116.

Quas, J. A., Goodman, G. S., Bidrose, S., Pipe, M. E., Craw, S., & Ablin, D. S. (1999). Emotion and memory: Children's long-term remembering, forgetting, and suggestibility. *Journal of Experimental Child Psychology, 72,* 235–270.

Quas, J. A., Schaaf, J. M., Alexander, K. W., & Goodman, G. S. (2000). Do you *really* remember it happening or do you only remember being asked about it happening? Children's source monitoring in forensic contexts. In K. P. Roberts & M. Blades (Eds.), *Children's source monitoring* (pp. 197–226). Mahwah, NJ: Erlbaum.

Quinn, P. C., Doran, M. M., Reiss, J. E., & Hoffman, J. E. (2009). Time course of visual attention in infant categorization of cats versus dogs: Evidence for a head bias as revealed through eye tracking. *Child Development, 80,* 151–161.

Quinn, P. C., & Eimas, P. D. (1996). Perceptual cues that permit categorical differentiation of animal species by infants. *Journal of Experimental Child Psychology, 63,* 189–211.

Quinn, P. C., & Eimas, P. D. (2000). The emergence of category representations during infancy: Are separate perceptual and conceptual processes required? *Journal of Cognition and Development, 1,* 55–61.

Rayner, S., & Riding, R. J. (1997). Towards a categorisation of cognitive styles and learning styles. *Educational Psychology, 17,* 5–27.

Read, C. (1971). Pre-school children's knowledge of English phonology. *Harvard Educational Review, 41,* 1–34.

Reed, S. K. (2006). *Cognition: Theory and applications* (7th ed.). Belmont, CA: Thomson/Wadsworth.

Reese, E., Haden, C. A., & Fivush, R. (1993). Mother-child conversations about the past: Relationships of style and memory over time. *Cognitive Development, 8,* 403–430.

Reese, H. W. (1962). Verbal mediation as a function of age level. *Psychological Bulletin, 59,* 502–509.

Reiss, A. L., Abrams, M. T., Singer, H. S., Ross, J. L., & Denckla, M. B. (1996). Brain development, gender, and IQ in children: A volumetric study. *Brain, 119,* 1763–1774.

Renninger, K. A., & Wozniak, R. H. (1985). Effect of interest on attentional shift, recognition, and recall in young children. *Developmental Psychology, 21,* 624–632.

Rescorla, L. A. (1980). Overextension in early language development. *Journal of Child Language, 7,* 321–335.

Resnick, L. B. (1989). Developing mathematical knowledge. *American Psychologist, 44,* 162–169.

Resnick, L. B., & Ford, W. W. (1981). *The psychology of mathematics instruction.* Hillsdale, NJ: Erlbaum.

Reyna, V. F., & Farley, F. (2006). Risk and rationality in adolescent decision making: Implications for theory, practice, and public policy. *Psychological Science in the Public Interest, 7,* 1–44.

Reznick, J. S. (2000). Interpreting infant conceptual categorization. *Journal of Cognition and Development, 1,* 63–66.

Richgels, D. J. (2001). Invented spelling, phonemic awareness, and reading and writing instruction. In S. B. Neuman & D. K. Dickinson (Eds.), *Handbook of early literacy research* (pp. 142–155). New York: Guilford Press.

Richland, L. E., Morrison, R. G., & Holyoak, K. J. (2006). Children's development of analogical reasoning: Insights from scene analogy problems. *Journal of Experimental Child Psychology, 94,* 249–273.

Roberge, J. J., & Paulus, D. H. (1971). Developmental patterns for children's class and conditional reasoning abilities. *Developmental Psychology, 4,* 191–200.

Roberts, K. P. (2000a). Introduction: Children's source monitoring. In K. P. Roberts & M. Blades (Eds.), *Children's source monitoring* (pp. 1–10). Mahwah, NJ: Erlbaum.

Roberts, K. P. (2000b). An overview of theory and research on children's source monitoring. In K. P. Roberts & M. Blades (Eds.), *Children's source monitoring* (pp. 11–57). Mahwah, NJ: Erlbaum.

Roberts, K. P., & Blades, M. (2000). Discriminating between memories of television and real life. In K. P. Roberts & M. Blades (Eds.), *Children's source monitoring* (pp. 147–169). Mahwah, NJ: Erlbaum.

Roebers, C. M., & Schneider, W. (2000). The impact of misleading questions on eyewitness memory in children and adults. *Applied Cognitive Psychology, 14,* 509–526.

Roebers, C. M., & Schneider, W. (2002). Stability and consistency of children's event recall. *Cognitive Development, 17,* 1085–1103.

Roediger, H. L., III. (1990). Implicit memory: Retention without remembering. *American Psychologist, 45,* 1043–1056.

Rogoff, B. (1990). *Apprenticeship in thinking: Cognitive development in social context.* New York: Oxford University Press.

Rosch, E. (1978). Principles of categorization. In E. Rosch & B. B. Lloyd (Eds.), *Cognition and categorization* (pp. 27–48). Hillsdale, NJ: Erlbaum.

Rosch, E., Mervis, C. B., Gray, W. D., Johnson, D. M., & Boyes-Braem, P. (1976). Basic objects in natural categories. *Cognitive Psychology, 8,* 382–439.

Rose, S. A., Feldman, J. F., & Jankowski, J. J. (2004). Infant visual recognition memory. *Developmental Review, 24,* 74–100.

Rosenstein, D., & Oster, H. (1988). Differential facial responses to four basic tastes in newborns. *Child Development, 59,* 1555–1568.

Rovee, C. K., & Fagen, J. W. (1976). Extending conditioning and 24-hour retention in infants. *Journal of Experimental Child Psychology, 21,* 1–11.

Rovee-Collier, C., & Barr, R. (2001). Infant learning and memory. In G. Bremner & A. Fogel (Eds.), *Blackwell handbook of infant development* (pp. 139–168). Malden, MA: Blackwell.

Rovee-Collier, C., & Barr, R. (2002). Infant cognition. In H. Pashler (Series Ed.) and J. Wixted (Vol. Ed.), *Stevens' handbook of experimental psychology* (3rd ed., Vol. 4, pp. 693–791). New York: Wiley.

Rovee-Collier, C., & Cuevas, K. (2009). Multiple memory systems are unnecessary to account for infant memory development: An ecological model. *Developmental Psychology, 45,* 160–174.

Ruble, D. N., & Frey, K. S. (1991). Changing patterns of comparative behavior as skills are acquired: A functional model of self-evaluation. In J. Suls & T. A. Wills (Eds.), *Social comparison: Contemporary theory and research* (pp. 79–112). Hillsdale, NJ: Erlbaum.

Ruff, H. A., & Capozzoli, M. C. (2003). Development of attention and distractibility in the first 4 years of life. *Developmental Psychology, 39,* 877–890.

Ruff, H. A., Capozzoli, M., & Weissberg, R. (1998). Age, individuality, and context as factors in sustained visual attention during the preschool years. *Developmental Psychology, 34,* 454–464.

Rumelhart, D. E., & Ortony, A. (1977). The representation of knowledge in memory. In R. C. Anderson, R. J. Spiro, & W. E. Montague (Eds.), *Schooling and the acquisition of knowledge* (pp. 99–135). Hillsdale, NJ: Erlbaum.

Ryan, M. K., & David, B. (2003). Gender differences in ways of knowing: The context dependence of that Attitudes Toward Thinking and Learning Survey. *Sex Roles, 49,* 693–699.

Saffran, J. R., Werker, J. F., & Werner, L. A. (2006). The infant's auditory world: Hearing, speech, and the beginnings of language. In W. Damon & R. M. Lerner (Series Eds.) and D. Kuhn & R. S. Siegler (Vol. Eds.), *Handbook of child psychology* (6th ed., Vol. 2, pp. 58–108). New York: Wiley.

Salapatek, P. (1975). Pattern perception in early infancy. In L. B. Cohen & P. Salapatek (Eds.), *Infant perception: From sensation to cognition* (Vol. 1, pp. 133–248). New York: Academic Press.

Salapatek, P., & Kessen, W. (1966). Visual scanning of triangles by the human newborn. *Journal of Experimental Child Psychology, 3,* 155–167.

Schmidt, S. R. (2004). Autobiographical memories for the September 11th attacks: Reconstructive errors and emotional impairment of memory. *Memory & Cognition, 32,* 443–454.

Schneider, W., & Bjorklund, D. F. (1998). Memory. In W. Damon (Series Ed.) and D. Kuhn & R. S. Siegler (Vol. Eds.), *Handbook of child psychology* (5th ed., Vol. 2, pp. 467–521). New York: Wiley.

Schneider, W., Kron, V., Hünnerkopf, M., & Krajewski, K. (2004). The development of young children's memory strategies: First findings from the Würzburg Longitudinal Memory Study. *Journal of Experimental Child Psychology, 88,* 193–209.

Schneider, W., & Pressley, M. (1989). *Memory development between 2 and 20.* New York: Springer-Verlag.

Shaffer, D. R. (2002). *Developmental psychology: Childhood and adolescence* (6th ed.). Belmont, CA: Wadsworth/Thomson.

Shatz, M., & Gelman, R. (1973). The development of communication skills: Modifications in the speech of young children as a function of listener. *Monographs of the Society for Research in Child Development, 38*(Serial No. 152), 1–37.

Sheingold, K., & Tenney, Y. J. (1982). Memory for a salient childhood event. In U. Neisser (Ed.), *Memory observed: Remembering in natural contexts* (pp. 201–212). San Francisco: W. H. Freeman.

Shipley, E. F., Kuhn, I. F., & Madden, E. C. (1983). Mothers' use of superordinate category terms. *Journal of Child Language, 10,* 571–588.

Siegler, R. S. (1981). Developmental sequences within and between concepts. *Monographs of the Society for Research in Child Development, 46,* 1–84.

Siegler, R. S. (1982). The rule-assessment approach and education. *Contemporary Educational Psychology, 7,* 272–288.

Simoneau, M., & Markovits, H. (2003). Reasoning with premises that are not empirically true: Evidence for the role of inhibition and retrieval. *Developmental Psychology, 39,* 964–975.

Singer, J. L., & Singer, D. G. (1998). *Barney & Friends* as entertainment and education: Evaluating the quality and effectiveness of a television series for preschool children. In J. K. Asamen & G. L. Berry (Eds.), *Research paradigms, television, and social behavior* (pp. 305–367). Thousand Oaks, CA: Sage.

Skyrms, B. (2000). *Choice and chance: An introduction to inductive logic* (4th ed.). Belmont, CA: Wadsworth/Thomson.

Slackman, E. A., Hudson, J. A., & Fivush, R. (1986). Actions, actors, links, and goals: The structure of children's event representations. In K. Nelson (Ed.), *Event knowledge: Structure and function in development* (pp. 47–69). Hillsdale, NJ: Erlbaum.

Slater, A., Mattock, A., & Brown, E. (1990). Size constancy at birth: Newborn infants' responses to retinal and real size. *Journal of Experimental Child Psychology, 49,* 314–322.

Slater, A., Morison, V., Somers, M., Mattock, A., Brown, E., & Taylor, D. (1990). Newborn and older infants' perception of partly occluded objects. *Infant Behavior and Development, 13,* 33–49.

Slaughter, V., & Gopnik, A. (1996). Conceptual coherence in the child's theory of mind: Training children to understand belief. *Child Development, 67,* 2967–2988.

Sloutsky, V. M., Kloos, H., & Fisher, A. V. (2007). When looks are everything: Appearance similarity versus kind information in early induction. *Psychological Science, 18,* 179–185.

Soja, N. N., Carey, S., & Spelke, E. S. (1991). Ontological categories guide young children's inductions of word meaning: Object terms and substance terms. *Cognition, 38,* 179–211.

Sousa, P., Atran, S., & Medin, D. (2002). Essentialism and folkbiology: Evidence from Brazil. *Journal of Cognition and Culture, 2,* 195–223.

Spear, L. P. (2000). Neurobehavioral changes in adolescence. *Current Directions in Psychological Science, 9,* 111–114.

Spelke, E. S. (1994). Initial knowledge: Six suggestions. *Cognition, 50,* 431–445.

Spelke, E. S. (2000). Nativism, empiricism, and the origins of knowledge. In D. Muir & A. Slater (Eds.), *Infant development: The essential readings* (pp. 36–51). Malden, MA: Blackwell.

Spelke, E. S., & Hofsten, C. von (2001). Predictive reaching for occluded objects by 6-month-old infants. *Journal of Cognition and Development, 2,* 261–281.

Spelke, E. S., Kestenbaum, R., Simons, D. J., & Wein, D. (1995). Spatiotemporal continuity, smoothness of motion, and object identity in infancy. *British Journal of Developmental Psychology, 13,* 113–142.

Stanovich, K. E., & West, R. F. (2000). Individual differences in reasoning: Implications for the rationality debate? *Behavioral and Brain Sciences, 23,* 645–726.

Sternberg, R. J. (1986). *Intelligence applied: Understanding and increasing your intellectual skills.* San Diego, CA: Harcourt Brace Jovanovich.

Sternberg, R. J. (1997). *Thinking styles.* Cambridge, England: Cambridge University Press.

Stroop, J. R. (1935). Studies of interference in serial verbal reactions. *Journal of Experimental Psychology, 18,* 643–662.

Tanaka, J. W., Kay, J. B., Grinnell, E., Stansfield, B., & Szechter, L. (1998). Face recognition in young children: When the whole is greater than the sum of its parts. *Visual Cognition, 5,* 479–496.

Taplin, J. E., Staudenmayer, H., & Taddonio, J. L. (1974). Developmental changes in conditional reasoning: Linguistic or logical? *Journal of Experimental Child Psychology, 17,* 360–373.

Tarlowski, A. (2006). If it's an animal it has axons: Experience and culture in preschool children's reasoning about animates. *Cognitive Development, 21,* 249–265.

Teale, W. H. (1987). Emergent literacy: Reading and writing development in early childhood. *National Reading Conference Yearbook, 36,* 45–74.

Texas School for the Blind and Visually Impaired. (2007). *Monitoring visual development.* Retrieved January 13, 2010, from http://www.tsbvi.edu/Education/infant/page7.htm

Thierry, K. L., & Spence, M. J. (2002). Source-monitoring training facilitates preschoolers' eyewitness memory performance. *Developmental Psychology, 38,* 428–437.

Thorndike, E. L. (1898). Animal intelligence: An experimental study of the associative processes in animals. *Psychological Monographs, 2*(Whole No. 8).

Thorndike, E. L. (1911). *Animal intelligence: Experimental studies.* New Brunswick, NJ: Transaction. (Original work published 2000; Lewiston, NY: Macmillan)

Thorndike, E. L. (1925). *Educational psychology: Briefer course.* New York: Teachers' College, Columbia University Press.

Thorndike, R. L. (1991). Edward L. Thorndike: A professional and personal appreciation. In G. A. Kimble, M. Wertheimer, & C. White (Eds.), *Portraits of pioneers in psychology* (pp. 139–151). Hillsdale, NJ: Erlbaum.

Tillman, C. M., Nyberg, L., & Bohlin, G. (2008). Working memory components and intelligence in children. *Intelligence, 36,* 394–402.

Tomasello, M. (2006). Acquiring linguistic constructions. In D. Kuhn & R. S. Siegler (Vol. Eds.), *Handbook of child psychology* (6th ed., Vol. 2, pp. 255–298). Hoboken, NJ: Wiley.

Tomasello, M., Akhtar, N., Dodson, K., & Rekau, L. (1997). Differential productivity in young children's use of nouns and verbs. *Journal of Child Language, 24,* 373–387.

Trevarthen, C., & Aitken, K. J. (2001). Infant intersubjectivity: Research, theory, and clinical applications. *Journal of Child Psychology and Psychiatry, 42,* 3–48.

Tulving, E. (1972). Episodic and semantic memory. In E. Tulving & W. Donaldson (Eds.), *Organization of memory* (pp. 381–403). New York: Academic Press.

Tulving, E. (1983). *Elements of episodic memory.* New York: Oxford University Press.

Tulving, E. (1989). Remembering and knowing the past. *American Scientist, 77,* 361–367.

Tulving, E., & Thomson, D. M. (1973). Encoding specificity and retrieval processes in episodic memory. *Psychological Review, 80,* 352–373.

Tyler, L. E. (1974). *Individual differences: Abilities and motivational directions.* Englewood Cliffs, NJ: Prentice Hall.

Urdan, T., & Mestas, M. (2006). The goals behind performance goals. *Journal of Educational Psychology, 98,* 354–365.

Usher, J. A., & Neisser, U. (1993). Childhood amnesia and the beginnings of memory for four early life events. *Journal of Experimental Psychology: General, 122,* 155–165.

Van Abbema, D. L., & Bauer, P. J. (2005). Autobiographical memory in middle childhood: Recollections of the recent and distant past. *Memory, 13,* 829–845.

Vandewater, E. A., Bickham, D. S., Lee, J. H., Cummings, H. M., Wartella, E. A., & Rideout, V. J. (2005). When the television is always on: Heavy television exposure and young children's development. *American Behavioral Scientist, 48,* 562–577.

Vukelich, C., & Golden, J. M. (1984). Early writing: Development and teaching strategies. *Young Children, 39*(2), 3–8.

Vuontela, V., Steenari, M., Carlson, S., Koivisto, J., Fjällberg, M., & Aronen, E. T. (2003). Audiospatial and visuospatial working memory in 6–13 year old school children. *Learning & Memory, 10,* 74–81.

Walker, L. J. (1984). Sex differences in the development of moral reasoning: A critical review. *Child Development, 55,* 677–691.

Ware, E. A., Uttal, D. H., Wetter, E. K., & DeLoache, J. S. (2006). Young children make scale errors when playing with dolls. *Developmental Science, 9,* 40–45.

Warren, A. R., & Swartwood, J. N. (1992). Developmental issues in flashbulb memory research: Children recall the *Challenger* event. In E. Winograd & U. Neisser (Eds.), *Affect and accuracy in recall: Studies of "flashbulb" memories. Emory symposium in cognition* (pp. 95–120). New York: Cambridge University Press.

Waterman, A. S. (2007). Doing well: The relationship of identity status to three conceptions of well-being. *Identity, 7,* 289–307.

Watson, J. B., & Rayner, R. (1920). Conditioned emotional reactions. *Journal of Experimental Psychology, 3,* 1–14. (Reprinted in *American Psychologist, 55,* 313–317)

Waxman, S., Medin, D., & Ross, N. (2007). Folkbiological reasoning from a cross-cultural developmental perspective: Early essentialist notions are shaped by cultural beliefs. *Developmental Psychology, 43,* 294–308.

Weaver, C. A., III. (1993). Do you need a "flash" to form a flashbulb memory? *Journal of Experimental Psychology: General, 122,* 39–46.

Wellman, H. M. (1992). *The child's theory of mind.* Cambridge, MA: MIT Press.

Werker, J. F., Pegg, J. E., & McLeod, P. J. (1994). A cross-language investigation of infant preference for infant-directed communication. *Infant Behavior & Development, 17,* 323–333.

Werker, J. F., & Tees, R. C. (1984). Cross-language speech perception: Evidence for perceptual reorganization during the first year of life. *Infant Behavior and Development, 7,* 49–63.

Werker, J. F., & Tees, R. C. (1999). Influences on infant speech processing: Toward a new synthesis. *Annual Review of Psychology, 50,* 509–535.

Werner, H. (1982). The concept of development from a comparative and organismic point of view. In J. K. Gardner (Ed.), *Readings in development psychology* (2nd ed., pp. 21–36). Boston: Little, Brown. (Original work published 1957)

Wetzel, N., Widmann, A., Berti, S., & Schröger, E. (2006). The development of involuntary and voluntary attention from childhood to adulthood: A combined behavioral and event-related potential study. *Clinical Neurophysiology, 117,* 2191–2203.

Wilson, J. F. (2003). *Biological foundations of human behavior.* Belmont, CA: Thomson.

Wimmer, H., & Perner, J. (1983). Beliefs about beliefs: Representation and constraining function of wrong beliefs in young children's understanding of deception. *Cognition, 13,* 102–128.

Windholz, G., & Lamal, P. A. (1986). Priority in the classical conditioning of children. *Teaching of Psychology, 13,* 192–195.

Woodward, A. L., & Markman, E. M. (1998). Early word learning. In W. Damon (Series Ed.) and D. Kuhn & R. S. Siegler (Vol. Eds.), *Handbook of child psychology* (5th ed., Vol. 2, pp. 371–420). New York: Wiley.

Wray, D. (1993). What do children think about writing? *Educational Review, 45,* 67–77.

Wright, J. C., Huston, A. C., Vandewater, E. A., Bickman, D. S., Scantlin, R. M., Kotler, J. A., et al. (2001). American children's use of electronic media in 1997: A national survey. *Journal of Applied Developmental Psychology, 22,* 31–47.

Wynn, K. (1992). Addition and subtraction by human infants. *Nature, 358,* 749–750.

Xu, F., & Carey, S. (1996). Infants' metaphysics: The case of numerical identity. *Cognitive Psychology, 30,* 111–153.

Yurgelun-Todd, D. A., Killgore, W. D. S., & Cintron, C. B. (2003). Cognitive correlates of medial temporal lobe development across adolescence: A magnetic resonance imaging study. *Perceptual and Motor Skills, 96,* 3–17.

Zelazo, P. D., Craik, F. I. M., & Booth, L. (2004). Executive function across the life span. *Acta Psychologica, 115,* 167–183.

Zelazo, P. D., Müller, U., Frye, D., & Marcovitch, S. (2003). The development of executive function in early childhood. *Monographs of the Society for Research in Child Development, 68*(3, Serial No. 274), 1–155.

Zillmer, E. A., & Spiers, M. V. (2001). *Principles of neuropsychology.* Belmont, CA: Wadsworth.

Zimmerman, F. J., Christakis, D. A., & Meltzoff, A. N. (2007). Television and DVD/video viewing in children younger than 2 years. *Archives of Pediatrics and Adolescent Medicine, 161,* 473–479.

Zoelch, C., Seitz, K., & Schumann-Hengsteler, R. (2005). From rag(bag)s to riches: Measuring the developing central executive. In W. Schneider, R. Schumann-Hengsteler, & B. Sodian (Eds.), *Young children's cognitive development: Interrelationships among executive functioning, working memory, verbal ability, and theory of mind* (pp. 39–69). Mahwah, NJ: Erlbaum.

AUTHOR INDEX

Ablin, D. S., **486**
Abrams, M. T., 278, **487**
Abramson, A., 132, **480**
Adams, A.-M., 197, **463**
Adams, J. W., 368, **477**
Ahmavaara, A., 423, **463**
Aitken, K, J., 136, **491**
Akhtar, N., 150, **491**
Akshoomoff, N., 179, **463**
Albert, J., 436, **478**
Alexander, K. W., 324, **486**
Alioto, A., 135, **475**
Alloway, T. P., 216, 217, **463**
Altenbaumer, H. E., **473**
Amso, D., 382, 383, **463**
Anderson, D. R., 184, 185, 186, 187, 189, **463, 469, 479,**
Angeard, N., 260, **482**
Angelillo, C., 354, **483**
Anglin, J. M., 143, **463**
Aronen, E. T., **491**
Arterberry, M. E., 60, 63, 67, 90 **479**
Asato, M. R., 398, 399, **463**
Asher, Y. M., 227, **483**
Aslin, R. N., 133, 134, 135, **463**
Astington, J W., 257, 259, 260, **475, 478**
Atance, C. M., 167, 180, 260 **463, 465**
Atkinson, R. C., 28, 89, 195, **464**
Atran, S., 332, **464, 490**
Austin, L., 401, **465**

Baddeley, A. D., 89, 195, 197, 276, 277, 288, 289, 388, **464,**
Bahrick, L., 321, **472**

Baillargeon, R., 88,108, 109, 110, 111, 112, 114, 117, 118, 159, **464**
Baker-Ward, L., 199, 211, 212, 214, 215, **464**
Baldwin, D. A., 103, **464**
Banich, M. T., **464**
Barch, D. M., 390, **466**
Barnard, P. J., 434, **483**
Baron, J., 399, **464**
Barr, R., 32, 81, 90, 91, 92, 93, **464, 488**
Barrouillet, P., 395, 396, **482**
Bartgis, J., 288, **465**
Barton, M. E., 227, **465**
Bauer, L., 8, **465**
Bauer, P. J., 87, 97, 98, 99, 106, 318, **465, 468, 481, 491**
Beach, D. R., 50, 198, 306, **472**
Beers, S. R., **470**
Behme, C., 126, **465**
Belenky, M. F., 439, 440, **465, 475**
Bell, M., 215, **485**
Benson, J. B., 58, 78, 101, **476**
Berko, J., 129, **465**
Bernstein, D. M., 170, **465**
Berti, S., 287, **492**
Bertocini, J., 135, **483**
Beyth-Marom, R., 401, **465**
Bialystok, E., 266, **465**
Bickham, D. S., 186, **477, 491**
Bidrose, S., **506**
Bisanz, J., 377, 378, **478**
Bjorklund, D. F., 201, 206, 246, 299, **465, 476, 489**
Black, J. E., 81, **476**
Blackwell, L. S., 423, **466**

NOTE: Terms appearing in bold indicate entries on references page.

495

SUBJECT INDEX

Ability differences, 413–415, **447**
Academic skills, 10, **447**
  math, 365–368
  reading, 355–358
  writing, 358–365
Accommodation, 20, 54, **447**
Achievement motivation, 418–424, **447**
Adaptation, 53, **447**
  See also Accommodation; Assimilation
Adolescence, 373–409, 411–445
  cognitive processes in, 383–407
  epistemological development in, 434–440
  identity development in, 440–443
  neurological development in, 382–383
  reasoning and moral development in, 424–434
  theoretical perspectives on, 374–383
Adult-directed speech (ADS), 134–135
Alerting network, 288, **447**
Amygdala, 36, 392, 393 (figure), **447**
Analytic cognition, 13–14, **447**
  See also Analytic versus holistic processing
Analytic system, of decision making, 400–401, 406, **447**
Analytic versus holistic processing, 162–163
Animism, 228, **447**
Antisaccade task, 387, 387 (figure), **447**
Appearance-reality distinction, 22, 239–242, **447**
Apprenticeship, 337, 353–354, **448**
Assimilation, 20, 54, **448**
Attention, 5–6, **448**
  disengagement of, 78
  divided, 178
  in adolescence, 385–388
  in early childhood, 177–183
  in infancy, 77–79

  in middle childhood, 287–288
  selective, 5, 177, 179, 287–288, 291, 295–296, **459**
  span, 29, 178–181, **448**
Attentional inertia, 183, **448**
Attentional network, 288, 289 (figure), **448**
Auditory perception, 129, **448**
Autobiographical memory, 194, 206–211, 311–319, **448**
Automatic processes, 6, 178, 385, 417, **448**
Automaticity, *See* Automatic processes

Babbling, 136, 138, **448**
Barney & Friends, 187–188, 188 (photo)
Basic cognition
  in adolescence, 383–393
  in infancy, 51–83, 85–119
  in early childhood, 157–191, 193–233
  in middle childhood, 273–301, 303–334
  See also Attention; Memory; Perception
Basic level, of a concept, 225–226, **448**
Between-subjects designs, 42, **448**
Biases, in decision making, 349, **448**
Blue's Clues, 186–187, 187 (photo)
Brain
  development of major structures in infancy, 34–38, 35 (figure)
  development in childhood, 278–280
  development in adolescence, 382–383
  functioning, studies of, 42–47
  imaging, 43–45, **448**

Capacity, 6, 89, 194–195, 276–277, 304, 379, 412–414, **448**
  See also Working memory

NOTE: Terms appearing in bold indicate glossary entries.

505

Supporting researchers
for more than 40 years

Research methods have always been at the core of SAGE's publishing program. Founder Sara Miller McCune published SAGE's first methods book, *Public Policy Evaluation*, in 1970. Soon after, she launched the *Quantitative Applications in the Social Sciences* series—affectionately known as the "little green books."

Always at the forefront of developing and supporting new approaches in methods, SAGE published early groundbreaking texts and journals in the fields of qualitative methods and evaluation.

Today, more than 40 years and two million little green books later, SAGE continues to push the boundaries with a growing list of more than 1,200 research methods books, journals, and reference works across the social, behavioral, and health sciences. Its imprints—Pine Forge Press, home of innovative textbooks in sociology, and Corwin, publisher of PreK–12 resources for teachers and administrators—broaden SAGE's range of offerings in methods. SAGE further extended its impact in 2008 when it acquired CQ Press and its best-selling and highly respected political science research methods list.

From qualitative, quantitative, and mixed methods to evaluation, SAGE is the essential resource for academics and practitioners looking for the latest methods by leading scholars.

For more information, visit **www.sagepub.com**.